Teaching Social Studies in Secondary Schools:
A Handbook

Teaching
SOCIAL STUDIES
in Secondary Schools
A HANDBOOK

LEONARD H. CLARK

JERSEY CITY STATE COLLEGE

Macmillan Publishing Co., Inc.
NEW YORK

Collier Macmillan Publishers
LONDON

MACMILLAN PUBLISHING CO., INC.
866 Third Avenue, New York, New York 10022

COLLIER-MACMILLAN CANADA, LTD., Toronto, Ontario

Library of Congress catalog card number: 72-87156

Printing: 1 2 3 4 5 6 7 8   Year: 3 4 5 6 7 8 9

To Mary

Preface

To secondary school social studies teachers and teachers to be.

This book is intended to be a useful tool for preservice or inservice teachers of secondary school social studies. I hope you will find it so. It can be used as a textbook in methods courses at the undergraduate or graduate level, or as a reference book by teachers in service. In any event, the book is intended to be practical and down to earth, no matter what use you put it to.

To make the book logical and easy to use, it has been divided into four parts. Part I presents the problem of teaching method (that is, how to select the most suitable strategy and tactics in view of the educational situation) and some of the variables that contribute to that problem. Part II tells how to carry out various general strategies and techniques. Part III makes specific suggestions for organizing and teaching courses in the various disciplines. Part IV tells where to find and how to utilize various materials and tools of instruction.

Although the parts and chapters have been arranged to follow a logical sequence, it is not necessary to follow that sequence. To make the book more useful to teachers the chapters and sections have been designed to stand alone. Read them in any order that you wish. An index has been provided so that you can use the book as a reference tool.

You will find the coverage of the book to be complete. Some topics not usually found in books of this type have been included. However, the main emphasis is on how to do things. For that reason I have explained many procedures step by step and included numerous examples of what one might do. Theory is emphasized only to provide a rationale for the methodology advocated.

I have tried to describe all the kinds of strategies and tactics that you will need to know, but the emphasis is on inquiry, problem solving, and discovery. Some attention is paid to the structure of each of the disciplines. These emphases result from certain basic assumptions: (1) There is no best way to teach. One should pick the teaching strategies and tactics most compatible to the teaching objectives and other elements in the pedagogical situation. (2) The nature of the social studies makes it imperative to emphasize open-ended problem-solving inquiry and discovery. (3) Because of the nature of the subject matter, social studies teachers should favor process over information, although fact should not be neglected. (4) How one teaches the social studies is important. To an extent the method of teaching and learning is the content in the social studies. (5) Social studies instruction today must relate to real life. There is no excuse for teaching the content of secondary school social studies courses as an academic abstraction in the 1970s. To this extent, then, this book is an expression of the new social studies, although history reminds us that the approaches advocated represent a very old tradition in the teaching of social studies and the humanities.

Variety gives spice to teaching. So do strategies and tactics that emphasize the real life elements in our subject matter. Therefore, I have included many different down-to-earth strategies and tactics in the hope that you will find some that will make your teaching more viable and lively. Try them. You may like them. If a technique does not seem to work for you when you first try it, do not give up on it. Try it again under different circumstances. It usually takes a little practice before one can execute even simple techniques with consistent success. Remember that today's failure may be tomorrow's standby.

During the writing of this handbook I have become indebted to many people. Among them are the many students at Jersey City State College who have seen much of the handbook in other forms, and the many secondary school teachers who have allowed me to sit in on their classes and have showed me the methods and materials they have found most effective. I am also especially indebted to Leo Alilunas, who reviewed the original draft manuscript and made numerous suggestions; to Lloyd C. Chilton, Jr., and his associates at Macmillan, Inc., who have been so helpful with this and previous ventures; and finally to my wife, who prepared the manuscript and took care of the innumerable secretarial, bookkeeping, and editorial details.

L. H. C.

Contents

APPENDIXES
SOURCES OF INFORMATION
AND TEACHING MATERIALS

Contents xiii

PART I

The Problem of
Method

CHAPTER 1

Teaching and the Problem of Method in Teaching the Social Studies

To teach is to try to help someone learn something. More formally, to teach is to help someone acquire or change some behavior; that is, some skill, attitude, knowledge, ideal, or appreciation.

THE PROBLEM OF METHOD

Teaching is much more than presenting information or even presenting ideas. It also includes, among other things, guiding pupils to learn by means of the probing, discovering, and analyzing and examining activities that we call reflective thinking, the subtle business of building attitudes and values, and the more straightforward tasks of skill development.

The Problem of Selection

The basic problem in pedagogical method is selection or decision making. Even to carry out a simple lesson you must

1. Select the instructional goals.
2. Select the strategy by which you hope to reach these goals. In mapping out this strategy you must select both
   a. Content.
   b. General method or approach.
3. Select specific tactics by which to carry out the strategy.
4. Select the materials and tools of instruction.
5. Select procedures by which to evaluate the success of your teaching and to follow it up.

Proper decision making requires good diagnosis. Without adequate diagnosis teachers tend to teach everything in the same way to everybody, and, as a result, their teaching becomes boring, frustrating, unsatisfactory, and unsuccessful. Really, the importance of diagnosis in teaching can hardly be overestimated.

Diagnosis in teaching is complicated by several variable factors.

3

1. The goal you are seeking.
2. The individual pupils you are teaching.
3. The subject matter you are teaching (including the nature of the discipline or disciplines concerned).
4. The tools and technology available to you.
5. The nature and dynamics of the group you are teaching.
6. Your philosophy of teaching.
7. The environment surrounding the school.
8. The school environment.
9. You yourself—your skills, knowledge, attitudes, prejudices, personality, and the like.

Let us examine a few of these variables.

SUBJECT MATTER

The subject matter to be taught should determine to a large extent the strategies and tactics to be used. Some subject matter is to be remembered, some to be used, some to be appreciated. Do not expect the same tactics and strategies to be equally successful in teaching different kinds of subject matter. What works well for one kind of content may not work at all for another.

The Structure of Subject Matter. Educational theorists use the term *structure of the discipline* to refer to the way disciplines are organized. The structure of a discipline consists of the organization of the concepts that make up the discipline and the processes by which one tries to ascertain truth in that discipline. It is largely formal, artificial, and arbitrary; however, once accepted by scholars, it is very useful.

Some modern educational theorists contend that the content of secondary school courses should center around structure of the discipline rather than information. Structure, they maintain, is more likely to be permanent than information or facts, which are likely to change overnight. On the other hand, the disciplines themselves are quite arbitrary divisions of subject matter. Some educationists seem to think them to be educational fictions. Certainly the subject matter and the structure of the various disciplines intertwine so much that the divisions between disciplines are often hazy. Perhaps it may be that all knowledge is really a unity. Perhaps we should not stress the different structures of separate disciplines so much, but rather the continuity and unity of subject matter. Certainly we ought to avoid erecting barriers between disciplines where no barriers naturally exist.

All this seems to mean that you must search for tactics and strategies that bring out generalizations and interrelationships—not only within the disciplines you teach, but in the interdisciplinary conglomerates that make up life.

The Doctrine of Contingent Value. In the social studies, the subject matter we teach is always a selection from a much larger mass of subject matter. No one can hope to cover the entirety of any subject. Most of the subject matter in a subject must be left out. Any teacher who feels he must cover the subject, or cover everything in the textbook, is either foolish, incompetent, or both.

Nevertheless, subject matter is important and necessary. Without it we would have nothing to teach. Because it is impossible to teach everything, we must carefully select the subject matter that is likely to be the most valuable to the pupils. To do anything else is wasteful. This is the doctrine of contingent value or relevance.

This doctrine does not mean that the curriculum should be narrowly vocational and materialistic. Subject matter that helps pupils understand themselves and their environment, or that makes their lives rich and enjoyable, is fully as useful as vocational subject matter. The point is that the subject matter needs to relate enough to the lives of the pupils so that they can see the relationships and utilize them. For this reason the social studies lend themselves particularly to teaching by variations of what has come to be called the inquiry method.

COMMUNICATIONS THEORY AND PEDAGOGICAL METHOD

Communications theory has many implications for instructional theory. Good teaching requires good communications. Communications theory, then, should be an important consideration in the selection of teaching strategies. The need for sophistication in communications skills is even more apparent when one realizes that the product the teacher has to sell is often not as glamorous as that of other communicators. Furthermore, teaching in classrooms presents one of the most difficult communication problems.

The Communications Problem. The communications problem in the classroom is difficult because it is so complex.[1] The teacher must communicate with a number of receivers all different from each other. In addition he tries to use a combination of a dozen or more media—oral, written, audiovisual, dramatic, and the like. The messages, too, are complex—they are not simply facts or skills, or even generalizations, principles, attitudes, and ideas, but such complicated matters as roles, values, and life concepts. All this is further complicated by the dynamics of groups. Individual interests and reactions may be sharply influenced by a group's dynamics. These complications become even more formidable when one realizes that boys and girls of today are used to expert professional radio and television communication. Compared to the professional productions pupils hear and see daily the efforts of teachers must often seem dreadfully amateurish.

The Engineering of Consent. Because of the importance and difficulty of classroom communications, teachers ought to adopt as much of the communications industry's expertise as they can. In the *Psychology of Learning and Teaching,* Bernard shows how procedures for the engineering of consent formulated for use by the communications industry by Bernays[2] can be used in teaching. As adapted for teaching the steps are

[1] Wilbur Schramm, "Educators and Communication Research," *Educational Leadership,* **13:** 503–508 (May 1956).

[2] Edward L. Bernays, *The Engineering of Consent* (Norman, Okla.: University of Oklahoma Press, 1955).

1. Define your objectives.
2. Study the pupils.
3. Modify the objectives in view of the study of the pupils.
4. Decide on strategy.
5. Set up motivational machinery.
6. Organize the plans.
7. Carry out the tactics.[3]

INSTRUCTIONAL OBJECTIVES

Instructional objectives deserve the serious consideration of all teachers. Many teaching failures occur because teachers do not select the correct strategies and tactics for their instructional goals. Still others occur because teachers do not have any real objectives clearly in mind.

THE CENTRAL PURPOSE OF AMERICAN EDUCATION

Most educators are convinced that the "central purpose" of American education should be intellectual. The rigors of life in a democracy make it mandatory that the schools encourage pupils to become independent thinkers and give them the tools with which to think. Social studies curricula and strategies of teaching should be designed with this goal in mind. Because of the necessity to encourage thinking and to give pupils practice in thinking, priority probably should be given to strategies that include discovery, problem solving, and other inquiry techniques. In teaching intellectual skills, it matters little what subject matter is used; the emphasis should be on the method. To paraphrase McLuhan, when one is teaching the higher cognitive processes, to a large extent the *teaching method is the content*.

THE HIERARCHY OF EDUCATIONAL OBJECTIVES

The Cognitive Domain.   Instructional objectives have been classified into three major categories: cognitive, affective, and psychomotor. The following is a hierarchy of educational objectives in the cognitive domain developed by Benjamin S. Bloom and his associates. Note that the objectives are arranged in a hypothetical order from the lowest to the highest mental processes. Pupils should have learning experience at all of these levels if they are to become able thinkers. All too often teachers never ask pupils to go above the very lowest levels.

A Condensed Version of the Cognitive Domain of the
Taxonomy of Educational Objectives

Knowledge

1.00 Knowledge
1.10 Knowledge of Specifics

[3] Based on and adapted from Harold W. Bernard, *Psychology of Learning and Teaching,* 2nd ed. (New York: McGraw-Hill Book Company, 1965), pp. 9–11.

1.11 Knowledge of Terminology
1.12 Knowledge of Specific Facts

1.20 Knowledge of Ways and Means of Dealing with Specifics
1.21 Knowledge of Conventions
1.22 Knowledge of Trends and Sequences
1.23 Knowledge of Classifications and Categories
1.24 Knowledge of Criteria
1.25 Knowledge of Methodology

1.30 Knowledge of the Universals and Abstractions in a Field
1.31 Knowledge of Principles and Generalizations
1.32 Knowledge of Theories and Structures

Intellectual Abilities and Skills

2.00 Comprehension
2.10 Translation
2.20 Interpretation
2.30 Extrapolation

3.00 Application

4.00 Analysis
4.10 Analysis of Elements
4.20 Analysis of Relationships
4.30 Analysis of Organizational Principles

5.00 Synthesis
5.10 Production of a Unique Communication
5.20 Production of a Plan, or Proposed Set of Operations
5.30 Derivation of a Set of Abstract Relations

6.00 Evaluation
6.10 Judgments in Terms of Internal Evidence
6.20 Judgments in Terms of External Criteria[4]

The Affective and Psychomotor Domains. Although intellectual goals may have the central position in education, instruction should not be narrowly intellectual. The cultivation of emotional responses, attitudes, appreciations, ideals, and sensitivity increasingly occupy a more important role in our schools as educators attempt to make education more humane and fulfilling. In *The Taxonomy of Educational Objectives,* the objectives of the affective domain are arranged into the following hierarchy.

The Affective Domain

1.   Receiving Attention
1.1 Awareness
1.2 Willingness to Receive
1.3 Controlled or Selected Attention

[4] Benjamin S. Bloom, ed., *Taxonomy of Educational Objectives, Handbook I: Cognitive Domain* (New York: David McKay Co., Inc., 1956).

2.0 Responding
2.1 Acquiescence in Responding
2.2 Willingness to Respond
2.3 Satisfaction in Response
3.0 Valuing
3.1 Acceptance of a Value
3.2 Preference of a Value
3.3 Commitment
4.0 Organization
4.1 Conceptualization of a Value
4.2 Organization of a Value System
5.0 Characterization by a Value or Value Complex
5.1 Generalized Set
5.2 Characterization[5]

The psychomotor domain has always been important in teaching the practical and vocational arts, but teachers have not always realized that psychomotor aspects are also important in teaching the humanities and social sciences. Both the affective and psychomotor goals contribute to fuller understandings. They cannot be divorced from cognitive learning, and they are essential for developing good thinking and for relevant education. Instruction limited merely to cognitive objectives will not suffice.

THE OBJECTIVES OF SOCIAL STUDIES EDUCATION

Several years ago a survey of the published objectives for the social studies found the over-all purpose of the social studies curriculum to be the promotion of good citizenship. Good citizenship is not the only aim of social studies curricula. Examples of more specific objectives for social studies instruction have been stated by the Pennsylvania Council for the Social Studies.

> The concern of the social studies program is the development of individuals who understand their own social world—the world of men, their activities, and their interaction—who desire to be productive and contributing members of a free society, who feel a responsibility for helping to conserve, transmit, and expand for the future generation the heritage of values and ideals of that society. To accomplish these broad general goals, it is believed that the social studies program must focus on providing learning experiences which will help the individual student
>
> 1. Understand that physical environment has conditioned when and how men live.
> 2. Understand how man in turn has attempted to adapt to, use, and control the forces and resources of his environment.
> 3. Understand that change is a condition of all human societies.

---

[5] David R. Kratwohl, Benjamin S. Bloom, and Bertram B. Masia, *Taxonomy of Educational Objectives, Handbook II, Affective Domain* (New York: David McKay Co., Inc., 1964).

4. Gain insight into the forces that bring about change in culture as well as into the problems of cultural change.

5. Appreciating the need for achieving a balance between change and stability.

6. Recognize and understand the implications of the growing interdependency of all people and nations of the world—the need for an appreciation of the value of difference, the acceptance of responsibility for the effects of our actions on other people and cultures, the need for group cooperation in meeting societal needs.

7. Appreciate and understand the role of all races, religions, and cultures in the cultural heritage.

8. Appreciate the problems of the peoples of Asia, Africa, Latin America, and the Middle East as well as Europe through an understanding of their history, their tradition, their religious beliefs and moral values.

9. Recognize and appreciate the dignity and worth of the individual as the all-important unit of society.

10. Understand and appreciate our American heritage.

11. Understand the basic structure as well as other principal functions of our democratic form of government.

12. Understand that a vital democracy depends upon an informed citizenry who are willing and capable of a responsible social role.

13. Understand that in a democratic society the people, through their government, have the responsibility for managing their national resource potential for the welfare of the greatest public.

14. Appreciate the need for and the problems of ever-widening group loyalties.

15. Acquire faith in the intelligence of free men to resolve the problems of our modern society and conflicts in our value system by the democratic processes of free inquiry.

16. Understand the structure and functions of our economic system and develop competence as a producer and consumer.

17. Develop greater competition and self-direction in the skills and techniques basic to the social studies.

18. Gain experience in the historical method of arriving at fact and valid conclusions.

19. Realize that our understandings of the past are ever changing as the result of the discovery of the new facts and new interpretations of the past.[6]

SOME PRINCIPLES OF LEARNING

Although learning theory is still young and still very soft in spots, there are numerous principles about which there is firm agreement. Choose strategies and tactics that are consistent with these general principles of learning.

---

[6] *A Recommended Curriculum in the Social Studies for the Secondary Schools* (University Park: Pennsylvania Council for the Social Studies, 1961).

1. Pupils learn best when they are ready. A pupil who is not ready to learn something cannot learn it efficiently at the time. Readiness is a combination of maturity, motivation, experience, ability, perception, aptitude, and other factors that make one ready for a given learning. If one uses the proper procedures it is quite possible to make ready pupils who are not yet ready.

2. Learning proceeds more effectively when the learner is motivated to learn.

3. Individuals learn at different rates and in different styles.

4. Pupils learn how to learn. Therefore, how one learns now tends to determine how one will learn in the future.

5. One's perception of a situation determines his conceptions and behavior in that situation.

6. The whole learner is involved in the learning process. Cognitive and skill learning have affective overtones and vice versa.

7. Learning always takes place in relation to some goal. Pupils learn better if the instructional goals are the same as their own goals and they are consciously working toward these goals. Teachers make little headway when they are combatting powerful pupil goals. Once pupils have reached the goals they have set for themselves, they seldom progress farther until they have set higher goals for themselves.

8. Learning depends on reinforcement. Both reward and punishment may be reinforcing but punishment is not dependable and may do more harm than good. A sense of self-satisfaction from having done something well and a chance to participate in new stimulating activities are among the most powerful rewards. To be most effective, reinforcement should follow learning immediately.

9. To learn one must do something. Anything one does may result in learning, but most school learning must be purposeful, hard work.

10. Pupils react unfavorably to overdirection.

11. Learning that does not transfer to new situations is useless. Learning inspired by incentive—that is, extrinsically motivated learning—does not transfer well.

12. Learning is not additive, it is integrative.

13. Pupils seem to learn more readily from their peers than from adults.

14. Pupils try hardest when the task they are to perform is within their range of challenge—that is, when it is neither too hard nor too easy.

15. Time spent in recalling something is more effective than rereading.

16. Pupils learn what they expect to be tested on.

17. Information that confirms one's opinions or attitudes is learned more readily than information that refutes them.

18. The opinion of one's peer group is a powerful motivation.

19. To form concepts pupils should encounter specific instances in which the distinctive attribute is present and others in which it is not present so that the pupils can infer the concept from specific instances. Then they should apply the concepts.

20. Skills learned in isolation do not function.

21. One learning product does not guarantee another.

22. Meaningful material is easily learned and transferred.

23. Everything else being equal, teaching by means of direct experience is ordinarily more effective than teaching by means of vicarious experience.

24. Psychomotor learning occurs best when there is explanation, demonstration, and meaningful practice.

25. Pleasant experiences are more useful for changing attitudes than unpleasant experiences.

26. Cognitive learning can be achieved both by rote association and by discovery techniques.[7]

SOME CHARACTERISTICS OF SECONDARY AND MIDDLE SCHOOL PUPILS AND IMPLICATIONS FOR TEACHING

Each pupil is unique. Because pupils differ, we must avoid stereotypic thinking about them and provide for differences in their programs, in our methods of teaching them, in the materials of instruction we use, and so on.

On the other hand, the young are more alike than they are different, so it is safe to make some general observations about the characteristics of youth, if the reader will remember to take them with a grain of salt.

1. A pupil is an entire organism. Anything he learns or does affects him as an entity. All activity has emotional, mental, and physical aspects. This applies to school learning as well as to other activities.
2. Pupils are plastic. They can be shaped, but in the process they interact with the environment. They are not just wax tablets to be written on. They are not passive, nor do they just react to environmental stimuli—although the environment has a great deal to do with what a pupil is, what he becomes, and how he behaves.
3. Adolescence is a period of change accompanied by rapid and uneven growth. These changes may cause many conflicts within a youth and in his social relations.
4. Secondary school age pupils and middle school age pupils tend to be emotional, moody, and flighty. Schools are likely to be sources of frustration, failure, humiliation, and punishment to them. They are a combination of naïveté and sophistication.
5. Secondary school pupils need to establish themselves as young men and young women. They need to learn how to live their roles in a heterosexual world and to make adjustments to their new evidence of sexuality and its attendant problems. In this connection, secondary school pupils have certain developmental tasks to perform. They, consciously or unconsciously, try to carry out those tasks by, quite properly, giving them a higher priority than schoolwork and other tasks. According to Havighurst these developmental tasks are:
   a. To learn to understand oneself, to live with and compensate for one's inadequacies, and to make the most of one's assets.

---

[7] *Learning Principles*, Madison, Wisc.: Wisconsin State Department of Public Instruction, 1964.

    b. To learn what it is to be a young man or young woman and to act accordingly.

    c. To develop a suitable moral code.

    d. To learn how to act one's part in a heterosexual society.

    e. To determine, prepare for, and become placed in his vocation.

    f. To acquire a suitable philosophy of life.

X   g. To build a system of values.

    h. To establish himself as an independent individual free from his mother's apron strings.

X   i. To learn how to make reasonable decisions in serious matters of his own responsibility without undue reliance on an older person.

    j. To master the social and intellectual level and knowledge necessary for adult life.

    k. To learn the skills of courtship and to establish close friendships with persons of the opposite sex as preparation for finding a suitable mate.

    l. To break away from his childhood home.

X   m. To learn what kind of person he is himself and to learn to live with himself.[8]

6. Secondary school pupils are trying to establish their independence. They tend to be very critical of adults and of the adult world and to reject adult authority and domination. They tend to associate school learning with adult domination and so reject it.

7. In spite of their desire for asserting their independence, secondary school age pupils have great need for security. They are greatly concerned about themselves—their bodies, social relations, future, image, status, and so on. This accounts for such phenomena as going steady, early marriage, conformity, and the like. It also accounts for many rapid extreme alternations in behavior. It follows then that secondary school programs should be supportive.

8. Secondary school pupils tend to be obsessed by conformity. Even the "nonconformists" are conformists. Adolescents tend to conform to the standards of the adolescent community rather than those of adults—although these standards may be the same.

9. In their efforts to establish themselves as grown-ups, youths are likely to experiment with undesirable behavior calculated to illustrate their independence, manliness or womanliness, and adulthood.

10. Secondary school pupils desire self-realization and so need to achieve to feel important, and to be accepted by their peers and by adults. They don't want to be talked down to or to be treated like children. They need responsibility. They need the chance to be leaders sometimes. Therefore teachers should give all pupils a chance to shine, to show off a little, and to assume some real responsibility.

11. Because of his desire for recognition and achievement the pupil of secondary school age is likely to be sympathetic to the desires of others, particularly the disadvantaged and downtrodden in their search for civil rights, economic

---

[8] Robert J. Havighurst, *Human Development and Education* (New York: Longmans, Green & Co., 1953), Chap. 1, pp. 9–15, 19, 20; also *Developmental Tasks and Education,* 2nd ed. (New York: Longmans, Green & Co., 1952).

opportunity, freedom, and so forth. Secondary school pupils tend to be "suckers for causes" whether well deserved or not.

12. Secondary school pupils are concerned about the meaning of life and self. They are concerned with vocational choice (some of them at least). They do not see much relevance or pertinence to most of the content in the secondary school curriculum.

13. Youth of secondary school age are more ready to learn through verbal means than younger ones. They are not as dependent on demonstration, manipulation, nonverbal perception, and the like as younger pupils are. On the other hand, they cannot learn everything from entirely verbal presentations. (Neither can adults for that matter.)

14. Pupils have long attention spans, but low tolerance to boredom.

15. Youth are self motivating. It is not a matter of getting pupils to do something so much as getting them to direct their activities into desirable directions. Schools and teachers need to provide relevant curricula, courses, and lessons that have meaning to pupils and that they can see real reasons for doing.

X 16. Pupils are interested by activity, novelty, adventure, and the like.

SOME PHILOSOPHICAL POSITIONS

Every teacher makes a good share of his curricular and methodological decisions on the basis of philosophical beliefs that cover some of the following questions. You will too. What is your position on them?

What are the proper aims of education? Should the principal object of the schools be to cultivate the pupils' souls, to develop their intellects, to make them good citizens, to prepare them vocationally, to educate them for complete living, or what?

Should education be preparation for the future (adulthood), or should it deal with the problems and concerns of the present and let the future take care of itself?

In educating for citizenship should one try to build an elite or should education be egalitarian? Can education be both "equal and excellent"?

Must one prepare pupils for freedom by first providing instruction and discipline so that they will be ready when allowed freedom, or should one let pupils live democratically, or freely, from the beginning and learn the self-discipline necessary for good living in a society by practice?

Should one (can one) indoctrinate for democracy so that pupils will know what is right, or should one allow pupils to draw their own beliefs?

What is the nature of man—particularly of learners? Is human nature fixed? Is man a finished product? To what extent is man a free agent? Can human nature be changed? Does it change all the time anyway?

To what extent are individuals different? Are we basically all the same with only surface variations, or are we truly individuals?

Should learning be passive or dynamic? Should the learner accept a rigid, cut-and-dried curriculum in which the facts and inferences are laid out in a disciplined way by authority, or should learning emphasize process and the construction of knowledge by the learner through problem solving and other dynamic learning experiences? Is there really an alternative, or does the nature of man as a learner mandate one or the other of these approaches?

Who should be educated? Everyone? If not, then who? If so, how?

What is mind? Is it like a muscle, or like a receptacle, or like a tablet to be written on, or is it something one creates for himself? Does one develop the intellect in pupils by disciplining it (the mind as muscle), through filling it (the mind as receptacle), by shaping it (the wax tablet), or must it be created by thinking out the solutions to problems?

What is the nature of knowing? When does one know something? How does one know? Does one create his own knowledge or does he discover it out there?

What is the nature of knowledge?

What is the nature of subject matter? What subject matter is of the most worth? Should one stress process or information? Should subject matter be taught for its own sake, for use, or simply as a medium for teaching the intellectual processes? Does subject matter have intrinsic value, or does it have only operational value—that is, value contingent on use?

What is the difference between process and content? Are they both subject matter?

What is the difference between liberal studies and vocational or practical studies? Are vocational and practical studies vulgar and demeaning or can they be humane and liberalizing studies too?

What is the nature of truth? Is truth absolute and constant, or is it relative, conditional, and changeable?

What is the nature of value? Is value absolute, fixed, objective, and intrinsic, or is it relative, changeable, conditional, or instrumental? Are things good or good for something?

Does subject matter have intrinsic value, or does it have only instrumental value?

Should the curriculum be fixed or flexible? Are certain things essential for all pupils to learn? Should certain things be required of all pupils—or all pupils with certain goals? Should we stick by the curricula and subject matter that have proven themselves in the past, or must we change with the times—in essentials, not just superficials? Is any content really essential?

Should education center on the group or on the individual? Should individual welfare and interest be subordinate to those of the group?

What is the role of authority in education? What should it be? Should one seek authority for ultimate decisions, or should one trust his own judgment?

PART II

General Methods of Teaching

CHAPTER 2

Basic Methodological Problems

LEARNING TO KNOW THE PUPILS

Good teaching is aimed teaching: if you are to aim your teaching well, you must know your target. Therefore, you must have considerable knowledge about adolescents in general and each of your pupils in particular.

METHODS OF LEARNING ABOUT PUPILS

1. Consult the cumulative record folder.
2. Observe the pupils—individually and collectively—both in class time and at other times. To objectify your observations
   a. Use rating scales and check lists. (See Chapter 7 for instructions in preparing and using rating scales and check lists.)
   b. Record observations as soon as possible. Use anecdotal reports and behavior logs.
3. Use pupil conferences. In conducting pupil conferences,
   a. Keep questions open.
   b. Avoid moralizing, judging, or condemning.
   c. Accept the pupil, his opinions, and his values.
   d. Listen. (Let him tell you. It is not necessary for you to comment or take a position.)
   e. Record the gist or important points immediately. Use anecdotal record, behavior log, or the like.
   f. Utilize class time, study-hall time, after-school time, and out-of-school time.
   g. Plan short, quick conferences. Several short, quick conferences can add up to more than one long one.
4. Utilize parent conferences.
5. Utilize material such as
   a. Autobiographies. (They often are assigned by the English department and are on file in cumulative folders.)
   b. Themes and other papers.

   c. Reading reaction sheets.

   d. Value sheets.

   e. Reaction sheets.

   f. Open-ended question sheets.

   g. Thought sheets.

   h. Autobiographical questionnaires. For example

      (1) Have you attended other schools? What were they like?

      (2) What do you plan to do after you have finished your education?

      (3) What is your father's vocation?

      (4) What are his hobbies or other interests?

      (5) What is your mother's vocation?

      (6) What are her interests and hobbies?

      (7) Do you have a job? Describe it. How long do you work?

      (8) How do you spend your leisure time?

      (9) What is your favorite recreation?

      (10) What do you do during your vacations?

      (11) Do you like to read? What have you read lately?

      (12) Do you go to the movies often? What movies do you like to see?

      (13) What are your favorite TV shows?

      (14) Do you like sports? What kinds?

      (15) Do you have a hobby? What is it? Why do you like it?

6. Use tests and other diagnostic devices. Both standardized and homemade tests are excellent sources of information. Use them as diagnostic devices.

7. Use sociometric devices. Sociometric devices are useful for showing the structure of groups and subgroups in a class, and to show the relationship of an individual pupil to the group and to his associates.

DISCIPLINE AND CONTROL

If teaching and learning are to make any progress at all, they must take place in a reasonably quiet, orderly setting. Much has been written, and will continue to be written, about control and discipline, and most of it will be disappointing to the neophyte. The truth of the matter is that no one can predict what techniques would prove most effective in any particular situation. And even if it were possible, it would be a rare beginning teacher who could remember what he had been told in the midst of a difficult disciplinary incident. However, here are some general principles and a few specific techniques that may help you.

To Achieve Control

1. Start establishing control the very first day of class. Begin the class at once and then continue in a businesslike way.

2. Start classes on time and end them on time. On the other hand, do not let the class begin until everyone is paying attention.

3. Keep the classroom atmosphere easy and informal, but purposeful. If possible, establish a mood for pleasant working conditions.

4. Plan and prepare carefully. Try to use methods appropriate to both the material to be taught and the pupils to whom it will be taught.
5. Try to make the class interesting to keep the pupils well motivated.
   a. Vary your teaching procedures and learning activities.
   b. Keep pupils active. Use visuals, discussions, and questions and answers to break up lecture and recitation periods.
   c. Allow for individual differences. Plan variations in the assignments so that pupils can occupy themselves profitably at different activities suited to their interests, needs, and abilities.
   d. Above all, make the classes worthwhile.

DISCIPLINARY TECHNIQUES

No matter how careful you are, some pupils will misbehave. In most cases pupil mischief is no more than an indication of youthfulness and you should take it in your stride. Nevertheless you must take steps to prevent recurrences.

1. Sometimes pupils who are restless and noisy can be calmed down by a "snap" quiz or a written assignment.

2. A similar technique is to pepper the noisy or inattentive pupils with more than their share of questions.

3. Sometimes you may be able to cultivate the ring leader and get him to declare himself on your side.

4. Conferences with the malefactors and/or their parents can be a great help also.

5. In some cases the bad actors should be referred to the guidance department for help, or to the principal's office for strong disciplinary action. You should not have to do this often, but you should not hesitate to do it when it is necessary.

6. In other cases you will be forced to punish the pupil yourself. When this time comes, punish him immediately and severely enough so that he realizes he is being punished and that being punished is not pleasant.

So that there is no doubt, set up a few reasonable rules that everyone understands. Infraction of these rules must result in almost automatic punishment. If pupils know that infraction brings instant impersonal punishment, they will avoid breaking your rules—particularly if the rules seem reasonable. Under no circumstances should you set up rules and then not follow through.

If it is at all possible, make punishment a constructive learning experience. To this end you may want to use suspended sentences for first offenders. Sometimes constructive penalties may be hard to find and the teacher may have to resort to such dead-end penalties as detention, isolating or ostracizing the pupil, and depriving him of privileges. In any case avoid questionable practices such as corporal punishment, sarcasm, ridicule, punishing the entire class for the faults of a few, or even the many, and assigning extra classwork. These practices seldom give the result desired, but rather arouse the indignation and enmity of the pupils toward the class and to the subject. Above all, avoid nagging and hollering. They only disrupt the class further and get you nowhere.

MOTIVATION

PROCEDURES THAT FOSTER PUPIL MOTIVATION

A person's motivation is part of his inner being. He provides his own motives and makes his own decisions in the light of his perception of the circumstances. About all you can do to influence motivation is to try to arrange the external situation so that the pupils will decide to act in the way you desire. Use these procedures to win and influence your pupils.

1. Make the activities and potential learning seem worthwhile.
   - X a. Be enthusiastic yourself.
   - b. Center activities around the everyday concerns of pupils whenever feasible.
   - c. Point out how classroom learning can be used in other classes and school activities, at home, and in social and community life both now and in the future.
   - d. Emphasize immediate rather than deferred values.
   - e. Provide enough variety so that pupils will find activities and material interesting and meaningful.
   - f. Encourage pupils to participate in the planning.
   - g. Avoid overdependence on marks and grades.
   - h. Be sure the activities and potential learnings really are worthwhile.
2. Utilize the pupils' motives.
   - a. Fit your teaching to their attitudes, interests, ideals, and goals.
   - X b. Capitalize on their curiosity.
   - X c. Preen their feathers. Provide plenty of opportunities for them to experience success and the approval of others. Give praise when praise is due.
   - d. Avoid threats and the use of fear. Sometimes one must resort to such procedures, but reserve them for the times when they are really necessary.
   - e. Make learning adventurous fun.
   - X f. Utilize group activities in which pupils can capitalize on their desire to socialize.
3. Help pupils establish suitable tasks and objectives.
   - a. Give clear instructions and assignments.
   - b. Be sure pupils know what they are trying to do.
   - c. Be sure pupils know the reason why they should do whatever it is they are supposed to do.
   - d. Be sure they know how to do what they are supposed to do.
4. Keep up the pace.
   - a. Make learning activities lively.
   - b. Involve pupils in their own learning. Let them dig it out themselves, rather than serve it up to them on a platter.
   - c. Provide a variety of activities.
   - d. Make the work difficult enough to challenge them but not so difficult as to discourage them.
   - e. Let them know how they are progressing.
5. Create a receptive mood.

a. Try to run a happy ship. Laughter, fun, humor, cooperation, pleasantness, and politeness all help to make the classroom a happy place. People learn better in a happy frame of mind.

b. Make your wares as attractive as possible.

6. Create an encouraging atmosphere.

Try to create an atmosphere that encourages each pupil to try out his ideas and do his best without fear of reprisals if he makes honest mistakes.

To Create a Supportive Atmosphere

Before pupils will accept the supportive nature of a class, the teacher must prove himself. As a rule, pupils have been disappointed too often to believe teachers who say they want pupils to think and act freely without recrimination.

1. Allow free but orderly interaction.

2. Refrain from forcing pupils to take part.

3. Guide but do not direct. The class should not be completely nondirective, but the pupils should not be *told* what to think.

4. Refrain from being overcritical. If pupils make errors in English, or errors in thinking, do not jump on them. If the error is important, correct it. If it is not, forget it. Perhaps you will want to question a pupil about his logic. But, whatever you do, don't discourage him from thinking.

5. Refrain from making speeches.

X 6. Ask open-ended questions.

7. Don't rush the pupils; give them time.

8. Refrain from upstaging the pupils. The pupils are the stars—not the teacher. The teacher is a supporting character.

9. Keep the atmosphere in the class informal, but polite.

X 10. Don't react negatively to strong feeling. Pupils have a right to get involved.

TEACHING SKILLS IN THE SOCIAL SCIENCES

One seldom thinks of the social studies as a skill subject. Yet prominent among social studies content are map skills, study skills, the skills of scholarship, and skills in critical thinking. The principles for teaching all skills—motor skills and others—are much the same: (1) the pupil must first learn the procedures involved in the skill either through instruction or by trial and error, (2) he must practice until he becomes skillful, (3) he must continue to use the skill in order to maintain it.

TEACHING UNDERSTANDING

How Concepts Are Learned

Although abstractions, concepts seldom exist in the abstract. Rather, each concept exists in the mind of someone, where it is that person's understanding of something—that is to say, the sum total of all the ideas or notions that that person has about a particular topic. Thus, one's concept or understanding of green is the totality of all one's ideas about green; one's concept of democracy, all one's ideas about democracy. Although a person's concept may be imperfect or incorrect, it is his and his alone. This is why no two people have exactly the same understanding of anything.

Evidently one develops a concept by a combination of locating the feature or features common to a class while observing that feature in numerous situations or examples and by separating it from other features in the situations or examples not common to the class. Thus we find that a child, after having had several meetings with warm and wiggly furry animals of various shapes, may begin to have some notions basic to the concept "doggie." Only later, when he has had some experience with another animal bearing slightly different features and "prickers in his feet," may he be able to separate the notions peculiar to doggie from "kitty." In short, then, the steps in the concept development are

1. Locating the common property or feature.
2. Isolating the common property or features
   a. By varying the concomitants.
   b. By contrast.
3. Labeling or sorting the categories.

SUGGESTIONS FOR TEACHING CONCEPTS

1. *Provide for a variety of experiences.*

   You cannot give another person an understanding—certainly not by simple exposition. The learner has to learn concepts through doing; for one attains concepts primarily by sorting out a collection of experiences and ordering them in one's mind. Note that these experiences are not intellectual only. The emotions, the senses, and physical activity are also involved. To understand clearly the pupils must have many opportunities to turn the concept over, handle it, view it from all sides and in different contexts, and approach it from different directions. Many pupils have incomplete understandings because their teachers did not provide them with a wide enough variety of experiences.

2. *Avoid overdependence on verbal activities.*

   Concepts are not learned by words alone. Overdependence on words leads to mere verbalism[1] rather than understanding. You will probably have to use all sorts of learning activities—role playing, audiovisual materials, discussions, construction activities, and many more—before your pupils will begin to build a clear understanding of the desired concept.

3. *Explain the official meaning of concepts clearly.*

   It is not enough that a pupil be able to explain his personal concept to you. He ought to be able to explain the *official* meaning in his own words and to

---

[1] That is, the repetition of words without understanding their meaning.

General Discovery Strategy for Teaching Generalizations

A discovery strategy for teaching a generalization—or concept is to
a. Select the generalization or generalizations.
b. Pick sub-generalizations, if necessary.
c. Diagnose the pupil's present understanding and need
d. Set up a problem situation.
e. Set up experiences that will bring out the essential elements during the problem solving.
f. Set up experiences that will bring out contrasting experiences.
g. Draw generalization or concept.
h. Apply the generalization or concept.

provide a number of examples. Ordinarily, teacher explanation and questioning are essential to achieve this high a level of concept learning.

4. *Use clarifying operations, for instance:*
   a. Ask the pupil to define what he means in his own terms.
   b. Ask the pupil to illustrate or demonstrate his meanings.
   c. Throw the pupil's idea back at him, perhaps rephrased, and ask him if this is what he really means.
   d. Ask him to consider the implications or logical consequences of his idea.
   e. Ask him to summarize or to prepare a precis in which he brings out the essential elements.
   f. Ask him to organize his meaning into a logical outline.[2]
5. *Use discovery techniques.*

   The greatest teachers of all times based their teaching on questions, examples, and parables. Today these and the other discovery techniques are considered to be the most useful in teaching concepts. The essential element in this type of teaching is for the pupils to derive their own concepts by inference from pertinent data under the guidance of a competent teacher.
6. *Provide opportunities for pupils to form concepts and generalizations by means of both inductive and deductive inferences.*

   Either type of inference is more likely to be effective in concept attainment than the common practice of teaching concepts as facts to be learned. One way to teach a concept or generalization by deductive inference, for instance, would be to
   a. Give the pupils a definition of a generalization as a proposition.
   b. Give the pupils a list of specific cases, some of which exemplify the generalization and others that do not.

---

[2] Adapted in part from Leonard H. Clark and Irving S. Starr, *Secondary School Teaching Methods,* 2nd ed. (New York: The Macmillan Company, 1967), p. 17. The original list was derived largely from Louis Raths' *What is Teaching?,* undated, mimeographed.

c. Have the pupils test the specific cases to see whether they fit the definition or not. Use forms like the following.

Definition of Concept or Generalization	
Exemplars that fit the definition	Exemplars that do not fit the definition

To teach pupils by means of inductive inferences use such methods as the problem-solving method, the case-study method, the Socratic method, the parable method, the inductive method.

In developing generalizations by way of the inductive or deductive processes, be prepared to give pupils a great deal of guidance. Help pupils make proper inferences by giving them hints concerning structure, strategy and tactics, principles, laws, and relationships.

7. *Pointing out the essential elements.*

Whatever your approach to concept teaching, be sure that the essential elements are conspicuous. Point things out verbally and visually, hint, and use leading questions.

8. *Use advance organizers.*

An advance organizer is a short—500 words or so—summary or overview of what is to be learned. In the advance organizer, the teacher provides the pupil with principles on which to hang the facts and concepts he will learn. It should help him relate the new learning with what he already knows. It should present the unifying concepts, as well as the discriminators (analogies and comparisons), that will help pupils to see the meaning and relationship of the new subject matter to be learned.

In preparing an advance organizer be sure that it

a. Gives an overview of what is to be learned.

b. Relates past learning with the new subject matter to be learned.

c. Provides organizing elements.

d. Is more abstract and general than the subject matter to be learned.

A study guide made up of questions and suggestions similar to the principles, concepts, and hints contained in the summation of the advance organizer can serve the purpose of an advance organizer.

9. *Foster divergent original thinking.*

10. *Cultivate critical attitudes toward one's own concepts.*

Socratic questioning, which introduces the pupil to information that does not fit his preset beliefs, is an excellent technique for creating critical attitudes.

11. *Encourage pupils to test their generalizations.*
    Encourage your pupils to test their own generalizations. The tests are those that are ordinarily used to test hypotheses in scientific study. (See "Teaching How to Think.")
12. *Emphasize generalizing rather than the generalizations.*

TEACHING ATTITUDES, INTERESTS, AND VALUES

Attitudes, appreciations, ideals, interests, values, and ethical moral character are all very much harder to teach than concepts and skills. Yet, if the nation and the world are to survive, we teachers must assume at least some of the responsibility for teaching them and teaching them effectively.

DEVELOPMENT OF ATTITUDES AND IDEALS

Development of Attitudes. We develop attitudes in a number of ways.

1. We develop attitudes by imitating other people either consciously or unconsciously. We tend to take on the attitudes of the people with whom we associate.
2. We develop attitudes by identifying with a model and attempting to copy the behavior of that model. Adolescents are likely to pick as models someone a little older than they are. Junior high school pupils model themselves after high school pupils and high school pupils after college students, for example.
3. We develop attitudes from emotional experiences. Good emotional experiences usually result in favorable attitudes; unhappy emotional experiences usually result in unfavorable attitudes.
4. We develop attitudes as a result of information. Thus, one's attitudes toward black people are likely to become more favorable if one realizes the great accomplishments of black individuals and societies. In this respect, casual, off-the-cuff information is as likely to be instrumental in causing attitude change as more formal instruction, particularly if it is repeated.
5. We may deliberately cultivate an attitude. To do this one deliberately sets up an ideal and tries to follow it until it becomes habitual.

Development of Ideals. Ideals are purposeful goals toward which we strive. Repetition and reenforcement tend to make them automatic and thus change them into attitudes.
For pupils to adopt goals as ideals several conditions must be satisfied.

1. The pupil must understand what the goal is.
2. The goal must be presented in such a way that the pupil sees it as desirable. For this purpose direct instruction is of little value. Appealing to personal concern and giving pupils models to follow are more likely to be convincing.
3. The pupil's awareness of desirability of the goal must be reenforced time and time again.

Development of Appreciation and Interests.   Appreciation and interests are special kinds of attitudes and are developed in the same way as other attitudes. In attempting to develop appreciations, however, one should pay particular attention to the affective tone of the presentations and the examples pupils have to follow.

To Develop Values.   According to Raths, Harmin, and Simon, if one wants to develop values in pupils, it would be well to

1. Encourage children to make choices, and to make them freely.
2. Help them discover and examine available alternatives when faced with choices.
3. Help children weigh alternatives thoughtfully, reflecting on the consequences of each.
4. Encourage children to consider what it is that they prize and cherish.
5. Give them opportunities to make public affirmations of their choices.
6. Encourage them to act, behave, live in accordance with their choices.
7. Help them to examine repeated behaviors or patterns in their life.[3]

SAMPLE TACTICS AND STRATEGIES FOR TEACHING ATTITUDES AND IDEALS

Fortunately, there are a number of strategies and tactics that one can use to teach attitudes.

1. Use informal activities in which there is plenty of give and take and casual, incidental remarks and questions. Avoid using lecture and recitation when trying to teach attitudes.
2. Arrange for pupils to meet the phenomena to which the attitude relates time and time again in circumstances favorable to the attitude.
3. Avoid preaching and dictating.
4. Provide models for pupils to imitate and identify with.
   a. Provide models by means of literature, history, and current events. Biographies can be especially useful.
   b. Avoid models that are unrealistic, overly dramatic, or too far removed from the experience of the pupils. Pupils relate most readily to people who are something like themselves. To be effective
   (1) The model must be consistent.
   (2) The model must be prestigious in the eyes of the pupil.
   (3) The model must be seen to gain satisfaction from conforming to the ideal.
   c. Try to be the type of person pupils will seek to model themselves after.
   (1) Treat the pupils like intelligent human beings.
   (2) Make the pupils feel that they can do the work. Be supportive.
   (3) Be patient.
   (4) Have wide interests.

---

[3] Louis E. Raths, Merrill Harmin, and Sidney B. Simon, *Values and Teaching: Working with Values in the Classroom* (Columbus, Ohio: Charles E. Merrill Publishers, 1966), pp. 38–39.

    (5) Be fair.

    (6) Cultivate a sense of humor.

    (7) Don't take yourself too seriously.

5. Present pupils with information and facts of a positive type. Casual information and explanations as pupils are working along oftentimes are more effective than long exhortations.

6. Let pupils find out the facts and information for themselves. Encourage them to check for facts as opposed to opinion or polemic.

7. Encourage pupils to draw inferences from their information. Challenge their thinking by asking: Where did you get that idea? Do the facts bear out your opinion? Can you prove it? Do you really mean what you have said? Is that thinking logical?

8. Use group procedures such as role playing and discussion groups; group pressures are powerful molders of attitudes.

9. Appeal to emotions.

10. Appeal to classroom leaders.

11. Use films to present attitudes. Be sure to discuss them with the class and try to influence the pupils to see things objectively. Prejudice and other attitudes are apt to cause pupils to perceive things quite differently from what you expected.

12. Use inductive methods, problem-solving case studies, and other approaches in which pupils find their own answers.

13. Use value clarifying responses, value sheets, and value continuums.

14. Use open-ended questions.

15. Play the devil's advocate. Present arguments for the other side. Let the pupils argue you down if they can.

16. Contrive incidents for pupils to discuss and draw conclusions from.

17. Utilize role-playing and simulation techniques.

TEACHING HOW TO THINK

THE THINKING PROCESS

Critical or reflective thinking has been defined as the process of rearranging and reorganizing information and knowledge to make new knowledge. Note that this definition speaks of a process rather than of a thing or an event. If you remember that thinking is a process, it may save you from making a number of pedagogical errors.

Convergent Versus Divergent Thinking. Reflective thinking may be convergent, divergent, or evaluative. Convergent thinking involves finding predictable answers—as in the solution of mathematical problems. Divergent thinking involves a free-ranging search for answers and is, therefore, not predictable. Evaluative thinking puts a value on things.

Each of these types of thinking is excellent for its purpose. The difficulty is to remember that each of the three has a place in classroom learning. Too much time is given to memory work, which is not thinking at all. Many teachers have a tendency to emphasize convergent thinking and to forget about the need for encouraging divergent and evaluative thinking.

Problem Solving. Most thinking involves problem solving — although thinking is not necessarily limited to problem solving. Problems may be of various types — static, dynamic; large, small; simple, complex — and may be solved in many ways. How we attack them is affected by many factors. Among the strategies people use to solve problems are intuition, trial and error, rationalization, dependence on authority or tradition, indoctrinated formulas, educated hunches based on past experience, wild guessing, or the inquiry technique that Dewey called the act of a complete thought.

In critical or reflective thinking, we go through the following processes.

1. We become aware of a problem (it may be started by the occasion, someone else, or ourselves), isolate it, and decide to do something about it.
2. We look for clues for the solution of the problem.
   a. We think up possible solutions (hypotheses) or approaches to take in solving the problem.
   b. We test the tentative solution or approaches against criteria that will help us evaluate them adequately.
3. We reject the tentative solutions or approaches that do not meet our requirements until we find one that is suitable, or give up. In making our conclusion, we may accept the first solution or approach that appears adequate, or we may test all hypotheses to find the best one.

Inferences. Reflective thinking of any kind is largely a matter of inferences. Inference may be deductive or inductive, but the heart of divergent original thinking is hypothesizing. Pupils need lots of practice in hypothesizing. They also need practice in checking out hypotheses. One of the primary faults of young people (and older ones too) is that often they go through the process of thinking up a solution, generalization, or conclusion, but do not really test the validity of the hypothesis.

To Test the Hypotheses or Generalizations

1. If data are drawn from authority, is the authority trustworthy?
   a. Are the findings of the authority consistent with those of other authorities?
   b. Does the authority base his argument on good evidence?
   c. Does the authority seem to be free of bias, self-serving, prejudice, or bigotry?
2. Is the hypothesis warranted?
   a. Is the sample on which the hypothesis is based adequate? Is it large enough and broad enough to give a faithful representation of the phenomenon being studied?
   b. Does the phenomenon repeat? As the sample is increased do the same characteristics continue? Even one instance that does not support a hypothesis makes the hypothesis suspect.
   c. Is the hypothesis consistent with what we already know? Does it harmonize with other generalizations and information? Does it explain all the relevant facts — not just part of them?
   d. Is the hypothesis simple systematically? The simplest hypothesis in this sense is the hypothesis that accounts for the most facts without adding as-

sumptions and that includes the fewest independent elements in its explanation of the phenomenon.

e. Is it the only hypothesis that adequately explains the phenomenon?
f. Is it fruitful? Does it lead to further investigation?
g. Is it subject to continual revision? No hypothesis is final. When new data
require changes in a hypothesis, it should be changed.[4]

To Check the Validity of Deductive Thinking

1. Determine the validity of the premises.
2. Determine whether the conclusions derive logically from the premises.

The first of these checks requires that premises be subjected to the proofs of
evidence. The second requires that the train of thought be tested logically; that
is, is it free from fallacy and errors in reasoning?

How We Learn to Think

Thinking is something we learn to do, it is not spontaneously generated. Our
thinking styles today are the culmination of skills, attitudes, and ideals we have
acquired over the years. Therefore, although it may be, as it is so often claimed,
that no one can teach another person to think well, it is possible to help pupils
develop the skills and attitudes necessary for efficient, effective thinking. Among
the skills needed for successful reflective thinking are

Finding, recognizing, and defining problems.
Finding evidence.
Observing accurately.
Interpreting and reporting correctly.
Judging evidence.
Detecting faulty arguments, polemics, bias, poor logic, and other evidences of
faulty reasoning.
Analyzing and evaluating data and alternatives.
Detecting relationships, seeing parts in relationship to the whole, tying ele-
ments together, recognizing similarities and differences.
Choosing between alternatives.
Making inferences and drawing conclusions.
Analyzing.

Attitudes and ideals needed for good thinking include

1. Ideal of suspended judgment.
2. Ideal of getting all the facts.
3. Objectivity.
4. Honesty.
5. Open-mindedness.
6. Critical mindedness.
7. Curiosity.

[4] See Maurice P. Hunt and Lawrence E. Metcalf, *Teaching High School Social Studies*, 2nd ed. (New
York: Harper and Row, Publishers, 1968), Chap. 5; and H. Gordon Hullfish and Philip G. Smith,
Reflective Thinking: The Method of Education (New York: Dodd, Mead & Co., 1961), Chap. 8.

8. Humility.
9. Thoroughness.
10. Self-respect.

Because thinking is so largely a skill, learning to think is largely a matter of practice. In the words of Comenius, one learns to think by thinking.

It follows, then, that pupils need plenty of opportunities to practice all the various types of thinking skills. The rules that govern any other practice also govern the practice of thinking skills.

Learning to think proceeds best in an atmosphere that supports the learner's ventures with the thinking process. As with other skills, the tyro in thinking makes mistakes. There is nothing evil about that. If the learner had already mastered the process, he would not need to learn it. It is important, however, that the learner get feedback from his mistakes so that he can learn to avoid them in the future. The reason that some people have never learned to think better is that they never had an opportunity to learn from the feedback of their thinking. Learning to think requires both freedom and discipline.

To Check Pupils' Thinking

To check the efficiency of pupils' thinking consider things like the following:

1. Is he interested in finding things out?
2. Does he stick with problems?
3. Is he rational? Does he think things through or jump to conclusions?
4. Does he test ideas?
5. Is he logical in his thinking?
6. Is he original, creative, or what?
7. How well can he recognize and define problems?
8. Can he formulate hypotheses?
9. Can he find and select pertinent evidence?
10. Can he draw valid conclusions?
11. Can he apply and test conclusions?
12. Can he judge worth of courses and evidence?
13. Can he distinguish fact from opinion?
14. Can he detect bias?

SUGGESTED STRATEGIES AND TACTICS FOR TEACHING PUPILS HOW TO THINK

Useful Teaching Strategies. Use such teaching strategies as the following. These categories are not mutually exclusive.

1. Inquiry.
2. Discovery.
3. Problem solving.

4. Socratic method.
5. Critical reading.
6. Debate.
7. Interviews.
8. Simulations—mock sessions.
9. Dramatizations.
10. Sociodrama.
11. Research assignments.
12. Discussion.

How Not To Teach Pupils
To Think

Formal logic
Formal discipline
Laissez-faire discussions, bull sessions, rap sessions
Teaching by formula

Specific Teaching Strategies That May Help Pupils Learn to Think

1. Emphasize understanding processes and reasons for correctness rather than correctness itself. Remember that thinking is a process, not an event or a thing. Give the pupils time to think, to investigate, to find alternatives to consider, to compare, to evaluate, and to make decisions.
2. Encourage pupils to gather information as a means by which to think rather than as an end in itself. Remember that information alone will not aid one's thinking. It is what one does with the information that counts. Do encourage wide reading and observation as tools for thinking, however.
3. Encourage pupils to check their reading for accuracy, logical thinking, polemics, and bias. (See Chapter 5.)
4. Be sure that logical thinking pays off. Reserve your highest rewards for careful, original, and logical thinking.
5. Utilize real problems that concern pupils. Encourage them to present problems that are important to them personally.
6. Encourage pupils to evaluate and criticize comments made in class by teacher and pupils.
7. Use many divergent and evaluative questions. Use both leading or probing questions as the situation may require.
8. Use lectures, texts, readings, and audiovisual aids as springboards to raise questions, to present problems, clarify problems or questions, and otherwise to involve pupils in the thinking process. Do not use lecture and telling techniques to present pupils with predigested answers![5]
9. Create problems to be solved.
   a. Adapt their own problems.

---

[5] See Chapter 4 for a fuller explanation of the use of springboards in inquiry teaching.

  b. Bring up conflicts; for example, the French position is _____; the British is _____; or the Conservatives favor _____; the Liberals _____.

  c. Bring up negative evidence that confutes their position. "Yes, but _____."

  d. Point out contradictions.

  e. Switch subject matter. "If this is so, how about _____?"

10. Let pupils do things themselves. Autonomy is a prerequisite for effective thinking. Let them be free to think and act. If they make mistakes, challenge them. Let them figure out what went wrong and why. Hold them to good standards of thinking. Do not allow yourself to curb pupils' thinking just because they come up with unpopular or bizarre conclusions. But do challenge them when their thinking seems ill-considered.

11. Give pupils plenty of opportunities to make decisions, both real decisions having to do with their own schoolwork, school, or community life, and simulated decisions in simulation games. Help them develop criteria for making decisions. Ask them to develop charts listing pros and cons. Let them live with their mistakes sometimes.

12. Use open-ended material. Allow disagreement. Encourage different solutions. Keep set solutions to a minimum. Never require a single right answer to a moot question. Show pupils that their ideas have value. Reward different and unusual approaches or solutions. Treat questions with respect. Welcome minority views.

13. Use problem solving. Let them enter into the entire problem-solving process: include selecting the problem, gathering data, finding possible solutions, and testing the solutions.

14. Give ample opportunity for criticism and evaluation. Criticism is just a verbally expressed evaluation. Ask the pupils to justify their criticism. Help them to build critical standards and to justify the standards. Use techniques such as the following:

  a. Select a topic for criticism; for example, a singer's performance.

  b. Evaluate the topic to be criticized.

    (1) Ask pupils to react. List their critical opinions about the topic (for example, the singer's performance) on the board.

    (2) Ask the pupils the reasons for their critical opinions. List them.

    (3) Ask pupils the reasons for the reasons. List these on the board.[6]

15. Encourage hypothesizing. Ask the pupils to find as many ways as they can to solve a problem or answer a question. Ask them to think of other possible solutions or alternatives than the ones presented in the book. Ask them to extrapolate from the information they have. Ask such questions as, "If this had or had not happened, then what?" Welcome divergent solutions and answers. Reward all answers and solutions even though they may appear ridiculous and will have to be rejected later. Don't always demand that pupils back up their ideas logically.

16. Encourage imagining. Have pupils provide endings for stories or plays; for example, "What might have happened if George Washington had decided to

---

[6] Mary Jane Aschner, "The Anatomy of Criticism," *The School Review*, **64**:317–322 (Oct. 1956).

try to capture Nova Scotia instead of sending Benedict Arnold to Quebec?"

17. Be sure pupils know what the words they are talking about mean. Ask for definitions. Help pupils to translate technical words into their own language. Try to impress on them the need for valid, reliable definitions. You can help pupils develop skill in defining and better understanding the words they use by asking them to make formal and informal definitions in their own words. Also ask questions that determine whether understandings of the words they use meet the stated criteria.

Standards for Acceptable Definitions

a. Be sure the definition is clear and unambiguous.

b. Be sure the definition includes the distinguishing attribute.

(1) Include only the attributes of the category being defined.

(2) Be sure all of the essential attributes of the category being defined are included.

c. State the definition positively.

d. Do not repeat the word or a synonym for the word being defined in the definition.

---

18. Have pupils look to see how alternate situations or events resemble or differ from each other. Ask such questions as, "In what ways are these the same?" "How do they differ?" "Are these really analogous?" Utilize statistical procedures—for example, scattergrams and correlations—to determine similarities.

19. Give pupils the opportunity to classify and categorize their evidence by type. This helps in organizing one's thinking, in comparing and contrasting, and in seeing relationships of the elements of a problem. Pupils should have experience in devising their own categories.

A useful device for developing systems of classifying data is the Data Retrieval Chart.[7]

Party	Conservative		Liberal	
Policy	Pro	Con	Pro	Con

FIGURE 2-1. *Data Retrieval Chart.*

[7] Charlotte Crabtree, "Supporting Reflective Thinking in the Classroom," in Jean Fair and Fannie R. Shaftel, eds., *Effective Thinking in the Social Studies,* Eighty-seventh Yearbook (Washington, D.C.: National Council for the Social Studies, 1967), pp. 105–106.

20. Have pupils explain the meaning and implications of what they read, see, and hear. For instance, what is the meaning of John's report? What is the significance of this passage? What did that film mean to you? What point was the author trying to make? Analyze documents. What do they say? What do they mean? What significance do they have?

21. Ask the pupils such questions as, "How did principle A operate in historical event B?" or, "On the basis of the situation as we know it and our understanding of such and such principles what would you expect to happen in situation X?" or, "How does situation Z illustrate principle Y?"

22. Encourage the attitude of proving. Require pupils to separate fact from opinion, prejudice, and the like. Require them to justify their assumptions. (On what assumptions is your position based? How do you know these assumptions are true?) Challenge the pupils' generalizations and other statements.

23. Organizing one's facts is akin to both categorizing and planning. Give pupils a chance to organize themselves and their material so that relationships become apparent. One way is to organize information into categories. Another is to ask pupils to arrange information into sequences — for example, temporal (chronological) or causal. For instance, you might give the pupils a scrambled list of facts at the beginning of the study of a topic and require the pupils to arrange these facts into a logical order as the topic is being studied.

Causes of Revolution

Revolution	Causes	
American		
French		
1848		
Russian		

Causes of Revolution

American	French	1848	Russian

Causes of Revolution

	American	French	1848	Russian
Despotic Rule				
Extreme Poverty				
etc.				

FIGURE 2-2. *Three Sample Organization Charts.*

Creative Thinking. Creative thinking is very much like critical and reflective thinking and problem solving. In most instances it is really the same. The steps in creative thinking are usually something like the following.

1. Preparation: The period in which one becomes familiar with the topic, gains the necessary background experience, and gets motivated and starts to work.

2. Incubation: The period in which the idea lies fallow and the creator relates and mulls over it.

3. Insight: The period in which the creator has his inspiration and produces his work.

4. Revision: The period in which the creator refines his creation.[8]

To Stimulate Creative Thinking

1. Show pupils you think their ideas are valuable. Treat their ideas and questions with respect. Even though their attempts may be crude at first, accept and encourage them.

2. Provide lots of opportunities for spontaneous expression—conversations, discussions, experimentation, projects, all sorts of experiences.

3. Avoid discouraging pupils. Do not set your standards too high. Be chary of gratuitous, negative comments. Sometimes let pupils do things without fear of being marked. (It is not necessary to mark everything a pupil does. In fact, your marks will probably be fairer if you consider most early attempts to be free trials or practice.)

4. Be patient. Take it easy. Do not rush them. Do not push them too hard. If a pupil is having trouble with one project, maybe you should let him change to another.

5. Take your time. Give the class a chance to relax and to ponder.

6. Do not drill on techniques until the pupil needs them. Then give aid as needed.

7. Once one has started, orderliness and system help, but do not sacrifice creativity on the altar of discipline.

TEACHING CONTROVERSIAL ISSUES

Any topic about which people hold strong, differing opinions can be considered controversial. It is because varying positions about social issues are held so strongly and emotionally that they cause special problems for the social studies teacher.

Controversial issues are open-ended. That is to say, the issues are never completely resolved. Even controversial issues of the past that may seem solved have a habit of raising their heads from time to time. Issues concerning the Reformation, the American Revolution, and the American Civil War, to cite only a few obvious examples, are still alive and perhaps will always be so. One should always treat them as live issues and avoid pat, dogmatic answers.

[8] William H. Burton, Roland B. Kimball, and Richard L. Wing, *Education for Effective Thinking* (New York: Appleton-Century-Crofts, 1960), p. 326. Copyright © 1960. By permission of Appleton-Century-Crofts, Educational Division, Meredith Corporation.

Why Teach Controversial Issues?

Controversial issues are important in the real life of a community. They are the topics of most importance in the social studies curriculum, because they concern vital problems. If you leave them out of your courses, you will not have much left to teach. That is exactly the trouble with many social studies courses. No wonder pupils find them boring.

In addition to making social studies courses more vital, the teaching of controversial issues gives pupils a chance to learn the skills and attitudes necessary for coping with the problems of modern society and for understanding the democratic process.

> Don't Neglect
> the Controversial Subjects
>
> Economics
> Race and Minority Groups
> Social Class
> Sex
> Courtship and Marriage
> Religion and Morality
> Nationalism
> Patriotism
> National Institutions

Choosing an Issue to Study

Before deciding whether or not to include a controversial issue in your teaching consider the following criteria:

1. Is the topic pertinent to your teaching goals? Will it further the achievement of those goals?
2. Is the topic pertinent to the course?
3. Are you competent and knowledgeable enough to handle it?
4. Is it significant? Is it worth taking the time?
5. Is it timely?
6. Can the pupils handle it? Are they mature enough? Do they have enough background?
7. Do you have time enough to do it justice?
8. Do you have, or can you get, enough suitable material to consider various points of view fairly and adequately?
9. Is the issue of concern to all rather than an individual matter?
10. Will it create more light than heat? Can it be discussed without overemotionality? Remember that it may be better to skip a controversial topic than to get pupils and parents so wrought up that the pupils cannot learn or think.

TEACHER RESPONSIBILITIES IN TEACHING CONTROVERSIAL ISSUES

To be successful in the teaching of a controversial issue, you will need extensive knowledge of the topic, teaching skill, tact and sensitivity, courage tempered with caution, discretion, and above all common sense.

1. Be sure that the topic is suitable for the pupils and the course.
2. Be sure that all necessary clearances are obtained, particularly if there seems to be any probability that the issues will cause the parents some concern.
3. Be sure that the pupils and the class are ready for discussion of the controversial issue.
   a. All necessary materials are at hand.
   b. Pupils have proper background.
   c. Teacher has proper background.
4. Be sure that all essential points of view are considered fairly.
5. Be sure that errors in fact or reasoning are pointed out to the pupils.
6. Be sure that pupils are allowed to formulate their own opinions and conclusions without undue influence, but with proper guidance.
7. Be sure to keep the topic under control. Remember that pupils (and their parents) have deep beliefs. To attempt to overturn these beliefs by direct teaching can result in heated battles that serve only to make people more convinced than they were before.
8. Stimulate and guide the pupils in their study of controversial issues, but do not overawe them or overpersuade them. Remember that controversial issues do not have easy or even right solutions and that your most dearly held beliefs may turn out to be wrong. On the other hand, you should feel free to tell pupils your opinions as long as you do not let your opinion keep them from thinking rationally.

SUGGESTED STRATEGIES AND TACTICS FOR TEACHING CONTROVERSIAL ISSUES

1. Use the indirect approach when studying hot issues that might flame up if approached directly. Instead of studying corruption in government in your own state or town, for instance, you might study it in Rome or in London.
2. Use problem-solving approaches featuring open-ended problems and research-type investigation.
3. Help pupils to discover and evaluate their own values. Use such procedures as value-clarifying responses, value sheets, value discussions.
4. Utilize such direct approach techniques as
   a. Debate.
   b. Panel discussion.
   c. Dramatics.
   d. Role playing.
   e. Simulation.
   f. Research techniques: interview, committee work.
   g. The jurisprudential approach.
5. Set up ground rules for the discussion of controversial topics:

    a. No name calling will be permitted.

    b. Facts must be supported by authority.

    c. Everyone must get a chance to express his opinion (even though he need not take it).

    d. All opinions and positions should be considered respectfully.

6. Simulate a town meeting, county council, party convention, or legislature, that is considering an issue.

7. To separate fact from opinion, keep a list on the board of what is fact and what is opinion, or use an opinion scale.

8. Try to help pupils understand the value conflicts concerned in the issue. A community opinion survey on the topic might bring out divergences in values and value conflicts.

9. To be sure that the pupils have a chance to look at all sides of the controversy, you may have to present some aspects of the topic yourself. Don't let them get the impression that things are just black or white when they may be many shades of gray — or pink or blue.

10. When presenting positions, say that some people take the position that . . . , or some people believe that . . . , rather than to give the impression that you are presenting a personal view.

11. Sometimes an introductory free-for-all in which pupils can really express their beliefs makes a good initiatory action. This way you may find out what the pupils' needs are and how they should be attacked.

12. Sometimes it helps to have pupils argue against their own point of view — that is, to present a position with which they disagree. This may help them to understand and respect the opinions of others.

13. Be sure pupils do not get hung up on the meanings of words. Many words have become emotionally charged: socialist, communist, capitalist. Pupils should learn exactly what such words mean and so avoid emotionality and misunderstanding because of semantic dysfunction.

14. Train pupils to check out sources for all information. Have them identify the sources and test them for authority, accuracy, objectivity, and timeliness.

15. Train pupils to check facts. To do so find statements that are questionable and show the pupils how to prove or disprove them. Then let them try some of their own.

CHAPTER 3

Planning

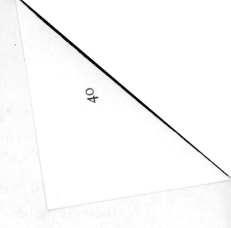

ALL good teachers plan. In the long run the success of any course or lesson depends on the excellence of the plan, and the skillfulness with which it is carried out.

Basics of Planning. Basically, planning consists of deciding (1) what one wishes to accomplish, and (2) how one wishes to accomplish it. It requires one to consider these questions for each plan:

1. What is to be accomplished?
2. Who is to do what?
3. How is it to be done?
4. When, and in what order, will things be done?
5. Where will it be done?
6. Why do we want to accomplish this, and why do we plan to do it this way?

Types of Planning. Planning for social studies instruction occurs on many levels.

1. Determining the place of social studies in the curriculum.
2. Determining the sequence of social studies courses or social studies content.
3. Determining the specific area to be covered by the various units or topics of the courses.
4. Planning the unit.
5. Planning the daily lessons.

Undoubtedly you will be called on to contribute to the planning at every one of these levels; however, curriculum building lies outside the scope of this discussion, which will consider only the planning of individual courses, units, and lessons.

39

PLANNING THE COURSE

Good course planning ensures that all the proper learnings are not only covered but given the proper emphasis.

PREPARING THE COURSE PLAN

These are the basic steps for preparing a course plan.

1. Determine the over-all goals for the course—just what it is that you want the pupils to get from the course and why.
2. Determine the principal specific objectives or terminal learning (that is, specific behavioral objectives) that you should include in the course in view of the over-all course objectives.
3. Determine the sequence of topics and the amount of time to be spent on each topic.
4. Determine the major assignments, references, texts, and approaches in light of the goals and topics to be discussed.

Establishing an Over-all Goal. If the over-all goal for your course is not stated in the syllabus or curriculum guide, it is your responsibility to do so. In determining this goal consider

1. The nature of the subject or discipline.
2. The needs of the pupils including their academic and vocational goals.
3. The previous experiences of the pupils.
4. The pupils' state of maturity, interests, and other characteristics.
5. The other elements of the curriculum both vertical and horizontal.
6. The philosophy of the school.
7. One's own philosophy of teaching.

Then write the goal out as a statement. This statement need not be long. All it needs to do is to set some limits to the teaching one is about to attempt, to suggest the types of approaches, to indicate the points of emphasis, and to set the direction.

Laying Out the Course. Once the over-all goal has been described, the time has come to determine the sequence of topics to be studied and the amount of time to be spent on each topic. In some social studies courses this may well be left to teacher-pupil planning as the course moves along. Frequently, however, the objectives of the course will be better served if you lay out the sequence of topics that will make up the course. Even so, the sequences should be regarded as tentative, for every good course plan is subject to change.

Ordinarily in laying out the course you should follow a procedure something like the following.

1. Divide the course into large topics or units. The typical course would contain about a dozen such units. This type of organization breaks the course into meaningful wholes and so facilitates the understanding of relationships.

For guidance in determining what topics to include you might turn to
a. The local course of study.
b. Courses of studies of other communities.
c. Suggestions for course plans included in bulletins of the U.S. Office of Education, state departments of education, the National Council for the Social Studies, and other professional groups.
d. A good textbook.

2. Decide how much time you want to allocate to each topic. Stress the important topics and soft pedal the less important ones.

Some Important Considerations

1. *The course should be psychologically organized.* To organize the course psychologically, center it around the pupils rather than the subject matter. When feasible use the pupils' help in selecting topics. See to it that the course does not limit the pupils to book learning, but that it is a judicious mixture of vicarious and direct experiences.

2. *There should be provisions for individualizing the course content.* Because all pupils are individuals, a predetermined selection of topics will not be appropriate for all pupils. Provide opportunities for differentiation within the units and, if necessary, for addition to, deletion from, or substitution for the units in the normal sequence.

3. *The course plan should be adjusted to the resources available.*

4. *The course plan should be flexible.* When the need arises, there should be no compunction about adding, deleting, or rearranging the topics in the sequence.

5. *The course should not be overstuffed.* In order to keep social studies courses manageable and still important, one must be skillful at leaving out content. Attempting to cover the entire subject, or the textbook, is hopelessly out of date.

6. *Teacher-pupil planning may be desirable.*

PLANNING THE UNIT

The social studies lend themselves to teaching by the unit method. Because some students find it difficult to visualize what the unit method is, let us look at an example of unit teaching.

AN EXAMPLE OF UNIT TEACHING

Early Civilization in the Tigris-Euphrates Valley.

Our first example describes a three-week unit on the beginning of civilization in the temple towns and early kingdoms of the Tigris-Euphrates area. To prepare for this unit the teacher decided what was most important for the pupils to learn and then wrote a short statement or overview of what he hoped the pupils would learn in the unit. Next he made a list of specific understandings, skills, attitudes, appreciations, and ideals that, if combined, would give the pupils the general understandings described in the general statement.

Once he had chosen his objectives, the teacher began to prepare the unit of work. To do this, he compiled a list of activities, problems, and readings that he thought would lead to the objectives he had laid out. From this list he selected a number of problems, activities, and readings that he would actually use in the unit. Some of these he decided should be required of all pupils, others he decided to make optional. The learning experiences he picked were largely problem solving activities, but he also included discussions and other activities, even a couple of lectures. He then decided how he would conduct the unit of work and prepared a study guide for pupils to use during the unit. He was now ready to begin teaching.

During the first class meeting, the teacher showed the pupils some pictures of the Sumerians and the Akkadians and their achievements that he had clipped from *Life* some time before, and discussed with them some questions about the beginning of civilization. He then discussed with them some of the things he hoped they might learn from the unit and passed out the study and activity guide. Then, after a short planning session, the pupils began work on the material in the study guide as individuals and committees. Except for a couple of classes in which the teacher lectured and showed audiovisual aids on Sumer and Akkad that he had ordered previously, the pupils worked on their individual and small-group activities for the next couple of weeks almost exclusively. Then the groups began to report what they had learned and to discuss their findings and their implications. Although the pupils had not done the same reading, it was quite possible for them to discuss the topics intelligently because the study guide and the teacher's guidance had kept them all aimed at the same objective. Although some pupils had more and sometimes slightly different information than others, all had studied about the same things and so shared enough common ground to discuss the civilization of Sumer and Akkad intelligently and profitably. The unit ended with a unit test.

CHARACTERISTICS OF THE UNIT

This description should make evident a number of the characteristics of units and unit teaching.

1. The unit consists of the study of a topic for a period of several weeks.
2. The unit is centered around some major understanding, problem, issue, or theme.
3. The unit consists of a variety of learning experiences: problem solving, independent study, reading, dramatizing, reporting, speaking, listening, and so on.

VALUES OF THE UNIT APPROACH

Because of the aforementioned characteristics — length of time, centralization on a theme, and variety of learning experiences — the unit approach provides a number of advantages not found in ordinary day-to-day teaching.

1. It provides greater opportunities for integrated teaching in which one can bring out the various relationships and interrelationships in the topics under discussion more easily than in the day-by-day approach.

2. It provides for continuity, whereas day-by-day teaching is fragmented.
3. It provides opportunities for flexibility not found in day-by-day teaching.
4. It provides greater opportunities for the individualization of instruction.
5. It provides greater opportunities for in-depth study.
6. It provides greater opportunities for pupil initiative and responsibility and for pupil participation in planning.

RESOURCE UNITS AND TEACHING-LEARNING UNITS

Educational literature sometimes classifies units by types: for example, experience units, subject units, appreciation units, problem units, process units, and the like. There are, however, only two types of units with which you need be familiar: the resource unit and the teaching-learning unit.

A resource unit is a general plan for a topic. It is not designed for a particular class, but as a resource that a teacher can go to when formulating his plan for teaching a particular unit or lesson. A teaching-learning unit is a plan developed for the teaching of a particular class; that is, the pupils in your tenth-grade World Cultures class at South Side Senior High School. In this chapter we shall consider the building of the teaching-learning units. Resource units will be discussed in Appendix A.

TO PLAN A TEACHING-LEARNING UNIT

Basic Outline of a Typical Teaching-Learning Unit.

Ordinarily the plan for a teaching-learning unit contains the following elements.

1. The setting or introductory information: for example, title, time duration, course title, and grade level.
2. An overview describing what the unit is about and a general description of what the pupils are to learn: this is the heart of the unit; it contains the target at which the teaching in the unit will be aimed.
3. The specific learning objectives: that is, the specific skills, understandings, attitudes, ideals, and appreciations that the pupils will acquire as a result of studying the unit. These objectives should be described as learning products or terminal behavior (behavioral objectives).
4. The unit of work or activities: that is, the learning activities in which you will engage during the unit. These learning activities include
   a. Introductory activities.
   b. Developmental activities.
   c. Culminating activities.
5. Methods, activities, and instruments to be used in evaluating the progress of the pupils.
6. Materials to be used in the unit.
7. Bibliography.
   a. Pupil.
   b. Teacher.

Many teachers also include an outline of the subject matter content to be included in the topic.

To Plan the Objectives

1. Become as familiar with the topic and materials on the topic as you can.
2. Consult courses of study, curriculum guides, curriculum bulletins, and resource units for ideas.
3. Decide what you feel the pupils should learn from the study of the topic and how you should approach it.
4. Write out a general statement or overview in which you summarize what you hope the pupils will have learned about the topic at the completion of the unit.
5. Prepare specific objectives.
   a. Include understandings, skills, attitudes, appreciations, and ideals.
   b. Be specific. Avoid vagueness and generalizations.
   c. Use behavioral objectives whenever feasible.
   d. Be sure that the specific objectives will contribute to the major learning described in your general statement or overview.

To Plan the Unit of Work.   The unit of work is the sequence of the learning activities that make up the teaching-learning unit. There is a tremendous difference in the way teachers organize the learning activities or the unit of work. Some teachers simply set up a series of daily lesson plans. Others conduct the unit of work as a classroom laboratory. Some teachers plan out all the activities themselves; others encourage a great deal of teacher-pupil planning. In general it is probable that units of work that are conducted as classroom laboratories and allow for a certain amount of teacher-pupil planning are more successful than teacher-centered and teacher-planned rigidly organized units.

No matter which approach you take, you will have to follow the same general steps in your initial planning.

1. Gather ideas for learning activities that might be suitable for the unit. Refer to curriculum guides, curriculum bulletins, textbooks, and the like.
2. Check these learning activities to make sure that they would actually contribute to the learnings that are your objectives. Throw out any activities that do not contribute directly to your goals.
3. Check to make sure that the learning activities are feasible in your situation. Can you afford to give them the time, effort, and expense necessary? Do you have the necessary materials and equipment? Are they suited to the maturity level of your pupils?
4. Decide which activities are so important that you feel that every pupil should participate in them at least to some extent in some way.
5. Decide which activities should be optional. In every unit there should be enough optional work to allow for some of the differences in pupil interests and abilities.
6. Decide how to introduce the unit of work. Provide for introductory activities that will
   a. Arouse the pupils' interest.
   b. Inform the pupils of what the unit is about.
   c. Help you learn more about your pupils — their interests, their abilities, and their present knowledge of the topics.

    d. Show the relationship with preceding units and offer courses.

    e. Give pupils opportunities to plan what they will do during the rest of the unit.

7. Plan developmental activities. Try to provide activities that will

    a. Keep up interest.

    b. Provide for individual differences.

    c. Develop the learnings cited in your specific objectives.

8. Plan culminating activities. Try to include activities that will

    a. Summarize what has been learned.

    b. Tie together any loose ends.

    c. Apply what has been learned to new situations.

To Plan for Evaluating Pupil Progress. Evaluating pupil progress should go on throughout the unit. Make plans to gather information of several types: informal observation, pupil performance, paper and pencil tests, and so on. Be sure that your plan for evaluating the progress of your pupils is actually keyed to the specific learning products or terminal behavior that were your unit objectives.

Preparation of Materials, Reading Lists, and Bibliographies. The unit of work cannot function without materials. Therefore you must plan for audiovisual materials, reading matter, dittoed materials, and community resources long before the unit of work begins. Reading matter that is not available to the pupils is not much help to them, even if it is in your bibliography.

Conducting the Unit of Work as a Learning Laboratory. The example given earlier in this chapter was conducted in laboratory fashion. The laboratory method of conducting units of work is recommended because it provides for individual differences, gives plenty of opportunities for independent creative thinking, usually provides high motivation, and is in general psychologically sounder than day-by-day teaching. See Chapter 6 for a description of a procedure for conducting laboratory classes.

LEARNING PACKETS

Learning packets, instructional modules, contracts, and similar innovations are variations of the unit plan. Instructions for constructing contracts and learning packets will be found in Chapters 6 and 16.

PLANNING THE LESSON

Although there are exceptions to the rule sometimes, you ordinarily should write out a plan in some detail for each lesson you teach. In this plan you should set forth (1) the objectives for the lesson, and (2) the procedure for attaining these objectives. In addition, the daily plan might also include (3) information concerning the subject matter under discussion, (4) notes on material to be used, (5) assignments to be made, (6) reminders concerning announcements, or other special items for you to remember.

THE ESSENTIAL INGREDIENTS

Objectives. The objectives of the lesson are what it is that you, the teacher, hope the pupils will have learned by the end of the lesson. You may wish to describe these learning products in the language of terminal behavior—that is, behavioral objectives. For instance,

> At the end of the lesson the pupil will be able to give an acceptable defini-
> tion of democracy in his own words and to identify democratic and un-
> democratic practices from a list provided with 75 per cent accuracy.

Such objectives are excellent for most lessons, although sometimes they are perhaps too difficult to write to be worth the extra effort. The merit of a behavioral objective is its specificity, which really gives one a definite target at which to aim, and a definite criterion by which to measure the success of the pupils' learning and your teaching. In the case of understandings the best practice may be to write the objectives in declarative sentences that prescribe the concepts that are to be learned. Attitudes can be described in the same manner or in terms of behavior. However, it is too much to expect to teach an attitude in one lesson.

Subject Matter and the Lesson Plan. The subject matter of the lesson may be described sufficiently in the objectives and in the activities of the lesson plan so that there is no need for a special section on subject matter in the lesson plan. Many teachers, however, like to outline the main points of the subject matter to be covered in this section. Here also the teacher may note the references in the text or other readings that the lesson covers. Do what you think best under the circumstances.

The Procedure or Learning Activities. The procedure is the part of the lesson plan in which the teacher lists the learning experiences he plans for the lesson. Each of these activities should be planned to bring about the major objective of the lesson either directly or indirectly through subordinate objectives. Any activities that do not contribute to the major objective should be deleted.

In the procedure you should include everything you plan to do and plan for the pupils to do. These are the activities. List these activities in order, step-by-step, to show what is going to happen during the lesson and the sequence in which they are going to happen. Be specific and go into some detail. Leave out nothing of importance. If an activity is going to be a discussion, note what is going to be discussed, the key points to be made, and the key questions to be used in the discussion. If you are going to ask questions, note which questions and which answers, and in the case of open-ended questions note the significant points and positions that should be heard.[1] If you are going to lecture, note the points of the lecture. If the pupils are going to do problems, note which problems, and their possible solutions.

The Need for Detailed Procedure. One cannot overemphasize the need for care in planning procedure in the lesson plan. Lack of planning at this stage can be

---

[1] Lest you forget!

disastrous. All too frequently beginning teachers assume that as long as they have determined the principal line of the lesson, they have done enough. Therefore, they limit their plan to such statements as "discuss the XYZ affair." Such planning does not suffice. One also needs to know what there is about the XYZ affair that needs to be discussed and how one should discuss it. Detailed planning will keep the class from drifting aimlessly and help ensure that the important points that should be considered are considered.

The details of the procedure should be in writing for two reasons: (1) to make certain that you really have a firm plan for action (too often plans that are not written down are only substanceless dreams) and (2) to give you something to refer to as the lesson proceeds. Teachers frequently forget. The lesson plan serves as a reminder.

Because teachers need reminders, the plan should not only be written down, it should be written in a format you can follow easily. The whole point of having a plan written out before you is to help you during the heat of the lesson. Write it so you can read it easily and quickly find the place. Usually this means to write it out as an outline, and to write large.

Provide a Beginning, Middle, and Ending. In almost every lesson the procedure needs a beginning, a middle, and an ending. One would think that these items would be essential for all lessons, but that is not so; some lessons are parts of units or other long-term plans. Most lessons, however, need to start off with some sort of introduction to prepare the pupils for the lesson, motivate them, and tie the lesson in with what has gone on before. The major part of the lesson should be given over to developing the principal objective toward which the lesson is being taught. Finally, the lesson should end with an activity that summarizes and binds together what has gone on in the developmental stages and that drives home the principal point — that is, the major objective.

Timing the Lesson. One of the most difficult problems in planning any lesson is judging the time. Probably the best plan is to estimate the amount of time needed for each activity and note it in parentheses after the listing of each activity. Do not, however, place much faith in the estimate. Discussions tend to run long if they are good and stop dead if they are not. Therefore, be sure to plan enough — if you plan too much you can use it in the next day's plan. If you do have time left over, you can spend it on review, going over the work for the next day, or discussing some current events.

Materials of Instruction. The section of the plan called materials of instruction merely gives one a place to note those materials or equipment to be brought to class or procured for the class. The purpose of this portion of the plan is simply to make sure that you know what material and equipment you need for the lesson and that you have it when you need it.

The Assignment. The assignment for the next lesson should be part of your lesson. It should be given at the propitious time in the lesson and given a space in the schedule of activities that makes up the class procedure. However, in order to have it stand out, it should appear in a section of its own in the lesson plan. Allow time enough in your lesson plan to develop the assignment and make sure that all the pupils understand it. To do this may take 5 to 10 minutes. In any case be sure that the assignment

1. Is clear.
2. Is definite.
3. Is reasonable, neither too long nor too difficult.
4. Gives the pupils background necessary for them to do it successfully.
5. Shows them how to do it sufficiently well so that they will not founder needlessly.
6. Provides for individual differences.

Special Notes. The recommended format leaves a special section for special notes to jog the teacher's memory. In many lesson plans there will be no need for such reminders, but to have a special spot for them makes it easier to find them when they are needed. The notes may concern announcements to be made, make-up work for certain pupils, and so on. These notes may be important or not, but they do need to be remembered.

RECOMMENDED LESSON PLAN FORMAT

What format you use in writing out your lesson plan is not particularly important. The important thing is to make up a plan that is easy to use — even in trying circumstances. Many different formats have been advocated by different teachers. You should pick the one that best suits you. One of the simplest and best formats seems to follow a simple outline:

1. Objectives.
2. Subject matter.
3. Procedure.
4. Instructional materials.
5. The new assignment.
6. Special notes.

Some examples of lesson plans using this format follow:

Sample Lesson Plan*

Objective (Major concept to be learned): The diversity of means of exchange helped confuse financial matters in the United States during the Revolution and under the Articles of Confederation.

Procedure:
  1. Brief introduction by teacher to set scene. Make following points and show samples of each.
     a. Back country and West — barter system
        (1) Put word *barter* on board

* The sample lesson plans in this chapter were prepared and used by students of Jersey City State College, Jersey City, N.J.

(2) Ask "What does it mean?"

8 min.

  b. After 1764 no paper money could be printed but some still in circulation.

  c. British, French, and Spanish coins in demand.

  d. Virginia—tobacco warehouse receipts used as money.

  e. IOUs to soldiers from Continental Congress.

  f. Promissory notes to European creditors.

  g. Each state had own paper money under Articles of Confederation.

2. Role Playing.

  a. Have pupils play parts of:

20 min.

    (1) Merchants (3 students).

    (2) Soldiers (3 students).

    (3) Continental Congress officials (6 students).

    (4) European creditors (3 students).

    (5) Residents of different states (10 students).

  b. Merchants sell to Continental Congress.

  c. Soldiers receive pay from Continental Congress.

  d. Continental Congress goes to European creditors (who sit at a distance).

  e. Residents of different states go back and forth trying to buy or sell.

  f. Easterners go to Kentucky and try to use their cash where only barter is used and vice versa.

  g. *In all cases*—each uses his own money and much trouble develops over various forms of currency.

3. Enter Alexander Hamilton (played by _____
_____).

5 min.

  a. Speech outlining financial policy.

    (1) Debts of previous govt. ($12 million foreign, $44 million domestic, $25 million state).

    (2) Where get money for new government?

    (3) How to strengthen credit?

4. Discussion.

12 min.

  a. Ask individuals what they learned from role playing.

  b. What were characteristics of system? (List on board.)

Elicit from class
{
    (1) Confusion.
    (2) Diversity.
    (3) Separateness of each political entity.
    (4) Animosity among people.
    (5) Much debt.
}

  c. What effect would Hamilton's program have on these characteristics? (List on board.)

Elicit from class
{
    (1) Clear up confusion.
    (2) Unify nation.
    (3) Sound credit.
}

Materials:

Play coins, play paper money, replicas of Colonial and Revolutionary currency, handmade IOUs, promissory notes, tobacco warehouse receipts, and objects for trade.

Assignment:
Read Thomas Jefferson's reaction to Hamilton's plan. What was his position and why?

Note: Speak to "Alexander Hamilton" before class.

Sample Lesson Plan

Objective (Major concept to be learned): Crises in Morocco and Bosnia built up tension before First World War.

Procedure:
1. Where is Morocco on map?
2. What was Moroccan crisis? There were *two.*
   a. 1904 — "cordial understanding." (Put on board.)
      What was it? (Eng/Egypt and France/Morocco).
   b. Germany upset.
   c. 1905 — Kaiser trip — speech (quote in text p. 407).
      Student to read aloud.
   d. *Looks like war.*
   e. Conference — What happened?
      ans.: All nations in attendance (even Italy) backed France, except Austria.
   f. What is Germany likely to conclude about conferences?
      ans.: She didn't get anything as might be expected and *conferences* were therefore *worthless.*
   g. What was second crisis called? Why? What was it?
      ans.: Agadir incident.
      France took over against agreement of conference.
      Gunboat into harbor — *no permission.*
      (Put all on board.)
   h. *Looks like war again!*
   i. *Both* backed down — Germany got territory in Africa and France got Morocco.
   j. What did Great Britain do at second crisis?
      ans.: Made plain in warning it would support France.
      Student to read text p. 408 aloud.
3. What did the Moroccan crises reveal concerning the great alliances? (Homework question.)
   ans.: Italy didn't support Germany. Only *Austria* with *no navy* supported.
      Aus. no tower of strength because of many *nationalities.*
4. Where is Bosnia?
5. What was Bosnian crisis?
   ans.: Aus-Hung annex Bosnia and Herzegovina.

6. What's wrong with that? Aren't they part of Aus-Hung?
    ans.: Slav peoples and Aus-Hung were only running those areas. They were actually part of Turkey but only technically.
7. Why didn't the Turks do something about it?
    ans.: Turkey becoming weaker.
8. Who backs down this time?
    ans.: Eng and France don't back up Russia.
    (3 crises didn't turn into war—*some* ally didn't support to point of war. Assassination—everybody supported everybody.)
9. What was the reason for the conflict of Russian and Austrian interests in the Balkans? (Homework question.)
    ans.: Russia supported unification of all Slavs (Pan-Slavism—put term on board) and Russia was allied with France and Gr. Britain. Serbia's expansion had to be opposed by Austria because Aus. saw Serbia as pawn of Triple Entente.
10. Did Russia consider Pan-Slavism primary??????
    In 1908, in a castle in Bohemia, Aus. and Russia agreed Aus. should have Bosnia and Herzegovina. Russia would take Bosporus. After taking Bos. and Herzegovina, Aus. played ignorant.
    Diplomatic double cross.
11. Read aloud—p. 494 from source book—letter from Francis Joseph to William II.
    How does he make annexation sound?
    ans.: As if Bosnia and Herze. are *eager* to be part of Austria.
        Doing it as favor to them.
12. Take out paper—self-correction quiz.
    Refer to map on p. 409 in text. Some questions can and some cannot be answered by use of this map.
    (On overhead projector—12 questions.)
13. Go over questions and clarify if necessary.

Materials: Overhead projector.
         Map of Europe.
         Pointer.
         Textbook.
         Primary source book.

Notes: None.

Assignment: Film tomorrow.
         Thursday—read to end of chapter.
         Question: How is each nation partly guilty for the start of the war?

Sample Lesson Plan

Objective (Major concept to be learned): To show pupils the turmoil and the difference of opinion at the Constitutional Convention.

Procedure:
1. Stage a mock Constitutional Convention in the classroom.
2. A two-day exercise. (Two class periods.)
3. First class period:
   a. Appoint some students to play the parts of:
      (1) George Washington.
      (2) James Madison.
      (3) George Mason.
      (4) William Paterson.
      (5) Alexander Hamilton.
      (6) John Dickinson.
      (7) Roger Sherman.
      (8) Benjamin Franklin.
      (9) William Livingston.
      (10) James Wilson.
      (11) Edward Randolph.
      (12) Charles Pinckney.
   b. The rest of the students will be on committees to represent:
      (1) Small states.
      (2) Large states.   (on representation)
      (3) Northern states.
      (4) Southern states.   (on slavery)
      (5) Northern states.
      (6) Southern states.   (on taxation)
   c. In class and at home the students are to find out the position that the character they are playing took in the Constitutional Convention. They will be given the rest of the period.
4. Second class period:
   a. Students assume the roles of the characters they are portraying.
   b. George Washington presides and leads discussion.
   c. James Madison takes notes. At the end of the class these notes will be dittoed and distributed at the next class.
   d. Students will run the class themselves.
   e. Students must not let their personal feelings enter the debate. They must take the opinions of the people they represent.

Materials: Mimeographed sheets (notes outlining position of various individuals and groups).

Sample Lesson Plan

Objective (Major concept to be learned): India's fight for independence was primarily nonviolent.

Materials: Film *Ghandi*   20 minutes

Procedure:
1. Place new vocabulary words on the board to be developed—ask class to distinguish meanings from the film.

      a. Civil disobedience.
      b. Caste system.
      c. Boycott.
      d. Pacification.
      e. Untouchable.

2. Introduce film.
      a. Why was Ghandi so popular?
      b. What was Ghandi trying to do?
      c. Why were his methods successful?
3. Show film.
4. Follow up discussion.
     Possible questions:
      a. Why did Ghandi want Indian independence?
      b. What methods did he use to get independence?
      c. How did he keep the struggle nonviolent?
      d. How did the boycott work?
      e. What kind of a man was Ghandi?
      f. Why was Ghandi so popular?
      g. In what ways were Ghandi's efforts similar to the efforts of civil rights marchers and demonstrators in the United States?
5. Summary.
     Ghandi's fight was long and hard, but nonviolent. Evidently nonviolent methods can work.

Assignment: Write a short story about the man Ghandi.

OTHER FORMATS

There are several other formats for lesson plans. One type commonly used lists the objectives in one column and the activities that are to bring about these objectives in another. This format has the advantage of pointing out which activity is designed to bring about each objective, and thus incidentally ensures that each activity is designed to bring about some objective. However, to at least one teacher the format seems to be harder to use in class. An example of this format follows:

Sample Lesson Plan

Objectives (concepts to be learned)	*Activities*
1. Bargaining and compromise were the principal methods of solving political difficulties in about 1850.	1. Map study, review the new territory added to U.S. 2. What was slave, what free? 3. On map find slave states. 4. List their representatives to Congress. 5. Why was it important to have control in Congress?

2. Proposals to settle the questions of slavery include
   a. Wilmot Provision.
   b. Missouri Compromise.
   c. Popular Sovereignty.
   d. Compromise of 1850.
3. Compromises failed to satisfy the leaders and the distance between the North and South widened.

6. List provisions of compromises affecting slavery on blackboard.
7. Discuss provisions that affected each section and why.

8. Discuss why the compromises failed. Why the leaders of both sides were displeased.

Assignment: Map study.
   a. Color slave states and territories red.
   b. Color free states and territories blue.

Another format for "developmental lesson plans" places the content in one column and pivotal or key questions in another.

Sample Lesson Plan

The Population Explosion

Aims: 1. To understand the reasons for the population explosion.
        2. To understand how the population explosion affects society.
        3. To realize how population growth affects them personally.

Motivation: Some nations are growing so fast that it is feared that they will soon have to go to war to gain control and to shelter their growing populations.

Content	*Key Questions*
1. Tremendous increase in population.	1. Define the term *population explosion*.
2. Reasons for population explosion.	2. Why is there such a growth in population?
a. Reduction in death rate—advances in modern medicine led to the reduction of contagious diseases, improvement in maternal and infant care, and the introduction of public sanitation.	
b. Changes in the economic patterns of the culture provided jobs for an increasing number of people.	
c. New lands in the Americas and elsewhere provided an outlet for the expanding populations of Europe and Asia.	
d. Fertilizers and power machinery have greatly increased the	

production of the world's food-
stuffs and commodities useful
in providing food and shelter.

3. Some countries may soon use war
to gain control of more land to
shelter their growing populations.

3. How rapid is the population explosion and what affect may it have
on foreign policy?

Country	1960	2000
China	710,000,000	1.6 billion
India	438,000,000	1.0 billion
Soviet Union	212,000,000	379 million
United States	180,000,000	280 million
Pakistan	84,000,000	230 million
Indonesia	93,000,000	220 million
Japan	94,000,000	150 million

4. How does the population explosion affect society?
   a. *Food supply*. Population growth
   is a major cause of starvation
   and undernourishment throughout the world today.
   b. *Scarcity of land*. With the expansion of population the amount
   of land available for living and
   for farming is greatly diminished.
   c. *War*. Population pressures have
   international repercussions
   when the "have not" nations
   gain hope and begin to demand
   more of the world's wealth.

4. What affect would such great
growth have on society?

5. How does the population explosion affect you?
   a. Overcrowding at school.
   b. Overcrowding at public places.
   c. Great transportation problems.
   d. Housing difficulties.
   e. Lack of open space available
   for recreation.
   f. Air pollution.
   g. Water pollution.
   h. Shortages.

5. In what ways does the population
explosion affect you personally?

6. Summary.
   Why should we be aware of the
   population explosion?
   What may be the final outcome
   of this problem?
   Is there anything we can do
   about it?

Materials:
Large map of the world.
Blackboard.
Charts.
Reference books.

Kenworthy[2] recommends that lesson plans be written on a series of cards in the following fashion.

Sample Lesson Plan

Card I

Topic: Who Started World War I?

Aims: 1. To show that the guilt for starting World War I is shared by many nations.

2. To point out that often nations blunder into wars.

Motivation: "Some damned foolish thing in the Balkans will ignite the next war."
Bismarck.

Discuss Bismarck's statement. Was World War I really the result of a damned foolish thing?

Card II

How much was Serbia responsible for the beginning of the war?

1. Serbian government knew about the assassination plot.

a. Make sure students understand that there is a <u>lack</u> of proof to back up this point.

b. Make connection between this and the United States government not always sure what the C.I.A. is doing.

2. At this time Serbia was trying to gain land. (Show on map what new territories had been gained.)

---

[2] Leonard S. Kenworthy, *Guide to Social Studies Teaching,* 3rd ed. (Belmont, Calif.: Wadworth Publishing Company, Inc., 1970), pp. 201–207.

Card III

What was Austria's share of the guilt?

1. Used the assassination to finally destroy Serbia.

    Refer back to first Balkan War, when Austria was against Serbia having a seaport, to show students Austrian, Serbian conflict. (Show on map the location of the seaport.)

2. Wanted their ultimatum to be rejected. (Hand out copies of the ultimatum's main sections to the students.)
    a. Demands apologies.
    b. Pledges to <u>refrain</u> from anti-Austrian propaganda in the future.
    c. Stipulates that Austrian representatives should <u>participate</u> in Serbian trials.
    d. Demands that Serbia remove from her employ "all officers and factions <u>guilty</u> of propaganda against the Austro-Hungarian Monarchy." (Write all of them on the board.)

      Show students why (c) is the main reason for Serbia's turning down the ultimatum.

3. They felt secure that Germany would come to their aid, but they never really told Germany about their true actions.

Card IV

What was Russia's share of the guilt?

1. Russian ambassador in Belgrade had knowledge of the Assassination.

    Make sure students understand that there is a <u>lack</u> of proof to back up this statement.

2. Russians started mobilization first. Why?

    a. They had to, because of the poor military set up.
    b. Czar stopped for a while, but started up again.

      Point out to students that in Russia, as well as in most European countries at this time, the military was running the countries.

Card V

What was Germany's guilt in starting the war?

1. Germany did give Austria a blank check.
2. Germany <u>tried</u> to prevent Austria from starting a war with Serbia, but when Austria did, Germany <u>tried</u> to prevent Austria from taking any more land than Serbia.

    a. Tell students German General Staff, unlike the government, wanted war, had the Schliffen Plan; explain the plan by using the map.
    b. Explain how hard it is to take back a blank check by making a comparison between the German government and the U.S. Congress giving the President the Bay of Tonkin Resolution.

Card VI

What guilt lies with France?

1. No documents on French plans.
2. Did very little to stop the war.
3. Was against peace conference between Russia and Austria.

Let students describe peace conference and why did France reject it.

Card VII

To what degree is England guilty for the war?

1. Not as guilty as the other countries.
2. Sir Edward Grey, foreign minister, made a secret naval agreement with France.
3. Attempted to hold peace conferences, but failed because of their poor organization of the conferences.
4. Did not have to enter the war because Belgium was invaded, but Grey used the issue to get the English into the war.

Card VIII

1. Map of Europe 1914.
2. Textbook.
3. Copies of the ultimatum.

TEACHER-PUPIL PLANNING

Pupils should have an opportunity to participate in planning their own learning experiences for a number of reasons.

1. Teacher-pupil planning offers one a laboratory in thinking, in making choices, in planning—in short, in democratic citizenship. The processes included in teacher-pupil planning help give the pupil the social and intellectual skills that make up skill in decision making.

2. Teacher-pupil planning also aids in motivation. When the young people select a topic or an activity, you can be fairly sure that it will be interesting to some of them at least. Also, often when the pupils have entered into the planning, the topic or activity becomes the group's activity and the pupils feel the responsibility and desire to see it carried through successfully.

SOME CAVEATS

In spite of its merits, teacher-pupil planning can be risky. Therefore you must provide the pupils with much guidance. Beware of asking pupils to make decisions for which they are not equipped.

TO CONDUCT TEACHER-PUPIL PLANNING

1. Initiate teacher-pupil planning in small steps.
   a. Ask the pupils' advice about coming assignments: Would they prefer to have the test Tuesday or Wednesday? Or would they prefer to study this unit or that unit next?
   b. Allow them to choose which activities they will do from a list of alternatives.
   c. Give the pupils a study guide or learning packet and allow them to plan how they will carry out the activities suggested and solve the problems proposed.
2. Gradually give the pupils more responsibility.
   a. Work out cooperatively with the pupils what they should learn in a unit and a plan for learning it.
   b. Increase the responsibility until pupils can take a major share in planning a course or unit.
   c. Help pupils to establish reasonable standards by which to guide their own work.
3. Finally, plan courses cooperatively with the pupils. To select the topics for study on a teacher-pupil planning basis follow the five major steps recommended by Zapf. These steps and criteria for judging the excellence of their execution are

> 1. *A clarification of the limits of choice.* How far am I, the teacher, able and willing to carry out pupil-teacher planned procedures? What are the subject-matter limits? What are the procedural limits? Must I use a textbook? How much freedom in the use of a text do I have? Do the pupils understand these limits?
>
> 2. *Establishment of criteria for topic selection.* Did the pupils have a major part in establishing the criteria? Are the criteria developed for a previous problem still satisfactory? How can they be improved so that better choices will be made? Are they being used?
>
> 3. *Development of a list of possible problem areas.* Was every pupil involved in building the list? Is it representative of the pupils' concerns? Has every item that pupils feel to be important been included? Have the items been checked against the criteria? Were the suggested topics discussed by the class with respect to possible specific problems for study, and to opportunities for activities such as field trips, hand work, etc.? Has the list been organized so that topics that belong together have been placed under common headings?
>
> 4. *Selection of one or more problem areas.* Did the method of choice focus attention on the values of the problem areas? Were the available resources checked before final choices were made? If a single area was

selected, was the decision reached by consensus rather than by majority vote?

   5. *Definition of problem.* Were all group members involved in the process of stating the problem? Is the statement of the problem broad enough to cover the major items the group wants to know, but specific enough to limit the study to a particular part of the entire topic area?[3]

SAMPLE PROCEDURES FOR COOPERATIVE PLANNING

A Sample Procedure for Cooperative Course Planning. To illustrate the procedure for planning a course via Zapf's steps, let us assume we are teaching a course in *Problems of American Democracy.*

1. Begin by introducing the pupils to the course and the notion that it is to be planned cooperatively.
2. Set up limits, for instance:
   a. The course will be limited to major problems of the United States, particularly problems having to do with government.
   b. We may consider any topics that really concern the class as long as
      (1) They are important problems of American democracy.
      (2) The resources for studying them are available.
   c. During part of the year we must study certain aspects of local and state government as required by school regulations.
3. Set up criteria for selection of the topics.
   a. Conduct buzz sessions in which each buzz group makes a short list of criteria to present to the class.
   b. Conduct a whole class session in which all the criteria recommended by the groups are listed on the chalkboard and discussed.
   c. By common consensus develop a final list of criteria.
4. Select the topics.
   a. For homework pupils individually make lists of the topics they would like to suggest.
   b. In class discussions the pupils decide on a list of topics.
   c. Before the class makes its final choice, committees should check the availability of materials for the various topics proposed and compile a bibliography.
   d. Choices should be made by consensus. Never take a formal vote if you can help it before a consensus of opinion seems evident, otherwise you can split the group into armed camps or be forced to accept a topic palatable to only a bare majority.
5. Use a similar plan to pick out the problems to be studied in the various units.
   a. Have pupils make lists of what they would like to learn about. Here you will have to give them help, because they may not know enough to realize the possibilities. These can be listed as a series of questions and pupils can choose from them the areas they particularly wish to learn. At this point it

---

[3] Rosalind Zapf, *Democratic Processes in the Secondary Classroom* (Englewood Cliffs, N.J.: Prentice-Hall, Inc., 1959), p. 197. Copyright © 1959. Reprinted by permission of Prentice-Hall, Inc., Englewood Cliffs, N.J.

is very important for you to help the pupil fix clearly in his mind what he is trying to do. If his understanding of his task is not clear, probably the understandings he gleans from his study will not be clear either.

b. Use discussion and consensus procedures to make the final selections.

An Example of Cooperative Unit Planning. An approach to teacher-pupil planning used in a unit conducted by a teacher in Massachusetts calls for less participation in the over-all planning. In this school, the teacher was working with a preselected unit prescribed by the course of study. The teacher also had carefully worked out an overview and objective. In her introduction she asked the pupils to develop the kind of things they would like to learn about most in the unit. On the basis of this discussion, a list of questions was drawn up and the class was divided into committees to prepare a bibliography of available material for use in answering the various questions. The committees then proceeded to investigate the topics and to prepare plans for reporting their findings and conclusions. For a few meetings the class met as a club with a pupil presiding to make decisions about the scheduling and reporting phase of the plan. An ad hoc committee selected by the pupils in their club meeting worked out the details. Each committee planned its own reporting technique in accordance with the general plan proposed by the ad hoc committee and approved by the class. After the presentations, the class discussed the presentations both as to technique and to content.

TEAM PLANNING

Courses of study, curriculum guides, and resource units are frequently worked out by teachers in committees. These committees may consist of teachers drawn from several levels of the school system, from many disciplines, or from the members of the department or the teachers who are teaching a particular course. In any case, the steps for such committee work are relatively easy to outline, although difficult to carry out.

1. Decide on goals.
2. Decide on topics.
3. Decide on materials.
4. Suggest resources.

Team teaching also requires team planning. In the case of the team consisting of a presenter and several follow-up teachers, the teachers must plan what the scope of each major presentation will be and work out the type of follow-up activities best suited for the small groups.

Another type of team planning requires the different subject matter teachers of a group of pupils to get together once a week or so to coordinate and correlate their activities and subject matter. In such planning perhaps the English and social studies teachers might agree to share the same assignment. Or they might agree not to give long, difficult homework assignments or tests on the same day. Members of such teams could discuss the strengths and weaknesses of various pupils and work out special assignments and activities for them to best serve their needs, interests, and goals.

In short, team planning is simply committee planning. It requires the members of the team to be courteous, considerate, and cooperative as well as industrious, alert, and responsible.

BEHAVIORAL OBJECTIVES

Learning is a process that brings about changes in behavior or tendencies toward behavior. Therefore it seems only reasonable that educational objectives should be stated in terms of behavioral change or of terminal behavior (that is, the behavior that results from learning). Educational objectives of this sort are called behavioral objectives. They are becoming quite common. They can—and perhaps should—be used in writing the objectives of courses, units, and lessons, because they provide clear, specific targets for teachers to aim at, and because they provide definite criteria by which to judge the success or failure of the instruction.

SIMPLE INSTRUCTIONAL OBJECTIVES

Educational authorities who have written on behavioral objectives differ in their conception of how statements of behavioral objectives should be written and what they should contain. For your purposes, probably simple descriptions of the terminal behavior sought will be sufficient. Such statements should identify and name "the observable act which will be accepted as evidence that the learner has achieved the objective."[4] In other words, they should describe what the learner must be able to do to demonstrate that he has learned whatever he was supposed to learn.

1. The pupils will be able to describe three causes of the Civil War commonly thought of as most significant.
2. The pupils will be able to trace the route of the Lewis and Clark expedition on a map.
3. The pupils will be able to locate map locations given in latitude and longitude.
4. The pupils will be able to summarize the arguments presented in the Declaration of Independence.
5. The pupils will be able to present principal arguments for and against the establishment of a strong central government during the days of the Articles of the Confederation.
6. The pupils will be able to apply the principles learned in the study of the causes of the Civil War to the study of states' rights arguments of today.

CRITERION-REFERENCED INSTRUCTIONAL OBJECTIVES

Although minimum-level objectives may suffice for some of our purposes, we also need more sophisticated objectives if we are going to properly evaluate the

[4] Robert F. Mager, *Preparing Instructional Objectives* (Palo Alto, Calif.: Fearon Publishers, 1962), p. 43.

learning of pupils and the effectiveness of our teaching. For such purposes, the statements of our behavioral objectives should not only identify and name the behavior act, but also "define the important conditions under which the behavior is to occur (given and/or restrictions and limitations)" and "define the criterion of acceptable performance."[5] Such criterion-referenced objectives are what McAshan calls desired level instructional objectives.[6] They are much more precise than the simple instructional objectives described in the immediately preceding paragraphs and so give one a much better target to aim at and a definite standard to use to measure both pupil and teacher success. Examples of such criterion-referenced instructional objectives follow:

1. Given the latitude and longitude of ten points, the pupil will be able to locate the points on the map in nine out of ten cases without hesitation.
2. At the end of the unit the pupil can define each of the following terms in his own words, so that the meaning of his definitions will match the textbook definitions in the judgment of the instructor.
3. Given five examples of non sequiturs, the pupil will identify the faulty logic in five out of six cases.
4. Given ten possible solutions to problem of racial integration in schools, the pupil can identify the solutions most likely to be favored by conservative whites and by militant blacks in eight out of ten instances.

[5] Ibid., p. 43.
[6] H. H. McAshan, *Writing Behavioral Objectives* (New York: Harper and Row, Publishers, 1970).

CHAPTER 4
Methods and Techniques

INQUIRY METHODS

Teaching by an inquiry method is teaching in which pupils find answers and draw conclusions for themselves. It is the opposite of expository teaching in which the teacher tells the pupils what it is they are supposed to know.

Advantages of Inquiry Teaching. The principle object in all inquiry teaching is for the pupils to think carefully about the ideas, problems, or issues under consideration. Contemporary authorities consider inquiry teaching to be particularly appropriate for social studies classes. In general, they recommend it as more effective for most social studies objectives than expository teaching.

1. It helps pupils to establish deep understandings and firm concepts, clarify processes and relationships, and to develop taste, values, and attitudes.
2. It helps pupils develop intellectual skills, including the ability to think rationally.
3. It has high motivating power.

General Characteristics of Inquiry Teaching. The procedures in the various types of inquiry teaching are much the same.

1. The teacher attempts to stimulate the pupils to think for themselves by
   a. Asking thought questions.
   b. Asking for interpretations, explanation, and hypotheses.
   c. Asking for application of principles to different situations.
   d. Asking for implications of data and information.
   e. Confronting pupils with problems, contradictions, implications, value assumptions, and value conflicts.
2. The teacher tries to keep the climate permissive and to encourage pupils to try out their own thoughts by
   a. Being supportive and acceptive.
   b. Accentuating the positive.

    c. Accepting and examining all legitimate attempts.

    d. Encouragement, approval, providing clues.

    e. Allowing pupils to be creative and independent.

    f. Encouraging pupils to exchange ideas and analyze the different ideas and interpretations that arise.

3. Most inquiry teaching involves some variation of problem solving either by individual or group problem-solving methods.

4. Inquiry methods are open-ended. Sometimes teachers engineer "discovery" lessons so that pupils end up with the "correct" generalization, but this practice is suspect in social studies teaching. Most social studies material worth teaching is open-ended and controversial, consequently most social studies teaching should be open-ended.[1]

THE SOCRATIC METHOD

The Socratic method is one of the oldest of discovery methods. It consists of a teacher's asking a pupil a series of questions designed to bring forth a certain concept or generalization, or to force him to think hard about some belief, problem, or issue. The main characteristics of the Socratic method as practiced today are that

1. The discussion consists of a series of leading questions designed to bring out certain answers.

2. The ideas are developed by asking the questions in logical fashion.

3. The motivation is natural coming as it does from the necessity to answer challenging questions.

4. The questions develop the idea to be learned as logically as possible. They must be well planned.

5. The pupil develops his own ideas as a result of the questioning.

6. Usually the questioning takes the learner to a predetermined learning, but sometimes the dialogue is open-ended.

The procedures for conducting a Socratic lesson are simple.

1. Elicit from the pupil a statement of belief or opinion that is controversial or questionable.

2. Ask probing questions that cause the pupil to reexamine his belief.[2]

CONTROLLED OR GUIDED DISCUSSION

A type of discovery technique often advocated by the proponents of the new social studies is the controlled or guided discussion. Briefly, what one does is

[1] For more information on the use of inquiry methods, see Barry K. Beyer, *Inquiry in the Social Studies Classroom: A Strategy for Teaching* (Columbus, Ohio: Charles E. Merrill Publishers, 1971), and Byron G. Massialas and C. Benjamin Cox, *Inquiry in Social Studies* (New York: McGraw-Hill Book Company, 1966), especially Chaps. 5 and 6.

[2] For an example of the Socratic method see Plato's *Meno*. For a careful analysis of the Socratic method see Ronald T. Hyman, *Ways of Teaching* (Philadelphia: J. B. Lippincott Co., 1970), Chap. 2.

1. Present pupils with information about a topic—perhaps by a reading or several readings, a film, a series of pictures, or what have you. In other words, some type of springboard.

2. Encourage pupils to draw principles and generalizations from the material presented by a series of questions.[3]

PROBLEM SOLVING

Problem solving is a kind of discovery learning. In it pupils, either as individuals or in groups, attempt to solve real problems. Group problem solving is advantageous because it draws on a greater range of background and so stimulates more ideas, more hypotheses, and more criticism. However, problems that require "sustained, closely integrated" reasoning are best solved by individuals.[4] (The characteristics of the problem-solving process are explained in Chapter 2.)

To Conduct Problem-Solving Activities.   Most problem-solving activities are long-term assignments that take several days or weeks to complete. To teach by the problem-solving method use the following procedure. The more pupils who participate in each of the steps, the better the learning.

1. Select the topic.
2. Frame the problem.
3. Plan the attack. Here pupils should plan with the teacher. What information will be needed? Where can it be found?
4. Prepare a study guide for the pupils that contains questions to be answered and facts to be gathered.
5. Gather a large amount of material. Provide readings, tapes, movies, slides, pictures, and so on. Be sure that the materials represent all the various sides adequately and state the facts (when the facts are known).
6. Let the pupils investigate the problem to find out the facts: different points of view and arguments pro and con. In their investigation, the study guide should give them the direction they need. Their investigations can be made as individuals or as small groups or both. Be sure all the pupils deal with materials representing various positions.
7. Let the pupils draw their own conclusions on the basis of the material they have read.
8. Discuss the findings, points of view, and arguments. Use discussion, panels, forums, symposia, debate, and so on. Do not, however, force pupils to defend their positions from attack. To do so may cause them to close their minds.
9. Close on an open-ended note. Be sure they realize that they have the right to their own beliefs as long as, and only as long as, they have been willing to examine them objectively.

[3] For good examples of a guided discussion, see Edwin Fenton, *The New Social Studies in Secondary Schools* (New York: Holt, Rinehart & Winston, Inc., 1966), Chap. 16.
[4] Robert L. Thorndike, "How Children Learn the Principles and Techniques of Problem Solving," in *Learning and Instruction,* 49th Yearbook, National Society for the Study of Education (Chicago: The University of Chicago Press, 1950).

PROJECTS

The project is a type of problem-solving activity usually undertaken by individuals or small groups. It differs from other problem-solving activities in that it usually results in some tangible product—a map, a model, a booklet—that has intrinsic value to the pupil or pupils who have produced it.

Projects should be selected, planned, and executed by the pupils. Projects laid out by teachers are not really projects but assignments.

Criteria To Use in Selecting and Approving Projects

1. Is it a real learning activity? (Too many so-called projects are busywork.)
2. Is it worthwhile to the pupil?
3. Is it pertinent to the objectives of the course?
4. Is the learning worth the time to be spent?
5. Are the equipment and material needed available?
6. Can it be done at a reasonable cost?
7. Can it be done in a reasonable time?

Procedure for Conducting Projects

1. Let the pupil select a project. To stimulate ideas for projects
   a. Provide a list of suggested projects.
   b. Suggest readings in which ideas for projects can be found.
   c. Conduct class discussion to uncover ideas for possible projects.
   d. Ask older pupils to visit the class and tell about projects done in the past.
2. Have the pupil secure teacher approval for his project.
3. Let the pupil make out a basic plan for completing the project. The plan should include timetable, source of information, procedures, and materials.
4. Once the pupil has had his plan approved let him go ahead to carry out the project. Check his progress from time to time. You don't want a last-minute job. Help him as necessary, but give him most of the responsibility.

INDEPENDENT RESEARCH PROJECTS

Research activities are a special kind of problem or project. Although academically talented pupils take to it most readily, all sorts of pupils can do research and enjoy it. However, there seems to be little point in insisting on this type of activity for less able pupils who are not particularly interested.

Research projects may be individual or group projects. Probably individual projects should be reserved for the academically able pupils; less able pupils can contribute to group projects. Whole-class projects seem to be the type of research project most likely to succeed at the secondary school level.

Surveys, Questionnaires, and Opinionaires. To do a survey seems deceptively easy, but unless the researchers are extremely careful in selecting their samples and in collecting and interpreting their data, they may come up with quite ridiculous findings and conclusions. Therefore surveys must be planned carefully and the pupils must be well trained in the techniques to be used. The procedures are as follows:

1. After setting up the problem decide how best to collect the data. Common ways are observation, interview, or questionnaire.
2. Build an instrument.
    a. If the data are to be collected by observation, it will be necessary to develop a check list or rating scale to guide the observer. He can use this check list or rating scale to record his observations.[5]
    b. If the data are to be obtained by interview, the questions to be asked should be written out. (When pupils interview it is probably best if they read out the questions and record the answers then and there.)
    c. If the data are to be gathered by questionnaire, the questionnaire or opinionaire must be designed. To make a good questionnaire is very difficult. Few questionnaires really deserve to be called good. In building the questionnaire
       (1) Be sure that you ask only what you want to know.
       (2) Do not ask for information you could find out in some other way with a little digging.
       (3) Be sure that your questions are clear. Try them out on other pupils and teachers. Explain and define terms that might be ambiguous. Word the questions carefully.
       (4) Make the questions easy to answer. Check-list and multiple-choice items can be answered more easily than free-response items.
       (5) Allow a place for the respondent's comments.
       (6) Set the questions up so that the responses will be easy to record and tabulate.
3. Determine the sample — that is, the group to be surveyed. If the survey information is to be useful, the sample must be representative of the total group about whom you are trying to get information. This is a quite sophisticated process. Before attempting research of this type, you should study something of sampling techniques. However, for many surveys the use of common sense will suffice.
4. Collect the data. The pupils should be carefully coached in the techniques to be used.
5. Tabulate and interpret the data. The interpretation may be simply a matter of inspection or it may involve simple statistics.
6. Draw conclusions.
7. Make the report.

The findings and conclusions of research activities of the survey type should be made public only if they are outstanding, free from error, and their release will enhance the relationship between the school and the community. In any case, before releasing information about the study, the teacher should clear publication with his immediate superior. The report should be carefully checked for proper research procedure, accuracy, interpretation of findings (including freedom from bias), and, of course, style and composition.

---

[5] See Chapter 7 for information on building check lists and rating scales.

SPRINGBOARD TECHNIQUES

A springboard is any type of presentation that can be used as a point of departure for further investigation or discussion. Some newer social studies textbooks are attempting to incorporate the springboard idea into their format. However, it should not be difficult for you to find springboards in the older standard social studies textbooks as well. Most of them have plenty of descriptions, ideas, and generalizations that could be used as a basis for discussion and for further inquiry. Role-playing, dramatizations, movies, pictures, archeological remains, and models are other examples of materials that can be used as springboards. In fact anything that lends itself to such questions as "How come?" "So what?" "If so, then what?" or "Why?" is springboard material. Usually the springboard must be aided by teacher questions that will bring out the ideas, relationships, or conclusions to be discovered or evaluated.

Contrived Incidents. Contrived incidents are incidents rigged to happen during a class. For instance, you might arrange to have two pupils start a name-calling argument as a means of launching an investigation of stereotypes. Use such contrived incidents to stimulate thinking and to make issues sharp and dramatic. They make excellent springboards.

The Method of the Parable. The parable is an ancient example of a springboard technique. To use the method tell some simple story the pupils can easily understand in order to point up a generalization or principle. Then ask them to draw their own conclusions.

THE CASE-STUDY METHOD

The case-study method of teaching consists of a fairly intense study of one individual, situation, institution, decision, or issue as a basis for making generalizations concerning the type. It is very useful because it gives people a chance to infer from a concentrated and deep study rather than from a cursory study of a number of cases. Otherwise, it has the same advantages and disadvantages of other discovery systems.

Procedure for Case Study

1. Set up a question or problem to be considered. This can be either open-ended or closed. The issue involved may be contemporary or historical.
2. Provide materials for pupils to study. These materials should describe one case in some detail. Usually the materials will be reading matter for pupils to study. However, they could include film, pictures, tapes, and so on.
3. Let the pupils study the materials presented and test them in various ways. Before they begin studying the materials, you should introduce them to the problem or issue and point out important questions to consider when studying. Sometimes a study guide is very helpful at this point. Some of the newer books have developed study guides to use with the various cases they present.
4. Discuss the material. Discussions can be supplemented by role playing,

panels, and the like. The main idea is to get the pupils to look carefully at their own thinking and to reach reasonable conclusions.

THE JURISPRUDENTIAL APPROACH

The jurisprudential approach is a special type of the case-study approach. According to Oliver and Shaver,[6] jurisprudential teaching differs from critical thinking in that it is an attempt to clarify and perhaps reconcile or resolve different points of view. It examines not only the facts of the case, but also the values and argumentative strategies. Basically it consists of analyzing controversial public issues.

In this analysis the pupils try to clear up

1. Problems of definition and communications. (For example, are the disputants arguing past each other because of differing definitions of key terms?)
2. Problems of fact.
3. Problems of value.

The problems of definition, communication, and fact are handled by the usual methods of scholarship and logic. The examination of values is usually made by looking at analogous cases. Studying analogies helps to define the differences in values incorporated in different points of view.

Procedure in Jurisprudential Teaching. The lesson plan, Little Rock I, proposed by Oliver and Shaver, well illustrates the jurisprudential procedure. This lesson is based on a three page summary of what happened at Little Rock, Arkansas, during the school integration crisis of September 1957. Notice that the lesson consists largely of a question for discussion, a dilemma, and analogies. Some of these questions are arguments that can be resolved by checking into the facts, but a number of them are subject to value judgment only. In jurisprudential teaching one moves from value judgment to fact determining and back again as the development of the issue demands.

Application of the Jurisprudential Framework

ILLUSTRATIVE LESSON PLAN
LITTLE ROCK I
I. Background Questions: Orientation to Case.
   1. In what year did the school crisis take place?
   2. Compare the percentage of Negroes in Little Rock to those in some of the other cities about which we have studied.
   3. What are some of the segregation practices in the city?
   4. What reason did Governor Faubus give for not wanting to integrate the schools?
   5. Over what court did Judge Davies preside?
   6. Why were U.S. soldiers sent into Little Rock?

---

[6] Donald W. Oliver and James P. Shaver, *Teaching Public Issues in the High School* (Boston: Houghton Mifflin Company, 1966), pp. 115–116. This is one of the best books on the jurisprudential approach. Reprinted by permission of the publisher.

II. Values: This case illustrates several important government principles.
1. Can you name some of the principles involved?
2. We shall focus on the dilemma of peace and order vs. equality. Which principle is Governor Faubus upholding? Which principle are the Negroes upholding?

III. Challenging the Student's Position with Analogies.
1. Analogies emphasizing fair treatment at the risk of violence.
   a. Should we have fought the American Revolution? After all, that meant resorting to violence, for example, the Boston Tea Party.
   b. Should this country have gone to war in 1941 against Germany? Is it worth fighting a war simply to guarantee freedom to somebody? What about Cuba or Hungary?
   c. Some nasty kids keep interfering with your ball game. You tell them to leave you alone in a nice way. If they refuse, do you have a right to fight with them in order to protect your right to play the game?
2. Analogies emphasizing the importance of peace and order at the expense of human rights.
   a. You are all dressed up going to church. You see a big boy picking on a smaller boy. You know if you start a fight you might lose and will get all dirtied up. Would you start a fight with the big boy to protect the smaller boy?
   b. Communist China is interfering with the rights of the peaceful Tibetans. This is a small country thousands of miles away. Should we start a war with China and risk hydrogen warfare over Tibet?

IV. Important Factual Assumptions Behind Conflict.
1. Will there actually be violence and civil strife if desegregation of the schools is attempted?
2. Will the violence be caused by the fact of desegregation rather than by radical or extremist groups who might be only a small minority? Was the violence in Little Rock caused by Faubus or by the original court order?

V. Definitional Problem.
Governor Faubus claimed that if integration took place there would be violence. What is "violence"? Is the intimidation of the Negro violence? Is the increase in racial tension violence? Are large and noisy meetings of extremist groups violence?

VI. A Problem of Prediction.
Governor Faubus made the claim that if integration took place there would be violence. How would you go about testing this claim in advance of the actual integration?[7]

THE USE OF VALUE SHEETS

Value sheets are springboards designed to raise issues and help pupils to clarify their own attitudes or values. They can be especially useful in the social studies for teaching attitudes, clarifying values, and clarifying issues.

Basically value sheets consist of a series of questions about an issue. The issue

[7] Ibid., pp. 164–165.

may be presented by a short statement on the value sheet, or in some other form—for example, in a reading or a recording. The pupils study the issue and then answer the questions in writing. After they have answered the questions, you should follow up with one or another of the following procedures.[8]

1. Have the pupils discuss their answers in small groups without your being present.

2. Have pupils turn in their completed value sheets to you. Read selected portions to the class aloud. Do not identify the writers of the papers unless they want you to.

3. Have pupils turn in their completed value sheets to you. Read them privately. Return them with comments but without grading them.

4. Have pupils turn in the papers to a committee that will select papers representing various positions for posting or to be read aloud.

5. Use the value sheets as a basis for a class discussion.[9]

A Sample Value Sheet

On Civil Liberties*

The National Defense Education Act of 1958 stipulated that a student wanting a federal loan for education purposes had to sign an affidavit stating that he "does not believe in, and is not a member of and does not support any organization that believes in or teaches the overthrow of the United States Government by force or violence or by any illegal or unconstitutional methods."

1. What do you think of such a requirement? (Check one)

_____ Seems reasonable. I would not mind signing such an affidavit.

_____ Seems unreasonable, but not seriously so. Not worth making a fuss over.

_____ Seems unreasonable, and seriously so. I would not accept money under such conditions and believe the law should be changed.

_____ (Any other positions; write it out here:)

2. Some persons did think such a "loyalty oath" serious and refused to accept money on that basis. In fact, some thirty-two of the nation's leading colleges and universities had officially notified the Office of Education that they had withdrawn from or declined to participate in the program specifically because of that requirement. Another sixty-three institutions participated, but under protest.

Why do you think some schools protested that oath?

3. The provision was repealed by Congress in the 1962 session. President Kennedy said when he signed the repeal that the oath was "offensive" to college students.

Under what conditions do you think the government should change laws when the people object?

4. Discuss your feelings about this matter further. Perhaps you will want to discuss the general relationship between citizens and government, or what you would have done in the specific situation described above, or what you will do in the future under such circumstances.

---

* Louis E. Raths, Merrill Harmin, and Sidney B. Simon, *Values and Teaching* (Columbus, Ohio: Charles E. Merrill Publishers, 1966), pp. 98–99.

[8] This section is based on Louis E. Raths, Merrill Harmin, and Sidney B. Simon, *Values and Teaching* (Columbus, Ohio: Charles E. Merrill Publishers, 1966), Chap. 6, which is perhaps the best reference on teaching values.

[9] Ibid., pp. 107–109.

ROLE-PLAYING ACTIVITIES

ROLE PLAYING

Role playing can be defined as an attempt to make a situation clear or to solve a problem by unrehearsed dramatization.[10] Role playing activities are useful for many purposes:

1. To motivate or launch units.
2. To culminate units.
3. To make clear historical or contemporary situations in which there are conflicting emotions, different points of view, biases, problems caused by differences in race, age, religion, nationality, or ethnic background, and so on.
   a. By making the pupils aware of the differences in points of view and their consequences.
   b. By making pupils aware of the attitudes and feelings of the people involved in the situations and to sensitize them to the feelings of others.
   c. By developing more vivid concepts.
4. To change attitudes.
5. To teach values.
6. To teach content having to do with human relationships.
7. To develop citizenship skills by showing both the successful and unsuccessful methods we use to solve intergroup and interpersonal problems, by providing practice in taking real life roles, and by practicing the democratic process.

Limitations and Disadvantages of Role Playing. You should be aware of a number of caveats before you attempt the use of role playing in your teaching.

1. Pupils who are not well prepared for role playing may not take it seriously. They may tend to "ham up" the roles, to laugh at each other, and generally turn the role playing into a farce.
2. Role playing will not work unless the atmosphere in the classroom is supportive.
3. Pupils find it difficult to enter the roles properly, especially if they are not well briefed on the assignments. For the role playing to be successful the pupils should identify with the characters whose roles they portray.
4. Role playing does not always take the direction one hopes. It may get bogged down or it may go off in unexpected directions. Sometimes it has an effect just the opposite to what was intended.
5. Role playing is time consuming.
6. For role playing to work well one needs a group of sensitive, imaginative, open-minded pupils who know each other well enough to be at ease with each other.

Conducting Role Playing. A step-by-step procedure for conducting role playing follows.

---

[10] Although simulations include the playing of roles they are not considered "role playing" for our purposes.

1. Preparation.
   a. Preparing for role playing.
      (1) Select a significant issue about which there are different views and several possible solutions. Avoid straining to find situations suitable for role playing. Take them from your ordinary classwork.
      (2) Brief the pupils on the situation and the problem to be faced.
   b. Selecting the players.
      (1) If possible, select volunteers. Do not force anyone to take a part if he does not want to.
      (2) As far as possible, select players who can identify with the role to be portrayed. *Never* allow pupils to nominate other pupils for the roles. (Pupils nominated may be unsympathetic, antagonistic, afraid, shy, or threatened by the roles or the role playing. You have a much better chance of avoiding embarassing either the pupils or yourself by sticking to volunteer players as much as you can.)
      (3) Select several casts. (You may need understudies. If you use reenactments, reenactments by different casts may be more satisfactory than reenactments by the same cast.)
      (4) Limit each cast to two to five players.
      (5) Avoid allowing pupils to play roles that approximate their real life roles.
   c. Preparing the audience.
      (1) Be sure the audience knows the situation and the purpose of the role playing. Be sure that they understand how role playing is supposed to work.
      (2) Brief them on how to behave. Tell them what to look for in the role playing. Sometimes it is useful to differentiate the assignments of the observers. Some may be asked to watch certain roles or to watch for certain types of reactions, for instance.
   d. Preparing the players.
      (1) Allow pupils plenty of time to prepare for their role playing. Let them work out the plan themselves with the absolute minimum of teacher direction consistent with their stage of sophistication. If they are inexperienced you may have to give considerable help; if they are experienced you probably should leave them alone.
      (2) Before the playing of the roles, be sure each player knows what he is going to do. Work out details of the acting such as the setting, the role of each player, what props are needed, and where the props are located. Be sure each player understands the situation, the setting, the characters, and the general direction the story line is to take.
      (3) The playing is all ad lib, but in order to get the playing started, it may be a good idea to plan the opening speeches in advance. Do *not* rehearse.
      (4) Set the stage. Provide for any props necessary. Be sure the pupils are familiar with the settings, stage directions, props, and so on.
      (5) Sometimes "small-group role playing" is a good way to launch a role-playing class. Divide the class into small groups; have each group play the roles. Then ask one group to play their interpretation for the entire class, or pick individual pupils from the different groups to make up a

new group to present a role playing to the class. This technique, by allowing everyone to participate actively, tends to break down tension and creates more interest and awareness in the audience.

2. The playing of the roles.
   a. Keep the role playing short. For beginners, five minutes is more than long enough.
   b. On the other hand, let the pupils play it out. Do not interrupt, except for emergencies.
   c. Let spontaneity be the key. Do not overdirect. Take it easy. Support their effort. Don't worry about things like errors in English, expressions of strong feeling, gaucheries, poor acting, and so on. Let the pupils interpret the roles as they see them, without your interference or interruption (except in a disaster). As long as a pupil's characterization is honest, he has a right to play it his way.
   d. Do not evaluate the acting, the language, and so on. Let the pupils play the roles free from marks and grades.
   e. If a player gets stuck you may have to follow one or another of these suggestions:
      (1) Guide him by asking such questions as "What type of person are you?" "How would you feel in such a situation?"
      (2) Select someone else for the role.
      (3) Cut the role playing and move to the follow-up.
   f. If the players get lost, you may have to try one or another of these suggestions:
      (1) Restate the situation and problem.
      (2) Summarize what has happened so far.
      (3) Stop and redirect the pupils.
      (4) Start over again after rebriefing the pupils.
   g. If a pupil is disruptive you may wish to:
      (1) Assign him a special role.
      (2) Remove him from the premises.
   h. Do not allow the audience to interrupt. If a pupil disagrees with a player's interpretation of a role let him take the part in a reenactment to show how he feels the role should go.

3. Following up the enactment.
   a. Discussion.
      (1) Follow-up by discussion. The discussion has great influence on pupils' attitudes and understandings—probably as much as the role playing. Unless there is a discussion afterward, there is no point to role playing.
      (2) The discussion should analyze the interpretations, solutions, reactions, and so on. In the analysis try to find the answers to such questions as:
          Why did the players act as they did?
          Why did the players react as they did?
          Were the players' actions and reactions related?
          What kinds of feelings did the various players express?
          In what other ways might they have portrayed their roles?
      (3) In the discussion try to evaluate what has been learned. What attitudes, ideas, principles, understandings, and the like were brought out? What were changed?

(4) In the discussion you may have to do some probing. Ask pupils open-ended questions that will dislodge their preoccupation with their own feelings and beliefs.

(5) Summarize the discussion so as to review what has happened, to make important points and inferences, and to tie things together.

(6) During the discussion consider the actors to be consultants. They can tell how they felt and why they interpreted the role as they did.

b. Reenactment.

Sometimes it is wise to follow up a role playing with a second or third role playing of the problem or situation.

(1) If the objective is to view a situation or problem in depth to show varying points of view or to develop sensitivity, it may be better to repeat the role playing immediately. At other times it is perhaps better to have some discussion and let the reenactment grow out of the discussion. If the purpose of playing the roles is simply to illustrate a situation or problem, or to start a discussion, then reenactment is usually not necessary or desirable. It may be advisable, at times, to let the pupils decide whether they wish to reenact the scene immediately, later, or not at all.

(2) The reenactment may be done by using:
   (a) An entirely different cast.
   (b) Different major characters, but the same supporting characters.
   (c) The same cast with parts interchanged or reversed.
   (d) The very same cast playing the roles again after having heard the discussion.

   Procedures (a) and (b), which utilize different personnel, have the advantage of involving more pupils in the playing and give additional depth by presenting more than one interpretation. Interchanging or reversing roles [procedure (c)] develops sensitivity in the role players and counteracts any tendency toward type casting or associating role characteristics with a particular role player; it also presents additional interpretations of the roles. Reenacting with the same cast [procedure (d)] gives the pupils a chance to reconsider and perhaps to change their minds, to learn from their mistakes, or to enlarge their vision.

(3) If discussion shows that someone feels an interpretation is wrong or inadequate, ask him to act the role as he sees it.[11]

DYADIC ROLE PLAYING

Leslie D. Zeleny and Richard E. Gross recommend dyadic role playing as a way to (1) help pupils better understand problems or situations, (2) develop em-

[11] Selected references on sociodrama and role playing include Mark Chester, and Robert Rox, *Role-Playing Methods in the Classroom* (Chicago: Science Research Associates, 1966); Fannie Shaftel, and George Shaftel, *Role-Playing for Social Values* (Englewood Cliffs, N.J.: Prentice-Hall, Inc., 1967); and Leslie P. Zeleny, *How to Use Sociodrama, How to Do It Series No. 29* (Washington, D.C.: National Council for the Social Studies, 1964).

pathy for the people in various roles in such situations, and (3) develop skill and experience in sociodrama before trying to role play more complex situations.[12]

To Conduct Dyadic Role Playing

1. Prepare pupils for the role-playing experience.
   a. Arouse interest.
   b. Help them acquire the necessary background information.
      (1) Identify two (or more) positions, statuses or behavior.
      (2) Identify roles associated with the statuses or positions.
2. Select two opposing positions or statuses.
3. Divide the class into dyads (pair groups).
   a. Each pupil in the dyad is to represent one of the opposing positions.
   b. If there are thirty pupils then there will be fifteen dyads.
4. Have the dyads play their roles simultaneously.
5. Have the pupils in each dyad reverse their positions and role play their new roles.
6. Have the pair-groups evaluate what they have done. In this phase they may
   a. Discuss how well each side was presented.
   b. Determine if more information was presented.
   c. Procure information.
   d. Replay as necessary.
7. Discuss and follow up the role playing.

Dyadic Role Playing Before the Class. When dyadic role playing is successful, it may be used as a basis for a class presentation. For example,

1. Pick a dyad that has worked successfully or compose a new dyad of two pupils whose presentations seemed promising.
2. Have this dyad role play the situation before the entire class.
3. Discuss the role playing.

SIMULATION EXERCISES

As used in social studies teaching, simulation combines role playing and problem solving. It consists of pupils performing in a simulated or contrived situation that duplicates a real situation as closely as is feasible so that the pupils will (1) understand the real situation and/or (2) learn how to perform in the real situation. Essentially what is required is that

1. The pupils be assigned roles to perform in a fairly well-defined situation.
2. The pupils be confronted with simulated real life situations that make it necessary to take action. As a rule, the actions and decisions made lead to further incidents. In these situations the pupils are not free to act in any way they wish. They must stay in character and keep their actions within the limits prescribed by the realities of the situation.

---

[12] Leslie D. Zeleny and Richard E. Gross, "Dyadic Role Playing of Controversial Issues," *Social Education* 24:354–358 (Dec. 1960). This is *the* reference on dyadic role playing.

Advantages of Simulation

1. It is highly motivating.
2. It allows both bright and less bright pupils to participate.
3. It gives practice in decision making.
4. It is not teacher dominated.
5. It encourages creativity and independent thinking.

Limitations

1. It may be time consuming.
2. Some simulations turn into entertainment.
3. Some pupils confuse the simulation with reality. Pupils may get erroneous ideas, particularly when they focus on facts rather than on generalizations or principles.

Procedure for Conducting Simulation Exercises. The over-all procedure for simulation games is quite simple.

1. Prepare the materials and equipment needed.
2. Introduce the pupils to the simulation and explain how and why it is to be played.
3. Assign pupils their tasks and brief them in their roles. (Sometimes the roles are described on cards that the pupils draw. It may be better for the teacher to give out the cards to pupils in accordance to his conception of their needs or abilities, or the pupils may volunteer for specific roles.)
4. The simulation takes place. Here the teacher may act as referee or umpire and score keeper. Pupils may assume these tasks if the occasion warrants.
5. The pupils discuss the situation, make generalizations, and draw conclusions.

Specific procedures are determined by the rules of the particular simulation. Many simulation scenarios have been published and are available for purchase. In playing these simulations, one merely follows the published directions. Other simulations are homemade. One of the best exercises possible is for pupils to make up their own simulations. Following is a description of a simple simulation. An outline showing how to prepare a scenario for a more ambitious simulation can be found in Chapter 16.

An Example of a Simple Simulation

The object of this simulation was to make clear to the pupils the differences of opinion and turmoil at the American Constitutional Convention. Two days were given over to this exercise. During the first class period the teacher explained what was to happen and assigned certain pupils to play the parts of key delegates: Washington, Madison, Paterson, Hamilton, Dickinson, Sherman, Franklin, Livingston, Wilson, Randolph, and Pinckney and listed the issues on the agenda of the convention. The rest of the pupils were divided into committees to represent (1) the small states, (2) the large states; (3) the Northern states (slavery), (4) the Southern states (slavery); (5) the Northern states (taxation), (6) the Southern states (taxation). The pupils were then given the rest of the day to find out the position taken by their characters or committees during the Constitutional Convention.

On the second day the pupils assumed the role of the characters and acted out the mock convention. George Washington presided, and James Madison took notes (these were dittoed later). The pupils ran this convention themselves. The only formal rule laid down by the teacher was that they had to "take the opinions of the persons" they were representing. They were "not to let their personal feelings enter into the debate."

After the convention the teacher used a discussion to summarize and to clinch various points.[13]

ORAL QUESTIONING AND ANSWERS

Questioning is among the oldest and best of the tried and true techniques. However, it should be borne in mind that questioning is only one of many techniques; that there are many kinds of questions, and that questioning in itself does not constitute a strategy. Questions should not be used as if they were ends in themselves. They are not ends; they are means.

To Develop Good Questioning Techniques

Questioning is a difficult technique to master because most of the give and take must be spur of the moment. The only way to master the technique is to practice. Nevertheless there are several tips that can help the neophyte as he develops his expertise.

1. Prepare carefully.
    a. Be sure that you clearly understand the goals of the lesson.
    b. Become as sure of the subject matter content as you can.
    c. Plan out your key questions to be sure that they are well worded and get at the goal desired. In this way you can ensure yourself from falling into at least some of the traps that accompany impromptu teaching.
    d. In making your plan check carefully to be sure that
        (a) Questioning is the best technique for your purpose.
        (b) You are using the right type of question for your objective.
        (c) Your key questions are well constructed.
2. Speak clearly and audibly. Be sure all can hear you. Then do not repeat.
3. Ask the group a question, wait a little, and then name the person to answer. However, when soliciting a response from an inattentive, slow, or shy pupil you may want to call his name first so that he will have time to gather his resources. If a pupil cannot answer because he has been inattentive, move on, but come back to him for another question later.
4. Try to be natural, easy, and informal when using oral questioning. Walk around the room so that all questions are not directed toward the front of the room. Mix the questioning up with other techniques.
5. Ask only a few *key* questions. A few deep questions are usually better than many shallow ones. Key questions may, of course, be supported by subquestions.

[13] A plan for conducting this simulation appears in Chapter 3. One of the most useful works on simulations for social studies teachers is William A. Nesbitt, *Simulation Games for the Social Studies Classroom* (New York: Foreign Policy Association, 1971).

6. Ask a series of questions that builds up from one question to another to develop a point.

7. Distribute questions evenly throughout the group. Give everyone a chance, but allow for individual differences. Usually shy, slow pupils should get the easier questions; bright, eager pupils, the more difficult ones.

8. Demand complete responses (not necessarily complete sentences, but complete thought units). Encourage extended answers, when appropriate.

9. Use a variety of questions. There should be some fact questions and some thought questions. Some questions should be convergent; some divergent; some cognitive memory; and some evaluative. The type of question to use depends on what you are trying to do, but a strategy that uses only one kind of question will undoubtedly fail. Try to use some questions that encourage pupils to go beyond classroom learning.

10. Try for an atmosphere that will encourage pupils to participate. Avoid cross-examining, baiting, heckling, tugging, or otherwise embarassing the pupils. Do not mark pupils on their answers to oral questioning.

11. On the other hand do not allow incorrect or incomplete statements to stand unchallenged. When you get a wrong answer:
    a. If the error is minor, correct it.
    b. If the error is major, ask other pupils to comment and correct (if the other pupils don't know the correct answer, tell them, or better still have them find out the answer for themselves).
    c. Reword the question (it may have been misunderstood). Sometimes putting the question in the negative or personalizing the question helps the pupil understand what is needed.
    d. When the pupil's answer is incomplete, ask supplementary questions that may bring out the answer desired.

12. In order that there be an open atmosphere, insist on courtesy from everyone.

The Use of Thought Questions.   If you want to attain the higher educational objectives in your classes, you must learn to use thought questions effectively. Therefore, practice using questions that go beyond the limits of the ordinary recitation. The following suggestions should be helpful.

1. Use developmental problem questions emphasizing how and why rather than who, what, where, and when.

2. Follow up leads. Build on pupils' contributions. Give pupils a chance to comment on each others answers; for example, ask questions such as, "Do you agree with John on that, Mary?" or "Do you think this argument would hold in such and such case, John?"

3. Be sure the pupils have the facts before you ask "thought" questions about them. One way is to ask fact questions first and then follow up with thought questions. Another way is to lead in by means of good summary questions. Other ways are to incorporate the facts in the question itself or to give the pupils fact sheets that they can consult as they try to think through suitable answers to the question. Similar results can be gained by putting the facts on the blackboard or the overhead projector, by allowing pupils to refer to their texts, or by simply telling the pupils the facts before beginning the questioning.

4. Remember that the best thought questions usually do not have correct answers. In such cases the thinking concerned is much more important than the answer derived. Be sure pupils back up their answers by valid, logical reasoning. Insist that they show their evidence and demonstrate why this evidence leads to their conclusion.

5. Encourage pupils to challenge each other's thinking and even that of their teacher. Good use of thought questions leads to true discussion rather than simple question-answer teaching.

PUPIL QUESTIONS

To Stimulate Pupil Questions. Do your best to stimulate pupil questions. Oftentimes they lead to more learning than teacher questions or comments do. To stimulate questions from the pupils

1. Always treat them courteously and considerately.
2. Ask them what was the most difficult part of the homework.
3. Let them develop questions for review.
4. Let them develop questions for class recitations, games, reviews, and so on. Try to get them to ask important questions; they usually tend to pick minute points.
5. Encourage them to ask questions regarding sources of information, other pupil statements and opinions, and so on.
6. Encourage them to challenge other pupils, texts, other readings, and even the teacher.

Handling Pupil Questions

1. Always treat pupils courteously.
2. Consider all questions.
   a. Answer them yourself.
   b. Ask some other pupil to comment.
   c. Have someone look it up. (Don't make a burden of this. You may never get any more questions.)
3. Use pupil questions as lead-ins. Toss questions to other pupils. Don't answer yourself until the other pupils have had a chance to think about it. Ask, "How would you answer that question, Joe?"
4. If you do not know the answer yourself, say so, and then find out—if it is at all relevant or important.
5. Refuse to be misled by the trivial and irrelevant. Turn off such questions in a courteous way.
6. If there are pupils who are overdemanding or attention seeking in their questioning, counsel them alone after class.[14]

[14] Excellent references on the use of questions are Edgar Dale, "The Art of Questioning," *The Newsletter* **34**:1–4 (Dec. 1968). Philip Grossier, *How to Use the Fine Art of Questioning* (Englewood Cliffs, N.J.: Teachers Practical Press, 1964). Norris M. Sanders, *Classroom Questions* (New York: Harper and Row, Publishers, 1966).

The Clarifying Response

The clarifying response strategy is a way of responding to a pupil so that he will "clarify his thinking and his behavior and thus clarify his values."[15] It consists of reacting to pupil statements, expressions, or actions by asking questions that will cause him to consider "what he has chosen, what he prizes and/or what he is doing."[16] Clarifying responses are short exchanges with pupils that "without moralizing raise a few questions, leave them hanging in midair, and then move on."[17] Raths and his associates list ten essential elements of a clarifying response:

1. The clarifying response avoids moralizing, criticizing, giving values, or evaluating. The adult excludes all hints of "good" or "right" or "acceptable," or their opposites, in such responses.

2. It puts the responsibility on the student to look at his behavior or his ideas and to think and decide for himself what it is he wants.

3. A clarifying response also entertains the possibility that the student will *not* look or decide or think. It is permissive and stimulating, but not insistent.

4. It does not try to do big things, with its small comments. It works more at stimulating thought relative to what a person does or says. It aims at setting a mood. Each clarifying response is only one of many; the effect is cumulative.

5. Clarifying responses are not used for interview purposes. The goal is not to obtain data, but for the student to clarify his ideas and life if he wants to do so.

6. It is usually not an extended discussion. The idea is for the student to think, and he usually does that best alone, without the temptation to justify his thoughts to an adult. Therefore a teacher will be advised to carry on only two or three rounds of dialogue and then offer to break off the conversation with some noncommittal but honest phrase.

7. Clarifying responses are often for individuals. A topic in which John might need clarification may be of no immediate interest to Mary. An issue that is of general concern, of course, may warrant a general clarifying response, say to the whole class, but even here the *individual* must ultimately do the reflecting for himself. Values are personal things. The teacher often responds to one individual, although others may be listening.

8. The teacher doesn't respond to everything everyone says or does in a classroom. There are other responsibilities he has.

9. Clarifying responses operate in situations in which there are no "right" answers, such as in situations involving feelings, attitudes, beliefs, or purposes. They are *not* appropriate for drawing a student toward a predetermined answer. They are not questions to which the teacher has an answer already in mind.

10. Clarifying responses are not mechanical things that carefully follow a formula. They must be used creatively and with insight, but with their pur-

---

[15] Raths, Harmin, and Simon, op. cit., p. 51. This book is the reference on the clarifying response.
[16] Ibid.
[17] Ibid., p. 55.

pose in mind; when a response helps a student to clarify his thinking or behavior, it is considered effective.[18]

OPEN-TEXT RECITATION

The open-text method is a technique in which pupils are allowed to refer to their books and notes during class discussions. The purpose of the open-book method is to encourage pupils to refer to their books (or other materials) for information with which to back up their assignment, to check on facts, and so forth.

Advantages of Open-Text Teaching

1. It frees pupils from the rote memorization and recitation of facts.
2. It helps pupils realize that facts are simply means to an end. Pupils learn to find and apply the facts.
3. It brings out important facts by using them.
4. It helps pupils learn the importance of checking and documenting.
5. It uses time efficiently. (The ordinary recitation in which pupils recite "facts" memorized from a book is almost always a complete waste of time.)

What Open-Book Exercises May Include

1. Interpreting and discussing maps, graphs, pictures, and the like.
2. Working out how to study an assignment or a selection.
3. Comparing the presentations in several books.
4. Introducing the text and teaching how to study.
5. Using texts to bolster arguments in class discussions.

LECTURE TECHNIQUES

Although the lecture method is an excellent tool for many purposes, it is greatly overused. It should not be the principal method for teaching secondary school social studies classes, because it is not really very effective for most instructional purposes.

DISADVANTAGES OF THE LECTURE TECHNIQUE

1. Pupils do not learn much from lectures and retain even less. There are several reasons for this failure.
   a. According to Alcorn, Kinder, and Schunert, experience shows that people generally remember
      10 per cent of what they READ
      20 per cent of what they HEAR
      30 per cent of what they SEE
      50 per cent of what they HEAR and SEE
      70 per cent of what they SAY

---

[18] Ibid., pp. 53–54.

90 per cent of what they SAY as they DO a thing.[19]
   b. Lectures tend to be boring and so lead to inattentiveness.
   c. Lectures provide little opportunity for reinforcement.
   d. Few pupils have ever learned how to listen or to take notes properly.
2. Lecturers can waste class time. Often it is better to mimeograph or ditto the information to be presented and use the class time for other purposes.
3. Lectures are seldom useful for changing attitudes or attaining the higher cognitive goals.
4. Lectures, because they provide little for the pupil to do and tend to be boring, may lead to problems of classroom discipline.
5. Lectures do not give pupils an opportunity to explore, to think, or to interact. They are not conducive to study in depth, but rather tend to make pupils gullible receivers of knowledge.

WHEN TO USE THE LECTURE TECHNIQUE

In spite of its disadvantages, properly used, the lecture technique can be extremely useful for a number of purposes.

1. Use the lecture technique to establish a general point of view or a state of mind rather than to teach specific facts, concepts, or ideas.
2. Use the lecture for giving out information quickly.
3. Use informal lectures and talks to arouse interest and so to motivate. Long formal lectures, however, kill interest more often than they arouse it.
4. Use some form of lecture or teacher talk to introduce new units and assignments, especially long-term assignments, to be sure that everyone starts off on an even keel.
5. Utilize lecture techniques as necessary in television and in large-group and some team-teaching schemes. Give lectures only when they are the most fitting technique or strategy, however. Do not give lectures simply because the mechanism (television, large-group instruction, or team teaching) seems to call for it. Be careful in such situations that "the tail does not wag the dog."

TO AROUSE AND MAINTAIN INTEREST IN LECTURES

1. Open with a challenging question, problem, or fact.
2. Puzzle them a little.
3. Tell them what you intend to do.
4. Relate the content to things they already know and like.
5. Use questions (both real and rhetorical).
6. Use demonstrations, projectors, flannel boards, and other instructional aids.
7. Utilize humor.
8. Give plenty of examples—the more specific and concrete the better.

---

[19] Marvin D. Alcorn, James S. Kinder, and Jim R. Schunert, *Better Teaching in Secondary Schools*, 3rd ed. (New York: Holt, Rinehart and Winston, Inc., 1970), p. 216. According to Alcorn, Kinder and Schunert these figures, which were originally developed by P. J. Philips at the University of Texas, Industrial Education Department, are only approximations and should be taken as such, but experience indicates that they are reasonably accurate.

9. Keep up the pace. Don't let the lecture drag or the audience relax.

10. Make use of dramatic effects. Pause. Ask questions. Change tempo and so on to avoid monotony.

ADDITIONAL HINTS FOR GOOD LECTURING

1. Aim the lecture. Try to cover only a few important points.

2. Combine the lecture with other methods and techniques. Utilize study guides, mimeographed outlines, fill-in outlines, summarizations, follow-up questions, and projects.

3. Hold the pupils responsible for what was said in the lecture. Require them to take notes. Occasionally, test to see how well they retain information. Check their notes from time to time. Once in a while have them submit outlines of lectures or summaries. Sometimes it is a good technique to have pupils write out questions to be used as the basis for a discussion following up the lecture the next day.

4. Teach pupils how to take notes.

5. Encourage pupil questions, but do not allow them to break the train of thought. Questions should come at natural breaks if possible.

6. Hit the same point several times in different ways. In a lecture, repetition is the only way to reenforce learning. Remember the old guideline for lecturers: Tell them what you are going to tell them; tell them; tell them what you have told them. In long lectures summarize frequently.

7. Modify your lecture as the situation demands. Watch the pupils for signs of boredom. Pause for class reactions. Change the tempo as needed. Move around the class.

8. Keep the lecture as short as possible.

9. Be sure all can hear. Get their attention before you start. Do not talk while others are talking.

10. Be clear and concise. Use simple vocabulary. Use concrete examples.

11. Keep the lecture friendly, informal, and conversational.

12. Avoid digressions, reminiscences, trivia, and distracting mannerisms.

Some Don'ts

1. Do not read the lecture.

2. Do not overuse your notes. Avoid following them verbatim.

3. Do not assume that pupils understand what you are saying. Check them once in a while.

4. Above all, do not talk too long before you say anything.[20]

To Make the Lecture Stick
Tell them what you are going to tell them. Tell them. Tell them what you have told them.

---

[20] For an excellent reference on the lecture, see Hyman, op. cit., Chap. 6, "Lecturing and Interaction."

REPETITION, PRACTICE, DRILL, AND REVIEW

THE NEED FOR REPETITION

Repetition is important in skill and concept development as it gives one a chance to renew and vary experiences; it gives opportunities to reenforce and refine skills and to amplify concepts. Use it

To polish or refine something already learned.

To fix something in memory; for example, formulas, dates.

To reenforce some learning; for example, symbolic learning needs continual reenforcement.

To provide overlearning.

To increase understanding.

To make something a habit.

To consolidate, clarify, strengthen, reenforce, and refine what one has already learned.

To learn arbitrary associations; for example, dates.

TO CONDUCT DRILL AND PRACTICE

1. Give pupils clear instructions, thus reducing the chance of their learning incorrect procedures and forms. In giving instructions
   a. Use oral instructions, written instructions, tape recordings, teaching programs, or whatever method seems most appropriate.
   b. Provide some method for checking to be sure the pupil understands what he is supposed to be doing and starts off correctly.
   c. Take your time. Avoid going too fast or telling pupils too much at a time. If the procedure is long or complex, break it into steps and teach only a few steps at a time.
   d. Provide a demonstration — either a live one or a canned one done on tape or film. Demonstrations make instructions clear.
   e. Use a positive approach. Tell the pupils what to do. Avoid telling them what not to do — it confuses them.
   f. Pay attention to form. Showing pupils the proper form in the initial stages can save time and effort. Just as ten-finger typing is more efficient than two-finger typing, going straight to the index is more profitable than leafing through the book when one needs to find a reference. These are matters of form — of using the right procedures correctly.
2. In using demonstrations
   a. Be sure everyone can see.
   b. Go slowly so that the pupils can follow the procedures.
   c. If the procedure is complex, demonstrate a few steps at a time. A good way is to demonstrate the entire procedure first and then to do it again a few steps at a time.
   d. Repeat the demonstration, or portions of it, as necessary. Pupils may need to watch a demonstration several times before they see what they have to do. After pupils have started practicing, additional demonstrations may be more meaningful and helpful.

e. Remember that when you are facing the pupils left and right are reversed.
3. Be sure that pupils have the proper tools and work under good conditions.
4. Keep practice highly motivated.
   a. Eliminate unnecessary drill and practice.
   b. Vary the kind of practice to make concepts fuller and practice less boring. Early practice should be concrete; later sessions can become increasingly more abstract.
   c. Use short practice periods. As pupils get better the periods can become longer with longer spaces between them.
   d. Keep the practice intense. Be sure they have goals and standards to work toward. Keep the practice moving swiftly, but do not sacrifice accuracy for speed.
   e. Use some pressure.
   f. Use such devices as games and contests.
   g. Include only pertinent and important material so the practice lesson will not get to be too dull.
   h. Make practice meaningful. Be sure the pupils understand what they have to do, why they have to do it, and how to do it. Be sure they have a goal and standards of excellence to shoot at. Point out why the drill is needed.
   i. Let the pupils contribute to the planning and evaluating of their own practice activities.
   j. Provide pupils with knowledge of their progress. It is an excellent motivator.
5. Keep practice as real and lifelike as possible. Simulations are useful for this purpose.
6. Carefully supervise practice. Point out errors and show how to correct them but avoid harsh criticism. Encourage pupils to criticize and evaluate their own work.
7. Structure the practice sessions. It is often necessary to pull skills out of context for formal practice. Use the part-whole method: that is, practice the whole operation, but take difficult parts out of context and practice them separately when necessary.
8. Individualize practice. Use diagnosis as the basis of each pupil's practice. Focus practice on individual pupil's weaknesses and gaps in learning. Use materials that can be automated. Self-correcting material, either purchased or homemade, is very useful. Exercises in which pupils work in pairs or small groups to help each other and correct each other can be excellent.
9. Make practice part of the regular work. Do not separate it for special instruction unless necessary. Use the regular school work for practice material. Keep it simple. In the beginning it may be necessary to take practice out of context and concentrate on it alone for short periods. Practice tends to get lost in the regular class situation, but keep such practice to a minimum.
10. Use a variety of materials. Homemade, mimeographed or rexographed material, workbooks, and other purchased exercises are all useful. Make a bank of such materials by saving exercises, items, workbook materials, programed materials, and so on.

MEMORIZING

Memorizing is a form of practice for all intent and purposes.

1. Avoid memorization for memorization's sake. Too much memorizing is anti-intellectual.

2. Have pupils memorize for a purpose only. Be sure pupils can see what the purpose is.

3. Have pupils study for meaning first.

4. Use the part-whole method when practicable.

5. Use the recall method (that is, study and then try to remember).

6. Otherwise, use the techniques suggested for other practice activities.

REVIEW

Review is not quite the same as drill or practice. It is a second look at the subject method to be taught. It does not require drill techniques so much as re-teaching. It should be used whenever there is need to tie up and consolidate learning.

When to Review.   Review daily at the end of a period or the beginning of the next period. Use this time to summarize, to tie together, and to show relationships among past, present, and future classes. Use review near the end of the unit or term to tie things together and to clinch important points, but do not wait until the end of the unit or term for this sort of review. Review at any time it seems that your forces need to be regrouped or reorganized and that loose ends need to be tied together.

Sample Tactics for Review Lessons

1. Have pupils summarize or outline.

2. Teach the lesson in a different context.

3. Utilize discussion in which principal points are brought out or applied.

4. Use problems based on material to be reviewed.

5. Have pupils prepare questions to ask each other. (This type of activity can be made into a game.)

6. Have pupils build charts, time lines, and the like to show various relationships and important points.

7. Dramatize material to be reviewed.

8. Have pupils apply the learning to other situations.

9. Have pupils write test questions.

10. Use broad questions.

A Warning About Review Classes.   The ordinary oral quiz in which teachers ask fact questions around and around the room is drill not review. It is usually not worth the effort.

DISCUSSION TECHNIQUES

DISCUSSION

True discussion is one of the most effective, yet the most difficult, of all teaching techniques. Learn to use it well as soon as you can. It is especially useful in social studies teaching.

Uses of the Discussion Technique

1. To solve problems.
2. To develop and change attitudes.
3. To present and make pupils aware of contrary viewpoints.
4. To develop communication skills.
5. To develop leadership skills.
6. To help pupils learn to formulate problems and principles in their own words and to guide application of the principles.
7. To encourage constructive, logical thinking.
8. To involve pupils in their own learning by making them responsible for their learning, by giving them opportunities to take stands, develop their arguments, defend their views, and live with the consequences by subjecting them to feedback and criticism from their peers.
9. To develop self-confidence, self-reliance, and poise.

Advantages of the Discussion Technique

1. Discussion tends to make pupils more tolerant as they become aware of different views.
2. Discussion helps to develop group feeling.
3. Discussion is likely to get at deep feelings. It can sometimes make real changes in attitudes and behavior that are too deep for other techniques to influence.
4. Because group discussion gets a high level of pupil participation and involvement, it tends to warm up the class.

Disadvantages of the Discussion Technique

1. The discussion technique is extremely difficult to use well.
2. Discussions can easily become a pooling of ignorance.
3. Discussions can become very discursive.

Suggestions for Conducting Discussions

1. Prepare for the discussion.
    a. Be sure the topic is discussable. The best topics are controversial problems that can be solved or clarified through discussion.
    b. Be sure pupils are well prepared. Make materials and equipment needed for the discussion available.
    c. Prepare a plan or agenda.
    d. Make an opening statement to point out the purpose of the discussion and to outline its ground rules. This opening statement should be suggestive rather than prescriptive. If the group wants them, adjustments should be made. In any case, the group members should all have a firm understanding of the purpose and the rules of the discussion before the discussion gets far along. In the rules one should include the agenda and time limits.
2. Use some sprightly device to launch the discussion. Among the types of tactics you might use are the following:
    a. Introduce a specific case or problem. This might be done by role playing, by presenting a written case study, or by relating an anecdote.

    b. Concoct a series of challenging open-ended questions.

    c. Show a film or present a skit or some other dramatic offering to arouse interest.

    d. Challenge the group with an evocative quotation or statement.

    e. Warm up the group by means of buzz sessions.

    f. Use a written exercise such as a quiz or pretest.

    g. Use a contrived incident.

3. Create an environment favorable to face-to-face expression.

    a. Arrange the room so that participants can see each other. A circle or semi-circle seems to be the best arrangement.

    b. Keep the discussion informal—but do not let it degenerate into a pooling of ignorance.

    c. Insist on courtesy at all times by everyone. (This means you, the teacher, too.)

    d. Encourage shy persons to contribute by directing easy questions at them from time to time. Sometimes questions such as, "Do you agree?" and "Would you like to comment?" will draw these people out. Gently but firmly cut off pupils who tend to monopolize the discussion. When more than one person wishes to talk, give preference to the one who has not spoken.

4. Keep the discussion moving.

    a. Try to keep the pupils on the track. At times this will require a restatement of the problem. A summary or partial summary in which you tell what positions and points have been made may also help. Backtrack when necessary to pick up loose ends and to reorient.

    b. Encourage cross-discussion as long as the amenities are followed. Throw questions around from pupil to pupil.

    c. Be sure all viewpoints get their day in court. At times in order to create discussion or to bring out unusual or unpopular topics you may have to play the devil's advocate. Present contrary opinions as views held by others—not as your own views. For example, say, "Some people disagree about the worth of doing that." If possible keep your own views under cover.

    d. Keep the discussion on an impersonal, rational level. This will mean that sometimes hotheads must be cooled and emotions calmed.

    e. Stop ineffective, immaterial, impertinent, or emotional discussions before they disrupt your class.

5. Try for a high level of thinking.

    a. Challenge inconsistencies, faulty logic, and superficiality. Be sure mistakes in fact are corrected. When necessary supply facts or correct facts yourself.

    b. Try to get pupils to clarify their ideas. Ask them why they say what they say and believe what they believe. Make them consider the consequences of their position. In other words, force them to examine their own ideas and the ideas of their colleagues critically. Do not allow unexamined opinions to go unchallenged.

    c. Try to reduce ambiguity. Ask pupils to give illustrations of what they mean. Ask them to rephrase and explain. Sometimes you will have to rephrase their statements yourself.

6. Try to bring the discussion to a head. Have pupils integrate and synthesize

the varying comments. Yet keep the discussion open-ended. Let the conclusions, consensus, and final positions be theirs not your predetermined ones. In any case be sure the discussion ends with a good summarizing activity.

Check List for Discussion Leader.

1. Did I lead rather than monopolize?
2. Did I introduce the topic well?
3. Did I keep the discussion moving?
4. Did I keep the group on the topic?
5. Did I give everyone a chance to participate? Did I encourage everyone to participate?
6. Did I draw out the shy ones? Did I keep the atmosphere permissive?
7. Did I prevent anyone from monopolizing?
8. Did I handle the overtalkative tactfully and kindly?
9. Did I keep the discussion open? Did I encourage fresh new ideas?
10. Did I discourage time-wasting side issues?
11. Did I clarify issues and questions?
12. Did I summarize as needed?
13. Did I close when we were finished?
14. Did the group accomplish its objective satisfactorily?
15. Was it a good discussion?

To Prepare a Flow Chart of a Discussion. Use flow charts to improve your class discussions. A flow chart is a diagram that shows the flow on conversation during a discussion. It can be made by one of the pupils, acting as an observer. It shows who participated and who did not. It sometimes helps to make pupils aware that they are monopolizing or not participating. To make the flow chart follow these directions:

1. It is easiest to make the flow chart if the pupils are seated in a circle. Semicircles and hollow squares make it more difficult to prepare the diagram. When pupils are sitting in rows, preparing the flow chart becomes virtually impossible.
2. Before the class starts, prepare a chart of the class showing where the participants are sitting.
3. As each pupil speaks, draw an arrow from his position to
   a. The center of the circle if he speaks to the group in general.
   b. The name of the person spoken to if he speaks to an individual.

Example

Interpret the model of a flow chart in Figure 4-1. What does it show about the discussion, about the leader, about the group?

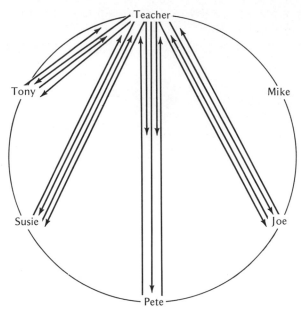

FIGURE 4-1. *A Simplified Model of a Flow Chart.*

SMALL-GROUP DISCUSSION

Form small discussion groups in your classes to get more pupil involvement and participation, to provide for individual differences, and to encourage reflective, original thinking. The procedures for such small-group discussions are the same as those for other discussion groups.

Use buzz groups to bring out various opinions; to clarify definitions; to expose points of view; to get definite proposals for next steps; to find what pupils really think; to evaluate films, materials, and activities; and to bring out pupils ideas, notions, and attitudes and to help launch large-group discussions.

Buzz Groups. Buzz groups are small groups of five or six pupils gathered together briefly for a few minutes to discuss a certain matter for a specific purpose.

1. Form buzz groups informally by some simple process such as "you six in the rear right corner make up one group," "you six in the first three seats of rows 1 and 2 make up another group," and so on.

2. Appoint a leader and a recorder for each group.

3. Be sure that the group members know what they are supposed to do. Buzz groups do no research. They simply talk about some point. The purpose is to loosen the group up, to get more ideas on the floor, and to get ideas out in the open.

4. Have buzz groups report the conclusions or suggestions to the class. Usually these reports are oral presentations by the recorders. Sometimes, however, panels, role playing, written reports, or other forms of reporting can be used.

PANELS, FORUMS, SYMPOSIUMS, ROUND TABLES, AND DEBATES

Formal discussions range from the quite informal round table to the extremely formal debate. They all have in common the factor of being largely audience activities and so are useful in large classes where informal whole-class or small-group discussions would not be feasible.

Types of formal discussion mentioned in the literature include the round table, panel, forum, symposium, debate, British debate, and jury trial.

In general, the procedures for preparing for these and other types of formal discussions are pretty much the same.

When to Use Panels, Symposia, and Other Formal Discussions. Use formal discussion techniques in the following situations:

1. As culminating activities.
2. To present points of view concerning controversial issues.
3. To present reports of pupil committees.
4. To present findings of pupil research.
5. In large classes as a means of involving pupils.
6. To utilize the talents and special preparation of certain students.
7. To give variety and change of pace to the class.

Suggestions for Conducting Formal Discussions

1. Let the pupils cooperate in selecting the topic but give them plenty of help.
2. Select the panel members. Assist them in selecting the positions to be represented.
3. Help the pupils prepare for the presentation.
   a. The panel may consist of representatives of committees. In this case divide the class into committees and supervise their work just as with other committees. In symposia, debates, and the like supervise the gathering and organizing of material as in any other report or research study.
   b. Help panel members develop their presentations. Help the students make up a plan for the presentation.
   c. Brief pupils on the procedure and their roles. Pupils should know what they plan to do. They should talk it over among themselves, but there should be no rehearsal.
4. Conduct the presentation.
5. Follow the presentation with a discussion.
6. Follow up and tie up any loose ends. A summary of important points or positions may be enough.

To Involve the Class in Formal Discussions

1. The more interesting the panel the more likely the students are to participate.
2. Give pupils a chance to ask questions.
3. Ask pupils to take notes on the panel presentation and discussion.
4. Ask pupils to summarize major points and different positions.
5. Ask pupils to list pros and cons.

6. Ask pupils to evaluate the arguments and logic of panel members but not their manner or skill of presentation.

Duties of the Chairman in Formal Discussions. In a panel discussion, the chairman is the key person. He, therefore, needs special help and briefing by the teacher. Probably the first panels should be chaired by the teacher himself. The duties the chairman must perform and the teacher must help him learn are

1. To introduce the topic, prepare the audience, and explain the procedures.
2. To introduce the panelists.
3. To ensure that the panelists do not talk too long.
4. To solicit questions from the audience. Sometimes it is wise to have some questions planted. Pupils can also be assigned to make up questions for homework.
5. To accept questions and refer them in such a way as to encourage more questions.
6. To sum up when necessary.
7. To redirect the flow of discussion when necessary.
8. To close the discussion.

(Usually you should select one of the ablest pupils as the chairman. Remember that students who are most academically able are not always the most socially able.)

BRITISH-STYLE DEBATE

To conduct a British-style debate

1. Divide the class into two teams (pro and con), each side having two principal speakers.
2. Have pupils on each side prepare their arguments.
3. Conduct the presentation.
   a. One member from each side gives a five-minute talk.
   b. A second member on each side gives a shorter (three-minute) talk.
   c. Other members of the teams make comments and ask questions from the floor. (So that each side will have an equal opportunity, alternate between affirmative and negative speakers.)
   d. One member from each side summarizes.
4. If time allows, follow up with a general discussion.

JURY-TRIAL TECHNIQUE

The jury-trial technique uses simulated courtroom procedures to discuss an issue or problem.

1. Select an issue or problem to debate.
2. Select lawyers, researchers, and witnesses, both pro and con.
3. Have all pupils research the problem. Lawyers and witnesses should get all the facts they can with the researchers' help.

4. Try to establish the facts in courtroom fashion.
    a. Witnesses present evidence.
    b. Lawyers question and cross-question.
    c. Lawyers from each side interpret the evidence presented trying to prove that it favors their position.
    d. The teacher, acting as judge, points out fallacious arguments, incorrect facts, and other obvious errors.
    e. After everyone has had a chance to share in the discussion of the merits of the cases presented by the two sides, the class, acting as jury, votes to see which side has presented the better argument.

SMALL WORK GROUPS AND COMMITTEES

There are many different bases for forming small groups in the classroom. Among the most common kinds of small groups are work groups or committees, discussion groups, buzz groups, ability groups, and interest groups. Ability and interest groups may be committees, discussion groups, or simply class subdivisions whose work differs from that of other groups.

VALUE OF SMALL-GROUP AND COMMITTEE WORK

Small-group techniques are very useful.

1. Small groups allow for individual instruction and help provide for the many differences in pupils by allowing them to participate in different roles and on different committees.
2. Small-group work promotes effective learning.
    a. Small groups seem to be more successful in problem solving than individuals are.
    b. Small-group techniques tend to develop critical discrimination.
    c. Small groups provide a wide range of information.
    d. Small groups provide opportunities for depth study and wide coverage.
    e. Small groups provide opportunities to develop research and study skills.
3. Small groups provide pupils with opportunities to learn social skills and to develop good social attitudes as a result of the give-and-take.
4. Small groups can help develop leadership ability.
5. Small groups can help develop self-reliance and self-direction.
6. Small groups add variety and interest to classes.
    a. They make it possible to match method with purpose.
    b. They give a change of pace.
    c. They provide release from the tedium of the ordinary class and give pupils an opportunity to work off their energy through active participation.

TEACHING BY COMMITTEE

Committee work is a special kind of small-group work. Use it
To carry out research projects.

To plan and carry out special projects.

To plan and carry out whole-class activities.

To plan and carry out service functions—keeping up the time line, fixing the bulletin board, and so on.

To help pupils learn communication and social skills.

To emphasize problem solving and research-like learning.

Procedure for Teaching by Committee. The following steps do not all apply to every committee. They represent a framework well suited for certain committees. Adapt them to other committees by changing or omitting steps.

1. Pick a leader and a secretary.
2. Define the task.
3. Set the objectives.
4. Set up a plan.
   a. What tasks must be done?
   b. What material and/or equipment must be secured?
   c. How will information be shared among the committee members?
   d. What records or notes need be kept?
   e. Who will do each of the various tasks? When will the tasks be done?
   f. What are the time limits?
5. Implement the plan.
6. Share the results with each other.
7. Plan how to report the findings.
8. Make the report.

How to Use Committees In a Unit

1. Begin the unit.
2. Discuss the objectives of the unit.
   a. What might be done?
   b. What must be done?
3. Prepare a plan including problems, subproblems, other tasks, and ways of reporting.
4. Provide committees for these various tasks.
5. Let each committee plan and execute its part of the plan.
6. Prepare for and execute a pooling of the experiences and findings of the committees.

PLANNING FOR GROUPS AND COMMITTEES

Selecting the Group Leaders. The key figures in a work group are the group leader, or chairman, and the secretary, or recorder. These functionaries can be selected in any of the following ways. Use the method that seems best in view of the total situation.

1. Teacher selected. This is a good procedure when pupils are unfamiliar with the process of working in committees. By choosing more mature pupils for leaders, the teacher gives the committee a better chance to be successful.

2. Elected by the committee itself after the committee has been formed. This is the normal procedure.

3. Elected by the class as a whole. This procedure makes it more likely to get the natural leaders in leadership positions, although interest and abilities are not always matched up.

Selecting the Committee Members

1. The number of committee members should range from four to seven—seldom, if ever, eight or more. Sometimes special committees of three are advantageous. If a committee has eight or more members, divide it into two committees.
2. There are several ways to select the committee. Choose the one most practical under the circumstances. Do not use the same technique all the time.
   a. Pupils' choice (interest).
      Let pupils select the committees with which they wish to work. If you have too many for any one committee, you can form subcommittees, but if you have too few you must either persuade someone to move to the unpopular committee, or drop the committee. Before taking drastic steps, however, remember that committees do not all need to be of equal size.
   b. Pupils' limited choice.
      Let pupils indicate three preferences for committee assignments. Then you can balance the committees by using second and third choices.
   c. Sociometric devices, such as sociograms.
   d. Arbitrarily.
      Pupils can be chosen alphabetically, or because they are in the first row, or because they are the five people in the rear left corner. Committees chosen in this way should be of short duration.
   e. Pupil steering committee.
      Let a pupil steering committee select the members of the committees.
   f. Skills or talents.
      Put certain pupils with special skills on certain committees.
   g. Ability levels.
      Group pupils of equal ability together or provide a mix of bright and slow in each group.
   h. Academic need.
      Group pupils who need help in certain areas together.
   i. By chairmen.
      Have chairmen nominated from the floor. Let the chairmen select their own committee members or let them act as a steering committee and divide the pupils among the committees.
3. Whenever possible, pupils should be assigned to committees they prefer and for which they have volunteered. Avoid forcing pupils into committees that are repugnant to them. To avoid embarrassment when choosing committees, pupils should write out their choices.
4. Do not let the same pupils work together all the time.

Committee or Group Planning. Planning small-group and committee work must usually be done cooperatively by teachers and pupils. In their planning the committee or group should

1. Discuss the objectives.
   a. What might be done?
   b. What must be done?
   c. How to accomplish the preceding requirements?
   d. How to report?
2. List subordinate problems and tasks. Outline what must be done.
3. List resources.
4. Divide the work.
     Use a form such as the following to record the work assignments of the various members of the committee.

Committee Work
Form for assignment of committee members.
Unit _____
Committee _____
Pupil _____ Job _____ Committee _____
1. _____
2. _____
3. _____
4. _____

---

5. Make provisions for pupils to share their work.

Frequently the initial plans made by a group are not realistic. Once the deficiency has been located, the pupils should alter the plans. You can help pupils see the deficiencies in their planning through open-ended questioning. Be careful not to cut off their search for their own solutions, however. Beware of direct interference or too-pointed suggestions.

SOME SUGGESTIONS FOR CONDUCTING SMALL-GROUP WORK

1. Before breaking up into committees or small groups, discuss the committee work and committee procedure. Be sure the pupils have a clear idea of what their task is, the procedures they can use, and the limits beyond which they may not go.
2. Teach the pupils how to work in committees and what is expected of them. Show pupils how to do the work. Often, you can use one group as a model. Sometimes it helps to have the poorer pupils act out the role of the good workers.
3. Mimeograph a list telling what a good committee does, or put this information on a chart on the bulletin board or chalkboard.
4. Provide good working conditions with plenty of reasonably quiet space. Keep the rules simple.

5. Circulate; visit all groups briefly. Listen to what is going on. You may find that pupils have misunderstood the assignment or are proceeding in the wrong way. Help by asking questions to make them think and by occasional suggestions. Keep direct suggestions to a minimum, however. Suggest that they consider such and such, or ask if they have considered such and such, but then let them make the decision and live with it.

6. Check to see that everyone has a job to do and is doing it. Check to see that pupils' goals are realistic—neither too high nor too low. Be sure that they have set up reasonable time limits.

7. Work with the various groups as needed. When a committee is having trouble it may help to have the whole-class discuss the problem.

8. Help pupils find materials. See to it that they have plenty with which to work. Have them check to be sure that material is available before they begin and become committed to the project. Help committees organize their material.

9. Work with individuals as needed. Chairmen and secretaries usually need help. From time to time, stop to discuss common problems.

10. Encourage pupils to be independent. Support them, but do not dominate. Allow and encourage them to do different things simultaneously.

11. Keep a record or log of what transpires.
    a. For the sake of continuity.
    b. As a basis for evaluation.
    c. So that you will know and remember.
    In it include committee assignments, committee members, tasks completed, leadership responsibilities, and so on.

12. Prepare a schedule of jobs showing when they are to be finished.

13. Ask for occasional progress reports—either oral, written, or both.

14. Vary the groups and the group work. Don't overuse group work.

15. In short, guide and help, but do not dominate.

Tips for Handling Some Problems in Committee Teaching

1. What does one do when a committee gets stuck?
   a. Ask the members to reconsider their objective. Is it reasonable? Do they want to continue with the same objective or do they want to change it?
   b. Ask them to consider the strategies and tactics they have adopted. Are they likely to reach the objective? Are there alternative strategies or tactics that might be better?
   c. If they do not see anything wrong with their objectives you may have to help them. If possible, draw out a new approach from the pupils by questioning them in the Socratic method rather than by telling them what to do. Ask such questions as: What do you want to do? Are there more reasonable goals? Are there more feasible goals? If the goals are changed, what tactics and strategies would be necessary? How can you avoid further difficulty and delay?

2. What do you do if a group gets out of control?
   a. Find out what the matter is.
   b. Work with the pupils that need help.
   c. Try role playing.
   d. Meet with the group.

3. What if one person monopolizes the group?
   a. Use role playing to try to show him how he behaves.
   b. Have a talk with him. Tell him that you appreciate his enthusiasm, but it would be fair to give others more of a chance.
   c. Make him a nonparticipating observer.
   d. Tape and play back a discussion and let him evaluate his own performance.
4. What if an individual causes trouble?
   a. Let him clarify his objectives, tasks, and strategies.
   b. Let him change roles if it seems advisable.
   c. Let him role play the part of an excellent group member.
   d. Talk things over with him.
   e. If all else fails, take direct action.
5. What about the shy pupil?
   a. Don't push him.
   b. Don't single him out.
   c. Let him choose his own role.
   d. Make frequent impersonal evaluations and checks.

Ways to Present Committee Reports

1. Oral reports.
2. Written reports.
3. Mimeographed (dittoed) reports.
4. Murals.
5. Diagrams.
6. Interviews, TV, radio.
7. Panels.
8. Time lines.
9. Map making.
10. Debates.
11. Majority and minority reports.
12. Charts.
13. Dramatizations.
14. Slides or pictures.

When pupils make their reports, other pupils should listen and look. Their responses to the reports will be more profitable if they take notes or prepare questions to ask the reporters during the discussion period to follow. Also one can utilize techniques such as buzz sessions, check lists, and questions from the class to involve the listeners.[21]

HOMEWORK

In most schools homework presents a sticky problem. Probably we teachers tend to depend too much on homework and not enough on learning in class. In

[21] For more information on committee and group work, see Louise E. Hock, *Using Committees in the Classroom* (New York: Holt, Rinehart and Winston, Inc., 1958), and Ned Flanders, *Teaching with Groups* (Minneapolis, Minn.: Burgess Publishing Co., 1954).

any case, the following suggestions should help you to ameliorate the homework problem.

1. Give only a reasonable amount of homework. Avoid overloading the pupils. The total homework load of all courses combined should be
   1–2 hours in grades 7–8.
   2–3 hours in grades 9–10.
   3–4 hours in grades 11–12.
To prevent superficial assignments and still keep within the one to two hours per day total, it may be wise to stagger assignments in grades 7 and 8. For example, science and math one night and English and social studies the next night. In the senior high school grades homework time should be equally divided among the courses, due allowance being made for major assignments and tests, of course. The use of weekly assignments or longer unit assignments can sometimes prevent the bunching of homework assignments.

2. Give homework assignments for which pupils do not need individual help. Avoid using new work for homework.

3. If you are in a situation where pupils do not do homework, do not assign it. Use supervised study and laboratory teaching instead.

4. Give homework that will enrich the pupils. Make it more than the simple reenforcement of classwork. Avoid mere repetition and busy work.

5. Individualize homework assignments. Give assignments that involve individual creativity, projects, field work, and the like.

6. Give reading and writing assignments.

7. Correct written homework assignments.

8. Be sure that pupils know how to go about doing the homework assignment. Avoid long, complicated assignments.

9. Make homework real. Avoid using it for punishment or extra credit.

10. Avoid using homework assignments as a major factor in assigning school marks.

SUPERVISED STUDY

Teachers should see to it that pupils do some studying under supervision in class time. Supervised study can also, of course, take place outside of class in the library, laboratory, resource centers, and elsewhere.

Some new teachers seem to think that for pupils to study in class is a waste of the class time. They are wrong. Studying is the core of learning. It should not be entirely relegated to homework. Neither should classes become merely lesson-hearing sessions or recitations in which the teacher checks on what the pupils have learned elsewhere.

Supervised study is useful for the following reasons:

1. The teacher can observe the pupils' study procedures and guide them in their studying.

2. The teacher can help pupils having difficulty.

3. The teacher can encourage pupils.

4. The teacher can make study materials available.

Suggestions for Conducting Supervised Study

1. Individualize. Diagnose pupils' needs, strengths, and weaknesses. Differentiate so that all pupils will be kept profitably busy but no one is overburdened. Pupils should not all have the same assignments. Vary your approach for different individuals.

2. Circulate. See how the pupils are doing and help where necessary. Check on their progress often. Asking questions about the ideas and content will give you better clues to how the pupil is progressing than will directly asking if he has any trouble. Observe pupils and confer with them on what they have learned, how they are progressing, what to do next, and what the implications of what they have learned are, how what they are learning relates to past and future learning, and the conclusions they have drawn.

3. Be sure each pupil knows what to do and how to do it. Be sure that the class understands the meaning and purpose of what they are doing. Be sure they understand the problem.

4. Show them how to study. Help the pupils evaluate their own study techniques. Give them practice in good study techniques. Work on skills with open books in large groups, small groups, or individually. Point out poor study skills and encourage good ones.

5. Encourage reading in the classroom.

6. Help the pupils locate and use sources of information.

7. Arrange the room to aid study. Be sure material is readily available.

8. Arrange for pupils to help each other.

9. Stop supervised study before the period ends in order to avoid control problems.

10. Give the pupils time enough to do the work. Avoid stopping them just as they are beginning to get involved.

CHAPTER 5
Reading and Studying

READING is difficult for many secondary school pupils. Pupils find social studies reading particularly frustrating. In the first place, there is so much of it. Secondly, it usually is difficult. As Herber[1] rightly states, much of the reading in social studies courses consists of abstractions presented in such a way that only persons who already understand them can understand them.

Therefore, all social studies teachers need to help pupils master such developmental reading skills as the ability

To read critically.

To separate fact from opinion.

To catch propaganda, polemics, and bias.

To define and analyze.

To use library and reference works well.

To use technical words with understanding.

In addition, some pupils need remedial help. Severe, stubborn cases of reading disability should be handled by a reading teacher. However, you will have to handle less difficult cases yourself. Consult works on the teaching of reading[2] for help in teaching remedial reading skills.

READING CRITICALLY

Reading critically is more than gathering information and making inferences from what is written. It consists of evaluating the worth of a selection and applying its message in other situations. It is made up of several elements.

1. Judgments about the accuracy of the information presented.
2. Judgments about the inferences and conclusions made by the writer.

[1] Harold L. Herber, "Teaching Secondary School Students to Read History," in *Reading Instruction in Secondary Schools, Perspectives in Reading No. 2* (Newark, Del.: International Reading Association, 1964), p. 83.

[2] For example Henry A. Bamman, Ursula Hogan, and Charles E. Greene, *Reading Instruction in the Secondary School* (New York: Longmans, Green and Co., Inc., 1961).

3. Judgments about the implications of the selection.
4. Judgments about the application of what is written.
5. Judgments about the style of writing.

To Read for Fact

Probably the most important step in thinking is to get one's facts, or premises, straight. No matter how well one thinks or how logical his inferences, if his original data were faulty, his conclusions will be no good. Yet, very few pupils learn how to find out the facts. At least part of the gullibility of adults is the result of textbook teaching in which the textbook is always the highest authority.

Here are some suggestions for teaching pupils how to ferret out facts.

1. Arouse in pupils an awareness of how difficult it is to get actual, factual information.
   a. Give pupils different readings about the same incident. Ask them to compare the facts as presented in the readings.
   b. Have pupils compare the presentation of certain events in different textbooks or to compare the textbook account with the presentation in other reference works.
2. Develop skills for spotting the difference between fact and opinion, inference, assumption, supposition, and other kinds of guesswork.
   a. Encourage pupils to ask: How does the author know? Does he really know or is he just guessing?
   b. Use exercises such as the following:
   (1) How much of this excerpt is fact and how much conjecture?

> While not disdaining contributions, Paul earned his livelihood, whenever possible, making tents. In the flourishing Greek city of Corinth, for example, he went into partnership with a couple from Italy. Their tentmaking workshop, open to the street, gave him a perfect base. Tradesmen and slaves, philosophers and idlers, women carrying water jars, sailors from the busy port, all would stop to chat. And Paul's magnetic personality, his charm, his talent for a well-turned phrase made many of them linger or come back for more. Soon, a feeling of "belonging" was born, of being members of a new community united by a common hope.[3]

   (2) Read the passage concerning St. Paul. List the things you consider to

Fact	Supposition

---

[3] E. O. Hauser, "Saint Paul—Apostle to All Men," *Readers Digest* **89**:149 (Sept., 1966).

be factual in the left-hand column in the illustration, and the things you consider to be supposition in the right-hand column.

   c. Use the pupils' textbook as the basis for practice in differentiating between fact and interpretation, or inference.

3. Teach pupils to check for accuracy and discrepancies.

   a. Check against original documents. For example, check the stenographic account of a court case, or congressional hearing, and compare it to a news account. Are there discrepancies?

   b. Tape a Presidential press conference. Compare the newspaper reports with the tape.

   c. Use the newspaper as practice material. (See Chapter 14.)

     (1) Check it for contradictions. Do the accounts in the news stories, editorial pages, and financial sections agree, for instance?

     (2) Check various newspapers against each other.

     (3) Compare newspaper accounts with accounts from other sources.

   d. Practice checking textual material in the textbooks against graphs, charts, maps, and other graphic and statistical devices. Give pupils plenty of experience interpreting statistics.

   e. Teach pupils to check their sources of information. Pupils should learn to ask and find answers to questions such as the following:

     What or who was the source of the information? How reliable is this source? Is the information the product of direct observation or hearsay? Was the observer a trained observer or not? What was the bias of the observer? Does the information check with that from other sources? Does the story check with known facts?

   f. Teach pupils to evaluate such phrases as "alleged," "a usually reliable source," "on good authority," and "a high government spokesman."

4. Develop skills for detecting propaganda and bias. Propaganda refers to attempts to sway opinion or action. It is not necessarily evil or pernicious, but it is purposefully one-sided. Advertising and political argument are two familiar examples. Bias is also one-sided, but not necessarily purposely so. Although we don't like to think so, most history and other social studies textbooks are biased. Therefore all pupils should be taught to test for bias and the use of propaganda techniques in even the staidest material. Advertisements, newspaper stories, and magazine articles make excellent sources of material to use in teaching pupils to detect bias and propaganda. Some examples of exercises useful in developing skill in propaganda analysis and detecting bias follow.

   a. Have pupils look through newspapers and textbooks for examples of colored words, glittering generalities, irrelevant authority, and other devices designed to persuade rather than inform.

   b. Have pupils look for signs of editorializing in newsstories and in textbooks. How much in each story seems to be hard fact and how much the reporter's interpretation or speculation?

   c. Have pupils write original advertisements using propaganda and polemic devices.

   d. List the various propaganda and persuasive rhetorical devices; have pupils search newsstories, editorials, and advertising for examples of them.

Colored or Loaded Words	False Analogy	Name Calling	Irrelevant Authority	Card Stacking

e. Project the following kinds of pieces onto a screen by means of an overhead projector or even an opaque projector as a basis for the discussion of faults of logic or the use of propaganda techniques. For example:

In the fall of 1964, the Ford Motor Company ran an advertisement featuring a picture of a young man, a beautiful girl, and a Mustang Hardtop, plus the following copy.

Two weeks ago this man was a bashful schoolteacher in a small Midwestern city. Add Mustang. Now he has three steady girls, is on first name terms with the best headwaiter in town, is society's darling. All the above came with his Mustang. So did bucket seats, full wheel covers, wall-to-wall carpeting, padded dash, vinyl upholstery, and more. Join the Mustangers! Enjoy a lot of *dolce vita* at a low, low price.

Then ask the pupils such questions as: What propaganda techniques does this ad use? In what ways does it violate principles of logic? What evidence of fallacious reasoning can you find? What evidence do they present to show that the Mustang is a good buy?

f. Use a chart like the following to rate advertisements.

Trait	Rating
Honesty	A B C D F
Rational Appeal	A B C D F
Information	A B C D F

ANALYZING, INTERPRETING, AND APPLYING ONE'S READING

In addition to determining accuracy and factualness, critical reading consists of analyzing, interpreting, and applying what has been read.

Fortunately, these activities are not difficult after one has had a little practice. What the reader must do is ask himself questions as he reads:

What is the author trying to say or do?

What is the point of the piece?

Are the author's conclusions logical?

How does what he says fit in with what I already know?

Does he present new evidence that should make me change my opinion?

Does his interpretation jibe with that of other authorities? If not, does it seem to be well supported?

At least some of the results of the reading analyses done by the pupils should be shared with the group. Small-group discussion, panels, and interviews are excellent for this phase. For the capable student, writing serious analyses can be a rewarding, mind-stretching experience. Even less capable pupils can gain from the experience, if given a real chance to try. The point is that reading should be used as a springboard to other intellectual activities wherever feasible, but if pupils do not learn to read critically, springboard reading and follow-up will be fruitless. Teachers can develop analytical skills by using exercises similar to those described for use in the section on reading comprehension and study skills.

To Check for Style. To check for style, have pupils consider such questions as

1. Is the style of writing appropriate to the writer's objective?
   a. Does the style enhance or obscure the writer's meaning?
   b. Does the style bring out the feeling or emotions desired?
   c. Is the style successful?
2. Is the writing sharp and sprightly or dull and turgid? What in the style makes the difference?

List Propaganda Devices and Other Signs of Bias

Pupils should be familiar with the various devices used in propaganda and polemics and with other signs of bias in writing. There is, however, no virtue in learning to list propaganda devices, in defining them, or even in learning them by name. What is necessary is that pupils learn to see through the devices and spot where the argument goes wrong. The point is not for pupils to recognize that an argument is *ad hominem*, but to recognize that the argument is irrelevant. In the following list, some of the common propaganda devices and signs of bias are defined.

Name calling: attempting to confuse by pasting negative labels on ideas, movements, groups, people, or policy either directly or indirectly.

Glittering generalities: attempting to confuse by associating vague, ambiguous virtue words or notions with an idea, group, or the like.

Transfer: attempting to carry over the aura of something prestigious to the thing one wishes to sell or put across.

Testimonial: attempting to curry favor by means of an endorsement by some prestige figure.

Plain folks: attempting to present an idea as that "of the people" and therefore good.

Card stacking: attempting to win favor by suppressing, distorting, or inventing facts.

Band wagon: attempting to influence by means of the argument that everyone is doing it.

Good old days: attempting to sell an idea because that is the way it used to be "in the good old days."

Rising sun: attempting to sell an idea because it is modern — the newest thing.

Guilt or virtue by association: attempting to convince by associating the idea, group, or whatever with something prestigious or unfavorable.

Irrelevant authority: attempting to influence by referring to a prestigious figure, body, or document not pertinent to the matter under discussion.

Closed mind: attempting to convince by use of untrue or half-true stock figures and beliefs, stereotypes, and myths.

Conversion by diversion: attempting to influence by the use of specious irrelevancies; for example, *tu quoque* (other people do it too), *ad hominem* (arguing in personalities rather than on the issue), *ad baculum* (use of threats), *ad misericordiam* (appealing to pity and sympathy, rather than speaking to the issue), *ad captandum vulgus* (use of irrelevant clichés, slogans, and other crowd-catching devices, and also by simply talking around the subject rather than to the point, or by introducing a red herring).

Emotion-arousing symbols: attempting to influence by use of catch phrases, colored words, slogans, pictures, and symbols that appeal to emotions rather than to reason.

Colored, or polluted, writing: attempting to influence by use of colored words, catch phrases, distorted emphases, and so on that change the meaning of factual accounts so that they seem to support a particular view.

Fallacies: using logical fallacies to support a position. [For example, *post hoc ergo propter hoc* (assumption that because A follows B, A caused B); *statistical fallacies* (for example, poor sampling, poor methodology, misinterpretation); *argument from insufficient evidence or argument from anecdote; ignoring exceptions; overvaluing exceptions* (exceptions treated as typical); *begging the question* (circular argument, argument in which the proof is simply the original in disguise); *complex question* (unanswerable question such as "Have you stopped beating your wife yet?"); *false analogy* (comparisons that don't compare in essentials).]

READING GRAPHS, CHARTS, TABLES, AND OTHER AIDS

Books in history and the social sciences frequently include maps, pictures, graphs, tables, charts, and other aids for the reader. Often, these devices carry the real meat of the work; the text merely embroiders or explains the information presented by them. For this reason, pupils must learn how to read these devices correctly and carefully. In the next few pages suggestions are made for teaching pupils how to use charts, graphs, tables, and pictures. The use of maps is considered in detail in Chapter 15.

1. Teach the reading of charts, graphs, and tables in context during regular lessons rather than in special lessons or units.

2. Instead of giving special lessons on charts and graphs, call attention to important graphic features in the texts, or other readings, as the class goes along — taking care that definite assignments concerning the reading and interpreting of such material are made at suitable intervals.

3. In your assignments, ask the pupils to use charts, graphs, tables, and so on to bring out ideas and to back up conclusions. For instance, in the French Embassy's pamphlet *France and Agriculture* (December 1961), the following table appeared:

Size of Farms (acres)	Number of Farms	Land in Farms (acres)	Percent & Distribution	
			Number Farms	Land in Farms
Under 25	1,265,070	12,979,850	55.8	16.4
25 to 49	532,400	18,614,167	23.5	27.4
50 to 124	375,200	27,582,984	16.5	34.7
125 to 199	74,900	12,271,454	3.3	15.6
250 to 499	16,700	5,425,489	0.7	6.8
500 and over	3,500	2,562,131	0.2	3.2
Total	2,267,700	79,436,435	100.0	100.0*

*From *France & Agriculture, Ambassade de France, Service de Presse et d'Information*, 972 Fifth Avenue, New York, N.Y. 10021 (Dec. 1961), p. 8.

When studying this table ask pupils to draw conclusions regarding the efficiency of the French system of agriculture in 1960, and to determine why the French ministry of agriculture desired to promote the consolidation of farms, in addition to asking questions of fact.

In ferreting out the answers to such questions, point out to pupils the use of such guides as captions, column leads, tabs, and so on.

4. In teaching graphs you will have to extend yourself to be sure that the pupils know what is going on. Probably you will have to do some direct teaching, using different kinds of graphs. Once this is done, let them make comparisons and draw inferences as with other materials. In teaching with the graph (Figure 5-1) from *U.S. News and World Report*,[4] you might use questions similar to the following.

> During what month of 1963 was business activity lowest?
>
> How does business activity in November 1963 compare with business activity in 1957–1959?
>
> What seemed to be the general trend in business activity during the four-year period, 1960–1963?
>
> How did business activity in November 1963 compare to activity in November 1962? In November 1961?
>
> What can a graph such as this one tell the reader?

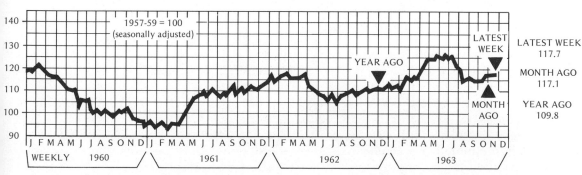

FIGURE 5-1. *U.S. News & World Report's Index of Business Activity, Dec. 2, 1963*

[4] *U.S. News & World Report*, 45:90 (Dec. 2, 1963). Copyright 1963, U.S. News World Report, Inc.

5. In teaching graphs and tables use the overhead projector to flash blank tables and graphs on the board. The pupils then can work on them in class. This procedure makes it unnecessary to encumber the board with graph lines ahead of time and makes the use of the board more flexible.

USE OF TEXTBOOKS

ADVANTAGES

Textbooks are valuable educational tools. Beginning teachers find them especially useful because

1. Textbooks can be a great help in the planning of courses, units, and lessons.
   a. They provide an organization or structure for the course.
   b. They provide a selection of content that can be used as a basis for selecting course content and determining emphases.
   c. They provide a certain number of activities and suggestions for teaching strategies and tactics.
   d. They provide information about other readings, sources of information, audiovisual and other aids, and other teaching materials and teaching tools.
2. Textbooks can be used as basic reading and as a launching pad for further activities such as discussions and research activities.

DISADVANTAGES

Textbooks have several disadvantages. The first and worst of these is that the teacher may depend on the text too much. Other disadvantages are

1. They are usually dull.
2. They tend to discourage real reading and studying.
3. They are liable to be superficial, because authors try to include something about everything and so say too little about too much.
4. They do not provide for differences in pupil ability or interest.

HOW TO USE TEXTBOOKS

1. Know the textbook before you use it.
2. Use the textbook as a basis for planning. Divide it into topics and arrange your course around them.
3. Use only the parts of the textbook that seem good to you; skip the other parts.
4. Supplement the text with other readings, audiovisual materials, and activities. Simulation, role playing, games, discussions, films, pictures, and so on can be used to give real meaning to the words of the text. Encourage pupils to read on their own.
5. Provide for individual differences by means of additional or substitute readings. Provide help for pupils who have difficulty reading.

6. Encourage pupils to read the text critically. Solicit reactions to and criticisms of textbooks. Compare text statements to statements in other texts, to commentaries, to source materials, and so on.

7. Teach vocabulary when necessary.

8. Adapt the textbook to the class. Be sure the assignments are reasonable.

TEACHING PUPILS HOW TO USE THE TEXTBOOK

The First Day.   Because the textbook is the principal tool in most courses, teach your pupils how to use it. Cartwright[5] recommends that on the very first day, before pupils begin to read their textbooks, you should examine the textbook with the pupils. In this examination the pupils should consider

1. The title page.
 What information does it give?
 When was the book written? Has it been revised?
 Who is the publisher? Where was it published? Do these indicate any likelihood of bias?
2. The preface.
 What does the author claim he intended to do? What was his purpose?
3. Table of contents.
 How much weight is given to various topics? How can we use the information contained in the table of contents to help us study the text?
4. The list of maps, charts, and illustrations.
 What is the importance of these devices? How can one use them to aid his study? Choose examples of each — maps, charts, tables, graphs, illustrations — and have pupils find essential information in them.
5. Appendix.
 What does appendix mean? What is it for?
6. Index.
 Use drill exercises to give pupils practice in using the index. These can be made into games or contests.
7. Glossary.
 What is a glossary? Why is it included? Utilize exercises that call for looking up words and then use them in sentences.
8. Study the aids at the ends of chapters.
 How can study questions be used? Which ones are thought questions? Which fact questions?
9. Chapter headings, section headings, paragraph leads, introductory overviews, preliminary questions, and summaries.
 What are the purposes of each of these? Use exercises that call for getting meaning from aids such as these without reading the entire text.

Developing Skill in the Use of Textbooks.   Use the following guide in developing skill in textbook use.

---

[5] William H. Cartwright, *How to Use a Textbook, How to Do It Series, No. 2*, rev. ed. (Washington, D.C.: National Council for the Social Studies, 1966).

1. Use the regular lessons and material in the order you would normally use them.
2. Work on one skill at a time.
3. Start with relatively easy work and make it increasingly more difficult.
4. Insist on good work.
5. Don't emphasize speed.
6. Teach when and how to skim.
7. Teach the parts of the book.
8. Teach the use of the aids and signposts.
9. Teach the use of charts, graphs, and illustrations.
10. Teach the vocabulary.
11. Teach pupils how to read for comprehension.
12. Teach pupils to read critically.

CAVEATS CONCERNING THE USE OF TEXTBOOKS

1. The textbook is a teaching tool. Use it as a springboard to launch investigation and discussion of the discovery type. Do not let it dictate your course content or lesson and unit plans. Do your own planning and teaching; do not become the slave of the textbook. It is not a Bible. Use other materials.
2. Do not expect pupils to know how to get the most out of texts without help.
3. Do not use the textbook as a means of avoiding hard work. The textbook is no excuse for poor teaching.

CRITERIA FOR SELECTING SUITABLE TEXTBOOKS FOR SOCIAL STUDIES COURSES

1. Perhaps the most important criterion to use in the selection of a book for a social studies course is, "Will it serve as a springboard to further thinking and inquiry by the pupils?" History and the social studies are all open-ended disciplines. Social studies textbooks should be open-ended too.
2. Is the information and interpretation presented up to date?
3. Who is the author? Is he competent in the field? Does he write clearly and well?
4. Is the book suitable for the objectives of your course? Does it cover the proper topics with the proper emphases?
5. Are the topics arranged in a desirable sequence? If not, can the sequence be altered or portions omitted without disrupting the usefulness of the book?
6. Is the content accurate and accurately presented? Is the book free from bias?
7. Are the concepts presented clearly? Are they adequately developed with sufficient detail? Is there a tendency to attempt to jam in too many ideas too compactly?
8. Are the vocabulary and language appropriate for the pupils of the class? Is the reading level appropriate?
9. Does the author make good use of headings, summaries, and similar devices? Does he give opportunities for the readers to visualize, generalize, apply, and evaluate the content?
10. Are the table of contents, preface, index, appendices, and glossary adequate?

11. Does the book provide suggestions for use of supplementary materials?

12. Does the book provide a variety of suggestions for stimulating thought-provoking instructional activities?

13. Are the illustrations accurate, purposeful, and properly captioned? Are they placed near the text they are designed to illustrate?

14. Does the book have suitable maps, charts, and tables? Are they clear and carefully done?

15. Is the book well made? Does it seem to be strong and durable?

16. Does the book look good? Is the type clear and readable? Do the pages make a pleasant appearance with enough white space?[6]

USE OF MULTIREADINGS

Although textbooks are valuable resources and have earned a place in social studies teaching, social studies teaching should probably *never* be limited to a single textbook. Multireadings, or a basic textbook plus supplementary readings, are almost always preferable. The common practice of using a set of books for one topic and another set for another topic is not a multireadings approach. It is a series of single textbooks used *ad seriatim*. The multireadings approach consists of using several readings for the same topic at the same time.

Procedure for Teaching by Multireadings. To conduct individualized reading with multireadings:

1. Select the goals to be learned from the unit. These goals should be expressed as concepts or ideas, or perhaps as skills, attitudes, or behavior. It depends, of course, on what you are shooting for.

2. Prepare a study guide containing questions that will guide pupils to discover the ideas, concepts, skills, attitudes, or behavior desired and suggested readings. Pupils can create questions for the study guide by discussing what they would like to learn in studying the topic. In any case, see to it that the questions are broad enough to require a lot of thinking.

3. Gather pertinent texts and other readings. (One can also include audiotapes, film strips, 8mm film loops, slide sequences, moving pictures, and the like.) Sometimes committees of pupils can perform this task.

4. Help individual pupils to select what they will read. The reading should be suitable to the pupil's reading ability. However, *no one should be kept from reading something he finds interesting and educational just because the teacher thinks it too difficult or too easy.* When pupils find that a work is too difficult or too simple, feel free to authorize a change.

Allow pupils to pick their own readings. Encourage them to consult sources not included in the study guide, but do not throw too much responsibility for finding the proper reading matter on to the pupils. It is not wise for pupils to hunt fruitlessly.

5. Follow up with a general discussion of the topic, panels, reports, and other activities.

[6] Leonard H. Clark and Irving S. Starr, *Secondary School Teaching Methods*, 2nd ed. (New York: The Macmillan Company, 1967), p. 274.

Beginning Multireadings. In the beginning, teaching with multireadings should be teacher-centered. During this phase, teach pupils to analyze and interpret. Encourage your pupils to develop their own questions to use in guiding their reading and study. While this is going on, it may be wise for the entire class to read and react to the same readings. However, as soon as the pupils become used to reading analytically, you should begin to individualize their readings.

At first keep the choices of reading matter limited. But be sure that there is choice enough to allow each pupil to find several things suitable to him. For optimum benefit, keep the books readily available in a classroom library. If this is not possible, a social studies resource center, laboratory, or the library will do. The purpose is to provide the pupil with an opportunity to browse under guidance — sampling and rejecting until he makes his choices.

Once the pupil has made his selection, let him read, analyze, and interpret his reading alone. The study guide, whether prepared by you or other pupils, or made up for the occasion by the pupil himself, should provide sufficient guidance. As you and the pupil become more confident with the technique, the choice of readings can become greater and the need for guidance will decrease. Use discussion periods and reports to tie everything together. If the pupils all talk about the same point, as described in a study guide, that not everyone has read the same readings will not matter.

Textbook Plus Supplementary Readings. Another approach is to use multireadings to supplement textbook assignments. In this type of teaching the procedure is similar to that used in other multireadings approaches, except that a standard textbook assignment is required as a basic reading.

Student-Prepared Guides and Reports. Pupils usually should be allowed to pick their own supplementary reading under the guidance of the teacher. Ask pupils to make short reports on 4×6 or 5×8 cards in which they tell something about the work, what parts were most interesting and useful, and so on. Keep these cards on file so that succeeding pupils can use them as guides. Pupil comments on the same work can be consolidated on one card. Note on the card what the work is about, some suggestions for getting the most out of it, and the degree of reading difficulty. Be sure to acknowledge the name and source of each pupil critic. These cards should be made up by pupils of all ability levels. The average or slow pupil may learn more from the comments of another average or slow pupil than from a bright one.

TO HELP A POOR READER

SOME RECOMMENDED PROCEDURES

1. Determine his actual reading level.
2. Use his listening comprehension as a guide to his potential reading level. The pupil should be able to learn to read at his listening comprehension level. To find a pupil's listening comprehension level
   a. Read a paragraph in a selection one grade higher than the pupil's reading level.

READING REPORT FORM

Student   Class   Date

Author

Title

Publisher

Summary of what the book was about.

What was good or bad about the book?

Do you recommend it? Why, or why not?

    b. Ask him to explain it to you in his own words.

    c. If he can give you the gist of the selection, try him on something more difficult.

    d. When you get to the point where he no longer can give back the gist of the selection, then you have reached the limit of his listening comprehension.

3. Use diagnostic techniques to find what the specific difficulties are.

4. Teach him the basic skills.

5. Encourage him to build up his sight vocabulary. He should continue to increase the number of words he recognizes by heart.

6. After having acquired a basic sight vocabulary, he should learn the word attack skills.

7. Utilize high-interest, low-vocabulary material as much as possible.

8. Help the pupil learn to read his social studies textbooks. As much as feasible, use his textbooks as the medium for learning reading skills.

9. Use graded reading material that becomes increasingly more difficult.

10. Use easy, nonacademic materials such as paperbacks, cartoons, popularized accounts, popular magazines, and the like. Remember, you are trying to help pupils learn, not to make the course academically respectable.

To Test for Reading Level

Pupils who have reading disabilities should not be expected to read material that is too difficult for them. Good readers should not be allowed to stick to a steady diet of easy reading.

There are several tests for determining a pupil's reading level. Not all of them are equally good or good for various purposes.[7]

An easy way to discover whether a book is too difficult for a pupil is to

1. Have him read a passage aloud. If he does not stumble over many of the words, the reading is probably not too difficult.

2. Ask him to tell about what he has read, in his own words. If he can give back the gist of the selection with supporting commentary, the selection was not too difficult.

By using this technique with graded reading material, as determined by one of the reading-difficulty formulas, it is possible to approximate the pupil's reading level. One can assume that if the pupil can read a passage without missing more than one word in twenty, he can read at that level providing that he can also demonstrate that he has understood the reading.

---

[7] Before using any test it is wise to consult such works as Glenn Myers Blair, *Diagnostic and Remedial Teaching*, 3rd ed. (New York: The Macmillan Company, 1967), and the various editions of O. K. Buros, *Mental Measurement Yearbook* (Highland Park, N.J.: The Gryphon Press).

To Determine the Reading Level of a Book. To determine the reading level of a book first check the teacher's manual or teacher's edition. If the reading level does not appear in them, use a readability formula.[8]

USE OF WORKBOOKS

In recent years, workbooks have had a bad reputation because

1. They frequently emphasize the obvious, the petty, and the immaterial.
2. They do not lend themselves to thinking but rather to rote work.
3. They are likely to be boring.

The truth of the matter is that workbooks are tools. They can be used well or badly. If you do use workbooks, try to find ones that try to help pupils see the larger aspects of the subject and that provide open-ended materials that encourage pupils to think.

Many of the new materials prepared by the social studies projects are really workbook materials in disguise. These should be viewed with the same jaundiced eye as other workbooks. If they encourage discovery, or thinking, then use them. If they merely ask pupils to find out more picayune facts, discard them.

TEACHING STUDY SKILLS

Pupils must learn how to study. The skills necessary for effective studying are difficult. We should not expect them to be learned incidentally by trial and error. Therefore they must be taught directly. Among the skills social studies teachers should expect to teach are

1. How to locate information.
2. How to read for information.
3. How to analyze problems.
4. How to plan for study.
5. How to review.
6. How to evaluate materials.
7. How to use charts, graphs, maps, and the like.
8. How to take notes.
9. How to concentrate.
10. How to outline.
11. How to use the library.
12. How to use reference works.
13. How to build a working vocabulary.[9]

---

[8] Typical readability formulas are described in the following references: Edgar Dale and Jeanne S. Chall, "A Formula for Predicting Readability," *Educational Research Bulletin* (January–February 1949). **27**:11–20, 37–54. Irving Lorge, "Predicting Readability," *Teachers College Record,* **45**:404–419 (March 1944). Use these formulas with caution. They are only rough indices at best.

[9] Clark and Starr, op. cit., p. 253.

RULES FOR STUDYING

1. Plan your studying. Make a schedule and stick to it. Have a definite place to work. Make your studying routine and part of your routine.

2. Start off immediately. Have your material ready before you sit down to work. Be sure you understand the assignment before you begin it.

3. Space your learning. Take two- to three-minute breaks. If possible, take your rests at natural breaks in the material you are studying. Try to master one lesson or selection before moving on to the next.

4. Study actively. Develop an interest in what you are studying. Try to find out something. React to the readings. Ask yourself questions. Recite. Work out examples. Illustrate principles. Apply your learning as soon as possible.

5. Vary your study techniques to suit the subject and your purpose. Learn materials in the form you expect to use them.

6. Avoid rote memorization. Memorize those things you need to memorize by the meaningful techniques of logical memory. Avoid mnemonics.

7. Evaluate your own work and study habits. Try to improve faulty habits. Try to increase your vocabulary; look up words you do not know. Make use of the aids provided in your books. Do not skip headings, marginal notes, questions, prefatory remarks, tables of contents, charts, and graphs. Use them.

8. Check your work and proofread your papers before handing them in. Take full notes, but do not attempt to rewrite the text or copy down each word of the lecturer.[10]

TO DEVELOP STUDY SKILLS

1. Study skills are probably best taught in regular classes using the regular class assignments. Careful assignments are an excellent help to the development of good study habits.
   a. Be sure that each pupil knows and understands the assignment.
   b. Be sure that each pupil knows how to do what the assignment requires of him.
   c. Be sure the assignment is complete enough to ensure that pupils understand what to do and how to do it.
   d. Use mimeographed study guides when feasible.
2. Use laboratory classes, workshops, and supervised study periods for teaching study skills and for pupils to practice using study skills.
3. Teach the specific study skills.
4. In supervised study sessions check pupils to see that in their studying (during labs) they direct their study by formulating objectives and carrying out SQ3R or similar techniques.
5. Be sure pupils know how to carry out the study assignment. One good way to do this is to have them discuss how they would proceed if no teacher were available. Do this while giving the assignment.
6. Work on one study skill at a time.
7. Use diagnostic techniques to find the strengths and weaknesses of each pupil.

---

[10] Ibid. p. 252.

Then work with him individually during supervised study periods, laboratory periods, and after school.

TO TEACH HOW TO OUTLINE

To teach the pupils how to outline correctly, the National Association of Secondary School Principals (NASSP) has recommended the following techniques, which have been well proven over the years.

1. Use easy materials and short selections in teaching pupils the mechanics of outlining. The following steps may be followed in teaching pupils to make outlines.
   a. Teacher and pupils working together select the main topics.
   b. Pupils, unaided, select the main topics.
   c. Teacher and pupils select the main topics, leaving space for subheads. Teacher and pupils then fill in these subtopics.
   d. Main topics are selected by the teacher and pupils and are written on the blackboard. Pupils then fill in the subtopics unaided.
   e. Pupils write the main topics and subheads without help.
   f. Pupils organize, in outline form, data gathered from many sources.
2. Train pupils to find the main topics and to place them in outline form. Use books with paragraph headings.
   a. Have pupils read the paragraphs and discuss the headings. Suggest other possible headings and have pupils decide why the author selected the headings he used.
   b. Match a given list of paragraph headings with numbered paragraphs.
   c. Have pupils read a paragraph with this question in mind, "What is the main idea in this paragraph?" Write a number of suggested answers on the blackboard. Choose the best one.
3. Provide practice in filling in subtopics.
   a. The teacher writes the main topics on the board or uses a text that has the main headings. Teacher and pupils then fill in the subheads.
   b. Have pupils skim other articles for more information and read carefully when additional material which is suitable for subheads is found. Add these new subheads. Do the same for new main topics.
   c. When pupils have gathered sufficient data, have them reread the complete outline and, if necessary, rearrange the order of the topics.
4. Give instructions in making a standard outline form. Many secondary-school pupils do not know how to make an outline. Emphasize the fact that in a correct outline there must always be more than one item in the series under any subdivision. If there is an "a" there must also be a "b"; if there is a "1" there must also be "2," etc. . . .
5. Have pupils use this outline form in preparing and giving oral reports.
6. To develop ability to draw valid conclusions, have pupils use facts and ideas which have been organized in outline form, not only as a basis for an oral report or as an exercise in outlining a chapter, but also as the basis for drawing conclusions. To check pupils' ability to make outlines, prepare lessons based on the following suggestions.
   a. List main points and subpoints consecutively. Have pupils copy these,

indenting to show subordination of subtopics and writing correct numbers and letters in front of each point.

b. List main topics and subtopics in mixed order and have pupils rearrange and number them.

c. List main topics with Roman numerals. List subtopics (all one value) with Arabic numerals. Have pupils organize subpoints under correct main points.

d. Present short paragraphs of well-organized material and have pupils write main topics and a specified number of subtopics.

e. Present part of a skeleton outline and have students complete it.

f. Have pupils outline a problem without assistance. Class discussion is valuable in checking a lesson of this type.[11]

To Teach Pupils to Take Lecture Notes

Taking notes at lectures is a very difficult skill. But all boys and girls who are planning to go to college need to master it.

The procedures used in taking lecture notes are quite similar to those used in outlining written material. The trick is to pick out the lecturer's main points and to subordinate the minor supporting points. Pupils who try to take down everything the lecturer says do not become good students. Here are some specific suggestions for teaching note taking.

1. Early in the course show the pupils how to take lecture notes.
2. Provide a skeleton outline for pupils to follow during the early lectures. Let them fill in the details during the lecture.
3. Gradually diminish the outline until the pupils can handle the whole process without any cues.
4. In lecturing give helps such as first, second, third, and so on. At times let the class know where you are in the lecture.
5. Lecture carefully. Stay on the topic, and follow your outline so that pupils can follow you.
6. Tape your lectures so that you can circulate around the classroom to help pupils while the lecture is in progress.
7. After your lecture, project your outline on a screen (use the overhead projector) so that pupils can see how their notes compare with your outline. Ask them to check to see if
a. They got the major points.
b. They got the important subordinate supporting points.

Selecting the Right Speed of Reading

Lately some teachers and many laymen have made a fetish out of rapid reading. Although there is no doubt that every pupil should learn to read as rap-

---

[11] "Teaching Essential Reading Skills." Reprinted by permission from the *Bulletin of the National Association of Secondary School Principals* (Feb. 1950). Copyright: Washington, D.C. Based on "How to Teach Pupils to Outline," *Teachers' Guide to Child Development in the Intermediate Grades.* Prepared under the direction of the California State Curriculum Commission, Sacramento, California State Department of Education, 1936, pp. 294–295.

idly as he comfortably can, he needs much more "to become as skillful as possible in using different approaches in his reading, and he needs to have good judgment in selecting that approach or combination of approaches compatible with his purposes in reading."[12]

Teaching How to Skim

1. Use direct teaching to teach pupils how to skim.
   a. Glance through the preface and table of contents to see what it is all about.
   b. Scan the book—read the headings, introductory paragraphs, and chapter summaries; sample the opening, middle, and final paragraphs.
2. Use practice exercises such as the following:
   a. Conduct a class discussion to determine what the pupils would like to learn from a chapter.
   b. Have pupils skim the chapter and then discuss what they found.

To Encourage Careful Reading and Study

1. Use directed reading lessons.
2. Introduce the SQ3R method (or something similar).
3. Use a sequence similar to the following:
   a. Begin with teaching pupils to study a paragraph.
      (1) Give them questions and let them find the answers.
      (2) Next have them summarize the content of the paragraph.
   b. Next teach them to study a section.
      (1) Again start with having them find the answers to questions.
      (2) Discuss what has been read in answering the questions.
      (3) Ask them to find key sentences.
      (4) Have them summarize.
   c. Next teach how to study a chapter.
      (1) Have a preliminary discussion concerning the chapter, where it fits into the course, what leads up to it, and so on.
      (2) Develop questions to be answered after the chapter has been read.
      (3) Read and discuss the chapter using the questions as bases.
      (4) Have the class reconstruct the author's main headings and supporting argument.
4. Have the pupils practice such techniques as these under guidance. Project examples of good questions and answers on the screen. Discuss them, allowing pupils to present alternate solutions.
5. Encourage pupils to use such techniques as these in independent study.
6. Use such exercises as:
   a. Writing headlines to illustrate principal parts of the chapter.
   b. Preparing a class newspaper giving the gist of the chapter.
   c. Preparing a telegram presenting the gist of the chapter.

[12] *Better Read, Curriculum Report No. 7* (Washington, D.C.: National Association of Secondary School Principals, The Curriculum Service Center, Nov. 1965).

DIRECTED READING LESSON

The directed reading lesson is a useful technique for developing pupils' reading comprehension and skill in studying. It is especially helpful for younger or slower secondary school pupils and for older, more sophisticated pupils who are studying difficult material.

To conduct a directed reading lesson:

1. Prepare the pupils by going over new vocabulary and ideas and reviewing old material and experiences so that they can see the relationships between the new and the old.
2. Have pupils skim the selection and look at pictures, headings, and so on.
3. Help pupils formulate questions about the selection to be read, for instance:
   a. What should a pupil try to find out when studying the selection?
   b. Is this the kind of selection that must be studied carefully?
   c. How does this selection connect with other lessons studied in the past?
      Three or four questions are quite enough. Too many questions may confuse and discourage the pupils. The questions should be pupil made rather than teacher made, if at all possible.
4. Let the pupils read the selection to themselves.
5. Discuss the reading. By using questions, help them see the relationships among the facts presented and also relationships to what has been learned previously.

The SQ3R Method. Directed reading lessons are meant for pupils who have not yet learned to direct themselves. As soon as possible, pupils should learn to direct their own reading and study. One of the best formulas for self-directed reading is the so-called SQ3R method. It is especially useful for studying social studies material. Teachers should insist that pupils learn how to use this method, or a similar one, in independent study as soon as possible.

The steps of the SQ3R method are

1. *Survey:* Quickly run through the headings to determine the major ideas and their sequence in the selection.
2. *Question:* Turn the first heading into a question so that you will know what you are seeking in your reading.
3. *Read:* Read to find the answer to your question.
4. *Recite:* From memory try to repeat the answer to the question.
5. *Repeat:* Repeat the steps for each section.
6. *Review:* Try to recall the points in the entire selection. Use notes only as necessary.[13]

To teach pupils to use the SQ3R method:

1. Begin with directed reading lessons.
2. Explain the SQ3R procedures.

---

[13] Francis P. Robinson, *Effective Study* (New York: Harper and Row Publishers, 1961).

3. Practice each of the three Rs as directed reading lessons.
4. Teach pupils to survey.
   a. If they do not already know them, teach pupils to use center heads, side heads, summaries, and so on.
   b. Ask pupils questions about the purpose of reading, as in the directed lesson.
   c. Have pupils develop their own questions.
   d. Have pupils practice surveying on their own, reporting to you what they have done and why.

CHAPTER 6

Providing for Differences in Individuals

O<small>NE</small> of the causes of past educational failures has been that neither the curriculum nor the methods of teaching in our secondary schools has taken the differences in pupils sufficiently into account. Therefore, in your teaching, try to provide for differences in pupils, in their interests, abilities, and goals.

INDIVIDUALIZING INSTRUCTION

In all your teaching try to provide for differences in pupils' interests, abilities, and goals by individualizing instruction as much as possible. Even in so-called homogeneous, or ability-grouped, classes there is a tremendous need for individualization of instruction.

STRATEGIES AND TACTICS FOR INDIVIDUALIZING INSTRUCTION

To really individualize instruction you must provide opportunities for pupils to work toward different goals and study different content. Just to vary the amount of work or the speed of progress through the coursework is not enough. Among the techniques and methods you can use to individualize your instruction are

1. Vary your tactics and techniques in classes according to the abilities and personality characteristics of your pupils.
2. Run your class as a classroom laboratory.
3. Utilize the facilities of the social studies laboratory or resource center.
4. Utilize small-group instruction.
5. Differentiate your classwork and homework assignments.
6. Give special assignments to individual pupils or small groups.
7. Use individual or group projects.
8. Encourage independent study.
9. Use the unit method and unit assignments (described in Chapter 3).

10. Use self-instructional materials such as self-correcting assignments, learning packets, programed materials, teaching machines, computer-assisted instruction, dial-access materials, and correspondence and television courses.

11. Give pupils special help.

12. Use the contract plan.

13. Use a continuous progress scheme. (You can run your course on a continuous progress plan even if the plan has not been adapted schoolwide.)

14. Use minicourses.

15. Use a variety of textbooks, readings, and other materials. (See Chapter 5.)

CONDUCTING THE CLASS AS A LABORATORY

Laboratory classes are work sessions. Here pupils work and study in an atmosphere that frees them to learn. Any class can be run as a laboratory class, and any classroom can be run as a laboratory. However, to be most effective, the classroom should be filled with materials of instruction and teaching tools. A social studies classroom in a New Jersey high school, for example, contains a film strip projector, an overhead projector, and a tape recorder on permanent loan. All of these are set up so that they can be used by individuals when they are needed. In addition, the classroom has two cupboards and several file cabinets full of materials, a couple of tables covered with reading matter, a long work shelf along the windows containing more materials (globes and the like), and of course book shelves, corkboards, chalkboards, and map racks.

To conduct a laboratory class:

1. Give out a general study guide, unit of work, or learning packet that outlines what is to be done in the unit. The activities may be required or optional.
2. Let the pupils select the activities they plan to do from the study guide or suggest activities themselves.
3. Let the pupils execute their plans. They may look things up in the pamphlets, books, and magazines. They may play the tapes and records or look at the films, film strips, or slides. They may do these activities as individuals or as committees and usually in any order they choose. They may confer with each other and help each other.
4. Help, guide, and supervise the pupils as they work.
   a. Observe pupils to diagnose poor study habits.
   b. Show pupils where to find information.
   c. Show pupils how to use the tools of learning.
   d. Clarify assignments.
   e. Show the pupils how to get the meat out of their studying.
   f. Help pupils form goals for study.
   g. Help pupils summarize.
   h. Point out errors and incorrect procedures.
   i. Suggest methods for attacking problems.

USING THE SOCIAL STUDIES LABORATORY OR RESOURCE CENTER

The social studies laboratory is a place pupils can go to study social studies. It should be extremely well equipped. Pupils should be able to go there during their

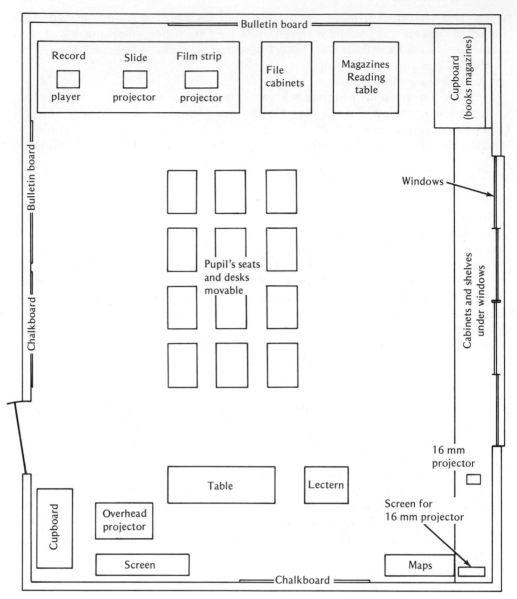

FIGURE 6–1. *A Classroom Laboratory.*

free time, or even in class time, to work individually on their social studies assignments. The techniques for using the social studies laboratory are the same as
those using a classroom laboratory. The social studies laboratory should be supplementary to classroom laboratories, not in lieu of them.

USING SMALL GROUPS AND COMMITTEES TO INDIVIDUALIZE INSTRUCTION

To use groups and committees for individualizing instruction,

1. Divide the class into groups by ability, by interest, by need, or by job or project (for example, into committees).
2. Utilize the procedures outlined for committee and small group work in Chapter 4. The different groups need not study the same topic. In fact, it may be better if they do not.

USING DIFFERENTIATED ASSIGNMENTS

Differentiate your classwork and homework assignments by giving various individuals and groups assignments that differ in (1) length, (2) difficulty, (3) type of work, or (4) topic.

To differentiate an assignment,

1. Set up teaching goals as behavioral objectives or concepts, skills and/or attitudes to be learned. If you wish, differentiate the goals so that there are different objectives for different individuals or groups. (Note that the object of the lessons is for pupils to achieve the objectives you have set forth. It does not matter what content pupils cover or activities they do, as long as they achieve the objectives desired.)
2. Give different assignments to different pupils or groups of pupils, for instance:
    a. Assign individual pupils, or groups of pupils, different activities on the basis of their interests and abilities. Thus, group 1 might do activities 1, 2, 4, and 7, while group 2 does activities 1, 3, 5, and 6; pupil A, activities 6 and 8; pupil B, 1 and 3; and so on; or group 1 might be assigned readings in book X, an advanced book; group 2 readings in book Y, the regular text; group 3 readings in book Z, an easy book.
    b. Give pupils who ordinarily work fast and well supplementary enrichment assignments. Enrichments should not be more of the same; rather enrichment should be study in greater depth.
    c. Give pupils of different abilities and inclinations quite different types of work. For example, assign John, an academically inclined boy, readings in advanced books; assign Jack, a poor reader, tape recordings on the same topic; assign Jane, a creative type, art work or composition on the topic.
3. Evaluate pupils in accordance with how well they achieve the goals. Tests should not be limited to any particular content because the pupils will not all have studied the same content.

GIVE SPECIAL ASSIGNMENTS TO SPECIAL PUPILS

Give special assignments to special pupils. These assignments may be in addition to regular work, instead of part of the regular work, or entirely divorced from the regular work. Let pupils do these special assignments individually in class time, as well as out of class. Work with the pupils at times during the class period or after class, before or after school, or during free periods.

USING INDIVIDUAL AND GROUP PROJECTS

Use individual and group projects to individualize schoolwork. Give the nonacademically minded relatively easy projects; the academically talented more difficult ones. Encourage pupils to choose projects compatible with their differences in interests and in life goals. Let pupils undertake projects that will exploit their abilities. One purpose of using projects is to allow pupils to shine, so let them do things at which they can shine.

USING SELF-INSTRUCTIONAL MATERIALS

Use self-administering and self-correcting materials (for example, learning packets and study guides) to individualize instruction. With such materials pupils can start, carry out, and evaluate activities on their own. Consequently, if you wish, when using such materials you can have every pupil doing something different at the same time. Use the materials to allow pupils to progress at different rates, to do different assignments, or to pursue different objectives.

Teaching Machines, Teaching Programs, Computer-Assisted Instruction. Teaching machines, teaching programs, and computer-assisted instruction (CAI) are sophisticated, self-administering, self-correcting materials. Use them as you would other autoinstructional materials: to differentiate assignments or to give pupils different or special assignments (there is no reason why pupils should not work on entirely different programs, if it seems desirable) or to allow pupils to proceed at speeds suitable to their backgrounds and abilities.

Dial Access. If a well-programed dial-access system is available in your school, use it to individualize instruction as you would use other programs. To do so you will have to provide pupils with study guides or work sheets that explain what they are to do and how to do it.

Correspondence and Television Courses. Correspondence courses can be procured from several state universities and commercial establishments. Use correspondence courses to provide individual instruction beyond the scope of the ordinary curriculum. Use correspondence course material as you would any other learning packets. Educational television courses designed for adults and telecasts by the Public Broadcasting System stations can be used in the same way.

Use of Self-Correcting Materials. Use self-correcting materials for instruction only. Do not use them as a basis for school marks. To do so may cheapen them and cause cheating. Provide mastery tests or similar devices when pupils are ready, if you need data for school marks.

USING INDEPENDENT STUDY TO INDIVIDUALIZE INSTRUCTION

Encourage the independent study of topics and courses just as you use projects to differentiate schoolwork. To conduct independent study,

1. Provide pupils with the necessary materials. Use learning packets, study guides, or correspondence courses to give pupils direction, to keep them from floundering, and to keep them from wasting their time by misdirecting their efforts.

2. Set up a timetable.

3. Provide for definitely scheduled tutorial sessions to check up on pupils' progress and provide help, direction, or redirection.

4. Provide for help and guidance at the times when pupils need it. When a pupil doing independent work finds himself in difficulty, he should have someone to turn to immediately.

PROVIDING SPECIAL HELP FOR PUPILS

See to it that every pupil gets special help. They all need it, although some need it more than others, so don't spare individual attention, encouragement, criticism, discipline, correction, and inspiration. It may be that a brilliant student needs a few leads to get him going on his project; or another brilliant student needs to be made to see the poor logic of his inferences; or that a less academically inclined pupil needs to be shown how to get started; or that another less academically inclined pupil needs to have some strong remedial instruction. Take time to look over each pupil's work, to compliment him on his progress, to suggest ways he might improve it, and give him special help during, before and after class, before and after school, and during breaks.

MAKING TIME FOR INDIVIDUAL INSTRUCTION

To make time to help individual pupils:

1. Allow pupils to do some of the planning, directing, and evaluating of their own work.
2. Use the laboratory class approach.
3. Allow and encourage pupils to help each other.
   (For the nonacademically oriented to help other nonacademically oriented pupils is most effective. It tends to remove the sting, if there is any, and provides natural motivation.)
4. Use the services of teacher-aides and assistant teachers.
5. Use autoinstructional materials, such as self-administering and self-correcting materials and study guides.

THE CONTRACT PLAN

The contract plan is a variation of the unit plan, in which the pupil agrees to do a certain amount of work during a time period.

Procedure for a Typical Contract. In preparing contracts you might follow a procedure something like the following:

1. Set up objectives and activities whereby pupils may achieve the objectives.
2. Decide which activities will be required.

3. Decide which activities will be optional.

4. Provide these objectives to the pupil in writing so he can study them.

5. Let the pupil decide how he will meet the requirements and what optional work he will do.

6. On the basis of the decision have the pupil make out a contract in writing. Each contract may be different from every other contract.

7. An example of a contract might be:

CONTRACT

John Jones   To be completed by May 1.

During the period of April 10 to May 1 I will

1. Read Chapters X–XIII of book A.
2. Do problems and exercises #1, 2, 4, 7, 8, 9, 11 of the study guide.
3. Participate on the map committee with Mike Smith, John Walsh, and Ted Burke.
4. Prepare a report on the topography of the area. and so on.

Signed _____
                                    Pupil

Approved _____
                                    Teacher

CONTINUOUS PROGRESS PLANS

Some schools have adopted continuous progress plans in which pupils move through the curriculum individually at a pace they set themselves without regard to grade levels. In essence the procedure is to

1. Divide the subject matter into modules.

2. Prepare instructional packets for each module—each instructional packet containing all the instructions and materials necessary for completing the module.

3. Prepare some sort of evaluative device to indicate how well the pupil has achieved the objectives of the module and some procedure for administering the device or otherwise determining when the pupil has satisfactorily achieved the objectives of the module and is ready to go on to the next one.

4. Supervise the pupils as they go on through their learning packets.

Supervision and guidance are important. Pupils should neither have to stand around waiting for help nor struggle alone through work they do not understand. Give all your attention to the supervision and guidance of individual pupils during class time. The purpose of learning or instructional packets is as much to give you a chance to work with pupils individually as it is to free pupils from the lock step of the recitation plan. To save time, utilize small-group instruction whenever feasible to help pupils who are at the same point in their packets or are finding the same difficulties.[1]

TEACHING THE ACADEMICALLY TALENTED

Most of the methods developed and used in the secondary schools were developed for use with academically talented pupils. Therefore, use them all. The important thing is to help academically talented pupils to stretch their minds. This means, of course, that above all else you must avoid spoon feeding your talented pupils. Use the suggestions that follow as a guide.

1. Avoid holding talented pupils back. If a pupil already knows the material, let him work on something else. Acceleration, depth study, or entirely different content may be appropriate.
2. Hold talented pupils to high standards. Make them think vigorously. Refuse to accept slipshod work or slipshod thinking.
3. Force talented pupils to learn to discipline themselves and their thinking.
4. Give talented pupils opportunities to learn the academic skills and insist that they do so.
5. Give talented pupils considerable responsibility for their own direction. Let them plan and evaluate their own work. Use teacher-pupil planning.
6. Give talented pupils difficult, challenging, interesting work.
7. Encourage talented pupils to dig into things. Encourage them to go to original sources.
8. Use a variety of materials; for example, original sources, adult materials, college textbooks, and the like.
9. Give talented pupils plenty of problem-solving, inquiry, and open-ended assignments.
10. Use the seminar method.
    a. Have the pupils present original papers for criticism and discussion.
    b. Let them all discuss in depth a topic they have all proposed.
    c. In either case hold them to high levels of analysis and logical thinking.[2]

[1] Among the best readings on individualizing instruction are Marvin D. Alcorn, James S. Kinder, and Jim R. Schunert, *Better Teaching in Secondary Schools,* 3rd ed. (New York: Holt, Rinehart & Winston, Inc., 1970), Chap. 8; Virgil M. Howes, *Individualization of Instruction: A Teaching Strategy* (New York: The Macmillan Company, 1970), particularly Part III; and, Virgil M. Howes, *Individualizing Instruction in Reading and Social Studies* (New York: The Macmillan Company, 1970).

[2] Three good references on teaching the academically talented are Association of Teachers of Social Studies of the City of New York, *A Handbook for Social Studies,* 3rd ed. (New York: Holt, Rinehart & Winston, Inc., 1967), Chap. 6; Nelda Davis, *How to Work with the Academically Talented in the Social Studies, How to Do It Series No. 21* (Washington, D. C.: National Council for the Social Studies, 1966); and Milton J. Gold, *Education of the Intellectually Gifted* (Columbus, Ohio: Charles E. Merrill Publishers, 1965).

TEACHING POOR ACHIEVERS

Here are some hints for helping pupils who are having a great deal of trouble with academic work. Not all of them apply to the teaching of all poor achievers. One must judge each case separately.

1. Use concrete, rather than abstract, subject matter.
2. Use activities in which pupils work with things, rather than just with words.
3. Take it easy. A slower pace may make all the difference. Present new work slowly. Take more and shorter steps than you would with more able pupils.
4. Try to build up the pupils' confidence in themselves. Encourage, praise, and help.
5. Try to integrate the subject matter and relate it to pupils' lives. Place considerable emphasis on current events and contemporary issues and problems.
6. Emphasize developmental rather than remedial instruction. Use frequent summaries and reviews. Emphasize opportunities to apply what has been learned.
7. Emphasize thinking skills.
8. Diagnose. Find out what the problems are and concentrate on them. Considerable instruction fails because the pupils have not learned the necessary background.
9. Avoid short cuts. Teach details. Give plenty of individual attention. Be patient, encouraging, and understanding. Help the pupils with their study skills.
10. Be sure your assignments and explanations are simple and clear, but do not talk down to the pupils. Keep your explanations concrete. Use many illustrations. Explain the meaning of words; write the words on the board.
11. Keep after poor achievers to keep them working well. They tend to become discouraged easily.
12. Use simple, easy, but adult material. Use shorter, easier problems. Utilize simplified texts and readings such as the Globe, Abramowitz, or Rand McNally Diamond series, or prepare your own simplified material.
13. Use dramatizations, pictures, illustrations, flannelboards, graphs, charts, puppets, dioramas, and other audiovisual aids to make things clear; but, keep films, dramatizations, and the like simple. An emphasis on one or two frames in a filmstrip may be enough.
14. Encourage pupils to help and learn from each other. This is ego building and helps remove the stigma of being "dumb."
15. Keep activities relatively short. Do not expect the pupils to keep at the same type of work all period.
16. Provide for considerable supervised study. It is usually better for pupils to work in class under supervision than to expect them to profit from homework.
17. Provide for group and committee work. In homogeneously grouped classes, poor achievers can handle leadership assignments satisfactorily if you do not ask too much of them.

Poor Achievers in Heterogeneous Classes. The methods described in the preceding section can be used in heterogeneous as well as homogeneous classes. In addition, the following suggestions may be helpful for teaching poor achievers in classes in which there is a wide range of academic ability.

1. Use activities that are not reading oriented so that poor readers will not be continually in competition with good readers.

2. Use committee and group work in which the academically less talented are given tasks in accordance with their abilities and interests.

3. Use many aids, illustrations, and visuals so that the less academically able can see the point.

4. Use a variety of readings. Let less able pupils read the short, easy materials.

5. Give these pupils easier assignments, and ask them easier questions than the more able pupils. Use many differentiated assignments.

6. Use pair groups in which more able pupils can help the less able.

7. Arrange for diagnostic remedial instruction.[3]

TEACHING THE CHILDREN OF THE POOR

Some General Suggestions. Because deprived youths may be disaffected and suspicious, you must make an extra effort. Use the same techniques for both poor and affluent youth, but change the tactics to allow for differences in the situation. Avoid watering down courses and course requirements; doing so may lead to further educational deprivation. On the other hand, do provide intensive remedial techniques wherever needed and make the coursework relevant to the lives of the pupils. More specifically,

1. Respect the pupils as people. If their culture is different learn their taboos and mores; respect their culture just as you hope they will learn to respect yours.

2. Pay great attention to motivation. Fight anti-intellectualism by showing pupils that the subject matter is worthwhile. Point out its practical value. Pick topics to study that have obvious importance.

3. Be sure the course content has meaning to the pupils and relates to their lives and interests. Be sure the content helps the pupils to understand themselves and their role so that they can learn how to function in society. Do not put this at a low how-to-do-it level, but at a high enough level so that they can understand what is really involved. Give them real work. Do not feed them pap. If the pupils cannot do the work required of them, substitute work they can do, but make it something respectable.

4. Give pupils opportunities to succeed. Praise them when they do well, but avoid gushiness. Make it evident that you expect them to learn just like everyone else, that you see no reason why they cannot, and that you intend to see to it that they really get their money's worth out of the course.

[3] Three good references on teaching poor achievers are G. Orville Johnson, *Education for the Slow Learners* (Englewood Cliffs, N. J.: Prentice-Hall, Inc., 1963); Newell C. Kephart, *The Slow Learner in the Classroom* (Columbus, Ohio: Charles E. Merrill Publishers, 1960); and William J. Younie, *Instructional Approaches to Slow Learning* (New York: Teachers College Press, 1967).

5. Be firm, strict, and definite, but not harsh. Harsh measures may seem to work on the surface but, as a rule, they make it more difficult to carry out any meaningful communication or real learning.

6. Use laboratory techniques, individual instruction, and individual help on basic skills. Adjust the subject content to the needs of the pupils. Because many of the pupils are physically oriented, they enjoy working on concrete projects. Begin at the pupils' level and then move toward the more abstract and academic.

7. Use simple language in the classroom. Worry less about the words pupils use and the way they express themselves and more about the ideas they are expressing. Let them use their own idioms without carping on grammar, syntax, and the like.

8. Use unstructured discussions of real problems. Unstructured discussions may help you understand the pupils and help them learn how to express themselves. In selecting problems to study,
   a. Be sure the problems seem real to the pupils.
   b. Be sure to pick problems they will accept.
   Sometimes they do not recognize problems as problems. Sometimes they do not want to. In such cases you may get them to see the truth by challenging their thinking. The Socratic method is useful for this purpose. Use it to pursue the faulty thinking of individual pupils. However, in doing so, be careful to let each pupil keep his self-respect. On the other hand, do not force pupils into discussions they would rather avoid. There is no point in discussing what they already know too much about.

9. Use inductive approaches. Pupils seem to respond better to open-ended questioning than they do to memorizing, for instance.

10. Sometimes pupils greatly enjoy and profit from role playing and dramatization. Simulations like *City I, Consumer,* and *Poor People's Choice* seem to go very well.

11. If pupils have not learned basic skills because of failures in the elementary school grades, help them learn those skills.

12. Use a variety of reading materials. Use multiple readings in laboratory fashion rather than the single textbook. Use adult material of low reading level. Use materials other than reading matter for pupils who cannot read: tapes, recordings, video, films, and pictures. Where no suitable reading matter is available, prepare your own.

To Prepare Reading Matter for the Educationally Disadvantaged. Paraphrase difficult reading matter so that the poor readers can read it. Try to make it informative, interesting, and adult, but easy to read and understand. Strive for clarity. Use short, direct sentences and basic everyday words. (Some of the better students in your classes can help you write these materials. You do not have to do it all yourself.)

Summary

1. Try to find subject matter that relates to the pupils.
2. Use many techniques to get the pupils working.

3. Try to be understanding and patient.

4. Respect the pupils and treat them with respect. Teach them respectable content.

5. Praise when praise is due.

6. Be prepared to walk the extra mile. You will have to do it to succeed, but with a firm commitment and perseverance you will probably do well.[4]

---

[4] Joseph O. Loretan and Shelly Umans, *Teaching the Disadvantaged*, (New York: The Teachers College Press, 1966), Part III; and Robert D. Strom, *Teaching in the Slum School*, (Columbus, Ohio: Charles E. Merrill Publishers, 1965), Chap. 5, contain many ideas particularly useful for teaching social studies to the economically deprived.

CHAPTER 7

Measuring, Testing, and Evaluating

Purpose of Evaluation. The basic purpose of evaluation in teaching and learning is to give feedback so that the pupil and teacher will have some basis for deciding what to do next. It is the heart of diagnosis and the basis of all good teaching. Your evaluation will be more likely to be valid if it is based on accurate measurement. Unfortunately, most of the measuring devices teachers use as bases for evaluation are not really very accurate.

SELECTING THE PROPER MEASURING DEVICE

If your evaluation is to be useful, you must use the types of measuring devices that will give you the information you need. The test items and devices listed here are examples of the types of test items that are useful for measuring different kinds of objectives.

Understanding	Skills	Attitudes, appreciations, and ideals
Objective test items	Observation	Observation
Essay test items	Rating scales	Rating scales
Problem situations	Check lists	Check lists
Essays	Sample work	Problem situations
Discussions	Problem situations	Interest inventories
Interpreting dates	Performance	Attitude tests and test items
Organizing and evalu-ating items	Performance tests and test items	Written work; for example, themes
Situation items		
Free-response items		

CRITERIA FOR DETERMINING THE WORTH OF MEASURING INSTRUMENTS

No matter what kind of measuring instrument one uses, it should meet certain standards of validity, reliability, objectivity, and usability. Publishers of commercially produced instruments should provide statistical information about these qualities. Teachers must check their own instruments by inspection or similar less accurate means.

Validity. Validity is the most important of all the criteria. A measuring device is valid when it measures what the measurer intends to measure.

Curriculum Validity. Curriculum validity means that the instrument measures what was supposed to be taught in the course. It is sometimes useful to think of curriculum validity as having two parts:

1. Content validity: the degree to which the instrument measures the content or subject matter of a course or unit.
2. Process validity: the degree to which the instrument measures academic skills, critical thinking, valuing, and so on that are part of the educational objectives.

Reliability. Reliability refers to the capacity of a measuring instrument to give the same information each time it is used. A yardstick that *always* measures a 36.00 inch yard is perfectly reliable.

Objectivity. Objectivity in a measuring instrument refers to the degree that the scoring is freed from human error or subjectivity. A machine scoring device that always scores in the same way is completely objective.

Usability. Usability in academic measuring emphasis refers to the degree of practicality or ease of use of the instrument in a particular situation.

Discrimination. Tests must discriminate between those who can and those who cannot; those who know and those who do not know.

WHEN TO TEST

Probably you should give a major (full period) test at the completion of every unit. Ordinarily one full-period test per month is reasonable. Do not give tests in different courses on the same day so that you will not have large numbers of tests to correct at once.

TESTS, MEASUREMENTS, AND DIAGNOSIS

The major purpose of measuring and evaluating should be to diagnose the educational status and needs of the pupils. All of the measuring devices mentioned in this chapter can be used for this purpose. An item analysis of test items is a useful technique for making this diagnosis.

To use item analysis for diagnosis:

1. Write out the instructional objectives.
2. Write test items that test the instructional objectives.
3. Give the test.
4. Correct the test.
5. Build an item analysis chart on a sheet of graph paper.
   a. List pupils' names at the head of the columns.
   b. List test items on the horizontal rows.
   c. Note what instructional goal each item was to test.
6. Record the accuracy of responses for each pupil. Use + for a correct response; − for an incorrect response.
7. Examine the chart.
   a. If a pupil answers the items that test an objective correctly, then he has achieved the objective.
   b. If a pupil does not answer the items that test an objective correctly, then he did not achieve the objective.
   c. If many pupils do not answer the items that test an objective correctly, presumably instruction for the objective was not successful and should be redone.
   d. If most pupils do answer the items correctly, presumably the instruction was successful.
8. Evaluate the results of the analysis and take the next steps accordingly.

Objective	Test Item	James	Joanna	Arthur	Mary
I	1	+	−	+	+
I	2	+	+	+	−
II	3	−	−	−	−
III	4	−			
I	5	+	+	+	+
II	6	−	−	−	−
III	7				
II	8	−	−	−	−

FIGURE 7-1. *Item Analysis Chart.*

CONSTRUCTING THE TEACHER-BUILT TEST

The steps in test building are quite simple.

1. List the teaching objectives for the course or unit as learning products or terminal behavior. These should be very specific. These objectives should, of course, be listed before the teaching begins.

2. Select test items that will test these objectives. This will give you validity.
   a. Be sure that the items are of the kind that will really measure the specific objective they are supposed to measure.
   b. Be sure that the items cover all the objectives.
   c. Be sure that the items in the test give the objectives the same emphasis they were supposed to have in the course or unit.
3. Arrange the test items in order. Keep items of the same type (multiple choice, matching, or essay) together.
4. Write clear directions.
5. Check the test and key for accuracy, clarity, difficulty, and ambiguity. Check for faults in format. Be sure the test is as objective as feasible. If possible, have someone else read the test to see if your items are clear and accurate.
6. Prepare a key.
7. Have the test duplicated.
8. Proofread the test and correct any errors.
9. Make the test as objective as possible to reduce scoring errors and inconsistencies.
10. Make the conditions for giving the test as standard as possible. Administer the test in the same way to all pupils. Avoid distractions. If possible, ensure that the physical surroundings will be comfortable, the lighting good, the heat and humidity in the classroom adequate, and so on.

WRITING THE TEST ITEMS

Objective Versus Essay Tests. There has been considerable debate about whether it is better to use objective or essay tests. The answer, of course, is that it depends on what you are planning to test. Both types of tests have valid uses and the social studies teacher who does not use both of them, plus other measuring instruments, is probably falling down on the job.

Advantages of Objective Tests

1. Objective tests allow the test builder to take wider samples than is usual in an essay test. This tends to give greater reliability and validity.
2. Objective tests force pupils to keep their answers relevant, thus eliminating the tendency of pupils to wander and "to throw the bull."
3. The scoring of objective tests is objective. Mechanical scoring can virtually eliminate human error and unfairness in scoring.
4. The scoring of objective tests is quite easy and can be done quickly by nonprofessional assistants.
5. Objective tests measure the knowledge of facts efficiently.
6. Objective tests encourage pupils to build up broad backgrounds.

Disadvantages of Objective Tests

1. Objective test items are very difficult to write. As a result, reliability may be lowered by poorly written—and particularly ambiguous—items.
2. It is difficult to test the higher mental processes with objective tests, although competent test builders can write objective items that will test higher mental processes such as infering, organizing ideas, comparing, and contrasting.

Advantages of Essay Tests

1. Essay tests are useful for testing higher mental processes. They are capable of testing
   a. Pure recall.
   b. Ability to organize.
   c. Ability to use material.
   d. Ability to apply knowledge.
   e. Ability to write.
2. Essay tests encourage pupils to learn how to organize and express their ideas.
3. Essay tests are relatively easy to write. Only a few items are necessary. (This advantage may be specious; teachers tend to forget that essay questions must be written carefully.)
4. Essay tests give the teachers the opportunity to comment directly on pupils' thinking and expression.

Disadvantages of Essay Tests

1. It is difficult to get an adequate sample; therefore validity may be low.
2. Irrelevancies in the writing and scoring as well as an inadequate sampling of content and processes may make essay tests unreliable.
3. Essay tests are very difficult to score. No matter how much one tries to objectify their scoring, it remains very subjective.

A FILE OF ITEMS

Because building good test items is very difficult, you should save all your good test items, be they objective or essay. To save such items is an easy matter. All you do is to cut the items from the test, paste or tape them on an index card (use 5 × 8 cards, if possible), and file them away under the proper course, topic, and objective.

TO MAKE TESTS FOR DIFFERENT SECTIONS

To prepare tests that are to be used for different sections of the same course:

1. Use the same items, but scramble them so that their numbering will be different.
2. Make a tremendously long test and then divide it into two or more tests by allocating every other item (or every third item) to a different test.
3. Revamp questions by making positive items negative, or by changing the distractors.
4. Create items that have different levels of difficulty for different groups.
5. Use the same maps, charts, graphs, and figures for the bases of the application, situation, analysis, interpretation, and similar items, but vary the specific questions about them.

WRITING OBJECTIVE TEST ITEMS

To write good objective test items requires much skill, care, and patience. For that reason, when writing objective test items, be on your guard to select the type of item best suited for your purpose and to avoid poorly written items.

CRITERIA FOR OBJECTIVE TESTS

To test the excellence of an objective test prior to giving it, use the following criteria.

1. Is it valid? Does it test what it was supposed to test?
2. Does it test all the goals of the course or unit?
3. Does it test the goals in proportion to their importance?
4. Is it free from catch questions?
5. Is it free from ambiguous items?
6. Is it free from giveaway items?
7. Is the physical format OK?
   a. Are items of the same type grouped together?
   b. Do the items run from easy to difficult?
   c. Is it free from typographical errors, items that go over the page, poor reproduction, and other errors of make-up?

After the test has been given, check for the following:

1. Was it too long or too short?
2. Were the directions clear?
3. Did the items discriminate?
4. How difficult were the items?
5. Is there evidence of ambiguity, giveaway, or the like?

ALTERNATE-ANSWER ITEMS

Alternate-answer items include true-false, right-wrong, yes-no, same-different, and any other items that require the pupil to choose between two alternatives. As a rule, alternate-answer questions are not strongly recommended for several reasons:

1. They allow at least a 50 per cent chance that pupils will guess correctly. Therefore, they encourage wild guessing.
2. They usually test only for memorized isolated items of information.
3. They are difficult to write so as to be really clear and unambiguous without giving away the answers.
4. They do not allow for exceptions to the rule and so may confuse good students.
5. When correcting such items, one should use the formula "to correct for guessing."

In writing alternate-answer items beware of emphasizing unimportant details — either by asking questions about them or writing questions that turn on obscure details — questions that do not have right answers, ambiguity, giveaway items, and trick items.

Some examples of alternate-answer items follow.

Example 1.

Circle the correct answer.

True–False   1. Columbus sailed to the West in 1492.
Right–Wrong   2. The Proclamation of 1763 opened the West to the English
                 colonists.
Yes–No   3. Were girls allowed to attend secondary schools in Colonial
                 New England?
Did–Did Not   4. Pontiac _____ succeed in his attempt to capture Detroit.

Example 2.

In the following, write *S* in the space provided, if the words are essentially
the same (synonymous); write *D*, if they are different.

( )   1. Alto Plano–Desert
( )   2. Estuary–Drowned River

ADAPTED ALTERNATE-ANSWER ITEMS

In order to eliminate some of the difficulties attendant on alternate-answer
items, some test writers have invented adaptions of these items. These adaptions
usually turn the items into multiple-choice or short-answer items.

Example 1.

In the space provided before each statement write plus (+) if it is true, minus
(−) if false, or *O*, if only an opinion.

( )   1. At the battle of Yorktown, Cornwallis was defeated by the French
          army and navy and the Continental forces.

Example 2.

Mark each of the following statements plus (+) if it is true, minus (−) if false;
if false, show why.

( )   1. The Proclamation of 1763 solved the Indian problem for the next
          decade.

MULTIPLE-CHOICE ITEMS

Multiple-choice items consist of a stem and several responses. The idea is for
the pupil to pick the correct or best response from the options listed. Some examples follow.

Example 1.

Place the letter of the best response in the parenthesis.

( )   Which of these statements best describes President Roosevelt's first
       inaugural address?
       a. It was primarily concerned with Latin American affairs.
       b. It was primarily concerned with domestic affairs.
       c. It was primarily concerned with European affairs.
       d. It was primarily concerned with cultural aspects of American life.

Example 2.

Circle (check or *X*) the letter preceding the correct answer.

What method did President Roosevelt use to fight the Supreme Court in 1938?
a. He called for the dismissal of all judges.
b. He asked Congress for power to broaden the Court's membership.
c. He asked all the Supreme Court justices to retire.
d. He asked Congress for the power to appoint ten extra judges.

Tips on Writing Multiple-Choice Items

1. In writing multiple-choice items be sure to have at least four options (one correct response and three distractors). Otherwise, you should use the correction-for-guessing formula when scoring multiple-choice items.

2. Writing multiple-choice items seems to go easier when the test writer first writes the stem as a question, and then, if it seems necessary, rephrases it as a statement. Usually, however, the stem of a multiple-choice item is better left as a question. In any case, the stem should pose one and only one central problem.

Dangers in Writing Multiple-Choice Items.

In preparing multiple-choice items be wary of the following dangers.

1. The correct choice may appear as the stem of another item and so give away the correct answer.

2. Unless one is careful to mix items well, pupils may guess the correct answer from its similarity in topic to immediately preceding or following items, especially if the distractors are not fairly homogeneous.

3. Obviously implausible distractors make it easier to guess the correct answer.

4. Avoid tending to place the correct response in a favored position. For example, some teachers never put the correct response as the first or last choice and so tend to give their answers away.

5. Avoid the use of specific words, grammatical clues, similarities of words in the stem and correct response, and other slips of language that can give away the correct response. Be particularly wary of number, tense, and gender.

6. Avoid making the correct response obvious because of its difference from the others. For instance, if the correct response is made too long or too specific, it will stand out. If necessary, make the stem long, but keep all the options brief.

7. Avoid writing items that can be guessed by applying a little common sense. For example, the correct response is one that would be true in any case; the correct response sticks out because it logically must follow the stem; the correct response is so broad and inclusive that anyone would tend to guess it to be the correct one.

8. Avoid putting unnecessary information in either the stem or the response. Doing so makes it appear that the pupil knows more than he does. Especially keep everything extraneous out of the stem. When the stem contains two concepts, usually only one functions.

9. Avoid items in which all possible attributes of the stem are accounted for in one or two of the options. The other distractors are valueless when all the possibilities are already accounted for.

10. Avoid using negatives in both the stem and options. Double negatives are always confusing.

11. Avoid items that concentrate on the picayune and unimportant.

12. Avoid opinion questions. If the correct answer is "iffy" or reflects an opinion, restate the question to include the if or to include the source of the opinion.

13. Avoid distractors that might be considered correct from other points of view.

MATCHING ITEMS

Matching items are items in which the pupil tries to tell which item in one group is associated with items in another group, for example:

Example 1.

Directions: Select the correct answer *from the right-hand column* and place the letter of the answer in the *left-hand column* next to the corresponding question.

Questions	*Answers*
_____ 1. Andrew Carnegie	A. Antitrust suits had top priority and right of way in the Federal courts.
_____ 2. Trust	B. Calls on the Congress to lay and collect taxes on income.
_____ 3. Protective tariff	C. Helped to regulate rail rates.
	D. The Populist party candidate.

Example 2.

Another type of matching item consists of matching the blanks in a paragraph with the words that would best fill them.

Dangers to Beware of When Writing Matching Questions

1. Too many matches make the item so long that it becomes a test of perseverance rather than knowledge. Five or six matches are usually enough.

2. All pairs of a matching item should be printed on the same page. A page break in a matching item may cause accidental pupil errors and so reduce the reliability of the instrument.

3. Be sure that there are several reasonable alternatives listed for each of the correct matches. For instance, in our first example only one option of those listed can logically match the Populist party candidate. All other questions refer to things, not people.

4. Be sure that the columns are uneven. Columns of even length make it possible to guess the last items by elimination.

KEY-LIST ITEMS OR CHECK-LIST ITEMS

Key-list or check-list items are excellent for checking facts. They can also be used for testing higher-level mental processes such as application and interpretation.

Example 1.

Check each of the following that is associated with or occurred during the administration of Franklin Roosevelt.

( )   1. World War II
( )   2. The Great Depression
( )   3. The Korean War
( )   4. The Bay of Pigs incident

Example 2.

Mark each of the items *R*, if they are associated with the Franklin Roosevelt administration; *T*, if associated with the Truman administration; *E*, if associated with the Eisenhower administration; and *K*, if associated with the Kennedy administration.

( )   1. World War II
( )   2. The Great Depression
( )   3. The Korean War
( )   4. The Bay of Pigs incident

COMPLETION ITEMS

Completion items are excellent for testing the ability to recall facts. They can also be used for certain types of situation or application tests. However, their nature makes them difficult to score when there is any chance for pupils to think for themselves. Scoring is further complicated by the fact that it is virtually impossible to write completion-test items in such a way that pupils will not come up with correct responses you did not anticipate.

Example 1.

Complete each of the following sentences by writing the correct name in the blanks provided.

The first President of the United States was _____ .

Example 2.

Write the word that will correctly complete each sentence in the blank preceding the number of the sentence.

_____ 1. The Lewis and Clark expedition was sent to explore the Northwest by President _____ .

Tips for Writing Completion Items

1. Use only one blank per item. (Sometimes two are OK, but that is the limit.)
2. Be sure there is only one definite response per blank.
3. Put the blank near the end of the sentence.
4. Do not use textbook wording.
5. Put a space for the correct answers to the left of the items.

SHORT-ANSWER ITEMS

Short-answer items are similar to completion items. They are simply questions to be answered by a single word, sentence, or paragraph. They are useful for testing the ability to recall facts and sometimes the ability to use the higher mental processes. The dangers inherent in writing short-answer items are about the same as those for writing completion items. The dangers can be avoided by making the questions very specific and explicit and by checking to see that the key includes all the possible correct answers.

Example

What was the principal purpose of the blockade of the South by the North during the Civil War?

ARRANGEMENT ITEMS

Arrangement items test the ability to organize and to remember.

Example 1.

Arrange the following events into chronological order by placing a *1* in front of the earliest event, *2* in front of the next event, and so on.

_____ The Constitution of the United States
_____ The Articles of Confederation
_____ The Albany Conference
_____ The Declaration of Independence

Arrangement items are easy to write if one keeps to fact questions. However, when it comes to testing the ability to interpret and to think it becomes extremely difficult to write clear items that can be keyed unequivocally, as example 2 illustrates.

Example 2.

Place the letter representing each of the following on the continuum below to indicate their relative position as democratic states.

Democracy   Dictatorship

├──┤

a. Hitler's Germany.
b. Russia under Stalin.
c. Russia under Kruschev.
d. Present-day USA.
e. Present-day England.[1]

---

[1] Two good references on preparing objective tests are Harry D. Berg, ed., *Evaluation in Social Studies*, Thirty-fifth Yearbook (Washington, D. C.: National Council for the Social Studies, 1965), Chaps. 3, 4, and 9; and Norman E. Gronlund, *Measurement and Evaluation in Teaching*, 2nd ed. (New York: The Macmillan Company, 1971), Chaps. 7 and 9.

BUILDING AN ESSAY TEST

To make good essay tests:

1. Be sure your objective is one that can be measured well by an essay test.

2. Be sure that your question is in enough detail so that the pupils understand what is expected. If it is not, the pupils will introduce different approaches, different styles, different lengths, and different points. Thus, in effect, the pupils will write different tests and you will have no common basis on which to base your judgment. The Educational Testing Service pamphlet, "Making the Classroom Test" (which you should own)[2] gives the following example to show how to make a vague discussion question more precise and delimited.

Example

Poor: Explain why you think the United Nations has been a success or a failure.

Better: An important function of the United Nations is to help settle disputes between nations. Describe how one dispute was handled successfully, pointing out how the settlement illustrates a general strength of the United Nations. Describe also how one dispute was handled unsuccessfully, pointing out how this illustrates a general weakness of the United Nations. Your essay should be about 300–400 words in length (two or three pages in longhand).

3. Determine what you expect the answer to include. Write out or outline the answer you believe to be acceptable.

4. Let the pupils know what kind of answer you expect. The following example cited by Robert J. Solomon in the NCSS Yearbook, *Evaluation in the Social Studies,* shows what pains a good test writer takes to make sure that the pupil knows what he is supposed to do.

Example

These questions are a test of your judgment, knowledge, and ability to present such knowledge in an appropriate manner. Cite specific facts to substantiate your generalizations. Be as specific as possible in illustrating your answers. Do not neglect to give dates where they are necessary for a fuller understanding of your response. Clearness of organization as well as the quality of your English will be factors considered in scoring your answers. Remember that you

---

The National Council for the Social Studies (NCSS) has published several very helpful compilations of test items. They include Howard R. Anderson, E. F. Lindquist, and David K. Heenan, *Selected Test Items in World History,* 3rd ed. (1960); Howard R. Anderson, E. F. Lindquist, and Harriet Stull, *Selected Test Items in American History,* 5th ed. (1964); Dana Kurfman, *Teacher-Made Test Items in American History: Emphasis on the Junior High School* (1962); and Horace T. Morse and George H. McCone, *Selected Items for Testing Study Skills and Critical Thinking,* rev. by Lester E. Brown and Ellen Cook, 5th ed. (1972).

[2] Educational Testing Service, *Making the Classroom Test, Education and Advisory Service Series, No. 4,* 2nd ed. (Princeton, N. J.: Educational Testing Service, 1961), p. 23.

have forty-five minutes to plan, write, and review each question. Be sure to number your answers, as the questions are numbered in the test.[3]

5. Avoid questions that deal just with facts or memorized generalizations. If you want to find whether pupils know this type of material, use objective test items.

6. Avoid "discuss" questions. They are too vague ordinarily. Be specific. Use the words define, illustrate, explain, compare, outline, summarize, or the like, which are better.

7. So that everyone will take the same test, require all pupils to answer the same items. Do not allow them any choice. To do so will disrupt your sampling and make it impossible to compare the achievement of the pupils.

8. In order to get a good sampling, it is better to use a number of short essays than a few long essays.

9. Allow time for pupils to think and compare their answers.

10. Essay tests lend themselves to situation or situation-type tests in which pupils react to a real, simulated, or hypothetical situation. Open-book essay questions, and questions given in advance to be answered during the test period, are useful adaptions of this type of item.

EXAMPLES OF ESSAY AND FREE-RESPONSE ITEMS[4]

Listing Items

List the major events leading up to the beginning of World War I from the beginning of the century to the invasion of 1914.

Arranging Items

List the major events leading up to World War I in chronological order.

Description Items

Describe "social class." In your answer tell what social class is, what determines one's social class, and what the differences of social class in the United States are.

Definition Items

In a short paragraph define "mercantilism."

Illustration Items. (In these questions pupils are asked to give examples or illustrations in order to show the depth of their understanding and their ability to apply their knowledge. Such questions are often combined with definition.) For example:

In history, what is meant by a "primary source"? Illustrate what you mean by giving an example of a primary source and show why it is one.

---

[3] Berg, ed., op. cit., p. 149.

[4] This list has been drawn from an unpublished paper by Ralph W. McCaw, Jersey City State College, Jersey City, N. J. which was partially based on a classification system set forth in Kenneth L. Bean, *Construction of Education and Personnel Tests* (New York: McGraw-Hill Book Company, 1953).

Explanation Items

A historian has said that the Hebrew religion has given birth to three major modern religions: Judaism, Christianity, and Islam. Explain how this came about.

Comparison and/or Contrasting Items. (In such questions pupils show the similarities and/or differences, or advantages and/or disadvantages, strengths and/or weaknesses of different things. The question may, or may not, call for the specific bases of the comparison.) For example:

In what essential ways does democratic government in the New England town meeting differ from ancient Greek democracy?

Summary of Outline Items

Summarize (or outline, or briefly review) FDR's foreign policy from the beginning of Germany's invasion of Poland until the bombing of Pearl Harbor.

Interpretation Items. (Interpretation questions require pupils to apply principles. They go much beyond rote memory. They are useful for checking the understanding of obscure or profound concepts when mere definition would not be sufficient.) For example:

Suppose that George Rogers Clark had not been able to conquer the British outposts in Illinois and that the Spanish and French had not given up control of the Louisiana country, what would the United States have been like in the nineteenth century?

Evaluation or Criticism Items. (This type of question asks the pupil to evaluate the worth of something in relationship to its correctness, adequacy, or impact. Often this type of item calls for judgment concerning changes that should be made.) For example:

It has been stated that the electoral college should be abandoned. State a case either for or against the continuance of the present electoral college system.

Creation of New Solutions or New Problems. (Such items require originality, creative thinking, and skill in the use of the subject matter field. Although they are difficult to prepare and to correct, they are useful for revealing higher mental processes and independent thinking. Such items are used mostly with advanced college students, but they can be used with high school students as well.) For example:

If the present electoral college system were to be discarded, what type of electoral system would you advocate that would be fair to all citizens in all the American states and territories?[5]

---

[5] For more information on preparing essay tests you may find the following helpful: Robert L. Ebel, *Measuring Educational Achievement* (Englewood Cliffs, N. J.: Prentice-Hall, Inc., 1965), Chap. 4; Gronlund, op. cit., Chap. 4; and Robert J. Solomon, *Improving the Essay Test in the Social Studies*, in Berg, loc. cit.

SITUATION AND SITUATION-TYPE TESTS

Situation and situation-type tests are useful for checking the higher mental processes, attitudes, and skills. Situation tests actually put the person in a real situation to which he must react. Situation-type tests present him with a simulated situation to which he responds or tells how he would respond. Such tests can be essay-type, performance, objective-type, construction, or almost any other form of written or unwritten test. Some examples follow.

Example 1. *Situation Type (Key List)*

INTERPRETING A FIGURE CHART

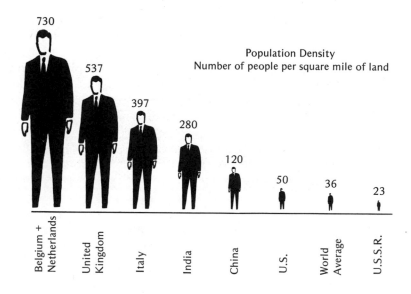

Write *T* if the statement is true; *F* if it is false; or *N* if there is insufficient data in the chart to answer the question.

_____ 1. The population density of India is more than five times that of the United States.
_____ 2. China has a greater population density than any European country.
_____ 3. The USSR has a larger population than the United States.
_____ 4. The USSR is more densely populated than the United States.
_____ 5. Belgium is overpopulated.

Example 2. *Performance Type (Key List)*

In a letter to Lady Delamere, an English friend, dated at Sagamore Hill, May 7, 1911, Theodore Roosevelt wrote:

> as for the attacks on me, the wave of popular disappointment, I literally do not care a rap. I am sorry to disappoint good, foolish people, but I am sorry

for their sakes not mine. I was really concerned about the overpraise, the overadmiration, and the impossible expectation; but I do not mind in the least when they go to the opposite extreme, and neither the praise nor the blame makes one particle of difference in my course.

Mark the following statements *A* if historical fact; *B* if probably true, but not completely established by the evidence presented here; *C*, probably not true, but the evidence is not conclusive; *D*, undoubtedly not factual; *E*, not pertinent to the data presented.

_____ 1. Theodore Roosevelt did not care what people thought of him.
_____ 2. Theodore Roosevelt was President of the United States.
_____ 3. Theodore Roosevelt had at least one friend in the English nobility.
_____ 4. Theodore Roosevelt wrote at least one letter to a friend in England.
_____ 5. Theodore Roosevelt claimed that whether or not people approved of his actions did not influence him.
_____ 6. Etc.

Example 3.   *Situation Type (Completion)*

The following graph is taken from an annual report of the Gulf Oil Corporation. Study it and answer the following completion (or fill-in) questions about it.

1. What were the approximate total assets of the Gulf Oil Corporation in 1963? _____ millions of dollars.
2. In the period from 1954 to 1964, the total assets of Gulf Oil increased _____ million dollars.
3. The Gulf Oil Corporation doubled its total assets in the period from 1954 to _____ .

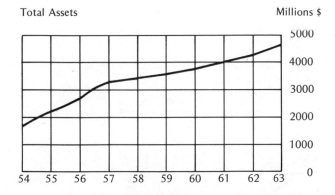

Example 4.   *Situation Type (Multiple Choice)*

Study the chart and answer the following multiple-choice items about it. Circle the letter of the best answer.

In June 1954 the total assets of the Gulf Oil Corporation were approximately a. $3,500,000,000; b. $2,000,000,000; c. $2,500,000,000; d. $1,900,000,000.

Example 5. *Situation or Application Item (Free Response, Short Answer)*

Place the following information on a time line.

Kościuszko, Tadeusz (1746–1817). Born at Mereczowszczyzna. In 1776, he joined the armed forces of the American Colonies. In 1791, he returned to Poland and attempted to get aid for the Poles from France. He took command of Polish freedom fighters in 1793. On April 3, 1794, he defeated the Russian army at Raclawice, but in October his army was soundly defeated and he was captured. On his release he returned to the United States where he stayed until 1798. He then returned to France. Because he did not wish to support Napoleon he retired to Berville near Versailles. Later he moved to Solothurn where he died on April 2, 1817.

Example 6. *Situation or Application Item (Free Response)*

To make it easier to score the preceding example one could provide a line such as follows. However, using this line reduces the difficulty of recall and application.

1725   1825
X ———————————————————————————————————— X

Example 7. *Performance Item (Free Response)*

If the RF of a map is 1 : 25,000, how far would it be from X to Y on the ground in the following example?

Example 8. *Performance or Application Item (Multiple Choice)*

The following map represents an island featuring one large river. In what general direction does the river Y flow?

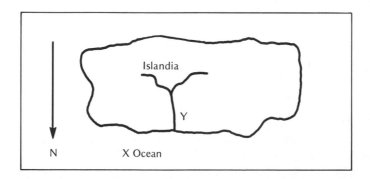

a. Northerly.   c. Easterly.
b. Westerly.   d. Southerly.

Example 9. *Performance Item (True-False)*

The following statistics represent the approximate dollar value of French imports during the ten-year period beginning in 1897.

1897	$790,000,000
1898	895,000,000
1899	905,000,000
1900	940,000,000
1901	875,000,000
1902	880,000,000
1903	960,000,000
1904	900,000,000
1905	955,000,000
1906	1045,000,000

On the basis of the data given in Example 9, check each of the following generalizations that seems to be true; line out those that seem to be false.

1. In general, French imports dropped during this period.
2. There was a slump, but the general trend was toward increased imports.
3. In general, the figures indicate a trend toward increased imports.
4. Etc.

Example 10. *Construction Item (Free Response)*

An oil company reports the following capital expenditures in the period 1954–1963. Make a line graph showing these expenditures.

Year	Millions $ Capital Expenditure
1954	290
1955	280
1956	475
1957	530
1958	400
1959	325
1960	330
1961	327
1962	520
1963	595

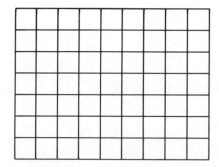

Example 11.   *Construction Item (Free Response)*

In the map indicate the route of the Oregon Trail.

Example 12.   *Application Performance (Free Response)*

Another excellent example of an application test that shows how well pupils can use their knowledge of words is the following test used in a geography class. In this test the teacher taped a number of color photos of scenes that illustrated different land forms to the chalkboard. Each picture was numbered, but had no other identification. Pupils then were given a list of the names of various land forms and asked to match the pictures with the names on the land forms by placing the number of the picture next to the name of the land form it represents. For example:

Picture	Land Form
B.	a. Arroyo.
A.	d. Drowned meander.
etc.	

OTHER EVALUATIVE DEVICES

RATING SCALE

To prepare a rating scale:

1. Decide which points you want to rate.
2. Make up a scale by which to rate them. Usually a five-point scale is about all one can expect to handle.
3. Label the points on the scale to make them clear.

Example 1. *Rating Scale for Map Work*

(Check the spot on each continuum that is most descriptive of the pupil's work.)

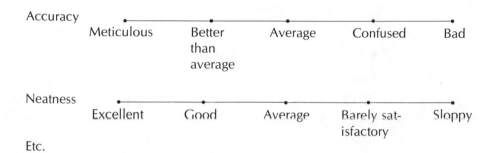

Accuracy
Meticulous   Better   Average   Confused   Bad
              than
              average

Neatness
Excellent   Good   Average   Barely sat-   Sloppy
                                isfactory

Etc.

Example 2. *Rating Scale for Written Work*

(Circle the number indicating rating. Code: 5, highest; 1, lowest; *NA*, not applicable.)

1. Originality: 5 4 3 2 1 *NA*
2. Clarity: 5 4 3 2 1 *NA*
3. Format: 5 4 3 2 1 *NA*
etc.

CHECK LIST

1. Decide which are the essential qualities that indicate the achievement of the goal you are seeking.
2. List the characteristics to check.

Example *Check List for Maps*

Check each item if the map comes up to standard in this particular category.

( ) 1. Accuracy.
( ) 2. Neatness.
( ) 3. Attention to details.
etc.

BEHAVIOR LOG

A behavior log is a record of significant behavior. It is easy to prepare. One simply devotes a sheet in a notebook to the pupil and notes significant occurrences on the page from time to time as they happen.

ANECDOTAL REPORTS

Anecdotal reports are short, objective accounts of significant pupil behavior. These are sometimes prepared for use by the guidance department. Sometimes you may wish to add your interpretation of the behavior, but usually it is better to report an incident without interpretation.

Anecdotal reports may help you gain insight into pupils' attitudes and beliefs. They are quite useful for judging one's achievement of affective goals in social studies teaching.

Example of an Anecdotal Report Form

ANECDOTAL REPORT

Name of Pupil:

Description of Incident:

Interpretation:

Reported by: _____

GATHERING SOCIOMETRIC DATA

Use sociometric data to find the social aspects of your class, such as the relationships among the individuals in the class.

General Procedure. Ask the pupils a question such as "Who would you like to have as a partner on the next field trip?" or "With whom would you like to team up to share a laboratory table?" The questions should probably represent a real, concrete situation on which you can take immediate action, rather than a vague, loosely defined question such as, "Who is your best friend?" The best data result when one allows the pupils to list as many or as few names in reply as they wish, both negative and positive choices. Additional information can be gleaned by asking the pupils to tell why they chose the people they did.

RECORDING AND PRESENTING SOCIOMETRIC DATA

Raw Data. A chart depicting raw data as presented by the answers to the pupils' questionnaires is useful when dealing with small classes. To make such a chart:

1. List the names of the pupils on the left side of the sheet and in the same order across the top of the sheet.

2. In the row following each pupil's name, place a plus (+) sign under the name of each person he chose and a minus (−) sign for each one he rejected. If pupils give several choices, these may be indicated by writing the appropriate numeral after the plus or minus sign. For example, +1 equals most desired; −1 equals least desired.

	John	Joe	Mike	Pete	Sam	George	Charles	Steve
John		+1		−2	+2		+3	−1
Joe	+1				+2			−1
Mike				+1		+2		
Pete		etc.		etc.		etc.		
Sam								
George								
Charles								
Steve								

(*Note:* It is helpful, when filling out forms such as this, to use graph paper or rows and columns to eliminate errors in posting.)

Sociogram. The sociogram, although rather time consuming to make, gives one a diagrammatic representation of the relationships in a group. To prepare a sociogram:

1. Record and tabulate the choices, keeping the boys and girls separate.

2. Using one symbol for boys and another for girls, diagram the relationships. Place the symbols for the most popular boys and girls in the center of the page, and those for the least popular on the fringes. Draw arrows between the choices to show who picked whom. When the choice is mutual, use a double arrow. Negative choices can be shown by dotted lines. Depicting second and third choices tends to make the diagram too complicated, but if one wishes, these relationships can be shown by color coding or by using some other symbol. An example of a sociogram appears as Figure 7-2.

Social Distance Scale. A social distance scale is designed to show the relationships of individuals with others. It is simple to make and gives excellent information.

a. Set up a scale as follows:

Like him very much	Like him some	No particular feeling	Dislike him some	Dislike him very much

b. Ask the pupils to rate their classmates according to this scale.[6]

[6] See Ruth Cunningham and Associates, *Understanding Group Behavior of Boys and Girls* (New York: Teachers College Press, 1951), for good examples of these and other devices.

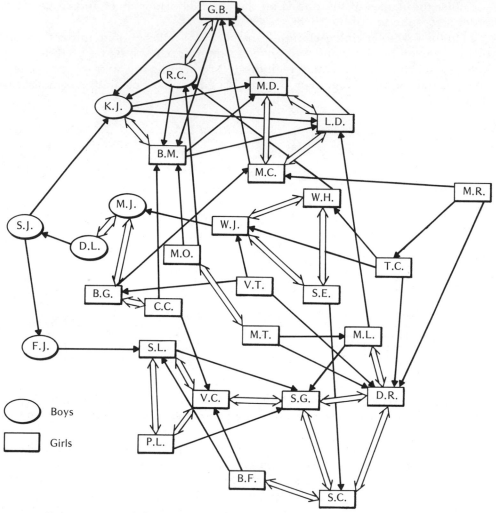

FIGURE 7-2. *A Sociogram.*

INTERPRETING SOCIOMETRIC DATA

Use sociometric instruments cautiously, for they can themselves be the cause of social cleavage if used indiscreetly. Who wants to know that his associates don't like him very much? Furthermore, the choices the pupils make may be merely ad hoc, transitory, or even spurious. Many a boy would be glad to work with a bright boy whom he would not pick for a social companion.

In order to get the full benefit of sociometric devices look for

1. Natural subgroups.
2. Natural leaders.
3. Popular pupils.
4. Pairs.
5. Chains.
6. Isolates.
7. Antipathies.

MEASURING SPECIFIC OBJECTIVES

TO MEASURE SKILL

One can measure a pupil's skill either by (1) observing the pupil performing the skill, or (2) observing a sample of his work. Neither technique is particularly difficult, although each requires some care.

Before attempting to measure skill it is necessary to define precisely what the skill is and to determine just what the standards of excellence for performing that skill are. This definition is needed so that the test maker and the scorer will know what they are looking for and how to judge whether the performance is excellent, good, bad, or mediocre. Use performance test, rating scales, and checklists to determine the degree of skill demonstrated by the pupils.

TO MEASURE ATTITUDES

Probably one can most accurately measure attitudes by direct observation of real behavior. Of course, this is extremely difficult to do in the classroom — or in the school at all for that matter. Therefore you will probably have to resort to contrived or simulated situations if you want to measure attitudes by direct observation. Observation of the way pupils behave and what they say in role-playing and discussion activities is usually productive. Sometimes indications of attitudes appear in pupils' themes, reports, essay tests, and other papers. Use check lists and anecdotal reports for reporting and recording your observations.

Written tests can also be used to measure attitudes. However, it is difficult to get any assurance that the response to any attitude test item represents a true attitude. Pupils generally tend to give the teacher the answer that they think he wants rather than what they really think. *Attitude tests should never be used for purposes of marking or grading.* Scale items are usually better suited for attitude tests than other types of items because of the necessity to allow for shadings. Some examples of attitude scale items follow:

Example 1.

Circle the word that you feel makes the sentence correct.

a. All   Most   Many   Some   No
_____ strikes are necessary for the welfare of union members.

Example 2.

Signify whether or not you agree with each of the following statements by encircling the appropriate word or words.

a. Japan must trade with Socialist Asian countries even if they should become Communist.
   Strongly Agree, Agree, Undecided, Disagree, Strongly Disagree.
b. Under no circumstances should the United States give economic assistance to a Communist country.
   Strongly Agree, Agree, Undecided, Disagree, Strongly Disagree.

Example 3.

Another type of attitude test is to present some sort of situation, either a real one (for example, a visit to a courtroom, attending the legislature, or participation in a getting-out-the-vote campaign), or a simulated one (for example, role playing, a story or a movie), and then ask such questions as:

a. What did you like or approve of?
b. What did you *not* like or approve of?

When presentations are made through movies, stories, role playing, or dramatizations, you can frequently utilize alternate-answer, check-list, or multiple-choice items to get at pupil attitudes, although free-response items are probably better, for example:

Example 4.

In the story you have just read (or heard or seen) circle the best answer.

Yes No a. Do you agree with Colonel Greene that Captain Warden made the only possible decision when he decided to fire his mortar at Colonel Nicholson and the other prisoners? (*The Bridge Over the River Kwai*)
          etc.

To Measure Skill in Thinking

It is extremely difficult to test the ability to think with ordinary paper and pencil tests. Perhaps the best technique to use is the essay—although most essay-test items tend to be tests of fact rather than of thinking.

Objective-type tests can be used to test reasoning fairly successfully. The great fault in using them for this purpose though is that one cannot easily find out why the pupil selected his answer.

Example 1.[7]

In the space provided, mark each of the following items *A*, if the argument is valid and the conclusion true; *B*, if the argument is valid and the conclusion false; *C*, if the argument is invalid and the conclusion true; and *D*, if the argument is invalid and the conclusion false.

( ) 1. Revolutions occur only when the people rebelling are better off than they have been before. The American Negroes are rebelling; the average American Negro is better off than he has ever been before.
     etc.

---

[7] This example is patterned after one of the several excellent suggestions contained in Dana G. Kurfman and Robert J. Solomon, "Measuring of Growth in Skills," in Helen McCracken Carpenter, ed., *Skill Development in Social Studies* (Washington, D. C.: National Council for the Social Studies, 1963).

Example 2.

Mark each of the following A, if the sentence is a definition; B, if the sentence is factual; C, if the sentence is interpretation.

( ) 1. St. Louis was the center of trade because of its location at the confluence of the Mississippi and Missouri Rivers.
( ) 2. The principal cause of the American Civil War was slavery.
     etc.

Example 3.

Choose the conclusion that follows from the premises given. Indicate your choice by circling the letter of the proper response.

Slave ownership is a property right, and the Constitution guarantees property rights.

A. The Constitution guarantees slave ownership.
B. Guarantees in the Constitution fail to protect antislavery men.
C. The Constitution must be changed to abolish slavery.

Example 4.

Consider the following generalizations (A) and the numbered statements listed below it. If any of the statements below the generalization can be used to support that generalization, mark it Y opposite the number of the statement. If the statement does not uphold the generalization, mark it N.

A.   The involvement of the United States in the war in Vietnam is immoral.
( ) 1. Many innocent women and children are being killed.
( ) 2. Several prominent American clergymen have declared that the war violates the provisions of the Geneva conference.
     etc.

Example 5.

Which of the following would be the most difficult to prove true or false? Place the letter of the option you select in the space provided.

( ) a. The treaty of Fort Stanwix sealed the doom of the Shawnees.
( ) b. There were more French than American military personnel at the battle of Yorktown.
     etc.

Example 6.

In the space provided, mark each of the following quotations F, if it represents a fact; or O, if it represents only the author's opinion or conclusion.

( ) a. "The other Indian nations directly involved, the Mingo, Delaware, and Shawnees, suffered, on the other hand, more by the treaty than they could have by a losing war."

( ) b. "What immediately transpired was that their generous and grateful
       Iroquois friends granted Johnson and Crogham 200,000 and 100,000
       acres, respectively, in New York. . . ."
   etc.

Sources of Critical Thinking Items. Wide-awake teachers are able to make
many adaptations and variations of the examples given here in order to test
thinking skills and thinking ability.[8]

RECOMMENDED PROCEDURES FOR THE EVALUATION OF COMMITTEE WORK

To evaluate the work pupils do in committees is quite difficult.

1. When evaluating individual contributions to committee work note that each
   pupil may contribute in a different way.
2. Encourage committees to evaluate themselves.
3. Use an overall discussion as a means by which the entire class can evaluate
   the worth of the committee work.
4. Keep a teacher's log.
5. Utilize the reports of observers.
6. Utilize the reports of secretaries.
7. Use reaction sheets at the end of the committee work.
   a. What part of your committee work went well?
   b. What part went poorly?
   c. What kind of progress did you make?
      Superior, excellent, good, fair, poor?
   d. What suggestions for improvement do you have?
8. Use
   a. Tests and quizzes.
   b. Rating scales.
   c. Check lists.
   d. Anecdotal records.
9. Let groups evaluate the reports of other groups. When you use this technique be sure that pupils are well briefed in what they are to use as a basis
   for their judgment.
10. Utilize a point system that considers a number of factors such as that in Fig-
    ure 7-3.

---

[8] Other examples of variations and adaptations of these types of test items can be found in The
Association of Teachers of Social Studies of the City of New York, *Handbook for Social Studies
Teaching,* 3rd ed. (New York: Holt, Rinehart & Winston, Inc., 1967); Helen McCracken Carpenter, ed.,
Skill Development in Social Studies, Thirty-third Yearbook (Washington, D. C.: National Council for
the Social Studies, 1963), Chap. 14.
  Examples of test items can also be found in the many texts on testing, secondary school teaching
methods, and methods of teaching the social studies.

UNITED STATES GOVERNMENT

UNIT

INDIVIDUAL POINTS BASED ON:
1. Teacher observation
2. Rating by other team members
3. Attendance
4. Self-evaluation
NOTE: Awarded by TEACHER (0-40)

GROUP POINTS BASED ON:
1. ORAL PRESENTATION . . . (0-20)
2. WRITE-UP . . . . (0-20)

TOTAL: Possible range of
        Individual points . . . . . (0-80)

STUDENT EVALUATION SHEET
RESEARCH TEAM NO. _____
CLASS HOUR   _____
DATE   _____

TEAM MEMBER	CONTRIBUTION	Abs.	INDIVIDUAL			GROUP		TOTAL Pts.
			Team Rating	Self	Teacher	Oral	Write up	

TEACHER'S REMARKS:

Teacher _____

FIGURE 7-3. *Evaluation Form Used to Evaluate Members of Research Teams. Form Used in Wichita, Kansas.*

UNITED STATES GOVERNMENT

"VOTER BEHAVIOR": SELF-EVALUATION

Name ___*K——, J——*_____
       (Print last name first)
                       Research
Hr. _____ Seat No. _____ Team: _____

> NOTE: This is a __CONFIDENTIAL__ evaluation sheet. NO ONE
> IS TO SEE THIS SHEET OUTSIDE OF YOU AND
> YOUR TEACHERS. HOW YOU ANSWER DOES NOT
> BIND YOUR TEACHERS IN ANY WAY IN AWARD-
> ING YOUR GRADE OR POINTS IN THIS UNIT.
> Be frank and to the point.

1. Did you get to know the members of your research team personally?
    __✓__ YES   _____ SOME   _____ NO

2. Who was really responsible for getting the job done on your team?
    __✓__ A.   Everyone played a key role.
    _____ B.   Success or failure depended on five or six people only.
    _____ C.   Most of the work was accomplished by only two or three.

3. Which of the following do you feel may account for the lack of TOTAL participation and involvement on the part of EVERYONE?
    _____ A.   They did not understand what was really involved.
    _____ B.   There was a basic lack of real interest in the project.
    _____ C.   There was too much confusion and lack of organization.
    __✓__ D.   This question does not apply to my group since there was total
              participation and involvement.

4. Which of the following best describes your role in your group?
    _____ A.   The outcome of my team's project depended mainly on my con-
              tributions, both in and out of class.
    _____ B.   Because of my high interest in this project, I did whatever had to be
              done, both in and out of class.
    __✓__ C.   I achieved whatever was assigned to me and no one can say that I did
              not do my share.
    _____ D.   I did only those things that I thought I understood, which wasn't
              very much.
    _____ E.   Somehow, I never really got involved.

5. What SPECIFIC contribution(s) did you make? (Be brief and to the point):
(DO NOT USE GROUP VOIDED "CONTRIBUTIONS")
    (a) *Made maps*_____
    (b) *Wrote pop characteristic; unemployment, males divorsed, females divorsed*
    (c) *Helped with the project as a whole.*
    (d) _____
    (e) _____

6. How many OUT-OF-CLASS hours did you devote to the project? _*0*_ Hrs.

FIGURE 7-4. *Self-rating Form. Form Used in Wichita Kansas. Names and Comments Have Been Added.*

7. If you were to rate yourself on a scale of points (from 0–40) for your individual contribution to the total outcome of your group's project, how many points would you award yourself? (Place an X somewhere on the scale to indicate your rank.)

```
0     5     10    15    20    25  X  30    35
!  .  .  !  .  .  !  .  .  !  .  .  !  .  .  ! X .  !  .  .  !  .  .  !
very              low             middle           high           very
low                                                               high
```

8. Of all the students in your group, list below the TOP four who you feel contributed most to the final outcome of your team's effort. Start with the number one student, then the student next to him or her, etc. DO NOT INCLUDE YOURSELF. (If you don't know a student's name, then leave that spot blank.)

    (1) _Wayne Lewis_

    (2) _Tom Williams_

    (3) _____

    (4) _____

9. How valuable do you consider this activity as a class project?

    _____ A. Extremely valuable
    __X__ B. Highly valuable
    _____ C. Some value
    _____ D. Doubtful value
    _____ E. Extremely non-valuable

10. Briefly explain your choice in number nine.

This gives each member of the group on opportunity to see how the city voted and possibly why the voted the way they did. It also gives the opportunity to work to gether.

11. What suggestions could you make of how this class project can best be improved:

There should be more emphasis placed on comparisons of the voting characteristic instead of facts, this should be given in the oral and written report.
Example.
In fact ? the colored pop voted such and such a way while the unemployed or the divorced voted another way.

Date _April 7_   _J——— a. K———_
                                  signature

FIGURE 7-4. (*Continued*)

CORRECTING TESTS AND PAPERS

CORRECTING ESSAY AND PERFORMANCE TESTS

Correcting essay tests is almost completely subjective under the best conditions and therefore quite unreliable. To make the correcting fair, it is necessary to make the tests as objective as possible by providing a key and by keeping the tests anonymous so that the reader is not influenced by knowing which pupil wrote the paper.

One method of attempting to make the reading of essay-test items objective is to

1. Write all the points that you think should be contained in, or you would be willing to give credit for, each answer.
2. Set up standards for what you consider to be A, B, C, D, or F work for each question.
3. Prepare a rating scale to rate each point. For example:

Political	A _____	F
Economic	A _____	F
Social	A _____	F
Geographical	A _____	F

4. Read each item separately, as in method 1, and note the excellence of the answers on the rating scale.
5. Average out the rating and assign this value to the item.
6. Average out the values for all the questions. This is your test score.

CORRECTING OBJECTIVE-TYPE TESTS

Correcting objective-type tests is relatively easy. It consists simply of preparing a key and then checking off the correct or incorrect answers to find the total number of items scored correctly. The raw score is the number of items scored correctly. It is obtained by counting the number of items right or subtracting the number of items wrong from the total possible.

To Make Keys for Objective-Type Tests

Type 1.

1. Set up the test so that the answers to the items appear at either the left or the right side of the paper in a column, or have the pupils write their answers on an answer sheet.
2. Mark up one test or one answer sheet with the correct answers. This is your key.
3. Place the key alongside the answers on the pupils' tests and mark the number of items right. It is best to complete the first page on every test before going on to the next page. (Some teachers find it easier to check the wrong answers and subtract to find the raw score because usually there are not so many errors.)
4. Put the total number of the correct answers at the bottom of each page. When all pages have been marked, add the totals of all the pages and place that number on the front page of the test.
5. When all the tests have been scored, place them in numerical order with the highest score on top of the pile. Then mark the tests according to their score.

Type 2. The Mask Key.

1. Prepare the test so that the pupils indicate their answers only by marking (circling, crossing out) the responses they believe correct. Answer sheets are especially good for this type of test key.

2. Place a sheet of light cardboard or stiff paper over the test. Make holes in this sheet where the correct answers should appear. This is your mask.

3. Place the mask over the tests. The correct answers will show through the holes in the mask. Count them to find the raw score.

To Correct for Guessing. When multiple-choice test items have fewer than four options, the chances that pupils may guess the answers correctly by sheer luck are quite high. Therefore, to eliminate the factor of luck, use a correction for guessing when scoring alternate-answer and three-option multiple-choice test items. The formula is

$$S = R - \frac{W}{(c-1)}$$

when S is the corrected score, R the number of correct responses, W the number of incorrect responses, and C the number of options provided for each item.

Therefore, for alternate-answer items the formula becomes

$$S = R - \frac{W}{2-1} \qquad \text{or} \qquad S = R - W$$

For items having three options, the formula is

$$S = R - \frac{W}{(3-1)} \qquad \text{or} \qquad S = R - \frac{W}{2}$$

CORRECTING ESSAYS, NOTEBOOKS, AND OTHER PAPERS

Notebooks and papers should be corrected in the same manner as essay tests. To objectify your impressions of the work use check lists or rating scales for which you have laid out appropriate standards. Thus, for a research paper, you might want to use something like the following.

Example 1.

	Excellent	Average	Unsatisfactory
Organization			
Logic			
Use of sources			
Bibliography			
Format			
Clearness of expression			
Accuracy			
Depth of research			
Conclusions			
etc.			

Instead of using a formal scale, many teachers simply indicate their estimate of each facet by a five-point scale—that is, 5, 4, 3, 2, 1, or excellent, good, average, fair, poor, for example.

Criteria for Correcting Essays. In correcting essays and other papers you may want to consider each of the following suggested criteria. The weighting of these criteria will depend on your estimate of the situation.

1. Content.
    a. Has he said something worthwhile?
    b. Is his conception accurate and complete?
    c. Does he make his point? Is he clear?
    d. Does he support his conclusions and document his facts?
    e. Does he develop his thoughts logically? Is his thinking logical?
    f. Does he show adequate knowledge of the subject?
2. Form.
    a. Does the essay have unity? Is there an identifiable central idea?
    b. Are the topic and viewpoint clearly stated?
    c. Is the paper free from vagueness, ambiguity, and indecisiveness?
    d. Does it have a strong beginning and ending?
    e. Is it coherent?
        (1) Is it developed in logical order?
        (2) Are the details bound together into a whole by proper use of transitional devices?
        (3) Is the paragraphing appropriate? Are the paragraphs well developed, logically constructed, and placed in natural sequence?
        (4) Is each idea given its proper emphasis?
    f. Is it effective?
        (1) Are the sentences clear and correct?
        (2) Is there variation in sentence structure and sentence strength?
        (3) Are subordinaton and coordination used appropriately?
        (4) Is the language and word choice effective, appropriate, and varied?
    g. Is the paper free from errors in grammar, spelling, punctuation, faulty construction, and mechanics?

Other Tips for Correcting Essays

1. Avoid covering the essay with red ink. If the paper is full of mistakes concentrate on a few. Let the rest go. Otherwise you just confuse and discourage the pupil.
2. Give two marks: one for content, one for composition.
3. When many pupils have the same difficulty, discuss it in class rather than mark up each paper.
4. Stagger written assignments so that you have only one set of papers to read at a time.
5. Have each pupil keep all his writing in a folder. If this is done, you will have all the papers available for conferences during laboratory periods.
6. Let pupils cooperate in correcting and criticizing each others work.
7. Make transparencies of essays or portions of essays and project them. (Pick papers to illustrate particular strengths and weaknesses.) Make corrections and comments directly on the transparency and discuss them. One can also project the transparency on to the chalkboard and correct the essay as projected on the board, thus saving the transparency to use again.
8. Project the essay or portions of the essay by means of an opaque projector. Discuss the strengths of weakness as in suggestion 7.
9. Mimeograph or ditto sections of papers illustrating strengths or weaknesses and discuss them in class.
10. Use a scale for evaluating students' writing as a guide for the grading of com-

positions. These will, of course, not be of great help in grading the particular content of an essay, but can be of great help in setting up standards for evaluating the "English" aspects of the paper.[9]

11. Dictate your comments to a tape recorder. When you use this technique keep these guidelines in mind:
   a. Have each pupil number his pages, so you can refer to specific places in the paper by page and line.
   b. At the end of the comment on each paper, ask the pupil to call the next pupil to the recorder.
   c. Be sure to note the count number at the beginning of the comment for each paper (so that you can find the comment quickly during the playback).
   d. Be sure not to talk too much or too fast.
   e. Provide earphones for the pupils (to cut down classroom noise and to make the comments private).
   f. Be sure the recorder is readily available.

Symbols Used in Marking Essays and Other Papers. Sometimes the school administration or the English department of the school will adopt a correction key to be used in checking themes and other papers. Where such a key has been adopted, it should be used by all teachers. The following symbols are suggested for use by teachers in schools that have not adopted correction keys.

Symbol	Meaning	Symbol	Meaning
Gr	— Error in grammar	Sl	— Slang expression; not acceptable
WW	— Wrong word	C	— Capitalization
Rep	— Avoid repetition	Agr	— Agreement
SS	— Sentence structure	t	— Tense
⌐P	— New paragraph	CS	— Comma splice
Sp	— Spelling (incorrect)	Red	— Redundant
D	— Diction; choose a better word	//	— Str. parallelism
ꙿ X	— Omit	⌣	— Make one word
∧	— Insert	tr	— Transition (needed)
?	— Not clear; what you have written is not understandable	frag	— Fragment
		ref	— Reference

MARKING

Marking systems are codes by which teachers represent their guesses concerning pupils' knowledge, abilities, attitudes, or other qualities that they need to report to the pupils, their parents, school authorities, prospective employers,

---

[9] Examples of useful scales are found in N. Field Winn, et al., *A Scale for Evaluation of High School Student Essays* (Champaign, Ill.: National Council for Teachers of English, 1960); Lois M. Grosse, Dorothy Miller, and Erwin R. Steinberg, eds., *Suggestions for Evaluating Junior High School Writing* (Champaign, Ill.: National Council of Teachers of English, nd); and Paul B. Diederich, "How to Measure Growth in Writing Ability," *English Journal,* Vol. 55 (Champaign, Ill.: National Council of Teachers of English, April, 1966), pp. 444–446. This scale is also reproduced in Leonard H. Clark, *Strategies and Tactics in Secondary School Teaching* (New York: The Macmillan Company, 1968), pp. 371–374.

college admission officers, and the like. It is important always to remember that, although marks may represent educated guesses, they always represent guesses. Completely accurate, objective marks do not exist.

MARKING SYSTEMS

There are several types of marking systems. The most common type is the five-point scale: A, B, C, D, F; 1, 2, 3, 4, 5; superior, good, average, fair, poor. There are also pass-fail systems, honors-pass-fail systems, and the 100 per cent system. None of these is really satisfactory, but the five-point system, in one or another of its forms, is generally considered to be the most satisfactory of all the marking systems presently available.

Marking on a Curve. In the past many teachers have used the normal curve of probability as a basis for computing school marks. Ordinarily this practice should be avoided.

1. The normal curve of probability applies to random samples where chance rules. Secondary school classes are not random groups, but selected groups.
2. The normal curve of probability applies only to large samples. Fifty is the bare minimum class size for which the normal curve can be used.

TO DETERMINE A TEST MARK

1. Determine the raw scores of the tests.
2. Arrange the raw scores from highest to lowest.
3. Convert the scores to a five-point scale by subjectively determining cut-off points for A, B, C, D, F on the basis of
   a. Evident difficulty of the test.
   b. How well the pupils seem to have attained the goals you thought they should.

TO DETERMINE COURSE, TERM, AND UNIT MARKS

Every mark should represent the teacher's best guess of the pupil's actual achievement. In determining term marks,

1. Obtain all the data you can. Give plenty of
   a. Tests and quizzes.
   b. Classwork, discussions, and the like.
   c. Papers, notebooks, and the like.
2. Record all data in your rank book.
   a. Record all test and quiz scores. It sometimes helps to record test and quiz scores as raw scores. At the end of the unit or marking period you can add up the raw scores and then translate the cumulated raw score into the terms of the five-point scale (for example, A, B, C, D, F). This system tends to make test scores more reliable. However, you may prefer to record each test on the five-point scale.
   b. Record other types of evidence. These can be recorded in the five-point

scale. In order to differentiate from tests and the like, you may want to record in symbols different from tests (for example, A, B, C, D, F; ★ + ✔ − 0; E, Vg, G, P, F; and so on), especially if they are to be weighted differently.

3. Compute the average.
   a. To determine the average of scores on a five-point scale, let the highest score be 5; the next highest 4; the next 3; the next 2; the lowest 1. Add the sum of the scores and divide by the number of cases.
   For instance, the average of 2 A's, 3 B's, and 2 C's is B.

$$2 \times 5 = 10$$
$$3 \times 4 = 12$$
$$2 \times 3 = \underline{6}$$
$$28 \qquad \frac{28}{7} = 4 \text{ or B}$$

   b. In averaging out the score to get the final score, you should be sure to weight each datum properly.

Using Unit Marks. A method strongly recommended is to draw off a mark for each unit by using the preceding system. When this has been done, the average of the unit marks will give you the term mark, allowing for the different weighting of units, if this is necessary.

Using Percentage Marks. Some schools require percentage marks. In this case convert the five-point marks to per cents by the following process: If the passing mark is 60, then let D equal 65; C, 75; B, 85; A, 95; F, 55 or less. If the passing mark is 70, A equals 95; B, 87; C, 80; D, 73; and F, 65 or less. When the school specifies the range for each mark, as A equals 93 to 100, use the mid-point of the range when you convert from the five-point mark to the per cent mark.[10]

SELECTING PUBLISHED TESTS

Use the following procedures to select tests published commercially.

1. Study your own school characteristics and testing needs.
2. Analyze the characteristics and capabilities of tests available.
3. Match
   a. The population of norm groups, of reliability samples, and of validity studies with your own school population.
   b. The content of the test to the curriculum and objectives of your school.
   c. The validity evidence, reliability data, scoring system, and interpretive material for the test with your own purposes and prospective uses of the test results.[11]

---

[10] For good references on interpreting test results and statistical procedures, see Paul B. Diederich, "Pinhead Statistics" in Fred T. Wilhelms, ed., *Evaluation as Feedback and Guide*, (Washington, D. C.: Association for Supervision and Curriculum Development, 1967); Robert L. Ebel, "Using the Results of Measurement," in Berg, loc. cit.; or Kenneth F. McLaughlin, "Interpretation of Test Results," OE-25038, *Bulletin No. 7* (Washington, D. C.: Government Printing Office, 1964).

[11] Adapted from "Selecting an Achievement Test, Principles and Procedures," *Evaluation and Advisory Service Series, No. 3* (Princeton, N. J.: Educational Testing Service, 1961), p. 31. This pamphlet is an excellent concise reference on the topic.

Things to Consider When Selecting a Published Test

1. What evidence is there that the test is valid for your purpose?
   a. Does it seem to test what you want it to test?
   b. Does it check the proper content?
   c. Does it check the content in the proper proportion?
   d. Is there evidence that the test results agree with other measures of pupil performance in the area?
   e. What types of performances can be predicted by this test?
   f. How accurate are the predictions?
2. What evidence is there that the test is reliable?
   a. Does the information about the test provide reliability coefficients: for example, coefficients of internal consistency (split-half or item analysis), equivalence (correlation between different forms), or stability (test-retest)? In evaluating the coefficients note that
      (1) Long tests tend to be more reliable than short ones, but they may not be as usable.
      (2) Coefficients of reliability tend to be too high in speeded tests unless speed is one of the elements to be tested.
      (3) The greater the range of scores of the sample population the higher the coefficient of reliability. Thus if a test publisher bases his coefficient of reliability on a sample with a wide-range of test scores, it may seem that his test is more reliable than a test whose coefficient is based on a sample with a narrow range when, in fact, it is not. For classroom purpose, coefficients based on "within class within school" data are more realistic than coefficients based on larger, more varied groups.
      (4) Because coefficients of reliability differ according to the "reliability sample," it is best if the group to be tested compares to the population on which the coefficients are based.
   b. What is the standard error of measurement? Although this measure cannot be used directly to compare tests, it does give you an index of confidence in the scores and differences between scores on any test.
3. Is the scoring of the test relatively objective?
   a. Is the test provided with a key that makes scoring automatic?
   b. In cases where subjective judgments must be made by the scorer, are guidelines provided to reduce the subjectivity?
4. Is the test usable?
   a. Can it be given in the time allotted?
   b. Can it be administered easily?
   c. Are administrative procedures standardized?
   d. Can it be scored easily and accurately?
   e. Is the format acceptable?
   f. Are adequate norms provided?
   g. Are provisions made for an easy, accurate interpretation of the scores?
   h. What does it cost to purchase, administer, score, and interpret this test?

SOURCES OF INFORMATION ABOUT PUBLISHED TESTS

1. A. K. Buros, *Mental Measurement Yearbook* (Highland Park, N. J.: The Gryphon Press, various editions. These yearbooks are not cumulative. Information in earlier editions is not included in later ones. Without doubt they are the best source of information about published tests.

2. A. K. Buros, ed., *Tests in Print: A Comprehensive Bibliography of Tests for Use in Education, Psychology, and Industry* (Highland Park, N. J.: The Gryphon Press, 1961).

3. Reviews of tests in professional journals, such as *Social Education.*

4. Catalogs of test publishers. Test services supplied by test publishers.

5. Brochures and pamphlets published by test publishers. For example, The Evaluation and Advisory Service Series published by The Educational Testing Service.

6. Pamphlets and other publications of professional organizations such as the National Council for the Social Studies.[12]

---

[12] For further information about selecting social studies achievement tests see Barbara A. Peace, "Published Tests in the Social Studies," Berg, loc. cit.; and "Selecting an Achievement Test: Principles and Procedures" op. cit.

PART III

Teaching the Disciplines

CHAPTER 8

Making History Live

HISTORY, Jacob Burckhardt says, is the record of what one age finds worthy of note in another. Although history is based on facts, it is more than just facts. History consists of facts seen through the eyes of the historian. In other words, history is not a science. Rather, it is a humanistic study of things past. It is characterized by the historical method, which, being a method of indirect rather than direct observation, differs substantially from the scientific method. Its generalizations, instead of being scientific laws that make it possible for us to predict the future with some accuracy, are seldom more than summary statements of what is known about the past. Moreover, history is more than a simple retelling of what happened. History seeks to determine causations and relationships and to interpret the meaning of the facts. This is why history is constantly changing. New history is created every year, not only by the discovery of new facts, but also by the reinterpretation of old ones. The new history grows out of the old history and so is continuous. Change and continuity are two key characteristics not only of what happens in history, but of history itself.

So we can say that history is a selective record of the past characterized by the use of historical method to determine the facts, by both change and continuity, and by attempts to go beyond the facts to determine their meaning in the past, present, and future.

HISTORICAL METHOD

Types of Sources. Only seldom is the historian fortunate enough to have been present at the scene of the events he is attempting to describe and interpret. Consequently, he must depend on indirect observation for his data. For this purpose he uses two basic types of information sources: traditions and remains. *Traditions* are the records by which people have tried to pass on to others information about what has happened. There are three kinds of traditions: written, oral, and pictorial. Written traditions include historical writing, records, reports, and other writings. Oral traditions include folk tales and legends. Many accounts now considered to be part of ancient history were first remembered as oral traditions. Pictorial traditions include maps and diagrams as well as pictures and sculptures. *Remains* differ from traditions in that they are unconscious, accidental survivals of the past. These may include artifacts of all kinds, and less tangible relics such as survivals in language, literary form, law, and customs.

Primary and Derived Sources. Sources are either primary or derived, but primary sources are the most trustworthy. They consist of direct material remains, eye-witness accounts, the actual texts of written documents, photographs, and taped recordings—in other words, firsthand evidence. Derived sources are secondhand information. The source may be secondary—that is, derived from a primary source—or it may be based on numerous retellings. The test is whether or not the evidence was learned directly. If it was not, the source is a derived source. One must judge its validity according to the distance the source is removed from the original and the reputation of the mediator.

Criticism and Synthesis. Historical method is characterized by two processes: criticism and synthesis. In criticism, the historian tries to determine what the facts are and what they mean by analyzing the evidence. In synthesis, he tries to put the facts together to form generalizations and conclusions. It is in this step that he writes his version of history.

In his analysis of the data the historian applies two kinds of criticism. First he tries to determine whether his data are what they seem to be. For instance, "How trustworthy are the sources?" This process is called external criticism. Next the historian tries to determine the significance and meaning of each item of data. This process is internal criticism. Thus, by external criticism you might determine whether or not a supposed eighteenth-century letter is really an eighteenth-century letter, and by internal criticism decide if it has any bearing on what you are studying.

During synthesis the historian tries to combine the evidence derived from his analysis to form an account of what actually happened and why.

What is Historical Fact? Because historical method is largely a method of uncontrolled indirect observations, it is often difficult to determine what the objective historical facts are. Pupils ought to have an understanding of this difficulty and a working knowledge of the rules of evidence that are permissible in historical research. These rules are simple and sensible. The first is that it takes at least two separate, independent sources in agreement to establish a fact. Exceptions to the rule exist, of course. Artifacts and other remains are self-validating. Moreover, sometimes, the rule of two does not hold because more convincing evidence may counter the two independent sources, or what we know of the situation or of natural laws makes the evidence seem plausible. In the long run, the determining of facts must be the result of inferences made by the historian on the basis of what he knows of the entire situation. Much history, therefore, is highly subjective—the result of personal interpretation.

HISTORY AND THE CURRICULUM

GOALS OF TEACHING HISTORY

What then are the particular goals for teaching history? Let us list a few:

1. To teach pupils to think historically—that is, to use the historical method, to understand the structure of history, and to utilize the past in studying the present and the future.
2. To teach pupils to think creatively.
3. To explain the present. This goal has two parts: it includes (a) learning how the present got to be the way it is, and (b) using the knowledge of the past to understand the present in order to help solve contemporary problems.
4. To understand the sweep of history, that is, that the status of anything today is the result of what happened in the past, and in time what happens today will, in one way or another, influence the future.
5. To enjoy history. If history teaching can make the love of history infectious, the teachers will have achieved much.
6. To help the pupils to become familiar with that body of knowledge that is history. Although many teachers seem to think this to be the only objective of history, historical information has real value only as a medium for bringing out the other objectives listed here. History should be used and enjoyed, not worshipped.

COURSE ORGANIZATION

Selection of Content. No matter what system you use, most of the history must be left out. So much has happened in every country in every period that to cover it all is always impossible. This undoubted fact makes the selection of content more and more important. In making your selection, consider the following:

1. What are the over-all goals of the course and the curriculum?
2. What content is best suited to the needs of youth and society?
3. What does history have to offer youth?
4. Where do the interests of the pupils lie? Remember, viable information and ideas that pupils can use now, and which relate the history to the present, will make history more useful, more interesting, and consequently better received.

"Post Holing." Because of the need for selectivity of content, and because teaching in depth is more likely to make history live than superficial ground covering, you should probably "post hole" your history courses. In other words, you should teach certain topics in depth and skip lightly over intervening topics. The arguments for this type of course organization are supported by Commager's statement that in history one should start with particulars and work up to generalities. His implication is that if one takes good care of teaching or

learning the particulars, the generalities will take care of themselves.[1] For many years advocates of the unit approach have been operating successfully on this same theory.

United States History. Typically, courses in American history are organized on a chronological basis. Some courses are organized topically, but the topics are treated chronologically, even though there is considerable evidence that starting with the present and then using history to explain the past is much more stimulating. Many American history courses combine the chronological and topical approaches. In these courses, the approach is frequently strictly chronological until the Civil War period; then it is centered on chronologically developed topics such as labor and industry, agriculture, and foreign affairs from the Civil War to the present.

An interesting variation of the combined chronological and topical approach is to center the course about important decisions that had to be made in the course of history, for example: "How should the Federal government raise money?" "How powerful should the central government be?" This type of course organization lends itself to the use of inquiry procedures, and to a better understanding of the complexities of the problems and the difficulties inherent in making reasonable decisions.

World History. World history encompasses so much content that it is almost impossible to find a logical course organization for world history courses. At the present time, most of the courses are organized chronologically; a few are organized topically; and a large number are organized around areas. In truth, however, almost all world history courses are conglomerates combining a mixture of chronological, topical, and perhaps areal features. Most chronologically organized courses, for instance, consist of units (for example, Ancient Greece and Rome) that overlap in time. Furthermore, many chronologically arranged courses include units on topics such as The Rise of Nationalism, or area studies such as China. Courses organized around culture areas may be chronological or they may be centered almost entirely around the area as it is today, with only flashbacks to its history from time to time.

To find the course organization best suited to your purpose, study the current textbooks. You will find a list of them in Appendix S. In any case probably you should choose a course organization that meets the following criteria proposed by Edith West.

1. Students should study Western European civilization as a basis for their own culture.
2. Students should study the USSR and China as the two competing leaders of the communist world.
3. Students should study India as the leading example of a noncommitted,

---

[1] Henry Steele Commager, *The Nature and the Study of History* (Columbus, Ohio: Charles E. Merrill Publishers, 1965).

underdeveloped nation whose economic progress through democratic means is being compared to other underdeveloped people with the progress made by Communist China.

4. Students should study one other underdeveloped area of the world.[2]

KEEPING ABREAST OF THE SUBJECT

Modern methods for the teaching of history require a really firm grasp of the content by the teacher. Unfortunately, history covers such a wide range of content that few young teachers feel very confident in subject matter when they first begin to teach. If you find yourself insecure in the history of any period that you must teach, your first recourse is to consult a good college textbook on the subject. Sometimes reading a good encyclopedia article on the topic will give you the orientation you need to get started. You should also provide yourself with

History Course Organization		
Chronological	Topical	Area Studies
Pro		
Best for developing time sense and sense of history and continuity.	Good for relating history to present.	Good for getting at non-Western world.
Emphasizes interrelationships.	Essential for problem solving courses.	Good for relating history and present.
Many many materials available.		Good for developing concepts from anthropology, sociology, economics, etc.
Can be told as an interesting story.		Good for teaching values and world understanding.
		Helps rid pupils of ethnocentric attitudes.
		Many materials available.
		More appealing to poor, less motivated pupils than chronological.
Con		
More difficult to develop concepts from other social sciences.	May lead to poor time sense.	Poor time relations.
Tends toward ethnocentricity.	Does not develop sense of history.	May lead to stereotype thinking.
Tends to be shallow and superficial.	Tends to leave out interrelationships.	Overabundance of content.
Difficult to bring in non-Western materials.		Difficult to teach the sweep and continuity of history.

[2] Edith West, "Promising Ways of Organizing World History Courses," in Shirley H. Engle, ed., *New Perspectives in World History,* Thirty-fourth Yearbook (Washington, D.C.: National Council for the Social Studies, 1964), p. 603. Reprinted with permission of the National Council for the Social Studies and Edith West.

basic references in the area. Some suggested references are listed in Appendix R.

SUGGESTIONS FOR MAKING HISTORY REAL

The crucial problem for the history teacher is how to make history real for pupils. History is the record of how human beings have acted, but pupils seldom see the actors as real people. Because they do not, they cannot participate in the drama and excitement that is history and so think of history as only dull abstraction. To make historical events and characters real you must let pupils stop and consider them. Understanding the reality in history requires study in depth. It is detail that makes history real. When Charles II was on the way home from his "travels," he and his officers amused themselves by measuring their heights against the wall of the ship's cabin, and Charles was the tallest. This simple detail is not important, but it is fun to know, and it gives us some inkling of Charles as a man rather than as a dim abstraction.

Sample Strategies and Tactics

1. Use problem-solving methods to make history real. The phrase "if so, then what," should be the history students' motto. Have pupils carry out activities that require a considerable amount of deduction.
2. Encourage pupils to observe relationships and see the analogies in different historical situations.

   What, for instance, were the similarities between the *Lusitania* incident in World War I and the *Alabama* affair during the Civil War? What similarities, and differences, are there between our favored-nation policies today and the French treatment of us when Jefferson was trying to negotiate favored-nation commercial agreements with France?
3. Use multiple readings to make history real. By reading several reports about the same event, pupils can develop both depth and perspective. Let them utilize differences in the readings to build an understanding of the need for ferreting out the truth.
4. Use novels, biographies, and other trade books of all kinds to help make history more realistic and lively. In this respect, the novels can be particularly useful. All novels are set in time and space, and so a surprisingly large number of them can be used to make history meaningful. Historical novels are important, of course, but novels written during the period represented can be even more revealing. They bring out the attitudes, beliefs, customs, and feelings of a period or group forcefully and authoritatively.[3]
5. Use original sources.
   a. Sometimes original sources can add considerable human interest, as with these names from the Halmote Rolls.

---

[3] For excellent bibliographies of historical fiction, see Hannah Logosa, *Historical Fiction* (Brooklawn, N.J.: McKinley Publishing Co.), and "World Civilization Booklist," *Bulletin No. 4* (Washington, D.C.: National Council for the Social Studies, 1968). Also see Appendix F of this book for suggestions.

Men	Women
John Jentilman	Agnes Redhead
Adam Barleycorn	Cicely Wilkinsdoughter
William Littlefair	Maud Malkynsmaydin
John Cherryman	Diote Jaksdoughter
John Merriman	Evote Wheelspinner
Gilbert Uncouth	Alice Robinsdoughter
Roger Mouse	Emma Andrewsmaydin
Henry Alansman	Margaret Ferrywoman
Thomas Marmaduke	Margaret Merry
John Fairjohn	Agnes Bonamy
Walter Mustard	Cicely Dansdoughter
Roger Litilannotson	Cicely the Pinderswoman*
John Stoutlook	
William Teddi	
Alan Paternoster	
Robert Benedicte	

* From G. G. Coulton, *Medieval Village, Manor, Monastery,* (New York: Harper and Row, Publishers, 1960), p. 103. Originally published by Cambridge University Press, London, 1925.

b. An analysis of original documents may clarify what actually happened in history, if the documents are not too difficult or obscure. Pupils might gain a quite different idea of the Stamp Act Congress than they sometimes do if they were to study the resolutions of the Congress and answer questions such as the following:
   (1) Is the document a primary, secondary, or tertiary source?
   (2) What did the Stamp Act Congress ask for?
   (3) On what grounds did it make the request?
   (4) Did the Congress state that there can be no taxation without representation? Prove your answer.
   (5) Did the Congress wish to be free from the British Crown?
   (6) Did the Congress wish to be free from the control of the British Parliament?
   (7) Would you call this an inflammatory document?[4]
6. Use pictures.
   Pictures can be extremely useful in making history real. A picture of the replica of the Mayflower docked at Plymouth can give pupils some idea of how cramped and crowded the Pilgrims were on the first Mayflower. For instance, a picture of the Indian dugouts can disabuse pupils of false ideas about Indian teepees and birch-bark canoes, just as pictures of the Pilgrims' thatched-roofed cottages can disabuse pupils of the log cabin idea.
7. Use cartoons, advertisements, magazines, newspapers, newspaper facsimiles, catalogs, and other materials of the period. Often, such materials will give pupils a real taste of the conditions, attitudes, and thinking of a period.
8. Use map study.
   Of all audiovisual aids, maps are the most necessary for understanding and teaching history. All historical events occur somewhere. Thus, pupils

[4] These questions might also be used as the basis for class discussion.

who read maps with understanding can visualize historical events more clearly than those pupils who cannot do so. A glance at a three-dimensional map of central and western Pennsylvania certainly can make the problem of transportation and communication between eastern Pennsylvania and the Pittsburgh area in the eighteenth century become clear, particularly if it is joined by the reading of an exciting story of the area at the time, such as Hervey Allen's *The Forest and the Fort.*

a. Make it a rule that every place of importance to the history being studied be identified on the maps by the pupils.

b. Use map study as the basis for research-type activities; for example, ask pupils to compare the route to Fort Duquesne laid out for General Forbes' Army by Colonel Bouquet with the route recommended by George Washington. In view of the situation, why was Colonel Bouquet's route more satisfactory?

c. Use map study to clarify historical events and policies.

For example, the aim of France in North America was to unite its holdings in Canada and Louisiana and so entrench France west of the Alleghenies that the British would be contained within the mountain barriers. Parkman describes the situation for us:

Years passed on. The new colony grew in wealth and strength. And now it remained for France to unite the two extremities of her broad American domain, to extend forts and settlements across the fertile solitudes between the valley of the St. Lawrence and the mouth of the Mississippi, and intrench herself among the forests which lie west of the Alleghenies, before the swelling tide of British colonization could overflow those mountain barriers. At the middle of the eighteenth century, her great project was fast advancing toward completion. The lakes and streams, the thoroughfares of the wilderness, were seized and guarded by a series of posts distributed with admirable skill. A fort on the strait of Niagara commanded the great entrance to the whole interior country. Another at Detroit controlled the passage from Lake Erie to the north. Another at St. Mary's debarred all hostile access to Lake Superior. Another at Michillimackinac secured the mouth of Lake Michigan. A post at Green Bay, and one at St. Joseph, guarded the two routes to the Mississippi, by way of the rivers Wisconsin and Illinois; while two posts on the Wabash, and one on the Maumee, made France the mistress of the great trading highway from Lake Erie to the Ohio. At Kaskaskia, Cahokia, and elsewhere in the Illinois, little French settlements had sprung up; and as the canoe of the voyager descended the Mississippi, he saw, at rare intervals, along its swampy margin a few small stockade forts, half buried amid the redundancy of forest vegetation, until, as he approached Natchez, the dwellings of the habitants of Louisiana began to appear.[5]

This passage could be the source of several types of map exercises. (1) You could locate the forts mentioned and the pupils could plot them on their maps. This would help pupils know the locations, but not much more. (2) The pupils could locate the spots mentioned and plot them on

[5] Francis Parkman, *The Conspiracy of Pontiac* (New York: Collier Books, 1962), pp. 74–75.

their maps. This would be better. (3) The pupils could locate the forts mentioned and plot them on their maps. Then they could consider whether these locations were appropriate for their purposes: Would they prevent the advance of the British if they could be held? Would they help bind the French settlements together? And so on. In answering these questions the pupils should consider the terrain, the transportation routes, and other geographic factors. Such an exercise would give a much greater understanding than the two exercises previously cited. (4) Another strategy might be to explain the problem, or have the pupils develop the problem, of the French government in America and ask the pupils to study the map to see where they would put their forts and settlements. They could then compare their solutions to those of the French as described by Parkman or others. This strategy, although time-consuming, would develop considerable understanding if the pupils really tackled the problem seriously. (5) Perhaps somewhat the same result can be achieved by still another strategy in which the pupils, after having been given the locations of the forts and settlements on maps, would attempt to determine the value forts located at these points would have in carrying out the French aim.

d. Use map making to clarify historical situations: maps of the route of the Santa Fe Trail, other westward routes, military campaigns, boundaries, crop distribution, and so on can be made quite easily. The aim is to have the pupils do the mapwork, rather than copy the work or sit idly by while the teacher does it.

9. Use deductive approaches: play the "what would have happened if" game. In this type of activity pupils attempt to forecast what might have happened if a particular event had not turned out as it actually did. For example, what would have happened if John Burgoyne had won the Battle of Saratoga? Or what would have happened if John Hancock had been made commander in chief rather than George Washington? Such an activity requires that the pupil begin with known facts and generalizations and then deduce the specific "might have beens." This method is particularly useful when pupils draw conclusions concerning why specific actions or policies were taken at specific times in history.

10. Have pupils reconstruct history.

a. Use oral activities such as debates, speeches, and dramatics in which pupils represent historical characters, movements, or incidents.

b. Use role playing. One might have pupils role play a conversation in which they take the parts of the "loyalists" and "patriots," or "Sons of Liberty," during the early days of the American Revolution. Such an exercise might well help pupils gain an understanding of some of the feelings and tensions of the time. However, during such role playing, one must be careful to discourage introduction of twentieth-century feelings and attitudes that are not representative of the period being depicted. Eighteenth-century standards and attitudes are not necessarily twentieth-century standards and attitudes.

c. Use simulation games.

d. Use activities in which pupils attempt to reconstruct the way a group lived in the past. The pupils might attempt to build models of homes and artifacts, or they could try to use some of the tools and techniques of a past era.

    e. Use activities in which pupils put themselves in the roles of people of the past by writing letters, diaries, or newspapers of the period.

11. Use recordings, films, or television programs that portray historical periods and events.
12. Use bulletin boards, models, and other displays and exhibits.
13. Encourage pupils to become expert on a spot of history, or the life and career of a historical figure.
14. Encourage pupils to read biographies and diaries, because if history is to be real, it must deal with people.

    Diaries and journals are particularly good to give the flavor of a period and to show what life was like at the time. Pepys' *Diary* is, of course, the prime example here, even though some pupils think it dull. One of the best is John Bakeless' *Journals of Lewis and Clark*—which should have adventure enough in it for anyone.

15. Use inductive methods that will encourage pupils to make their own meaningful generalizations of what happened in history.
16. Encourage pupils to make their own cartoons, advertisements, models, or pictures to illustrate the period.
17. Introduce the music of the time, such as English ballads, our own folk ballads, Western music, the sentimental songs of the World Wars, and the formal music of the eighteenth century. Consider what music and songs tell us about people and their lives.
18. Encourage pupils to make charts or diagrams illustrating what happened in history and why: for example, a flow chart showing causation for the beginning of an armed conflict.

SAMPLE STRATEGIES AND TACTICS TO TEACH HISTORICAL METHOD

If learning to think historically is to be a real objective of history teaching, learning the historical method must become a real part of history courses. Use such strategies as the following:

1. Teach to give pupils an opportunity to practice both external and internal criticism.
2. Give exercises in critical analysis verisimilitude by using materials contemporaneous with the events being studied. For example:

> In the year 1860, the Abolitionists became strong, strong enough to elect one of their men for President. Abraham Lincoln was a weak man; and the South believed he would allow laws to be made which would deprive them of their rights. So the Southern States seceded, and elected Jefferson Davis as their president. This so enraged President Lincoln that he declared war, and has exhausted nearly all the strength of the nation in a vain attempt to whip the South back into the Union. Thousands of lives have been lost, and the

earth has been drenched with blood; but still Abraham is unable to conquer the "Rebels," as he calls the South. The South only asked to be let alone.[6]

Is this a primary, secondary, or other source? Where did the author get his information? How much of this selection is true? How much opinion? How much propaganda? Compare this description of President Lincoln with that in your history text. What differences do you find? Why must statements like this one be taken with a grain of salt?

What does this selection show about the feelings of at least some of the people in the confederacy?

3. Encourage pupils to learn to check the accuracy of what they read and see. There should be plenty of opportunities for them to find out that historical representations are not always accurate. One technique is to have pupils compare statements in the history texts with statements from other sources.

4. Use inductive teaching.

In this type of teaching the object is for the pupils to draw inferences from historical facts and thus develop their own concepts or generalizations. The teacher does not teach the pupils facts or generalizations as information to be learned, but rather teaches facts as material from which to make generalizations. In this way he helps pupils to think historically.

5. Use exercises in which pupils attempt to solve real or simulated problems of historical analysis. For example:

   a. Present the pupils with artifacts from a site and let them try to reconstruct as much as they can of the life of the people who lived at that site.

   b. Have pupils reconstruct and write local history.

WRITING HISTORY

Recently, many secondary school teachers have encouraged their pupils to learn historical methodology by actually doing some historical research and writing. Although projects of this sort require considerable diligence, they are not as difficult to conduct as one might imagine.

In secondary schools historical research is usually best done as a group project with teams or individuals working on various aspects of the research problem. Group projects of this type are easier to control and guide than individual projects. In any case, you will find that secondary school pupils will require much help and guidance in determining topics to study, in locating source material, in evaluating the evidence, in drawing conclusions, and in reporting their findings. Such projects should not be taken lightly. It is probably better not to attempt the job at all than to give pupils erroneous ideas about historical methods through using sloppy investigative procedures.

References on Writing History. This chapter obviously is not the place to tell how one goes about writing history. There are many references on this topic. Make yourself familiar with them, if you do not already know them. Two

---

[6] "For the Dixie Children," *A Primary Geography Written for Confederate Children* (Raleigh, N.C., 1864), p. ix.

resources especially useful in guiding writing projects in history are the *Historian's Handbook* and Lord's *Teaching History With Community Resources.*[7]

A Procedure for Research in History Classes

1. Introduction.

    Although academically talented pupils take to research and writing most readily, all pupils can do it and enjoy it. However, there is little point in insisting on this type of activity for less able pupils who are not particularly interested.

2. Sources of research topics.

    Topics for original historical research abound in local history. Here are a few examples of topics that may be appropriate:
    a. The settling of the town.
    b. The birth of the educational system—or of their own school.
    c. The change in the community in a particular period.
    d. The development of economic aspects of the community.
    e. The impact of a war (for example 1812, 1861–1865, 1898, 1914–1918, 1939–1945).

3. Selection of topics.
    a. In selecting a topic for study, use the following criteria:
        (1) Of what value is it?
        (2) Can it contribute some new knowledge?
            (a) Has anyone studied it previously?
            (b) Is there a possibility that the investigation could turn up new evidence, new facts, or a new interpretation?
        (3) Is it feasible?
            (a) Are the resources available?
            (b) Do the pupils have the necessary abilities?
            (c) Can the pupils complete it in the time and space allotted?
        (4) Does it have some central focus that will give the study direction?
    b. Insofar as possible, the pupils themselves should select the topics to be researched. However, because pupils lack maturity, information, and skill, teachers must help them. You can help by
        (1) Providing lists of possible topics.
        (2) Conducting discussions and other activities that may open up topics for research.
        (3) Allowing for teacher–pupil planning.
        (4) Providing sample materials.
        (5) Allowing time for background reading.
        (6) Advising about the probable availability of information.

4. Launching cooperative group research.
    a. Conduct a discussion in which the group decides a topic.
    b. In class discussion consider
        (1) The data needed.
        (2) Where data may be obtained.
        (3) Who should search for various items.

---

[7] Wood Gray, *Historian's Handbook,* 2nd ed. (Boston: Houghton Mifflin Company, 1964), and Clifford L. Lord, *Teaching History with Community Resources* (New York: Teachers College Press, 1964).

5. Continuing the research.
   a. Make individual assignments by teacher-pupil planning.
   b. Let each pupil work on his assignment.
   c. From time to time call the pupils together for progress reports and an evaluation of each person's program.
      (1) Pupils report both what they find and what they have difficulty finding.
      (2) The group discusses ways to solve any problems that have arisen.
      (3) The group makes decisions concerning the next steps.
6. Writing up the research.
   a. Each pupil should write up his findings and conclusions.
   b. A writing committee prepares a draft report based on the rough copy prepared by the individual researcher.
   c. The writing committee submits its draft to the class.
   d. The committee revises the draft in light of the class discussion.
   e. The research is published.

Sources of Data for Historical Research Projects

1. Local and state histories.
2. Libraries.
   a. Manuscript collections.
   b. Histories, biographies, and the like.
3. Historical societies.
4. Newspaper accounts.
5. Government records and reports.
6. Magazine articles.
7. Census materials.
8. Local historians.
9. Old-timers.
10. Physical remains.
    a. Furniture, buildings, and so on.
    b. Pictures.
11. Business concerns.
    a. Records and reports.
    b. Advertising.
12. Diaries, letters, and family archives.

Avenues for Publishing Pupil Research

1. Class publication.
2. School papers, yearbooks, and so on.
3. Local newspapers.
4. Local historical societies (including junior societies).
5. Local television and radio.
6. Local PTA and other bulletins.[8]

---

[8] In spite of its being more than thirty years old, Henry Johnson's *The Teaching of History,* rev. ed. (New York: The Macmillan Company, 1940), is still the best book on how to teach history. Other useful references are Gerald Leinwand and Daniel M. Feins, *Teaching History and the Social Studies in Secondary Schools* (New York: Pitman Publishing Corp., 1968); Morris R. Lewenstein, *Teaching Social Studies in Junior and Senior High Schools* (Chicago: Rand McNally & Co., 1963).

TEACHING TIME CONCEPTS

History occurs in time and space. It is, therefore, necessary for a pupil to develop a sense of time, depth, and knowledge of chronology if he is to have a reasonable understanding of history. Because developing a time sense is particularly difficult, and is usually too much for elementary schoolchildren to master, the burden of this responsibility necessarily falls on the secondary school teacher. Evidently, one can expect little success teaching time concepts to children whose mental age is less than 12.

In general, the development of time concepts follows three steps or stages. In the first of these concepts based on the here and now are developed. These are usually taught quite well in the elementary grades. In the second stage the pupils' numerical or mathematical chronological concepts are developed. This stage is begun in the elementary school, but must be continued in the secondary grades. In the third stage, social meaning is applied to chronology; it depends and builds on the first two stages. It is in this third stage that the pupil develops a sense of time relations, including the understanding of time continuity and duration. Actually, it is in this third stage that chronology is given its meaning and value in historical study. Because of its importance and difficulty, the stage begins in a pupil's secondary school years and should continue as long as he remains an active learner.[9]

TEACHING DATES AND CHRONOLOGY

Dates and chronology must be taught and taught carefully. Do not leave them to incidental learning. On the other hand, dates must be taught in context. Drilling on dates or special units on chronology will add little besides boredom to history teaching. Instead, you and your pupils must be perennially date conscious. Do not let any important historical events in any unit get away before they have been tagged conspicuously with a date.

Which Dates to Teach.   Naturally you cannot expect pupils to learn the dates of all the events in their history books. Here are a few guidelines that may prove helpful in determining which dates the pupils should learn.

1. Dates should not come from a list handed out ahead of time, but should be drawn from the content of the course as the pupils study it.
2. No pupil should be asked to learn the dates for any event until he has had an opportunity to learn about the event itself. Under such conditions, it is frequently possible and advantageous for pupils and teachers to decide together which dates are the ones to be remembered.
3. Concentrate only on the important dates.
   a. Famous dates like 1066, 1492, 1776, and 1789.
   b. Dates marking the beginning (or ending) of historical periods, such as the dates of the Nicene Creed, the Hegira, or the Battle of Hastings.

---

[9] Helen McCracken Carpenter, ed., *Skill Development in Social Studies*, Thirty-third Yearbook (Washington, D.C.: National Council for the Social Studies, 1963), p. 188.

4. Remember that dates are both definite and indefinite. For historical purposes, 10:30 P.M., 13 December 1970, is a date. So is Sunday, December 13, 1970 and so also is the twentieth century. For periods, reigns, lives, and other events, the date includes the entire duration; therefore, both the beginning and ending must be shown. Similarly some dates are approximate. The "c." in c. 800 is an essential part of the date.

5. There is always some question about how definite the dates pupils learn should be. Undoubtedly, the answer depends on the subject under discussion. In ancient history dates may be quite vague. Often, the century is near enough. On the other hand, in some areas, such as in the events leading up to a declaration of war, for instance, knowing specific dates down to days and hours may be essential for students to visualize the relationships of the events. This is particularly important when one is trying to establish implications.

Suggestions for Teaching Chronology

1. To fix dates in pupils' memory use short periods of drill at the beginning of the period. These drills ordinarily should last only two or three minutes.

2. Make longer drills interesting by introducing games, such as the following one suggested by Fraser and West.

> Famous Dates Game. Students divide into groups of six or eight. Each group has a set of cards which has been prepared by students. Each card has the name of an era or an event on one side, and the appropriate date or dates on the other. The first player draws a card and shows one side of it to the student on his left. If the latter can name the event or date connected with what he sees, he wins the card. If he fails to do so, the next player has a chance, and so around the group. Then the second player draws a card and the game proceeds. The object is to win the most cards.[10]

More mature students are likely to prefer quick oral or written drills that they know are for practice and will not affect their grades. Drill exercises, can be mimeographed or dittoed for students to use, or the teacher can place them on the chalkboard or project them with the overhead projector.

3. Develop the practice of always mentioning dates when speaking of an event. In this way, remembering the date tends to become automatic.

4. In order that pupils have opportunities to see the significance of the dates and their interrelationships, provide for considerable review and try to bring out time durations, changes, and continuity in the progress of events that make up the history course.

5. Emphasize how difficult it is to tell with certainty what the dates of certain events really were. Ancient dates are exceptionally formidable, but modern dates are not always easily discernible either. Pupils should have opportunities to face up to such questions as: "How is it that Jesus is now believed to be born in 4 B.C.?" or "Why, if George Washington was born on February 11, do we celebrate

---

[10] Dorothy McClure Fraser and Edith West, *Social Studies in Secondary Schools* (New York: The Ronald Press Company, 1961), pp. 181–182. Copyright © 1961, The Ronald Press Company, New York.

his birthday on February 22?" In this connection, pupils need to learn not only how unreliable tradition can be, but also that there were and are other calendars and that differences in time throughout the globe influence dating. Examples are simple enough to find. As far as calendars are concerned, pupils should be familiar with the fact that the Romans and Greeks could not have used the Christian A.D. and B.C. and that the Chinese, Persians, and Jews today utilize different calendars and celebrate the New Year at different times. The Greeks reckoned time according to Olympiads of four years, extending from 776 B.C., and the Romans figured their calendar from the founding of the city (AUC). It might be fun to translate dates from the Christian calendar to AUC or to Olympiads.

The difference in time around the world is also easy to see, but somewhat difficult to reconcile. A short time ago a group of educators from Sydney, New South Wales, talked to another group of educators in New York. In Sydney it was Sunday morning; in New York it was Saturday evening. Was the call made on Saturday or Sunday?

6. Adhere to the following principles summarized by Wesley and Wronski.

1. List related events in the order of their occurrence.
2. Ascertain approximate dates by reference to specific dates.
3. Give the length of time between two related or similar events.
4. Relate specific events to periods or general movements.
5. Compare the duration of two movements.
6. Associate the contemporary events that occur in different countries.
7. Place events by centuries, decades, or years.
8. Assign events for each of the years in a list.
9. Associate men and events and apply the dates for either to the other.[11]

TEACHING TIME DEPTH AND DURATION

Making concepts clear is extremely difficult. Time concepts, particularly concepts of time depth and time duration, are especially difficult in this respect because one usually has so little basis on which to make comparisons and contrasts. Probably no one has a really meaningful conception of what a millenium is. Even a decade is hard to realize. Ten years is not the same to the octogenarian as it is to the twelve-year-old. Nevertheless, the task needs to be undertaken. Authorities generally advocate four basic principles to follow in the attempt:

1. Teach the meaning of the terminology as clearly as possible.
2. Compare historical times with times and time durations that pupils already know and understand.
3. Use spatial representations to show time relationships.
4. Use chronology as a framework on which to hang history.

The following paragraphs will investigate each of these principles in greater detail.

---

[11] Edgar B. Wesley and Stanley P. Wronski, *Teaching Social Studies in High School*, 5th ed. (Boston: D. C. Heath & Company, 1964), p. 445. Reprinted by permission of the publisher.

Teaching Time Vocabulary. Most junior high school pupils and many older pupils, including a surprisingly large number of adult students, are quite hazy about the meaning of terms used to denote time. For this reason make a special effort to ensure that the terms denoting definite and indefinite time used in your courses become part of the pupils' working vocabulary. There are a number of strategies and tactics useful for teaching terms.

1. Ordinarily, it would probably be better to use definite dates—for example, in the decade from 1875 to 1885. However, you will have to use indefinite terms at times. When you do, try to explain what the term means, or—better yet—ask one or more of the pupils to explain it so that everyone knows. This can be done simply: ". . . during the last half of the eighteenth century. What years would that include approximately, Charles?"

2. Teach the unfamiliar terms in context as they come up. Terms such as decade, millenium, century, and generation, will usually have to be taught directly to junior high school pupils by the use of practice or drill.

3. Attempt to make the concepts truly meaningful. The pupils should learn not only that the term decade means ten years, but they should also get some idea of the span of time that ten years represents. For a 15-year-old, ten years is two thirds of his life; a decade ago he was in kindergarten. By helping him to realize this fact, the teacher may help him to get some feeling for the time involved.

4. Two words that cause confusion for pupils are generation and century. One simple device for teaching pupils the duration of both of these periods is to ask every member of the class to find how old his father was when the pupil was born. Usually, this will average out to about thirty-three years. Thus, by extension, the pupils can determine not only that a generation is the time distance between the birth dates of father and son, but also that a century is three generations long. A century ago, then, would probably be when a pupil's great grandfather was a boy of his age.

5. Pupils, college students, and gray-haired scholars all have difficulty with such phases as the nineteenth century, the fifth century B.C., and so on. A good way to teach pupils which century is which is to construct a single time line extending from several centuries B.C. to several centuries A.D. By counting and observing on such a line, pupils can see that 370 B.C. is in the first quarter of the fourth century.

$$400 \quad 300 \quad 200 \quad 100 \quad | \quad 100 \quad 200 \quad 300 \quad 400 \quad 500$$

FIGURE 8-1. *Time Line for Teaching the Centuries.*

Teaching Time Depth. By time sense we mean a real understanding of time depth that is more than just words or numbers, plus an understanding of time interrelationships such as before and after, contemporaneity, duration, and continuity. To develop real time depth is most difficult, even for adults. Short times and long times get mixed up in our experience. To a certain extent, time sense seems to be a function of age. Younger pupils seem not to have lived long enough to have much sense of time depth and time duration. Therefore, teachers must consciously work to develop time sense in secondary school pupils.

1. Compare the time concerned with a known period or with our own lives. For a pupil 15 years old in 1973, World War II began two and one-third lifetimes away, or not quite four times as long as he has been in school. World War I began two thirds of a century ago, a length of time approximately four times his lifetime and six and a half times the length of time he has gone to school. Similarly, the length of World War II was about as long as the time a pupil spends in junior and senior high school.

2. Use dates and periods that the pupil has already mastered to establish new time-depth concepts. How, for instance, does the length of the existence of the Roman Empire in the West compare with the length of time that the United States has been a nation so far? What is the chronological relationship between our War of 1812 and the Napoleonic Wars? And would it not be worthwhile to note that the American Revolution, the British Conquest of India, and the settling of Australia all occurred during the reign of George III?

3. Use spatial representations of time. Among the types that have proved useful are time lines, parallel time lines, time charts, time scrolls, and time clocks. Essentially, all of these devices use the same principle, the representing of time by linear distance.

   a. Time lines are particularly useful for showing the time relationships and the duration of periods. In making time lines, care must be taken to ensure that the line is made to scale and that the dates put on it are accurate. Although you will want to use your own time lines for illustrating chronological facts, pupils benefit most from building and filling in time lines of their own. Pupils can also learn by spotting events in the proper place on large time lines placed over the chalkboard or bulletin board, or on a time line made of a cord strung across the room on which events and periods can be hung.

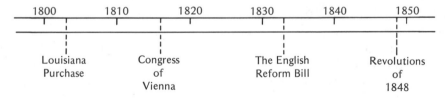

FIGURE 8-2. *Example of a Time Line.*

   (1) Parallel time lines, which compare different events in the same periods (for example, European history and United States history), are especially useful. So are time lines presented by overhead projectors on which colored flip-ons can be added to show the overlapping of events and periods.

   (2) Making time lines is an excellent culminating exercise, for it provides a way for the pupil to tie together some of the knowledge gleaned from the unit. Similarly, they are, of course, excellent material for pupils to keep in their notebooks, providing that they make their own time lines and that they are checked for accuracy.

   b. Time charts are really multiple time lines. Two common types are illustrated in Figure 8-3. They are extremely useful for showing relationships.

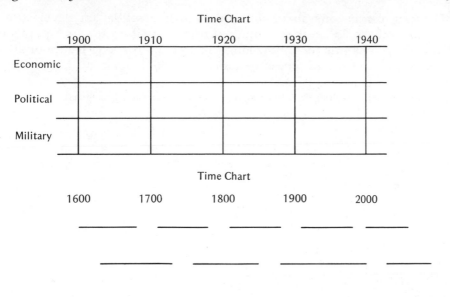

FIGURE 8-3. *Examples of Time Charts.*

As with the time lines, they are most useful when the pupils keep them themselves.

4. The time scroll is another device for pupils to keep up as they proceed through the course. It consists of a long sheet of paper rolled up from both ends like a scroll with the centuries, quarter centuries, and decades marked out on it by light parallel lines. Each pupil would have a scroll of his own on which to record all the significant historical events he studies in the units of the course. Because the pupils will need several events for the same year or period, the paper will need to be wide enough for parallel entries. If one wishes, time duration can be indicated by vertical lines.

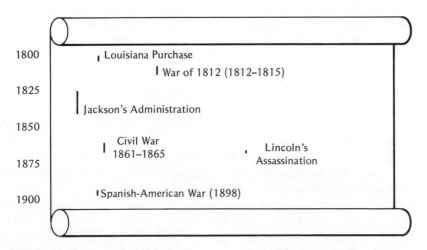

FIGURE 8-4. *A Time Scroll.*

5. Drawing conclusions about time duration is essential for developing time sense. You should be able to think of many activities in which pupils determine how long this took, how long this lasted, how long before or after this happened, and the slowness or rapidity of the course of various developments.

6. Genealogical devices are also useful in establishing time sense.

FIGURE 8-5. *Genealogical Device to Clarify Time Depth.*

7. Use chronology to develop a sense of time depth and time relationships.
   a. Chronology provides the framework of history. Its key dates give us both a framework for understanding the long course of history in general and a framework for understanding the course of specific events or periods such as the life of Napoleon or World War II. Because this is so, chronology provides a useful means for developing a time sense. Its value becomes particularly apparent when we remember that the use of such indefinite phrases as "a long time ago," and the like, has little meaning to pupils. Obviously, the way to teach time sense is to use definite dates wherever that is possible.
   b. One of the first things then is for pupils to place events according to key dates. There are many exercises for this purpose. Ordinarily, it is better to use them in the regular course of the class discussion, than to make special assignments of them. (1) In one type of exercise a date is given and then pupils are asked to tell whether other events occurred before or after it. (2) Another exercise is one in which certain events are identified as having happened after one event but before another. (3) Still another exercise is to

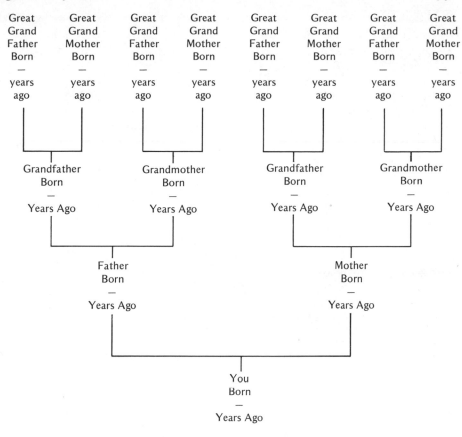

FIGURE 8-6. *A Family Tree.*

place a number of historical events in chronological order: for example, The Declaration of Independence, the Articles of Confederation, the Constitution. (4) Another exercise, which can be considerable fun, is to make up fictional anecdotes describing a period, with a number of clues thrown in, and ask pupils to guess the date of the supposed event. This can be turned into a game in which the pupils make up the anecdotes. (5) Still another device is to present pupils with an account in which key time words are underlined and ask them to give the dates of the key words.[12]

---

[12] Two of the best references on teaching time concepts are Fraser and West, op. cit., and Alice W. Spieseke, "Developing a Sense of Time and Chronology," in Carpenter, loc. cit.

CHAPTER 9

Geography

GEOGRAPHY is the study of spatial relationships. Although its subject matter includes physical, biotic, and societal elements, it can be differentiated from other disciplines by its focus on the distribution and relationships on phenomena according to place.

STRUCTURE OF GEOGRAPHY

The genius of geography is that it takes facts from various disciplines and integrates them into new wholes by interpreting them according to their spatial relationships.

ORGANIZING AND INTERPRETING THE DATA

Establishing Spatial Distributions. Once gathered, geographical facts are assembled into sets according to their distribution in specific places at specific times and are compared. Traditionally, this recording and comparing is done by mapping, although other techniques are available. The assembled sets of data give us a picture of spatial or geographical distribution from which we can draw generalizations. In plotting these distributions, it is important to note that in order to establish a spatial or geographical distribution (1) one needs to have many facts; and (2) these facts must maintain three similar elements: time, location, and essential characteristics. If in portraying the distribution one introduces information from a different time, location, or group of essential characteristics, one no longer has a distribution, but simply a collection of information. Examining and comparing distribution gives one the basis for drawing generalizations about the data collected.

The areal scope, or scale, in which data are investigated and portrayed affects the type of distributions and consequently the generalizations one can draw from them.[1] Large-scale map studies, for instance, tend to yield many generalizations of limited scope, whereas small-scale map studies are more likely to give fewer but more general conclusions. In other words, a large-scale investigation will reveal more about a smaller area, whereas a small-scale investigation will gloss over many specifics but show findings of a more general character.

---

[1] In this context, scale refers to the scale of the map on which the geographical data are, or could be, plotted. Scale is discussed in Chapter 15.

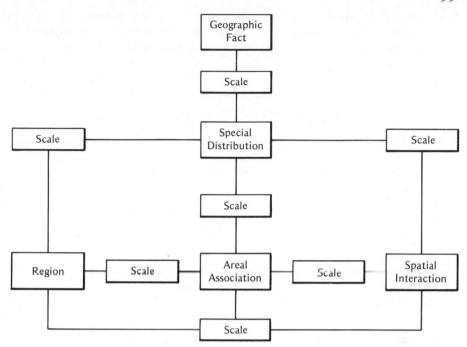

FIGURE 9-1. *Structure of Geography.* [*Edwin N. Thomas, in Clyde F. Kohn, ed.,* Selected Class Room Experiences: High School Geography Project (*Normal, Ill.: National Council for Geographic Education, 1964*), *p. 45.*]

Regions. Regions are areas that are homogeneous in one or more respects. There seem to be two basic types of regions: (1) uniform regions identified by formal features of areal association, and (2) the nodal or functional regions characterized mainly by spatial interaction.

Formal regions are made up of areas in which one element seems to vary with, and be related to, the distribution of another element or other elements. Features that vary similarly in different regions are called accordant features. Because the pattern of areal associations for accordant features of different regions conform, such regions are called uniform, or formal, regions. By comparing such regions, it is possible to find differences and similarities in the distribution of other phenomena that may explain the differences and similarities of the areas, and from which generalizations can be drawn.

Nodal, or functional, regions differ from formal regions in that they are not primarily bound together by areal associations. Rather, the functional region is *centered around a focal point* (for example, a city). The region is the area around the focal point that is controlled or influenced by it. Thus, if the focus of a functional area is a large city, the functional region consists of the suburbs and exurbs that form around and depend on the city, and that interact with it by providing it with markets, workers, and the like. The various parts of such a region are tied together by a *pattern of circulation* (for example, a transportation and communication pattern).

Furthermore, functional regions are primarily societal in nature; formal regions may be biotic, physical, societal, or any combination thereof. Functional regions tend to be dynamic and functional; formal regions, static and morphological. Nevertheless, all regions are located somewhere and have relationships with other regions, and so functional associations take on the characteristics of areal association. It is, therefore, possible to compare functional regions to find areal differentiation and to draw conclusions concerning the geographic phenomena of the regions and their relationships.

THE METHOD OF GEOGRAPHY

Basically, the method of geography involves three steps:

1. To seek out information.
   a. By observation in the field.
   b. By searching through primary and secondary documents.
2. To record and categorize what has been found.
   a. By mapping.
   b. By statistics.
   c. By other records and reports.
3. To interpret and draw conclusions from the information recorded and categorized.
   a. By logical inference.
   b. By statistical analysis.
   c. By map analysis.
   d. By a synthesis of the elements.[2]

OBJECTIVES

CURRICULUM OBJECTIVES

According to Gopsill the aim of geography

> is not so much the acquisition of factual knowledge, as the development of an enthusiasm for the work, an insight into the knowledge which geography has to offer, together with a wider contribution to the general education of children in the shape of a positive attitude toward work and the development of sound habits of study.[3]

SPECIFIC OBJECTIVES

More specifically, the objectives of geography teaching include

Attitudes

To teach attitudes and the value of careful observation.
To respect orderly, objective methods of scientific investigation.
To understand the value of seeing for ones' self.
   a. Through actual first hand observation.

[2] Excellent discussions of geography as a discipline may be found in Phillip Bacon, ed., *Focus on Geography*, Fortieth Yearbook (Washington, D.C.: National Council for the Social Studies, 1970), Part I; Jan O. M. Broek, *Geography: Its Scope and Spirit* (Columbus, Ohio: Charles E. Merrill Publishers,

   b. Through primary sources (for example, reports by someone who was
      there).
To develop love for maps.
To develop curiosity about knowing where places are.
To develop the atlas habit.
To develop curiosity about places.
To develop a sense of the uniqueness of places.
To realize that change of one of the elements may change the other elements
   and to some extent the personality of the place.
To respect the natural environment.
To realize that although "man can modify the environment, his modifications
   can have undesirable consequences as well as good ones."
To realize that the significance to "man of the physical and biotic features of
   the earth is a function of man's own abilities and that a natural resource is
   not a resource at all unless men have the ability to use it."
To develop a sense of responsibility toward society.
To develop understanding and sympathy to people of other places.

Geographic Concepts

To realize the interrelationship and interdependence of people all over the
   globe.
To understand the regional concept.
To understand that neither man nor land is dominant, but that dominance
   depends on circumstances. The relationship of man and land is an interrela-
   tionship in which each influences the other.
To understand that "natural resources aren't really resources" until men want
   to and know how to use them.
To understand all locations as relative locations.
To learn to search for the significance of location.
To learn that a distribution is "the pattern or arrangement of places classified
   according to one characteristic or the pattern or arrangement of a group of
   places which have the same characteristics."
To realize that spatial covariation is not necessarily a sign of cause-and-effect
   relationships.
To know that there are element complexes consisting of groups of elements
   usually found together and interconnected by functional relationships.
To know that the generalizations of geography, in part at least, depend on the
   scope or scale of the area being studied.
"To understand that, in addition to their static aspects, spatial relations also
   have a dynamic aspect which is expressed in movements from one place to
   another."

Geographic Facts

To know where certain places are.
To learn basic criteria for comparing distances, altitudes, populations, areas,
   and the like.

1965); and Richard Hartshorne, *The Nature of Geography*, several editions (Washington, D.C.: American Association of Geographers).

   [3] G. H. Gopsill, *The Teaching of Geography*, 2nd ed. (London: Macmillan & Company, Ltd., 1961),
pp. 17–18.

To know the general worldwide distribution of continents, landforms, climatic types, population density, transportation, temperature, rainfall, language, religion, natural resources, industry, and the like.

To know the standard sources of gathering geographic information.

Geographic Skills

To be able to read and interpret maps.

To be able to read geographic material.

To be able to observe and record geographic phenomena objectively.

To be able to prepare accurate maps.

To be able to describe an area.

To be able to formulate geographic hypotheses.[4]

GEOGRAPHY IN THE CURRICULUM

GEOGRAPHY: CURRICULUM STATUS AND TRENDS

Presently, geography seems to have a firm grip on only one of the junior-senior high school years. This year is quite likely to consist of a required seventh-grade course in either the geography of the world, the geography of Asia, Europe, and the Middle East, or sometimes the geography of the Western Hemisphere. In addition, there seems to be some movement toward the introduction of more courses in world geography in the tenth grade. Nevertheless, there seems to be plenty of evidence to indicate that geography should be taught at every grade level so that pupils can learn to understand the world in which they live and make intelligent decisions as citizens of their country and the world.

RECOMMENDATIONS OF THE NATIONAL COUNCIL FOR GEOGRAPHIC EDUCATION

A Commission of the National Council for Geographic Education recommends that geography be offered in grades K–12 in accordance with the following standards:

> In summary, the committee recommends that a geography program should steadily give evidence of (1) articulation of geographic learning, grade by grade, from K–12, because education is a continuing process, (2) procedure from a less complicated geographic region, at a given educational level to a more complicated area, (3) frequent application of the principle of adjacency in selecting a sequence of areas for study at a given educational level, (4) recognition of individual differences as far as possible, and (5) realistic experiences in geography education in contrast to mere memorization and recitation of facts and verbalistic generalizations. It should be remembered that learning takes place most easily and naturally through actual experiences and participating in activities which will give not only understandings, but control

---

[4] Based on *Advisory Paper for Teachers Associated with the High School Geography Project,* mimeo (Boulder, Colo.: The High School Geography Project, Aug. 1962), Chaps. II–IV.

over geography concepts. Consequently, we recommend much activity, experimentation, field trips, and definite opportunities for "socializing and exploratory" experiences for each learner.[5]

The sequence that the Commission recommended for the secondary grades follows. Note that there are several alternatives at the various grade levels.

Suggested Sequences of Courses for Geography

JUNIOR HIGH SCHOOL

Grade 7.   A Course on one of the following:
1. Eurasia.
2. Eastern Hemisphere.
3. Europe, the USSR, North Africa, and Southwest Asia (Arctic Ocean).
4. Our United States in the Working World.
5. Europe and the USSR.

Grade 8.
1. Local Community, State, and the United States in their larger geographic settings and world relations.
or

2. Topical Study of the United States.

Grade 9.
1. World Geography (recommended as a year's course for this grade).
or

2. Earth Science or Physical Geography.

SENIOR HIGH SCHOOL

Grade 10.
1. World Geography (if not taught in Grade 9).
or

2. World Patterns of Economic or Commercial Geography.
or

3. Economic Geography—World Distribution and Exchange.

Grade 11.
1. Geography of Latin American and Other Special Areas—depending on Current World Problems.
or

2. Geography of Local Areas within the Framework of Historical Geography of the United States.

Grade 12.
1. Geography of World Cultures.
or

2. Geography of Selected Areas.
or

[5] Wilhelmina Hill, ed., "Curriculum Guide for Geographic Education," *Geographic Education Series, No. 3* (Oak Park, Ill.: National Council for Geographic Education, 1964), p. 32.

   3. World Political Geography.
                    or
   4. Geography of Current World Problems (to be developed by teachers).

Other Suggested Courses for Senior High School

Grade 10.

   World Geography and the Geography of Selected Areas are recommended
as year courses for this grade level, but which should be offered first will be
left to the curriculum designers in individual school systems.

Grades 11 and 12.

   The following courses may be offered as either two-semester or single-
semester courses.
   1. Physical Geography or Earth Science (which stresses: (1) earth and the
      universe, (2) land and landforms, (3) minerals and rocks, (4) water and
      waterbodies, (5) weather and climate, (6) soils, (7) plant and animal
      ecological geography, and (8) relative location or spatial relations).
      Show relation to population patterns.
   2. World Patterns of Major Economies and Resources.
   3. Conservation of Resources.
   4. Elementary Meteorology.
   5. Geography of World Cultures (Nation and State).
   6. Geography of Selected Areas — Strategic Areas.
   7. World Political Geography (Geography of Current World Problems,
      other names).[6]

BASIC CURRICULUM APPROACHES TO GEOGRAPHY

   There seem to be two approaches to course organization in geography — one,
topical, the other regional. In the former, one studies a phenomenon, or set of
phenomena (that is, a topic), as it is distributed throughout the world. In the
other, one studies the phenomena that occur in an area or region. These two
approaches are not mutually exclusive; topical studies, also called systematic
studies, must always be conducted in places — that is, in regions; and regional
studies must always concern phenomena — that is, topics. It is the emphasis that
really makes the distinction.

   The Topical Approach.   At the moment, most school geography is based on
regional study. However, a movement toward more use of the topical approach
seems to be beginning. Where teachers adopt the topical approach, they can, and
perhaps should, group the topics around a regional framework.
   An example of this type of strategy is Dale Lott's unit, "The World Is Rich and
Poor," in which pupils compare two regions, one a "have" nation and one a
"have-not" nation, and draw conclusions about them.[7]

---

   [6] Ibid., pp. 40–50. A suggested sequence of units for each of the courses is listed in the report.
   [7] Dale R. Lott, "The World Is Rich and Poor," ditto (Jersey City, N. J.: Jersey City State College,
nd).

The Regional Approach. Where the regional concept retains favor, there seems to be a movement away from regions based on continents, or even on nation-states, to cultural areas. James, one of the foremost authorities on the teaching of geography, argues for cultural areas based on the impact of the industrial and democratic revolutions on preexistent cultures.[8] The culture areas proposed by James are

> European (Western, Southern, and Northern Europe).
> Soviet (The Soviet Union and Eastern Europe).
> Anglo-American (Canada and the United States).
> Latin American (Mexico, Central America, South America, the Antilles, and the Bahamas).
> North African–Southwest Asian (The Moslem countries from Morocco to Afghanistan and Israel).
> South Asian (India, Pakistan, Ceylon, and border countries).
> Southeast Asian (The "shatter belt" between India and China).
> East Asian (China, Japan, and bordering countries).
> African (The countries south of the Sahara).
> Australian-New Zealand (The countries of British origin in Australasia).
> Pacific (The islands of Melanesia, Micronesia, and Polynesia).[9]

Any region consists of three major components: people, the physical environment, and societal phenomena. The region must also have areal extent, be located somewhere, and exist in time. But the quality that really identifies a region is the homogeneity or near homogeneity of certain characteristics or criteria. In cultural areas this homogeneity is societal. Warman suggests that the criteria for definition of cultural areas should be

> Land.
> Labor.
> Capital.
> Governmental systems.
> Behavior of inhabitants.
> Attitude of people.
> Locational efficiency.[10]

Warman's Nine Major Concepts. Warman also suggests that geography courses be centered around nine major concepts: Globalism, The Round Earth on the Flat Paper, The Life Layer, Areal Distinctions, Differences and Likenesses, The Region (and Regionalism), Resources Culturally Defined, Man—The Chooser, Spatial Interaction, and Perpetual Transformation.[11]

At every grade level, whatever region is being studied, the content of the

---

[8] Preston E. James, "Geography," in *The Social Sciences and the Social Studies*, The American Council of Learned Societies and the National Council for the Social Studies (New York: Harcourt Brace Jovanovich, Inc., 1962), pp. 80–81.

[9] Ibid.

[10] Henry J. Warman, "Suggested Guidelines to the Content of Geography in Secondary Schools," *The Social Studies*, **54**:207–211 (Nov. 1963).

[11] Henry J. Warman, "Major Concepts in Geography," in Hill, op. cit., Chap. II.

course should, according to his thesis, be aimed at furthering pupils' under-standing of the nine concepts. Although there may not be general agreement on details, Warman's and James' theses seem to be fairly well accepted among ex-perts in geography teaching. They are included in the course sequences suggested by the Commission of the National Council for Geographic Educa-tion mentioned earlier.

Summary. As we can see from the foregoing, up-to-date geography courses are usually regionally organized, although some may be organized topically, and are designed to build up general geographic concepts, the habit of thinking geo-graphically, and skill in using the tools and methods of geography. They are not usually concerned with facts, except as facts serve to build up larger under-standings. Similarly, place location is no longer an end in geography teaching. A certain amount of knowledge of place location is necessary, of course, but, again, only as it serves as a tool for higher understanding.

STRATEGIES AND TACTICS FOR TEACHING GEOGRAPHY

The foregoing discussion of the structure of geography should give us a number of clues concerning the strategies one should use in teaching geography. The way to learn about geography is to examine or analyze distributions, com-pare salient factors in the distribution, and synthesize new facts and general-izations from these analyses and comparisons. It follows, then, that geography should be taught largely by inquiry strategies and tactics. To be most successful, geography classes should be conducted as laboratories. The following maxims make a good guide:

1. Study effects before causes.
2. Study human activity before physical conditions.
3. Study small areas before large areas.
4. Present descriptive data before asking children to do relational thinking (which is the essence of geography).[12]

TEACH THE TOOLS OF GEOGRAPHY

To carry out the type of teaching implied by the proceeding discussion and the structure of the discipline, you must teach the tools of geography.

1. Maps. Pupils need to learn to read, interpret, and make maps. The ability to place information on maps and the ability to interpret a map's message are para-mount in geographic study. (Map skills are discussed in detail in Chapter 15.)
2. Statistical analysis. Pupils studying geography should not only have prac-tice in reading charts, graphs, tables, and the like, but also experience in making them. In addition, senior high school geography students should have experi-

---

[12] *Report of the Commission on the Teaching of Geography in School,* International Geographic Union, Eighteenth International Geographic Congress (Rio De Janeiro: Aug. 9–18, 1956). Reprinted by Denoyer Geppert Company, Chicago, Ill., p. 15.

ence with such simple statistics as measures of central tendency, measures of spread, indices of correlation, scatter diagrams, and the like.

3. Photointerpretation. Although photointerpretation is a highly sophisticated art, aerial photos can be, and should be, used in geography classes to illustrate topographical elements and show the topography of a region. Both vertical and oblique photos can be read after a minimum of instruction. Stereo-pairs require only a little more instruction and give the advantage of a three-dimensional picture of the area.

4. Field study and observation. Pupils should have experience in the field observing, mapping, and reporting geographic phenomena, for example, patterns of circulation, population density, land use, and the like.

5. Study of documents. Documentary study consists of analyzing and interpreting data gathered by others. It is essentially the same technique used by the historian, or any other scholar, when he attempts to study phenomena he has not observed directly.

TEACHING THE GEOGRAPHIC SKILLS

The pupils should learn the geographic skills as soon as possible. Types of skills useful for activity-centered classes and out-of-doors geography include

1. Developing a sense of space and time distance.
2. Observing, identifying, recording, and interpreting out-of-doors data, scenes, and landscapes.
3. Identifying geographic specimens and scenes within buildings.
4. Making, reading, and interpreting maps, and reading and interpreting globes.
5. Taking, reading, and interpreting pictures.
6. Making, reading, and interpreting models and graphic forms such as sketches, diagrams, graphs, profiles, cross sketches, and three-dimensional illustrations.[13]

FIELD STUDY

Insofar as it is feasible, pupils should study geography in the field. Examples of field activities include

1. Observation of the sun.
2. Observation of cultural and physical features.
3. Measuring distance, area, and extent.
4. Locating and giving direction to places.
5. Mapping.
6. Keeping a daily record of the weather: record temperature, precipitation, wind direction, wind speed, cloud cover, and so on.
7. Observing weather signs: check weather instruments, study local weather maps, and predict the next day's weather.
8. Measuring precipitation: use a straight-sided can and measure with a ruler.

[13] Thomas Frank Barton, "Geography Skills and Techniques," in Hill, op. cit., p. 54.

9. Making terrain sketches.

10. Making transects.

11. Keeping a geographic diary for short periods of the year: for example, at the time of the equinoxes and solstices. Information recorded in the diary could include:

> Time and direction of sunrise.
> Time and direction of sunset.
> Length of day.
> Daily maximum temperature.
> Daily minimum temperature.
> Daily mean temperature.
> Amount of rain recorded in previous twenty-four hours.
> Air pressure.
> Wind direction and velocity (at time of maximum velocity).
> Relative humidity.
> Clouds—type, amount of sky covered.
> Copy of weather map.
> Notes on the interrelationships of the pattern of isobars, wind direction and
>   force, temperature, rainfall.[14]

12. Estimating the degree of slope: use a table similar to the following, if the pupils cannot compute gradients.

Table 9-1. To Estimate Degree of Slope*

Angle	Gradient	Descriptive Term	Difficulty of Movement
45°	1:1	Extremely steep	Very hard going; hands help; dangerous.
25°	1:2	Very steep	Formidable obstacle; best walked on a zig-zag course.
18°	1:3	Steep	Walking requires definite effort; dangerous for motor traffic.
11°	1:5	Fairly steep	Steep gradient for modern motor traffic; troublesome for heavy vehicles.
6°	1:10	Moderate	Requires slight effort when walking. Taken at reasonable speed by modern cars; heavy vehicles use low gears; cyclists walk if it involves a long uphill approach.
3°	1:20	Gently sloping	Limit for easy cycling.
1°	1:60	Almost level	Movement is easy; can be undesirably steep for steam locomotives.

* See footnote 14.

STUDY OF LOCAL GEOGRAPHY

Local field study can be one of the most profitable of geographic studies.

1. It arouses pupil interest.

[14] The Faculty of Education, Sydney Teachers College, "Local Geography in the Secondary School," *Sydney Teachers College Research Publication, No.* 1 (Sydney, N.S.W.: The College, 1962), p. 8.

2. It provides for individual differences through individualizing assignments and projects.

3. It assists pupils in formulating accurate concepts through firsthand, real experiences.

4. It develops skills in using the methods and tools of geography.

5. It allows for pupil planning and self-directions.[15]

Selecting the Area of Study. In selecting the area for study, use the following· criteria:

1. Will study of the area develop fundamental geographic concepts?
2. Are data concerning the area available?
3. Is it accessible to the pupils?
4. Is it large enough to provide pupils with opportunities to observe significant geographical phenomena and interrelationships?
5. Is it small enough so that pupils can really observe it?

It may be necessary to conduct several studies of one aspect or to study various aspects of the area successively.

Organizing Local Studies. In organizing the local field study, give particular attention to the following considerations:

1. The preparation of a programme which provides both for the gradation of study of the local area and for the integration of its study with that of other geographical topics and areas.
2. Possible adjustments in the school timetable to enable pupils to work out-of-doors.
3. Attention to details for the organization and conduct of field work, such as making arrangements for transport, selecting points from which observations will be made, planning the particular work to be done at each point.
4. Work to be done by pupils, prior to out-door study, to assist them to benefit from field work, e.g. drawing a cross-section for use in the preparation of a transect.
5. Types of assignments designed to direct observation in the field, e.g.,
   a. Answering a questionaire.
   b. Landscape sketching.
   c. Working exercises in map interpretation.
   d. Drawing a form line map of observable landforms.
   e. Recording information on a base map.
   f. Preparing a transect.
   g. Collecting and labelling specimens.
   h. Completing a table noting essential features of the landscape by regions.
   i. Collecting material to be used in the preparation of an essay on a particular topic.

[15] This list and much of the discussion following have been adapted from "Local Geography in the Secondary School," which is one of the best references on using local geography in teaching.

      j. Taking photographs and annotating them to show location and signifi-
         cance.
   6. Use to be made of secondary sources of material.
   7. Work to be done by pupils following observation in the field.[16]

Suggested Content for Local Field Study

1. Description of area.
   a. Natural elements.
      (1) Landforms.
      (2) Climate.
      (3) Vegetation.
      (4) Soil.
   b. Cultural elements.
      (1) Population.
      (2) Land use.
      (3) Settlement.
      (4) Transport and communication.
2. Interrelationships of the elements.
3. The origin of the geographical elements.
4. Syntheses into generalizations.
5. Development of global concepts.

EXAMPLES OF LEARNING ACTIVITIES IN GEOGRAPHY

1. Use many map activities.
   a. Compare phenomena by plotting them on maps.
   b. Compare phenomena as plotted on maps.
   c. Use map transparencies. Use flip-ons to show phenomena.
   d. Let pupils prepare map transparencies and flip-ons.
   e. Make a collection of special purpose maps. Pupils can find them in maga-
      zines, newspapers, and the like.
   f. Build terrain models.
   g. Make distribution maps (for example, population, weather, and world-
      pattern maps from data gathered by pupils).
   h. Check generalizations presented in texts by maps and mapwork.
   i. Let pupils identify terrain features on the ground from map information.
      Give close attention to symbols.
2. Ask pupils to sketch an area described in their geography book. Emphasize
   that the idea is not to create great works of art, but to show the idea. This
   activity is good for summarizing and testing.
3. Have pupils make shadow boxes, terrain models, layouts, dioramas.
4. Use models, shadow boxes, layouts, and dioramas to illustrate geographical
   principles.
5. Use pictures. In geography, pictures are a must. When pupils cannot see
   things on the ground, they should see pictures of them. Geographical abstractions can be difficult to understand; pictures can make them concrete.
   They are excellent for building up basic concepts, stimulating thinking, and

---

[16] Ibid., p. 18.

catching pupil interest. As a rule, still pictures are more useful than moving pictures, and color pictures more useful than black and white.

   a. Present pupils with pictures. From these pictures let them draw inferences concerning the nature of the land, rainfall, economics, and culture. In doing so,

      (1) Direct pupils' attention to significant factors.

      (2) Ask pupils to explain what they see.

      (3) Ask pupils to interpret and make inferences from what they see.

      (4) Compare pictures of one place with those of another. Let pupils pick out and explain the similarities and differences, for example:

Florida	California

   b. Have pupils collect and exhibit pictures that show different landforms, weather, climatic conditions, crops, and so on. Arrange them and present them so that they tell a story (for example, the difference in crops as one moves from cold to hot areas, or from wet to dry areas).

   c. Have pupils prepare murals. This activity is excellent for pupil committees.

   d. Have pupils make individual desk murals. Use them for summarizing, review, or research.

6. Use posters to brighten up classes and to give information. They are especially useful for motivation and as bases for discussion. Posters can be procured from travel agencies, railroads, airlines, steamship companies, and foreign governmental information agencies. Pupils can also prepare their own posters.

7. Have pupils make charts and graphs.

8. Let pupils make up newspapers or magazines featuring geographic events. The finished newspaper or magazine can be duplicated or posted on the bulletin board. Include in it such material as,

   a. Newstories of a geographical nature with commentary explaining geographic aspects.

   b. Editorials explaining the geography behind the news.

   c. Weather.

   d. Special features, such as articles about travel, the dress and costumes of people in other lands, unusual facts, and so on.

   e. Advertisements of products of various countries and regions.

   f. Pictures, drawings, illustrations, and other art work.[17]

9. Let pupils plan and prepare a booklet about a country or region. One com-

---

[17] See Linnie B. James and LaMonte Crape, *Geography for Today's Children* (New York: Appleton-Century-Crofts, 1968), pp. 237–239, for more suggestions for preparing pupil newspapers.

mittee can be charged with the planning, another with the artwork, and so on. Each pupil could be responsible for a page. What to include could be worked out by class and teacher in a whole-class planning session. The booklet can be duplicated and distributed to the pupils.

10. Let pupils make up radio and television commercials advertising the products or advantages of an area.

11. Encourage pupils to prepare travel brochures or pamphlets advertising the area being studied.

12. Study the foods of an area.
    a. Have pupils procure and serve samples of the food characteristic of the area being studied.
    b. Prepare menus characteristic of the areas and compare them with other menus.
    c. Put on a dinner in which foreign food is served. This can be great fun and is enjoyed by youths and adults alike. Sometimes adult groups will help. Ethnic societies are often glad to participate.

13. Bring in visitors and speakers. Travelers, American natives of foreign countries, visitors from other nations, and representatives of foreign governments can sometimes be persuaded to visit the school and tell pupils what it is like in other countries. Some schools have adopted ships and have been visited by the masters. Airlines pilots and stewardesses, representatives of travel firms, and so on, are likely to be well versed on information important to geography classes. So also are employees of the departments of agriculture, resources, and commerce; port authorities; and international industrial concerns.

14. Use problems. There are many ways for the geography teacher to use problem-solving and inquiry techniques. Some have already been mentioned. Other suggestions are to
    a. Examine distribution maps. What accounts for the differences in distribution?
    b. Make a simple barometer.
    c. Give pupils a map and a physical description of an area. Let them individually interpret these data and determine the type of housing, clothing, food, crops, work, exports, imports, and the like that one would expect to find in such an area.
    d. Study a local area in depth.
    e. Give pupils maps and data sheets about an area. Where would they put an industrial plant? Where a supermarket?
    f. Investigate problems such as
       (1) Where is there need for another canal to supplement the Panama Canal? Where should it be put?
       (2) Why are certain places densely populated? Why are others not? Why did New York become the major port rather than Boston or Halifax?[18]

15. Use simulation games, such as the Game of Agriculture, in which pupils take the part of farmers during a certain historical period.

[18] For an excellent example of how to conduct problem solving from the beginning to the end, see Bertha Boya Thompson, "An Experiment in Problem Solving," in Kohn, ed., op. cit., pp. 1–4. For further suggestions on teaching geography, particularly good references are Gopsill, loc. cit.; Raymond H. Muessig and Vincent R. Rogers, "Suggested Methods for Teachers," in Broek, loc. cit., Ch. 11; and Thralls, loc. cit.

CHAPTER 10

Political Science and Citizenship Education

POLITICAL SCIENCE

THE STRUCTURE OF THE DISCIPLINE

For our purposes, political science can be defined as

> a contextual discipline, committed to the description and evaluation of the institutions of government and also to finding ways in which the highly specialized knowledge of any or all disciplines can be used to guide policy.[1]

Driscoll goes on to say that

> Presumably, then, the function of the political scientist is to study and describe the actions and probable consequences of the action of modern governments, to study and explain the beliefs and values on which such actions are based, and to evaluate both the beliefs and the actions.[2]

Important Ideas and Relationships. David Easton, of the University of Chicago, has developed a list of the important idea relationships of political science and a diagram of their relationships. His list includes the following ideas:

> 1. Members of society have many wants which they hope to satisfy.
> 2. Some of these wants will be satisfied through the economic system, family system, educational system, and religious system. Wants that cannot be satisfied by any of these systems are channeled to the political system.
> 3. As the people's wants enter the political system for satisfaction, they become demands. These demands are screened.

[1] Jean M. Driscoll, "The Nature of Political Science," in *Political Science in the Social Studies*, Donald H. Riddle and Robert S. Cleary, eds., Thirty-sixth Yearbook (Washington, D. C.: National Council for the Social Studies, 1966), p. 31.
[2] Ibid., p. 39.

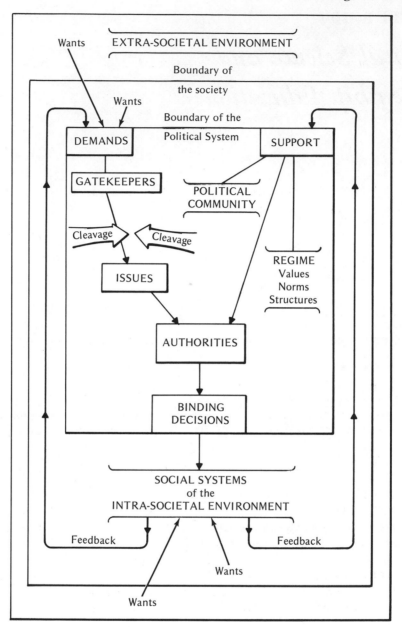

FIGURE 10-1. *Systems Analysis of Political Life.* [*See Footnote 3.*]

4. The screening process operates through formal or informal organizations. These organizations act as gate keepers. Some of the demands vanish.
Others become issues debated in the political community (a group who share
a desire to work together as a unit in the political solution of problems).

5. The issues are molded by cleavages in the political community and by
the authorities which translate these demands into binding decisions.

6. The binding decisions affect the social systems and the participants in
them, generating positive or negative support.

7. The support may be directed toward the political community, toward the regime (a political system which incorporates a particular set of values and norms, and a particular structure of authority), and/or toward the authorities (the particular persons who occupy positions of political power within the structure of authority).

8. The binding decisions generate new wants which appear again at the gate of the political system asking for recognition.

9. The source of the support for the political community, regime, and authorities may originate from the social systems in the form of education, patriotism, and other mechanisms.[3]

A diagram showing the relationship of these ideas appears as Figure 10-1.

POLITICAL SCIENCE IN THE CURRICULUM

Curriculum Objectives for Political Science Courses. According to Cleary and Riddle,[4] the objectives of political science in the curriculum should be

1. To learn how to gather information.
2. To learn ways of using political science knowledge and methods.
3. To learn to think critically about political phenomena; in short, to be an educated man.

In addition the broad goals of teaching political science and government probably should include citizenship education goals:
Understanding the nature of political science, its scope, and methodology.
Knowledge of governmental and political structures and how they work.
Skills in political and governmental processes.
Attitudes favorable to participation in political and governmental processes in order to promote the general welfare of the entire community at every level: local, state, national, and international.
Appreciation of the goals, values, and ideals of the American way of life.
The determination to live by the goals, values, and ideals of the American way of life, to preserve them, and to help achieve those not as yet achieved.

Courses in political science and government offered in most schools do not achieve these objectives.

Present Status of Political Science in the Curriculum. The courses in the government area most frequently offered in secondary schools are civics, govern-

---

[3] Lawrence Senesh, "Organizing a Curriculum Around Social Science Concepts," in Irving Morrissett, ed., *Concepts and Structure in the New Social Science Curricula* (New York: Holt, Rinehart & Winston, Inc., 1967), pp. 28–30. Copyright © 1967. Reprinted by permission of Holt, Rinehart & Winston, Inc. For a fuller discussion of political science as a discipline, see such works as Vernon Iredell, "Political Science," in John V. Michaelis and A. Montgomery Johnson, eds., *The Social Sciences: Foundations of the Social Studies* (Boston: Allyn & Bacon, Inc., 1965; Riddle and Cleary, eds., op. cit.; and Francis J. Sorauf, *Political Science: An Informal Overview* (Columbus, Ohio: Charles E. Merrill Publishers, 1965).

[4] Op. cit., pp. 8–9.

ment, and problems of democracy. As a rule, the political science in these courses is simply a description of institutions. This approach is not satisfactory. Rather, the content of courses dealing with government and political science should be oriented toward pupil involvement in the processes of government.[5] It is for this reason that courses are being increasingly centered on pupil development of central ideas, the inference of basic generalization, and the use of the methods of inquiry.

Recommended Curriculum Content. If courses in government and political science are to fulfill their objectives, the content of the courses must include, among others, such topics as
    Nature of the American Party System
    Social Structure of Society
    Nature of Representative Government
    Influence of Economic Groups
    Public Opinion
    Capitalism
    Labor and Management
    Progress Toward Political Democracy: Success and Failures
    Democracy versus Totalitarianism
    Meaning of Freedom and Equality
    The United States and the World Community
    Defense and Security
    Current Political Issues
    Racial Conflict
    The Pluralistic Nature of American Life: Contributions of and Problems
      Caused by the Variety of Racist, Religious, and Ethnic Groups
    Law and Order
The important consideration here is that the matters discussed be real, important, and pertinent to the goals of government-oriented courses. They should not be part of an ivory-tower attitude; they can and must be controversial; they should also be solid.

The topics studied in political science courses should allow for frank discussions of social problems. In studying the topics, the pupils should have plenty of opportunities to develop skill in political analysis so that in the future they will have the abilities necessary for facing and answering new social questions. Practice in forming generalizations, drawing inferences, predicting possibilities, and explaining new phenomena is essential. Furthermore, as Robinson points out, the methodology, content, and school climate must be attuned to the conditions pupils see in their own lives, or else civic education becomes an exercise in futility and is "likely to be a vehicle for self-deception."[6]

Teaching Methodology for Political Science Education. In keeping with this curriculum, government oriented courses should feature laboratory practice

[5] Norton E. Long, "Political Science," in the American Council of Learned Societies and the National Council for the Social Studies, *The Social Studies and the Social Sciences* (New York: Harcourt, Brace Jovanovich, Inc., 1962), pp. 104–105.

[6] Donald W. Robinson, *Promising Practices in Civic Education* (Washington, D. C.: National Council for the Social Studies, 1967), p. 38.

in citizenship, jurisprudential teaching, role playing, problem solving, simulation, and open-ended and divergent questioning.

CITIZENSHIP EDUCATION

Although most of the preceding discussion has been aimed at political science courses, all of it applies to citizenship education, the primary difference being that citizenship education has a much broader scope than government-oriented courses, and that it is simultaneously the business of all the courses and other activities in the school.

SAMPLE STRATEGIES AND TECHNIQUES FOR CITIZENSHIP EDUCATION AND GOVERNMENT-ORIENTED COURSES

Activities Concerning Government

1. Have pupils study a situation, as in Golding's *The Lord of the Flies* or Stewart's *Earth Abides*, for instance, where people try to live without a government.
2. Have pupils compare the form of the local government with that of other towns and cities.
3. Have pupils prepare a booklet describing the government and life in their school.
4. Have pupils examine the town report (or the local budget), analyze it, and compare it with those of other towns or cities.
5. Have pupils discuss the state and national budget. What is the money spent for? Compare it with past years. What trends can be seen?
6. Have pupils make a list of services of the local government. Let them discuss how these services affect them.
7. Have pupils investigate and discuss such topics as the following.
   a. Suppose you were a legislator who wanted the state to pass stronger legislation about pollution. What would you have to do?
   b. Suppose you were a citizen who wanted the law passed. What could you do?
8. Have pupils invite officials and government employees to the class to explain the problems, procedures, and services of their agency or arm of government.
9. Have pupils study, analyze, and discuss crucial court cases. In their study they might give special emphasis to the constitutional rights of defendants.
10. Have pupils discuss what could happen if there were not the Fifth Amendment, or similar provisions in our constitution and laws.
11. Have pupils discuss how the Bill of Rights or some other measure affects youth. How does it apply to high school pupils?
12. Encourage pupils to take part in school politics by giving them a real role in the management of their school and class affairs.
13. Have pupils study and discuss incidents of graft and dishonesty, but counter them with studies of cases of real service.

Activities in Propaganda Analysis. Study propaganda in politics and government. Have pupils use exercises and activities similar to those described in Chapter 5.

Activities Concerning Issues

1. Have pupils compare editorials in newspapers on a current issue with editorials on the same issue a decade or more ago.
2. Tape portions of radio and television programs such as "Face the Nation" or "Meet the Press," and replay them as bases for class discussion.
3. Have pupils analyze the speeches and press statements of the President, governor, mayor, and other officials as printed in newspapers of record or broadcast on TV or radio.
4. Have pupils conduct opinion polls on some current issue.
5. Have pupils make a list of organizations and predict what positions they would take on various bills and why.

Outside Civic Activities and Projects

1. Work for a few hours per week as volunteers in local settlement houses, neighborhood centers, and so on.
2. Conduct a community survey that would provide useful data for the school or community (for example, traffic or pollution problems) and make recommendations.
3. Study a bill and actively work for its passage (or defeat) by obtaining signatures for petitions, by attending and speaking at hearings, and the like.
4. Participate in such civic activities as planting lawns and flower beds, soliciting for the United Fund drive, clean-up campaigns, and the like.
5. Investigate candidates' stands on election issues, inform the community of them by means of speeches, publications, and visits to civic groups.
6. Plan and conduct assemblies.
7. Conduct a student city-government laboratory. Nominate and elect city officials: mayor, clerks, and councilmen. Follow the local election laws and procedures, modified as necessary during the campaign and election. After the elected officers have been chosen, they should select the appointed officers. Once elected or appointed, the pupil officials study the positions to which they have been elected. After this preparation, both elected and appointed pupil officials carry out the duties of their offices for a day under the guidance of the real officials.

Charts, Graphs, Bulletin Boards, Flannel Boards, and Exhibits

1. Have pupils, as individuals or in committees, prepare world maps illustrating the types of governments in various countries and countries in the various political blocks.
2. Have pupil committees make wall charts, flannel graphs, bulletin boards, or exhibits that illustrate the agencies of the Federal, state, or local government; the United Nations; a comparison of the structure, provision, and powers of the student council with the provisions of the United States Constitution; how a bill becomes a law, and so on.

Dramas, Role Playing, and Simulations

1. Hold mock sessions of Congress, legislative hearings, and the like.

2. Enact the passing of a law. Divide the class into a lower and an upper house, with the necessary functionaries, and let the pupils go through the procedures necessary in passing a law.

3. Utilize simulation games.

4. Have pupils role play prominent figures being interviewed on certain issues, or presenting their views on topics in speeches. Pupils will have to prepare themselves to know something of the issues involved and the position of the person whose role they are playing.

5. Have pupils role play a conference of a group of persons who are to set up a colony on the moon, or some uninhabited island. What laws, agreements, and rules would they need in the new settlement so that they could get along?

6. Make up a group of fictitious legislators, each with certain characteristics (for example, rural Southern, college graduate, farmer, elderly, Protestant, widower, childless, Democrat). Have pupils role play the positions these characters would probably take on such and such a bill.

7. Have pupils prepare and present mock television or radio programs on government, issues, or what have you.

Debates, Panels, and Forums

1. Have pupils conduct a debate, panel, or forum on an important issue. If feasible, make the presentation at a school assembly, a club meeting, another class, or at a meeting of an adult civic club or similar organization.

2. Have pupils conduct a mock court in which they argue the pros and cons of some contemporary issue, proposed legislation, or whatever. (See Jury Trial Technique, Chapter 4.)

Collecting Activities

1. Have pupils collect newspaper clippings, cartoons, pictures, and other materials illustrative of such topics as the machinery of local, state, or national government, current issues, or proposed legislation. There is much free and inexpensive material available. Have pupils write for it.

2. Encourage pupils to take pictures of places connected with a local issue or problem, or to illustrate larger ones.

3. Encourage pupils to take pictures of local governmental activities, or local aspects of state or national government.

4. Have pupils make a notebook of clippings illustrating activities of the Congress, the state legislature, or governmental activities. Each clipping should have commentary written by the student explaining the significance of the clipping.

5. Have pupils collect and make into a booklet stories about things done to make democracy really work.

Trips

1. Have pupils attend political meetings.
2. Have pupils visit the state legislature, a town meeting, a meeting of the city council, a legislative committee meeting, court hearings, and the like.

3. Have pupils attend meetings of community groups.
4. Have pupils participate in exchange programs.
   a. Inner city with suburbia and/or vice versa, for a day.
   b. Exchange programs abroad.
      (1) School Affiliation Service of American Friends Service Committee.
      (2) The Experiment in International Living.
   c. Exchange with communities in other parts of the country.
5. Perhaps it might be possible to arrange a field trip similar to the unusual and exciting program at Verde Valley School in Sedona, Arizona. In this program pupils visit the Hopi and Navaho Indian Reservations for a week and spend their spring vacation in Mexico. These trips give the pupils opportunities to hear explanations of civic problems by civic leaders and officials. In Mexico the pupils live in Mexican homes.

Investigations and Reports. Encourage pupils to engage in both individual and group research activities. Among the types of research activities pupils might try are:

1. Trace the history of a problem or issue (race relations, for example) over a period of years.
2. Prepare a background paper on a governmental agency.
3. Prepare an annotated bibliography of source readings by writing synopses and comments about supplementary readings on index cards. The pupils' cards can be collected, alphabetized, and used as a bibliography for future classes.
4. Rewrite newspaper stories as they probably would be written in a dictatorship.
5. Compare the output of the legislature during the first month of a session with that of the last month of the session. Why the difference?
6. As a whole class or committee, compile a booklet in which the public services of government agencies are listed.
7. Write to the local state senator or assemblyman to ask him why he took the position he did on a certain bill or question.
8. Conduct a public opinion poll. Analyze and report.

Interviews

1. Have pupils interview prominent functionaries about their jobs, their responsibilities, and their headaches. Let them report on the interviews or tape the interviews to replay for the class. A telephone interview in which all pupils can hear the interviewee and even ask questions can be very interesting and not so terribly expensive or difficult to arrange. Items that might be asked in the interview would include,
   a. Offices held.
   b. Education.
   c. Hobbies.
   d. Academic interest in school.
   e. Extracurricular interest in school.
   f. Reasons for becoming interested in the career.
   g. Tips concerning the political life.
   h. Facts about the job.

2. Similarly, have pupils interview people from foreign lands or who have lived under different forms of government.

Election and Voting Activities

1. At election times, have the social studies class cover the elections. Pupils can study the parties, campaign methods, election rules, and voting procedures. Encourage pupils to campaign for the parties or candidates of their choice. Hold an election to see who is the winner as far as the class or school is concerned.

2. Send representatives to the League of Women Voters' "Meet the Candidates" meetings. Have them report back to the class.

3. Investigate and debate the platform of the parties and candidates.

4. Conduct class and school elections as in a regular campaign. Study campaign and party politics and election procedures at this time. In some schools the social studies classes carry out the elections. In this activity they set up the election rules, appoint the election officials, prepare the tests for nominees and voters, report the vote, and so on.

5. Help the pupils conduct a political rally. Have campaign managers for the major parties. Let them arrange for a presentation of the platform, campaign speeches, the distribution of campaign literature, and the like.

6. Have pupils work with the party of their choice. After they have declared their affiliation, they can volunteer to help get out the vote. In such a project pupils would be encouraged to attend political meetings and rallies and to volunteer to work with campaign committees.

7. Conduct a political practicum.

8. Conduct a mock election.

TO CONDUCT A MOCK CAMPAIGN

1. Separate political science or civics classes into two parties and nonpartisan groups active in the community election. Once pupils find suitable positions in these parties and groups, they carry out the actual activities persons in such positions would perform.

2. The mock parties form platforms and select candidates to represent actual campaigners.

3. The mock candidates and campaign managers map out detailed strategies with mock party workers. The strategies should include
   a. Distributing literature.
   b. Canvassing homerooms.
   c. Speeches by candidates.
   d. Rallies for students.
   e. Debates between candidates.
   f. Fund-raising projects.
   g. Coordinating the activities of nonpartisan groups.
   h. Conducting a poll among the student body.
   i. Setting up registration and voting procedures.

4. Encourage cooperation and competition among all the groups to learn the actual give-and-take process of practical politics.

5. During the mock election the total student body serves as the public. As potential voters they
   a. Register as voters on a voluntary basis.
   b. Are available as subjects for the preelection polls conducted.
   c. Participate in rallies, attend speeches, and the like.
   d. Participate as a public that needs information. Thus
      (1) Demonstrating the need for an informed electorate.
      (2) Acting as a check for the mock campaigners' effort, as compared to actual public inclinations.[7]

POLITICAL PRACTICUM[8]

The political practicum is a program of laboratory and field activities in the realm of practical politics conducted in the community prior to and during primary and general elections. In this practicum, students serve with political leaders in the local political organizations in their neighborhoods at the precinct and ward levels. It is hoped that by working directly with political leaders for two weeks or so, and by correlating their classroom learning with laboratory field practice, pupils will learn about such political realities as registration of voters, campaigning for votes, and how elections are won and lost. Ordinarily a political practicum would be a part of a course in United States Government, but it could be used as well in a Problems of American Democracy course.

PLANNING THE PRACTICUM

Planning the political practicum requires much detailed work in order to ensure that there are no loose ends. Begin to make plans at least six months in advance.

If the practicum is to take place before and during the November election, plan to spend September discussing the political parties, their nature, structure, and function in our democracy, and registration procedures. It is advisable for pupils

---

[7] Among the most promising sources of ideas for teaching civic education are Donald W. Robinson, et al., *Promising Practices in Civic Education* (Washington, D. C.: National Council for the Social Studies, 1967) and William S. Vincent, ed., *Laboratory Practices in Citizenship* (New York: Citizenship Education Project, Teachers College, Columbia University, 1958).

[8] This account of the political practicum is taken, somewhat abridged and modified, from "Preparation for Active Participation in Government," a resource unit in the social studies for the twelfth grade, prepared by a group of Jersey City State College juniors under the supervision of Professor Norman W. Beck, Director of the Practicum in Practical Politics at the college. The students making up the political practicum resource unit committee were

Juliet Caruso, editor	James Norris
Vincent Baldassano	Robert Scala
Carol Collins	Marlene Securda
Andrew Cornelia	Sonia Spector
Mary Ann Gogliucci	Sharon Smith
Clara Ketten	Edward Spencer
Robert Kulessa	Judie Stele
Robert Lutter	Judith Wiuff

The resource unit prepared by these students is based on their own experiences in the political practicum conducted by Professor Beck.

to begin work with cooperating leaders in time to help out in the intensive registration drive.

In making your plans, you should consider and provide for a number of administrative details and problems. In this connection, you will probably find it necessary to make plans that will provide for

1. The preparation of a guide for each pupil. This guide should list
   a. The goals of the practicum.
   b. Conditions and guidelines that must be observed.
   c. Required activities.
   d. Optional activities.
   e. Other necessary instructions.
2. Identification of the ward and election districts in which class members live, and the names of the party leaders.
3. Provision for sample representation at events when the number of pupils is too large for full attendance. These representatives will report their observations to the whole class.
4. Keeping the number and the size of the tasks manageable. Guard against the involvement of pupils in the practicum to the extent that it encroaches upon their other classes.
5. Correlation of practicum activities with activities of other courses being taken by the pupils at the same time.
6. Preparation, with the help of the pupils, of lists of significant points for attention during specific experiences, such as
   a. Key questions and procedures to be used in interviews.
   b. Procedures to be used in canvassing.
   c. Procedures to be used in voter round-ups.
7. Maintenance of contact with cooperating leaders and pupils.
   a. The teacher should be available whenever problems and questions arise.
   b. The teacher should foster harmonious interpersonal relationships by
      (1) Timely action in case of illness, personality clashes, inactivity on the part of either the pupil or the person with whom he is working. (A bad experience may cause a pupil to lose all interest in the program.)
      (2) Seeing to it that each pupil is getting a sufficiently diversified program to provide a well-rounded picture of the process of the selection of public officials.
8. Processing and following up pupils' progress reports. These reports should enable the teacher to ensure the steady and progressive development of the program. Each report should include a description of each contact with the program. Pupils should list dates, nature and length of time spent, as well as their evaluation of the experience. These reports should be submitted by each pupil weekly.
9. Preparation and distribution to news media of significant accounts about the development of the program.

To Initiate the Political Practicum

1. Sound out key people on the acceptability of the practicum.
   a. Draw up an explanation of the practicum that includes

      (1) Precedents, procedures, and involvement of time and personnel.

      (2) Materials, expense, total school program, and so on.

      (3) Channels for approach to political and community leaders and resources.

  b. Consult with school officials. Gain their approval, accept suggestions, and modify your plans if necessary. All this must be done well in advance of practicum time.

  c. Consult with leaders of political parties and pressure groups.

      (1) Confer with key leaders. Incorporate their suggestions into the plan and solicit their approval.

      (2) Invite school authorities, public officials, and political leaders to discuss the proposal and court their interest in it. Include an agenda of the discussion with the invitation.

      (3) At the discussion to be attended by school authorities, public officials, and political leaders,

        (a) Enlist their help in formulating objectives, program, and conditions.

        (b) Get a preliminary indication of their respective "grass-roots" leaders.

2. Present the political practicum program to pupils.

  a. Relate human interest aspects of local campaigns (present and past).

  b. Explain place, precedents, and procedures.

  c. Distribute and discuss mimeographed copies of the class work plan. This plan should include

      (1) Statement of purpose.

      (2) Principles underlying the practicum in politics.

      (3) Initial steps for the practicum.

      (4) Program for the cooperating political leader.

      (5) Suggested activities to schedule with cooperating political leaders.

      (6) Responsibilities of the students.

      (7) Instructions to students.

      (8) Some questions for guiding students to significant observations.

  d. Request each pupil to supply you with his home address, election district number, and the addresses of political clubs in his area.

3. Introduce the political practicum to the parents.

  a. Invite the parents to a meeting to consider the practicum proposal.

  b. In the program for the meeting include consideration of both the general and specific objectives of the practicum.

  c. At the meeting solicit their suggestions and cooperation. Parents can cooperate by

      (1) Attending club organization meetings, rallies, and so on.

      (2) Assisting in the promotion of effective relationships with cooperating leaders.

      (3) Assisting and encouraging their children.

4. Introduce the political practicum to other groups in the community.

  a. Consult with the League of Women Voters, Chamber of Commerce, civic groups, union locals, and so on.

  b. Explore possible avenues of cooperation with these organizations — such as attendance at the League of Women Voters' nonpartisan candidates' meetings, distribution of literature, and the like.

ESTABLISHING FIELD RELATIONSHIPS

1. Establish contact with leaders of political parties in the community with
   a. A letter from the high school principal inviting cooperation in the program.
   b. A letter from, or visit by, the teacher to explain the details of the pupils' apprenticeship and to discuss suggested activities for pupils in the field.
   c. An endorsement by heads of the political organization communicated directly to the cooperating leaders who have been chosen by pupils in their own neighborhoods.
2. Have pupils arrange interviews with their cooperating leaders.
   a. To establish an acquaintanceship and to consider the goals of the program.
   b. To request permission to be apprenticed during the campaign and election.
   c. To consider possible ways to observe and to participate in political processes from registration through election.
   d. To formulate a schedule of participation that would be practical and worthwhile both for the leader and pupil.
3. Have conferences with your pupils regarding proposed schedules.
4. Arrange a meeting of teacher, cooperating leaders, and pupils (perhaps at a tea).
   a. Arrange to have one or two brief, inspiring speeches about the role of the politician in government.
   b. Arrange to have a suitable question-and-answer period—informally conducted—to establish rapport between pupils and leaders.
5. Arrange to have political leaders as guest speakers during regular class sessions, by invitation of teacher or pupils. At these sessions candidates or other interpreters for both parties will discuss
   a. Personalities, issues, strategy, and election work.
   b. Relevant structural and/or procedural aspects of canvassing, registration, administration of elections, guarantees of secrecy of the vote, and the integrity of election.
   c. Phases outside the range of observation by high school pupils, such as
      (1) How money is raised.
      (2) How publicity is handled.
      (3) How rallies are planned and arranged.
   d. Postelection analysis of returns and issues by political leaders.
   e. How young people can get into politics.
   f. Official interpretation of the duties of the officers after they have been elected.
6. Arrange a postelection meeting for school officials, cooperating political leaders, faculty members of the department, and pupils involved. If possible, include the parents of the pupils. At this meeting
   a. Express formal appreciation to all for their cooperation during the political practicum.

b. Call on one political leader from each party to speak regarding the value of the practicum; the highlight of the program; and possible changes, additions, or deletions in future programs.

c. Provide a question-and-answer period for a free discussion of anything pupils deem relevant to the practicum.

ALTERNATE PATTERNS FOR ORGANIZING PUPILS' PARTICIPATION

The ideal way in which to carry out the political practicum is to assign each pupil to a cooperating leader in a political party at the precinct or ward level. However, this may not always be feasible. Therefore, the following are suggestions for modifying the program:

1. Form groups or squads of pupils who live in the same neighborhood to work as a unit with one cooperating leader in the party of their choice.
   a. Allocate the laboratory experiences to be used. Rotate teams of two or four pupils so that maximum diversification can be achieved.
   b. Consider the individual differences of pupils in setting up the program.
2. Choose representatives elected by the class to work in the field, and act as liason between the political party and the rest of the class. These pupils will
   a. Report to the class on their experiences and the progress of the campaign.
   b. Distribute campaign literature to the class.
   c. Report and discuss issues, procedures, and strategy.
3. Choose representatives of the class to work with pressure groups and nonpartisan groups and report to the entire class.
4. Set up a dual program—combining participation with a political club, where it can be arranged, and a mock campaign and mock election in the school.
5. Form a High School Voting League through which pupils can apply their understanding of party politics.

SUGGESTED CLASSROOM ACTIVITIES DURING THE PRACTICUM

1. Individual activities.
   a. Ask each pupil to write "My Political Autobiography" and include his own definition of politics. If his parent has been active in politics, a pupil may interview him about his experiences.
   b. Give reading assignments and conduct discussions on topics correlated with field activities; for example,
      (1) Political parties: their nature, structure, and function.
      (2) Candidates: how they are chosen and who supports them.
      (3) Issues involved: party platform, referenda, and so on.
      (4) Party organization: the hierarchy of committees, how they are chosen and how they perform.
      (5) Registration requirements.
      (6) Campaign financing.
      (7) Election laws.

    c. Have each pupil select a party affiliation for the practicum on the basis of
       (1) Issues involved.
       (2) Candidates covered in newspapers.
       (3) Interviews with members of a neighborhood political club.
    d. Have each pupil systematically prepare predictions concerning the election. These predictions should be placed in sealed envelopes and filed with the teacher.
       (1) In October, a prediction should be expressed in percentages.
       (2) On the eve of election day, a prediction and a statement describing the basis for the prediction — that is, whether it is based on canvas, polls, political leaders, or what — should be made.
       (3) Conduct a postelection evaluation of the predictions in light of the results of the election. Newspaper comments may be used to support the analysis.
    e. Have a suggestion box in which pupils from time to time deposit written suggestions for possible improvements over methods used during the practicum in both field and classroom. Open the box at the end of the practicum and let the whole class evaluate the suggestions.
2. Group activities.
    a. Discussions on pressure groups, lobbying, and political parties.
    b. Debates on issues of the campaign.
    c. Panel discussions regarding campaign strategies and the differences in method used by opposing parties.
    d. Brief campaign speeches followed by a question-and-answer period.
    e. Poll of the student body regarding election results. Analysis of results and presentation of findings to class.
    f. Postelection round table discussions of the value of the practicum together with considerations of the suggestions in the suggestion box.
3. Outside Sources.
    a. Invite guest speakers, such as party members, political leaders, and elected officials to address the class, to be followed by a question period.
    b. Integrate contributions from the mass media: TV, radio, newspapers, and magazines.

Suggested Laboratory Experiences

Campaign Activities. The bulk of the practicum will consist of laboratory or field experiences conducted by individuals, squads, or groups during the campaign. Among the activities pupils might perform are to

1. Interview appropriate officials regarding the duties of the respective offices to be filled in the election.
2. Visit the county Board of Elections to survey its functions and to secure official materials on registration and voting procedures.
3. Attend one or more organization meetings of a local political club and, if possible, a county committee meeting.
4. Visit the office of the County Clerk to secure voting statistics and other information.

5. Attend political rallies and nonpartisan candidates' meetings (for example, the League of Women Voters).

6. Attend fund-raising dinners, teas, and the like.

7. Accompany the cooperating leader on door-to-door canvassing for registration, distribution of literature, contact with new voters, needs for special services, and nonparticipants.

8. Act as an apprentice to the political party treasurer. Prepare a chart on how campaign funds are spent.

9. Interview candidates.

10. Distribute literature, both partisan and nonpartisan.

11. Accompany the leader on the campaign trail, in caravans, and on broadcasting sound trucks.

12. Act as an apprentice to the cooperating leader and perform services at the club.

Election Day Activities.   Election day should be a day of real activity. Pupils can, among other things,

1. Observe procedures at the polls.

2. Watch the setting up of the polls (usually between 6:30 and 7:00 A.M.).

3. Distribute campaign literature and ride sound trucks during the final effort.

4. Help check off poll lists as voters come in.

5. Telephone to club headquarters the count of the vote and the percentage of those eligible who have voted.

6. Make visits or telephone calls of reminder to party members who have not yet voted.

7. Serve as babysitters to enable mothers to go to the polls.

8. Work at the club or headquarters.

9. Help demonstrate how to use the voting machine.

10. At end of the vote, watch the opening of the machines and tallying of the votes.

11. Receive returns in various headquarters and at clubs.

12. Hold an election night watch at the school or, by prior arrangement, at the clubs. This is an excellent time for the parents to participate. Watching the returns as received over television provides an exciting climax.

After Election Day

1. Arrange for pupil representatives to interview political leaders in the county regarding the significance of the election.

2. Arrange for pupil representatives to interview the candidates who were elected.

Over-all Reporting Activities.   During the entire practicum the teacher should require

1. Each student to keep newspaper clippings that are pertinent to candidates, issues, polls, and the election in general in a scrapbook.

2. Each student to keep an individual notebook in which he can record activities, observations, and questions that are relevant to aspects of politics that are not clear to him.

CHAPTER 11

Economics

THE STRUCTURE OF ECONOMICS

DEFINITION OF ECONOMICS

Economics is concerned with the ways in which we manage our productive human and natural resources and the goods that result from the employment and use of those resources. It starts from the simple, undeniable proposition that mankind does not have and never will have enough human, natural, and produced resources to enable all men to have all they want of goods and services.

Because there are not enough goods and services to go around, we must choose between alternatives. The difficulty is to make intelligent choices from among the various competing alternatives. These choices should be made on the basis of a firm knowledge of the facts, economic principles, logical analysis, and rational inferences.[1] All other economic problems are outgrowths of this basic problem.

Basic Ideas of Economics. Senesh has identified five fundamental concepts of economics:

> 1. The central idea of economics is the scarcity concept, namely, that every society faces a conflict between unlimited wants and limited resources.
> 2. Out of the scarcity concept a family of ideas emerges. Because of scarcity, man has tried to develop methods to produce more in less time, or more with less material and in shorter time. Various types of specialization were discovered in order to overcome the conflict between unlimited wants and limited resources. We specialize geographically, occupationally, and technologically. The third family of ideas grows out of specialization.
> 3. Because of specialization, we are interdependent; interdependence necessitates a monetary system and a transportation system. The fourth idea emerges from the first, scarcity, and from interdependence.

[1] *Economic Education in the Schools,* Report of the National Task Force on Economic Education (New York: Committee for Economic Development, 711 Fifth Ave., 1961), p. 14.

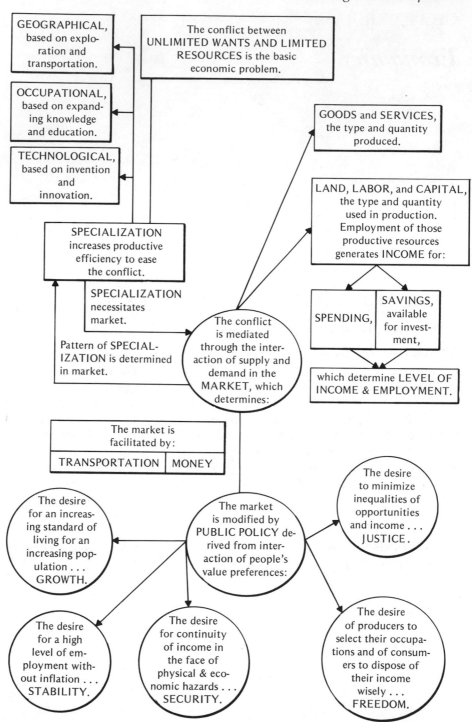

F I G U R E   11-1. *Fundamental Ideas of Economics.* [*See Footnote 2.*]

4. Men had to discover an allocating mechanism and this is the market, where through the interaction of buyers and sellers price changes occur. Prices determine the pattern of production, the method of production, income distribution and the level of spending and saving, which, in turn, decide the level of total economic activity. The fifth family of ideas grows out of the fact that the economic system is a part of political society.

5. The market decision is modified by public policies, carried out by the government to assure welfare objectives. These welfare objectives are determined in the United States through the political interaction of 200 million people which generates thousands of welfare objectives which I have reduced to five: our attempts to accelerate growth, to promote stability, to assure economic security, to promote economic freedom, and to promote economic justice.[2]

In Figure 11-1 the relationships of these ideas are shown diagramatically.

Method of Inquiry. The method of determining economic truths is basically scientific. The nature of the subject matter, however, forbids the use of controlled experimentation. Because the controlled experiment of natural science is barred to him, the economist has turned to statistical approaches. These are the steps in this adaption of the scientific method:

1. He observes the data or phenomena carefully. The data may be self-gathered or recorded by others. From these data the investigator may find a pattern appearing.

2. On the basis of this pattern, he creates a hypothesis (for example, if X is so, Y must follow).

3. He then sets out to verify his hypothesis by finding new data and analyzing them statistically. If analysis upholds the hypothesis after sufficient trials, he then assumes that the relationship is a fact (that is, if X, then Y).

4. He then sets out to determine the reasons behind the fact (that is, to theorize). In economics, most theorizing is done deductively.

Theories, or models, as they are often called, also provide the researcher with useful, analytical tools and approaches. For instance, Figure 11-2 presents a model of the American economy.[3] This model explains the main features of American economic life. Models such as this are useful because

1. They isolate the main variables under study and show at least some of the main relationships among the variables.

2. By simplifying they highlight the main variables and their relations.[4]

In this way models make it possible to observe phenomena free from the burden of detail that obscure the phenomena in the real world. Thus, they make ex-

[2] Lawrence Senesh, "Organizing a Curriculum Around Social Science Concepts," in Irving Morrisett, ed., *Concepts and Structures in the New Social Science Curricula* (New York: Holt, Rinehart & Winston, Inc., 1967), pp. 24–26. Copyright © 1967. Reprinted by permission of Holt, Rinehart and Winston, Inc.

[3] Richard S. Martin and Reuben G. Miller, *Economics and Its Significance* (Columbus, Ohio: Charles E. Merrill Publishers, 1965), p. 4.

[4] *Economic Education in the Schools,* op. cit., p. 19.

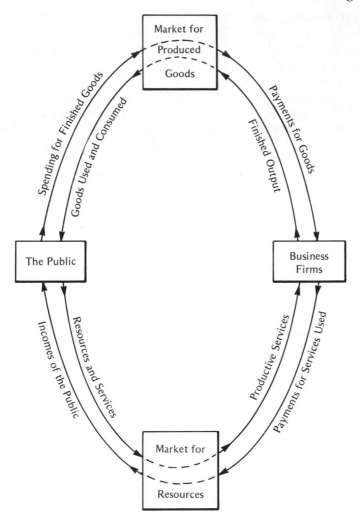

FIGURE 11-2. *A Model of the American Economy.* [*See Footnote 3.*]

cellent jump-off points for thinking about particular situations or problems. In addition to being devices by which to carry on objective rational analysis, they are useful teaching tools.

Testing for economic truth is also difficult. One test seems to be how well the theory predicts what actually happens in the real world. If historical experiences and empirical observation uphold an economic law, then the law can be considered valid. Another test is the validity of the assumptions and of the logic used. If the assumptions are really true, and the inferences drawn are really logical, then the theory can be assumed to be valid also. Obviously, the more ways one tests economic laws and theories, the more likely one is to find out the truth.[5]

---

[5] For exceptionally good discussions of the nature of economics, see Ben W. Lewis, "Economics," in American Council of Learned Societies and the National Council for the Social Studies, *The Social Studies and the Social Sciences* (New York: Harcourt Brace Jovanovich, Inc., 1962), and Ronald H. Wolf, "Economics," in John U. Michaelis and A. Montgomery Johnston, eds., *The Social Sciences* (Boston: Allyn & Bacon, Inc., 1965), on which this discussion is largely based.

ECONOMICS IN THE CURRICULUM

NEED FOR ECONOMIC EDUCATION

Economic understanding is a requisite for good citizenship. The principal objective for teaching economics is, or should be, to provide the economic understanding necessary for responsible citizenship.[6] Both leaders and citizens need to understand basic economic concepts and principles well enough to enable them to understand, appreciate, and seek to improve the economic situation; to face up to public economic issues; to vote intelligently on economic questions; and to use their knowledge for their own and the social good. Otherwise we shall all suffer.[7]

PRESENT STATUS OF THE ECONOMICS CURRICULUM

Economics has never achieved a high place in the American school curriculum. When offered, economics courses are likely to be half-year elective courses for seniors. Sometimes, economics courses are offered in the business and commercial curricula. Problems of Democracy and other social studies courses frequently include economics content, as do courses in homemaking and mathematics. Usually, however, the subject matter taught in these courses is largely superficial consumer education.

RECOMMENDED CURRICULUM IN ECONOMICS EDUCATION

In the early 1960s several groups began campaigns to upgrade economic education. In general, these groups have tried to promote economic education through existing courses, rather than through the addition of more courses in economics. The report of the National Task Force on Economic Education was one of these efforts. In this report, the committee calls for "the understanding of a few essential concepts and a few major economic institutions, plus an understanding of how these fit together in the functioning of an economy." Most important, they emphasize, is the need for replacing unreasoned judgment by objective, rational analyses and "teaching that leads students to examine and think through economic problems for themselves."[8]

Specifically, the Task Force recommended

1. That more time be devoted in school curricula to development of economic understanding. In particular:
   a. That, wherever feasible, students take a course in economics or its equivalent under another title, such as Problems of American Democracy, in high school; and that in all high schools of substantial size there be at least an elective senior year course in economics.

---

[6] Lewis, op. cit., p. 107, ff.

[7] Franklin Patterson, ed., *Citizenship and a Free Society*, Thirtieth Yearbook (Washington, D.C.: National Council for the Social Studies, 1960), p. 119.

[8] Ibid.

   b. That where economics is not required, courses in Problems of American Democracy (now taken by approximately half of all high school students) devote a substantial portion of their time to developing economic understanding.

   c. That more economic analysis be included in history courses, which are taken by nearly all students.

   d. That business education curricula include a required course in economics.

   e. That development of economic understanding be emphasized at other advantageous points throughout the entire school curriculum, beginning in the lower grades.

2. That major emphasis be placed on an objective, rational way of thinking about economic problems, as well as on knowledge of fundamental economic institutions and concepts for analyzing economic issues.

3. That objective examination of controversial issues be included in the teaching of economics, as an important part of helping students develop the ability to reach their own conclusions on important social problems; and that school boards, administrators, and the public support the right of students to this educational experience.[9]

The Task Force also recommended that the content of the economic curriculum should include

1. Fact of scarcity.
   a. Need for economizing.
   b. Costs—opportunity (alternative) and money costs.
   c. Productive resources—factors of production.
   d. Division of labor, specialization and exchange.
   e. Economic production—conversion of resources into desired outcomes.
   f. Saving, investment capital formation.
   g. Labor productivity.
   h. Principle of diminishing returns.
   i. Demand, supply, price.
   j. Market.
   k. Competition.
   l. Profit, profit incentive.
   m. Interdependence.
   n. Price and market system.
   o. Economic efficiency.
   p. Monopoly, antitrust laws.
   q. Corporation, balance sheet, profit and loss statement.
   r. Government expenditures of taxes in allocating resources.
   s. Taxes—corporate income tax, personal income tax, property tax, sales tax, payroll tax.

[9] *Economic Education in the Schools, Summary of the Report of the National Task Force on Economic Education* (New York: The Committee for Economic Development, 711 Fifth Ave., 1961), p. 13. A fourth point is omitted because it deals primarily with staffing, teacher education, supply of materials, and the like.

        t. International specialization.

        u. Balance of payments, balance of trade.

        v. Tariffs.

2. Economic growth and stability.

    a. GNP, national income, per capita production and income.

    b. Money and real income.

    c. Price level.

    d. Aggregate demand (total spending) and components of aggregate demand (consumer spending, business spending, investment, government spending).

    e. Business cycle, depression, inflation.

    f. Money—bank deposits and money creation through banklending.

    g. Central bank—Federal Reserve System.

    h. Government budget, fiscal policy, public debt.

    i. Economic growth.

    j. Underdeveloped areas.

    k. The population problem.

3. Distribution of income.

    a. Income as payment for services—productivity as a basis for receipt of incomes.

    b. Personal distribution of income.

    c. Real and money wages.

    d. Labor unions—collective bargaining.

    e. Strikes, picketing, closed shop, featherbedding.

    f. Economic security as a goal.

    g. Social security, unemployment insurance, old-age insurance, private security measures.

    h. The farm problem.

4. Communism, socialism, and capitalism.

    a. Central planning versus free demand.

    b. Individual economic incentives, much the same.

    c. Importance of capital accumulation and economic growth.

    d. Stability of communistic versus free enterprise systems, that is, booms and depressions.

    e. Ownership of capital.

    f. Success in attaining a high standard of living.[10]

THE ECONOMICS COURSE

Discrete economics courses are often taught as electives in the senior high school—usually at the twelfth-grade level. Such courses should probably have the following characteristics.

1. They should center on the "economic problem."

2. They should be realistic and down to earth, dealing with the real problems, issues, and controversies of the world today and relating to the pupils' roles in economic life.

[10] *Ibid.* p. 13.

3. They should be policy-oriented; that is to say that they should be oriented toward the study of policy problems that face us in the real world.

4. They should be based on creating a lifelong interest in economics.

5. They should introduce pupils to the concepts, facts, principles, and processes that a person needs to know if he is to function as a responsible citizen and be able to make decisions necessary in a democratic, private-enterprise economy.

6. They should provide pupils with background and skills so that they can cope with later courses in the field.

7. They should develop a way of thinking about economic problems. In this connection they should develop sufficient skill in economic analysis so that they can explore new economic issues.

8. They should be selective rather than encyclopedic.

9. They should present an overview of our own and alternative economic systems.[11]

ECONOMIC CONTENT IN OTHER SOCIAL STUDIES COURSES

The following examples are topics that could be used to illustrate economic principles in other social studies courses.

United States History.
    Economic Factors Leading to Revolution.
    Hamilton's Financial Program.
    Jackson and the United States Bank.
    Economics and the Civil War.
    Economics and the Westward Movement.
    The Populist Movement.
    The Cross of Gold.
    Setting Up the Federal Reserve System.
    The New Deal.

World History.
    Economic Policies in the Roman Empire.
    Manors.
    Trade in Medieval Europe.
    Mercantilism.
    The Industrial Revolution.
    Economic Causes of the French Revolution.
    Colonialism.

Problems of Democracy and Government.
    Financing State, Local, and Federal Governments.

---

[11] This list is based largely on Edward C. Prehn, *High School Economics: The Analytic Approach* (New York: Pitman Publishing Corp., 1968), Chap. 5. This book is one of best works on teaching economics. The best source of information on materials for teaching economics is the Joint Council for Economic Education. Write the Joint Council for their *Checklist,* which describes all their publications. See the Council's annual publication, *Economic Education Experiences for Enterprising Teachers,* for excellent teaching strategies and techniques.

National Economic Priorities.
The Federal Budget.
Inflation and Employment.

SOME STRATEGIES AND TACTICS FOR TEACHING ECONOMICS

1. Use a combination of analytical and other experiences. For instance, you could use business and financial reports to illustrate principles of economics as they are studied.

2. Tie economics teaching to the concrete, urgent problems of youth and society.

3. Personalize the course: How much economic freedom are you ready to sacrifice for economic security? How much are you willing to pay for pollution-free water? Such questions are good for research, simulation, or role playing.

4. Utilize a centralizing theme, such as the role of high school pupils in the American economy, throughout the course.

5. Every so often base current events on economics in the news.

6. Have pupils prepare position papers on such topics as "The Government Should Enforce Strong Price Controls."

7. Debate such questions as what to do about inflation, after first learning the theoretical reasons for inflation and ways of stopping it.

8. Survey the economic factors in the local community.

9. Study the changes in the economic life of the community over a period of time.

10. Compare old catalogs with new ones. Why the difference in price and products offered for sale?

11. Have pupils construct price indexes. Use old catalogs and newspapers to learn past prices.

	Past Price	Current Price	Index
Refrigeration			
Food			
etc.			

12. Utilize simulation games such as Diminishing Marginal Utility.[12] Several games are on the market.

13. Organize a mock company.

14. Conduct a simulated business.

15. Use games such as Monopoly.

16. Simulate playing the stock market. Let pupils study market operations.

[12] Jane Caskell, "Diminishing Marginal Utility," in George G. Dawson, ed., *Economic Education Experiences of Enterprising Teachers* (New York: Joint Council on Economic Education, 1971), Vol. 8.

and the companies in which they want to invest. (As a club activity it may be possible to actually buy stocks and follow the market.)

17. Let pupils role play economists debating economic issues.

18. Let pupils role play interviews of famous economists about their beliefs.

19. Dramatize or role play collective-bargaining sessions, a corporation board meeting, a town council budget meeting, and the like.

20. Use simplified models to illustrate economic principles. Later use more complex models. Vary parts of the model to show relationships.

21. Invite experts in to discuss economic problems.

22. Have an economics current events bulletin board featuring local, state, and national economic news.

23. Have students do posters, charts, graphs, tables, and diagrams to illustrate economic principles.

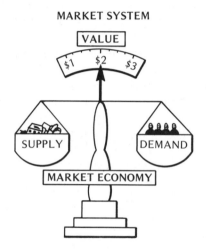

FIGURE 11-3. *A Poster Illustrating an Economic Principle. This Poster Is one of a Number Made by Twelfth-grade Students of Mr. Dennis W. Cambier of Lincoln High School in Midland, Pennsylvania, one of the 1969–1970 Award Winners in the Kazanjian Foundation Award Program for the Teaching of Economics.* [*George G. Dawson, ed.,* Economic Education Experiences of Enterprising Teachers (*New York: Joint Council of Economic Education, 1971*), *Vol. 8, p. 75.*]

SOME STRATEGIES AND TACTICS FOR TEACHING CONSUMER ECONOMICS

1. Compute the cost of operating an automobile.

2. Compute the cost of buying a car on credit, as compared to paying cash.

3. Have pupils build and use a budget for an imaginary family.

4. Analyze television commercials.

5. Give practice in "buymanship." Have pupils shop to find the best buy in a particular product (for example, a portable radio). Let them compare advertising, labels, brands, government and consumer test agencies, and the like.

6. Simulate investing.

7. Role play an incident involving consumer economics, such as installment buying, and then discuss it.

CHAPTER 12

The Behavioral Sciences

T H E behavioral sciences share a common structural feature — they are sciences and their truths are established via the methods of scientific inquiry. The basic content of all of them is conceptual — that is, it consists of broad generalizations or principles that are derived from the observation and analysis of many specific cases and from which inferences concerning specific action and phenomena may be drawn. Because of these structural characteristics they all lend themselves to teaching methods based on inquiry, induction, and problem solving.

Because the number of really dependable generalizations in the behavioral sciences is small, probably their focus in the secondary schools should be on method rather than on information. Therefore, McKeachie suggests the following as goals for courses in the behavioral sciences.

Attitudes.

1. Curiosity about human behavior.
2. Appreciation of scientific methods and their applicability to problems of human behavior — with awareness of their limitations.
3. A critical attitude toward generalizations about human behavior.
4. Increased skepticism about the finality of our present state of knowledge. Greater ability to get along without absolute answers to every problem. Recognizing that all scientific generalizations must be viewed as tentative in nature, subject to modification in light of new evidence.
5. Recognition of the influence of needs and cultural values upon the acceptance of generalizations about human behavior and a desire to separate values from observation.
6. Willingness to recognize one's own needs and values as sources of error and bias — the fallibility of man as a student of man.
7. Appreciation of the importance in the scientific process of fresh perspectives, of creative imagination, and of freedom as a factor influencing creativity.

8. Increased objectivity in approaching social problems.

9. Attitudes toward people . . . a heightened sensitivity to the feeling of others and to an understanding of their needs.

Understandings and Abilities.

1. Understanding of the elements of scientific methods as applied in social science.

2. Increased ability to formulate testable hypotheses about behavior.

3. Increased ability to recognize assumptions involved in generalizations about behavior.

4. Increased ability to discriminate between reasonable and unreasonable generalizations in terms of the evidence upon which they are based.

5. Awareness of some of the major tools and methods of psychology and other behavioral sciences.

6. Understanding the purposes of the behavioral sciences, the nature of their subject matter, and their limitations.[1]

ANTHROPOLOGY

Anthropologists study the biotic, psychic, social, and cultural aspects of man and try to look on them in a way that will show *"how* man has adapted to his environment and *why* he does *what* he does."[2] To gather the information necessary for such a broad view and to solve the problems that must be solved before understanding can be achieved, anthropologists turn to the areas of other disciplines and then try to weld them into a new whole that will show how man acts and why.

THE STRUCTURE OF ANTHROPOLOGY

The Fundamental Ideas. The diagram in Figure 12-1 shows the twelve fundamental ideas of anthropology and their relationships. These principles, as described by Senesh, are

1. Man may be looked upon as a
   a. mammalian animal,
   b. social animal, and
   c. cultural animal.
2. Man, in these three capacities, has needs.
3. Man's needs are satisfied within a social structure.
4. Social structure itself has needs (called "requisites") which must be satisfied if it is to persist.
5. Needs are satisfied within a particular set of patterned behavior: tradition.

[1] W. J. McKeachie, "Psychology," in the American Council of Learned Societies and the National Council for Social Studies, *The Social Studies and the Social Sciences* (New York: Harcourt Brace Jovanovich, Inc., 1962), pp. 173–181.

[2] Paul Bohannan, *Anthropology,* Publication No. 106 of the Social Science Education Consortium (Lafayette, Ind.: The Consortium, 1966), p. 3.

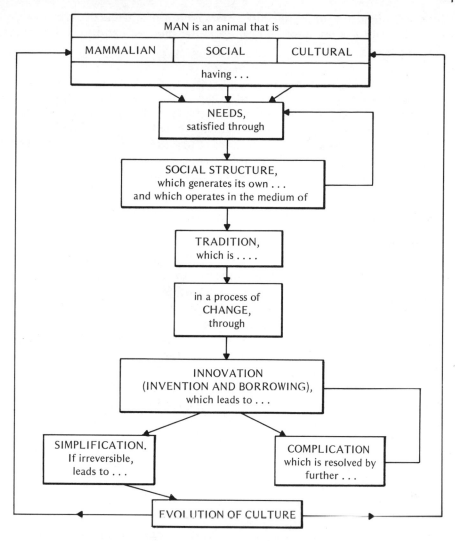

FIGURE 12-1. *Fundamental Ideas of Anthropology. [See Footnote 2.]*

6. All traditions leave some wants unsatisfied.
7. Dissatisfaction leads to changes in traditions.
8. Changes take the form of invention and borrowing: innovation.
9. Innovation leads to complication and simplification.
10. Complication leads to social dislocations. Problems caused by dislocations may be resolved through further innovations.
11. If simplification is of such a magnitude that it forms an irreversible base for man's behavior (for example, the use of fire), it leads to evolution of culture.
12. The evolution of culture affects man in his three capacities as a mammalian, social, and cultural animal.[3]

[3] Lawrence Senesh, "Organizing a Curriculum Around Social Science Concepts," in Irving Morrisett, ed., *Concepts and Structures in the New Social Science Curriculum* (New York: Holt, Rinehart & Winston, Inc., 1967), p. 34. Copyright © 1967. Reprinted by permission of Holt, Rinehart & Winston, Inc.

Of all these ideas probably the one of greatest importance is the idea of culture, in other words the accumulation of patterns of learned behavior passed on from one generation to another.

Methods of Studying Anthropology. As we have seen, anthropology is a generalizing science. Although, in general, it uses the methods of science, anthropology differs from other sciences in that it makes considerable use of analogy and comparison between cultures in interpreting data.[4] Furthermore, because the object of anthropology is to study the variety of and differences in man's behavior, it does not so much look for universals as it attempts to use universals as a framework within which to place differences.[5]

ANTHROPOLOGY IN THE CURRICULUM

Curriculum Aims and Justification for Secondary School Anthropology. Basically, the aims of instruction in anthropology are (1) to give pupils a broad view of human behavior and (2) to teach pupils to think objectively by eliminating ethnocentric thinking. "By giving students accurate and extensive information about other cultures" anthropology stretches the experiences of pupils and puts them in a much broader context.[6] Because of its broad view of the study of man and his culture, anthropology offers a good background for studying the other social studies. It also tends to supplement the usually ethnocentric biases of other social studies.

Content of Anthropology in Secondary Schools. Anthropology has seldom had a place as a separate subject in the American secondary school curriculum, although the curriculum does embody a sizeable amount of anthropological content in other social studies courses. Recently, however, anthropology has been gaining recognition as a separate subject in secondary school curricula. This change is partly the result of the work of such projects as The Anthropological Study Project, which has prepared course and unit materials for secondary school anthropology courses.

Much anthropological subject matter is now included in courses in other subjects. Probably this is a good practice and should be encouraged. Anthropological content that might well be included in courses in other social studies includes,

History.
    The continual change in behavior (the cyclic, contingent, and cumulative nature of change, cultural evolution, diffusionism).
    Prehistory (transformation from *hominoid* to *hominid*; beginnings of agriculture, prehistoric civilizations).
    Methods of anthropological historians (archaeology, ethnology).
Sociology.
    Subhuman societal organizations (bees, ants, gibbons, gorillas).
    Subhuman use of language.

[4] Alfred K. Guthe, "Anthropology," in John U. Michaelis and A. Montgomery Johnston, eds., *The Social Sciences: Foundations of the Social Studies* (Boston: Allyn and Bacon, Inc., 1965), p. 184.
[5] Bohannan, op. cit., p. 4.
[6] Ibid., p. 5.

Cross cultural study of institutions.
Cross cultural study of individual socialization.
Political Science.
Universality of government.
Universality of law and coercive sanctions.
Economics.
Noneconomic ways in which goods and services circulate.
Cultures in which the price-fixing market system does not exist.[7]

Anthropology Courses. When anthropology is taught in separate courses, the content of such courses should, it would seem, develop the fundamental ideas of anthropology described earlier in this chapter. The foremost of these concepts is, of course, the concept of culture. Questions such as the following ones, developed by the Anthropological Curriculum Study Project for its experimental course, *Patterns in Human History*, serve admirably as a basis for studying cultures.

> What did culture have to do with the evolutionary process that produced man as we know him today? What does culture have to do with humanness, with human nature? What have been the broad patterns, the crucial disjunctions, in the evolution of culture? How have differences in cultural capacity affected the relations between societies? What are the implications of tribal culture or peasant culture or industrial culture for the life experience of the individual? What kinds of cultural change are involved when a society attempts to "modernize"? What generic qualities of culture explain the difficulties of planned social change?[8]

The type of anthropology course probably best suited for the secondary school curriculum and its place in the curriculum are well illustrated by the Anthropology Curriculum Study Project's statement concerning plans for their course, *Patterns in Human History*.

> Patterns in Human History is seen as coming early in a secondary social studies sequence, perhaps most appropriately as the first semester of a world history or a world cultures course. It will be a foundation course in every important respect since it provides:
>
> 1. An analytic basis for describing and comparing societies; this involves a technical nomenclature for talking about the structure and processes of society and a typology that makes broad classification of societies on the basis of complexity and institutional capacity possible.
> 2. The basis for seeing new significance in conventionalized historic particulars, for example, the classical Greek city-state had a tribal past and the persistence of pastoral tribal traits can be observed in the classical literature; the Greek experience is one of the evolution from tribal-grade society to civilized society.

[7] Douglas Oliver, "Cultural Anthropology," in the American Council of Learned Societies and National Council for the Social Studies, op. cit., pp. 136–140.

[8] Anthropology Curriculum Study Project, *Newsletter*, 8:2 (Fall 1969).

3. Theories about culture change which illuminate both historical and contemporary events.

4. Models for hypothesizing. A number of direct opportunities for making sense out of data are offered; in addition, students are confronted with the awareness that scholars disagree about the meaning of evidence more commonly than is popularly appreciated.

5. A social scientific perspective, which prompts looking beyond crises and personalities for general significance and pattern—a perspective which has been underrepresented in the social studies. For example, one can focus attention on peasant groups only at those times when they rebel against the established order or one can be concerned about peasant groups in the context of larger social systems, with an interest in the distribution and legitimation of power and privilege in such traditional systems and in the question of how peasant culture is adaptive to the larger social environment.[9]

SOCIOLOGY

STRUCTURE OF THE DISCIPLINE

Definition. Sociology has been described as "the science that deals with social groups: their internal forms or modes of organization, the processes that tend to maintain or change these forms of organization and the relations between the groups."[10] In other words, sociology, like anthropology, is a study of culture.

The Structure of Sociology. Perrucci has worked out a fundamental structure for sociology. This structure, he says, presents the "fundamental categories and concerns" of sociology.[11] The structure is presented diagrammatically in Figure 12-2. As one can see, "the general structure consists of six different levels of society: values, social institutions, organizations, groups, positions, and social roles." At each of these levels there is great diversity. To see society as a whole, Perrucci tells us, we must look down the levels of society and across each of the levels and search out the relationships among the various parts.[12] The basis of the entire structure is the idea of values and norms.

1. It is values and norms that give energy to the system.

2. It is values and norms that shape the social institutions, thus becoming the *raison d'etre* for organizations and groups, and ultimately determine the positions and role relationships of the individuals in groups. In other words, values

[9] Ibid. For a good discussion of both anthropology as an academic discipline and methods of teaching anthropology in secondary schools, see Pertti J. Pelto, *The Study of Anthropology* (Columbus, Ohio: Charles E. Merrill Publishers, 1965).

[10] Harry M. Johnson, *Sociology: A Systematic Introduction* (New York: Harcourt Brace Jovanovich, Inc., 1960), p. 2. Quoted by William E. Cole, "Sociology," in John U. Michaelis and A. Montgomery Johnston, eds., op. cit., 1965, p. 198.

[11] Robert Perrucci, *Sociology*, Publication No. 101 of the Social Science Education Consortium (Lafayette, Ind.: The Consortium, 1966).

[12] Ibid., p. 34.

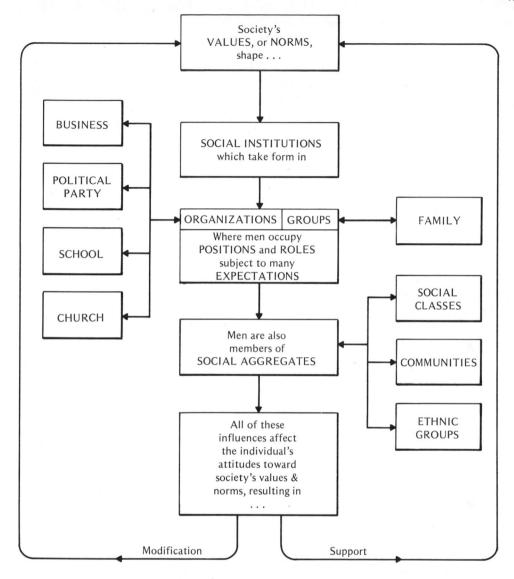

FIGURE 12-2. *Fundamental Ideas of Sociology.* [*Senesh, op. cit., p. 31.*]

and norms "shape the structure of society" and "become the meaningful ideas about which men organize their lives."[13]

3. At the same time, men's values and norms are affected by the pressures of their positions and roles. Because of these pressures, individuals support existing values or norms or seek to modify them. In this way they reshape their positions, their groups and organizations, and finally the value systems of their society.

4. Once the new values have been formed, the process starts over again. The new values reshape the institutions, roles, and positions, and the institutions, roles, and positions reshape individual attitudes, and so on *ad infinitum.* "Both

[13] Ibid.

persistence and change of social forms is achieved by this process of mutual influence."[14]

Methods of Research in Sociology. Like anthropology, sociology uses the methods of science. However, because of its particular concerns, sociology has adopted and developed investigative techniques specially designed to serve its purposes. Among these techniques we find

Questionnaire.

Interview.

Projective testing.

Quantitative content analysis (that is, how many times does a phenomenon occur in such and such context).

Logical analysis.

Historical analysis.

Case study.

Life history or biography.

Controlled experiment.

Direct observation as a participating observer.

Simulation of social situation.

Building of models.

SOCIOLOGY IN THE CURRICULUM

Status. Sociology courses are relatively rare in social studies curricula. However, considerable social studies content is included in courses such as Problems of American Democracy. Whether or not separate courses in sociology are desirable, is moot. There is no doubt, however, that curriculum should give more attention to the subject matter and concepts of sociology.

1. A knowledge of sociology should help a person understand his place in society, and his own roles, motivations, and responses.

2. Sociological knowledge, like psychological knowledge, helps one to understand the behavior of others.

3. Sociological knowledge should lead to an understanding of the social systems into which people are born and in which they live.

4. While sociology is first of all a normative social science, concerned with nondeviant conditions, and behaviors, individual and group deviation is a fact; and sociology does aid in the understanding of deviation.

5. To many people working at professional and lower levels in sociology and in related fields, sociology serves a useful vocational purpose.[15]

Thus sociology is useful because it helps to explain "human motivation; behavior, value system, as related to striving for goals; and individual and group deviation and disorganization,"[16] — things that are necessary for pupils to understand if they are to have any real comprehension of themselves and the world they live in and how to cope with them.

[14] Ibid.

[15] Cole, op. cit., p. 192.

[16] Ibid.

Content of Sociology Teaching. Whether sociology is taught as a separate subject or as part of other social studies courses, its content should bring out the functional orientation of sociology, for it is "this functional conception that unites the diverse inquiries of sociologists and provides a common framework into which we can fit the many things and empirical studies of social behavior."[17]

According to this conception, society is viewed as a system of interacting parts. Therefore, sociology must answer two basic questions: (1) What keeps the system going? and (2) What causes the system to change and develop new patterns?

To implement this functional conception and its fundamental questions it is suggested that six major topics be included in the curriculum. All of these topics should serve to bring out the structure of sociology (as shown in Perrucci's model, for instance).

1. Physiological needs.

Every society must provide for the acquisition of adequate food, clothing, and shelter by its members.

2. Reproduction.

All societies must provide for the raising of children so that the society will not die out. This topic contains two fundamental subtopics: (1) demography and (2) the family.

3. Socialization.

Because very little human behavior is innate, every society is faced with the necessity of teaching its children values, skills, knowledge, and other aspects of behavior necessary for the preservation of the society.

4. Production and distribution of goods and services.

Every society must provide some method for producing and distributing the goods and services needed by that society.

5. Social Control.

All societies must find ways to control its members.

6. Meaning and motivation.

If a society is to be preserved, it must instill in its members the necessary values and goals to motivate them to sustain the society and develop the institutions that give life meaning and coherence, such as religion, art, and ethics.[18]

In addition, the study of sociology should help pupils learn the basic methods of scientific research in sociology. Instruction in methods of research should be carefully coordinated with the rest of the program. Pupils should do research of their own, but only if it is real and meaningful—not busywork—so that they will get a feeling for the methods of conducting scientific research and also acquire the scientific attitudes necessary for such research.[19]

[17] Gresham M. Sykes, "Sociology," in the American Council of Learned Societies and the National Council for the Social Studies, op. cit., p. 160.

[18] Ibid., pp. 162–165.

[19] Ibid., pp. 166–167. For further discussion of sociology as a discipline, see Cole, op. cit., Chap. 7, and Caroline B. Rose, *Sociology, The Study of Man in Society* (Columbus, Ohio: Charles E. Merrill Publishers, 1965). This work also contains an excellent chapter on suggested methods of teaching sociology.

PSYCHOLOGY

The Structure of Psychology

Psychology is the study of individuals rather than groups. Originally it was defined as the study of the human soul or mind, but it has come to include any human behavior. Thus, it overlaps biology, anthropology, and sociology. However, the focus is on discovering as much as can be learned about individual human behavior—group behavior, except as it influences individual behavior, is not a concern of psychology.

The methods of research in psychology are about the same as those in the other behavioral sciences, except that psychology allows for much more use of controlled experimenting of the kind associated with the natural sciences.

Basic Generalization of Psychology. The California State Curriculum Commission has published a list of generalizations to be used as the basis for social studies curriculum development. The generalizations selected for psychology are

Behavior.

1. Behavior is caused and is not its own cause. Each form of individual behavior has a pattern of causes that are multiple, complex, and interrelated. Behavior is not capricious or random. The discovery of causes leads to an understanding of behavior.
2. Human behavior is purposive and goal-directed. The individual may not always be aware of basic purposes and underlying needs that are influencing his behavior. The study of psychology attempts to bring about a greater awareness of the underlying causes of behavior.
3. Behavior results from the interaction of genetic and environmental factors. Through genetic influences, all individuals have a potentiality for development and learning; yet these genetic factors produce differences among individuals. The character of the physical and social environment promotes or limits the degree of realization of the individual's potentialities.

Influence of social groupings.

1. As a biologic organism, the individual posesses at birth certain physiological needs, but the methods of satisfying these needs and their subsequent development are to a great extent socially determined by his particular cultural unit.
2. Through the interaction of genetic and social and physical environmental factors, the individual develops a pattern of personality characteristics. This pattern includes motives for action, the organization and development of self, values and standards of conduct, and relationships with other individuals.
3. Individuals differ from one another in personal values, attitudes, personalities, and roles; yet, at the same time, the members of a group must possess certain common values and characteristics.

4. Social groupings develop as a means of group cooperation in meeting the needs of the individuals. The basic unit of the family makes it possible for two individuals to cooperate in producing and training children. Similarly, other social groupings—such as communities, social organizations, and nations—enable individuals to work together toward satisfaction of common needs. The nature and structure of groupings tend to change and become more complex with the circumstances under which man lives.

5. Every individual is a member of several social groups, each of which helps to satisfy his needs. The child starts life as a member of a family but soon establishes additional memberships in school, neighborhood, church, and other groups. As he matures, he extends his membership into a greater variety of groups.

Society and the individual.

1. Each of the social groups to which an individual belongs helps shape his behavior. Members of different societies learn different ways of acting, perceiving, thinking, and feeling. Groups exert pressures on their members so that they will accept and follow group ways and mores. The behavior of any individual reflects in many ways the influences of group pressures.

2. Differences are important in the personality structure and behavior of individuals and make possible the infinite variety of work and recreation activities that characterize modern culture. Differences also furnish a basis for flexibility and creativity, which are essential to social change and development. In any social group, the range of differences among individuals is likely to be greater than the differences between any two groups.

3. Socialization processes, such as methods of child training, differ markedly in different social classes, groups, and societies. Personality structure and behavior are largely influenced by these processes. Individuals develop standards of values that reflect these influences as they seek to relate themselves to the group and to satisfy personal needs.

4. The satisfaction of social needs is a strong motivating force in the determination of individual behavior. Values placed on learning, as well as levels of aspiration, are largely attributable to the mores of the individual's "reference groups." What sometimes appears to be nonconforming behavior may be in reality conforming behavior in terms of a particular group in which an individual seeks status. The strong human tendency to conform to social pressures often prevents individuals from seeing reality. The stereotyping of individuals because of racial or cultural backgrounds is another example. In general, noncooperative, aggressive behavior indicates that the individual's need for social acceptance has been frustrated. The individual displaying such behavior usually has been forced, through repeated experiences of rejection, to develop an attitude of defeat and inferiority.

5. The behavior of individuals is related to the structure and organization of the group in which they are placed. A range of roles, such as leadership, followership, aggression, and submission, may be exhibited by the same individual in different groups. The "need-satisfying" quality of a group and the member-to-member relationship influence behavior.

6. For preservation of its identity, a social group resists change through the phenomena of cultural lag and conservatism. A social group also changes in various degrees to preserve its identity when new conditions arise.[20]

PSYCHOLOGY AND THE CURRICULUM

Status of Psychology. Like economics, psychology has not had much of a role in the secondary schools. Lately, however, psychology has been gaining in popularity—usually as an elective in the twelfth grade.

Content of Psychology. Some high school psychology courses have centered around problems of adjustment. Psychologists feel that such practice is a mistake for several reasons.

1. Knowledge of psychology does not seem to be greatly helpful in solving problems of adjustment.
2. The direct approach does not seem to be effective.
3. The contribution of psychology is its scientific approach to the study of human behavior. Courses emphasizing adjustment seem likely to subvert psychology's principal contribution—"its systematic knowledge and methods as a scientific discipline."[21] Consequently, it is probable that the secondary school psychology courses should center around the methods of determining any psychological facts and concepts to be found in such general areas as:
The biological background of behavior.
Perception.
Learning.
Motivation and emotion.
Personality.
Measurement of abilities and traits.
Social psychology.[22]
Specific generalizations that might be included under these headings can be found in the California Commission Report previously quoted.

SOME STRATEGIES AND TACTICS FOR TEACHING THE BEHAVIORAL SCIENCES

You will find some specific suggestions for strategies and tactics for teaching behavioral sciences in this section. Remember: the structure of the behavioral sciences requires that you place at least some emphasis on problem solving and inquiry teaching.

1. Use multiple readings (paperbacks).
2. Use problems (for example, archaeological problems using evidence cards,

---

[20] State Curriculum Commission, Social Studies Framework for the Public Schools of California (Sacramento, Calif.: California State Department of Education, 1962), pp. 89–109, reprinted in Michaelis and Johnston, op. cit., pp. 306–339, and elsewhere.

[21] McKeachie, op. cit., pp. 178–179.

[22] Ibid., pp. 182–189.

site maps, photographs, facsimile documents, models, casts, wall charts, film strips, and recordings from which pupils try to piece together the evidence and draw conclusions).

3. Use role-playing activities.
   a. Role play situations that illustrate roles, for example:
      (1) Pupils at school, pupils at a party, pupils at home, pupils at a club meeting.
      (2) Members of a family.
   b. Role play situations that illustrate expectations.
   c. Role play the behavior of people of such and such a culture faced by such and such a situation.
   d. Role play the reactions of persons of different cultures in a certain situation (for example, a teenage boy finding a certain girl attractive).
4. Provide opportunities for pupils to analyze material statistically. Let pupils build scattergrams, profile charts, and histograms; compute correlations; study charts, graphs, and tables; and draw inferences from them.
5. Use films, television, and radio programs to show
   a. Culture differences.
   b. Different solutions to common problems.
   c. Cultural determination of behavior.
   d. Problems of a changing culture.
   e. And so on.
6. Use pictures to illustrate roles, stereotypes, culture differences, artifacts, and so on.
7. Encourage pupils to adopt pen pals in other communities or countries.
8. Compare differing ideas held about certain institutions (for example, marriage or child-adult relationships) and discuss them.
9. Use music, stories, plays, and the like to bring out beliefs, customs, and attitudes.
10. Use readings as springboards for discussing social problems and various cultural solutions to human problems, and so on.
11. Use adjective check lists for rating several types of people; for example, ask respondents to check the type of person each adjective describes best, as in the following form:

	Physician	Clergyman	Professor
Scholarly			
Poor			
Young			
Well dressed			

Such exercises are good for studying stereotypes, role expectations, and similar phenomena.

12. Do a case study or depth study of a certain phenomenon, incident, or human problem (for example, a comparative study of youth's attitudes toward marriage, Negro leadership, or the society of your school).

13. Have pupils prepare specialized maps showing one or more types of socio-
    logical data (for example, the locations of shopping centers, homes, business
    districts, census information, and the like. You could provide outline maps
    of the area so that pupils would not have to spend too much time on busy
    work).
14. Conduct research projects.
    a. Investigate the sources of American customs, words, names or the like
       (for example, See George E. Stewart, *Names on the Land* (Boston:
       Houghton Mifflin Company, 1967).
    b. Investigate the impact of an innovation (for example, the advent of the
       automobile).
    c. Search through old magazines and catalogs for advertisements. What do
       they show about change in our culture?
    d. Study some aspects of the school or community.
       Use survey techniques.
       Use interviews.
       Use questionnaires or opinionaires.
       Use source material such as newspaper reports and census material.
15. Perform simple psychological experiments.[23]

---

[23] For further ideas for teaching the behavioral sciences, see Rose, op. cit., Chap. 6, and Pelto,
op. cit., Chap. 6.

CHAPTER 13

Integrated Programs, Current Events, and International Relations

INTEGRATED AND INTERDISCIPLINARY COURSES

The real world is not divided into disciplines. The disciplines are figments of scholarly imaginations concocted to aid them in their research and study. More and more in the world of research the borders between disciplines have had to be broken down because the nature of the real world defies investigation limited to single disciplines. Perhaps the barriers between school subjects should also be broken down. At least that is the opinion of numerous educators who have been attempting to establish multidisciplinary or interdisciplinary courses for at least half a century.

SOCIAL STUDIES AS A DISCIPLINE

Since World War I there has been a movement to teach the social studies as a fused whole rather than as separate courses in geography, history, and the various social sciences. The late Samuel P. McCutcheon, for instance, believed that the social studies could and should constitute a discipline in its own right made up of four components:

The societal goals of America.

The heritage and values of Western civilization.

The dimensions and interrelationships of today's world.

A specific process of rational inquiry and the tenets of good scholarship.[1]

Other educators have devised other centers for fused social studies courses. Miller[2] suggests a fused course built around social change as viewed by behavioral scientists. Sandberg[3] recommends a fused course for the talented called In-

---

[1] Samuel P. McCutcheon, "A Discipline for the Social Studies," *Social Education*, **27**:62–63 (Feb. 1963).

[2] Stuart C. Miller, "The Interdisciplinary Approach to Teaching Social Studies," *Social Education*, **28**:195–198 (April 1964).

[3] John H. Sandberg, "An Independent Study Course for Able High School Students," *Social Education*, **28**:199–200 (April 1964).

troduction to the Social Sciences. The subject matter of this course includes sociology, anthropology, political science, psychology, and economics. The focus of
the course is what social scientists do and how they do it.

Recently there has once again been a movement toward courses that integrate
not only the contents from the social studies, but also from other academic areas.
Examples of broad integrated courses include humanities courses, unified
studies courses, area studies, core curricula, and block-of-time courses. Such
courses are characterized by the broadness of their scope. Oftentimes they are
also characterized by multiperiod classes and teams of teachers.

Some interdisciplinary courses are pupil and problem centered. Such courses
tend to ignore subject matter lines, to take up subject matter and skills as they
are needed rather than in any fixed sequence, and to provide for individual differences through the use of laboratory techniques, individualized instruction,
and similar methods. Unit topics typical of such courses include

Problems of school living.
Problems of economic relations.
Problems of intergroup relations.
Problems of finding values by which to live.
Problems of relations with minority groups.
Problems of technological change and modern living.[4]

Most interdisciplinary courses are subject and teacher oriented even though
they are made up of a number of subjects that have been fused into a single
course sequence. Humanities and area studies courses are usually of this sort.
Humanities course content may be drawn from history, philosophy, the fine
arts, or what you will. (The humanities include history, literature, dance, music,
and philosophy.) Usually it centers on some topic or theme, frequently a great
issue or a great man, and draws content from whatever sources seem most relevant. Its purpose is to give pupils an opportunity to meet the great issues and
great men of all time, and to expose pupils to the world's best thinking and
expression. It is hoped that such courses will open up pupils' minds and make
them more aware of the world and of their culture. A problem area studied in a
humanities course might well be "Problems of Finding Values by Which to
Live," or "Problems of Technological Change." A topic in a less venturesome
humanities course might well be "The Age of Elizabeth" or "The Romantics," in
which history, literature, and the fine arts are combined.

Area studies are unified studies focused on a single area or region such as the
Near East, Latin America, India, the Soviet Union, or the USA. The subject
matter of area studies courses may be drawn from any subject field pertinent to
the topic, although some area studies are limited pretty well to social studies
content. Trow, for instance, suggests an area study social studies curriculum in
which the social sciences would contribute concepts that would aid in understanding the life of people in different locales and periods; for example:

> Anthropology. (How do they live?) The people, their beliefs, traditions,
> customs; religion, recreation; archeological artifacts. The curriculum might
> be called anthropology, in the sense that it is the study of man in different

---

[4] William Van Til, *Modern Education for the Junior High School Years* (Indianapolis: The Bobbs-
Merrill Co., Inc., 1967), pp. 266–267.

cultures. Certainly the point of view should be maintained. Appropriate data will be included whether they were turned up by anthropologists, social psychologists, or others.

History. (What have they done?) The sequence of events, cause and effect; factors affecting stability and change. History is recognized as providing the time line for the underlying structure which symbolizes the contemporaneity and succession of events, so students will construct parallel time lines relating different periods. The lessons of the past are difficult to interpret in the changed context of the present, but little of the present can be understood without a knowledge of the past.

Geography. (Where do they live?) Surface structure, ecological factors; land masses, waterways; flora, fauna; divisions: natural (altitude, soil, climate), and political (states, countries). Geography provides the maps which symbolize the spatial relationships and influences. So students will learn to make, read, and interpret maps. The why of what occurs cannot be answered without knowing the setting, the where as well as the when.

Psychology. (What is their nature?) Growth, development, attitudes, knowledge, skills.

Sociology. (How do they live together?) Groupings, social class; leadership, communication, institutions.

Economics. (How do they make a living?) Wealth, occupations, products, imports; transportation; science and technology.

Political Science. (How are they governed?) Sources of power, governmental forms, political parties; law making, interpretation, enforcement; power groups—external, internal; war and peace.

Health, Education, and Welfare. (How do they take care of themselves?) Medicine, education, and social work. (All the social sciences and other disciplines contribute in one way or another to the development of these professions. But because of their importance in any culture, these call for special consideration.)

Art. (How do they express themselves esthetically?) Crafts, architecture, sculpture, painting, literature, music, dance. (Included in Area Study, though classed with the humanities rather than the social sciences.)[5]

ORGANIZING INTEGRATED COURSES

The basic principles for organizing core curriculum, unified studies, humanities, and area studies courses are the same.

1. Establish the objectives.
2. Select integrating themes or threads.
3. Select the problems, themes or topics that will be the units.
4. For each problem, theme, or topic select unit objectives.
5. Select content and activities that will attain the objectives, from any appropriate subject or discipline.
6. Execute.

[5] William Clark Trow, "An Area-Study Social Studies Curriculum," *Social Education*, 29:142–146 (March 1965). Reprinted with permission of the National Council for the Social Studies and William Clark Trow.

The planning of multidisciplinary or interdisciplinary courses, then, is not different from the planning of other courses, except that the content is chosen from a larger reservoir and it is more necessary to provide coordinating themes or threads because there is no disciplinary structure to provide them. However, planners of such courses would do well to stick to the problem-and-topic approach. There is always a danger of making courses too academic.

Another danger in planning interdisciplinary courses is the temptation to include too much. Just because one has content of all sorts of material from many disciplines available, it does not follow that one must use it all. It is much more satisfactory to be selective, to study relatively small topics in depth, and to allow pupils a chance to mull over what is being studied.

METHODS OF TEACHING INTEGRATED COURSES

Integrated courses have no magic that makes them easy to teach. In fact, they are likely to be somewhat more demanding of teachers than lesser courses.

Integrated Versus Intergrating. The purpose of integrated courses is to provide course work that is more meaningful and, therefore, more usable for adolescents. The mere fact of serving up multidisciplinary or interdisciplinary courses does not meet this purpose. The courses must be integrative as well as integrated, or they will not succeed. In the final analysis, the integrating of the learning in a course must be done by the learner. It follows, then, that courses must be taught in such ways that the pupils draw inferences and conclusions and so gain the skills and attitudes necessary for mastering the new learning and integrating it into their personalities. Interdisciplinary courses that do not integrate learning are simply courses in which the subject matter is served in a different way. A spoiled pie tastes just as bad when it is cut in squares as it does when it is cut in wedges. Interdisciplinary courses give teachers more room to maneuver, but it is the way teachers teach that gives them their value.

The Method of Inquiry. As we have seen McCutcheon claimed that the method for teaching the social studies should be the method of problem solving. Undoubtedly, the use of problem-solving strategies and the method of inquiry will help pupils to (1) learn the methods of the social sciences, (2) help them shape their learning into more meaningful usable units, and (3) integrate their new learning into the body of knowledge they have already learned. It has much to recommend it.

TACTICS AND TECHNIQUES SUITABLE FOR INTEGRATED COURSES

The strategies and tactics used in integrated courses are the same as those used in discrete courses in the disciplines. What works well in one should work well in the other, except that the teacher of integrated courses has an advantage in that he has more room to maneuver because of the broader base of integrated courses.

Some suggestions concerning teaching strategies for integrated courses follow:

1. Use multireadings. Avoid single-textbook recitation approaches.
2. Concentrate on inquiry and discovery.
3. Center the course around problems—preferably real problems of youth and society.
4. Utilize laboratory procedures.
5. Make many provisions for individual differences. The nature of integrated courses lends itself to individual research projects, committee and small-group work, and similar techniques.
6. Use multimedia approaches.
7. Use one discipline to strengthen another; for example,
   a. Have pupils illustrate the antebellum period by painting a mural, drawing pictures, acting out a dramatic production, role playing, staging a ballet, or playing music of the period.
   b. Have an exhibit of gadgetry from another culture.
   c. Bring in music of the lands or periods being studied.
   d. Stage dramatizations.
   e. Show and analyze films.
   f. Play a recording of John Gay's *The Beggar's Opera* to illustrate history.
   g. Use slides of Hogarth's paintings to study eighteenth-century England.
   h. Read the Cavalier Poets to illustrate Restoration Culture.
   i. Compare the *Three Penny Opera* with the *Beggar's Opera* to bring out similarities between the eighteenth century and the 1920s.
8. Use much depth study.
   a. Research the fashions of Louis XIV's court and design dresses for the period.
   b. Learn to dance the minuet, the galop, or some other dance of a period or country.
   c. Study in detail the life in a frontier fort and build a model of a typical fort.
   d. Study the caveman's technology and attempt to fashion some stone tools.
9. Use experts to discuss their specialities. Also use humanities films and film lectures, television and radio programs, and the like to give the course life and breadth. Use these as springboards on which to base discussion and further study.
10. In short, use content from the various fields as they are most useful. In the words of Scott Heyman, use "the freelance approach"; that is, include "bits and pieces whenever they seem relevant. . . . If an imaginative approach can be developed in a unified lesson, well and good. Method must suit the individual teacher and the particular situation."[6]

CURRENT EVENTS OR CONTEMPORARY AFFAIRS

OBJECTIVES OF CURRENT EVENTS TEACHING

The study of current events, or contemporary affairs, is essential in the social studies curriculum. Use it:

[6] Scott Heyman, "And Music," in Thomas F. Powell, ed., "Humanities and the Social Studies," *Bulletin No. 44,* (Washington, D. C.: National Council for the Social Studies, 1969), p. 86.

1. To create in pupils an awareness, understanding, and interest in the problems and issues of the day.

2. To instill in pupils the habit of keeping up with the news.

3. To help pupils learn how to deal with problems and issues.

4. To develop skills in the use of the news media and the evaluation of information.

5. To illustrate and pinpoint generalizations and principles in history and the social sciences.

6. To bring the historical record up to date.

7. To introduce topics in social studies courses.

8. To motivate the study of social studies courses.

9. To make history and the social sciences more interesting, exciting, and alive.

10. To show the relationship between past and present.

11. To give substance to thought questions in social studies courses.

12. To break down the gap between school and the real world.

CURRENT EVENTS AND CONTEMPORARY AFFAIRS AS CONTENT

Current events are continuations and extensions of what has gone on before and are presagers of what will happen in the future. They are never isolated, for they are components of the total pattern of events that makes up the milieu at one time. Therefore, it seems proper to state categorically that *current events should never be studied in isolation, but should always be studied in relationship to other events,* past, present, and future. The study of current events requires depth and continuity to be meaningful. A conglomeration of separate current events has no value. *The common practice of teaching current events as discrete entities, usually by having pupils bring in clippings that they read during the current events period, without any real attempt by the teacher to introduce, follow up, or correlate the current events reading with other social studies teaching, is worthless and inexcusable malpractice.*

Wherever possible, then, integrate current events into the social studies unit you teach. Make historical, geographical, sociological, economic, political, or psychological considerations part of current events study. Help pupils see how the current events of the day illustrate the generalizations and principles found in history and the social sciences.

There are, of course, current events that are so important that you should teach them immediately, even if they do not seem to be pertinent to other course work being studied at the time. In such a situation, temporarily put aside the regular course work so that one can study the significance, background, cause, and implications of the event at hand. The rule in favor of integration of current events and other content still applies, but in this type of an instance the current event becomes the center on which the other content is focused.

What Content in Current Events? Briefly, current events lessons should include

1. Current events of significance — that is to say, current events that make a difference in the world, nation, community, or in our lives.

2. The background of the current events, what factors caused them or influenced them, and their relationships to other events and factors.
3. Important issues and problems facing contemporary society at the local, state, national, and international levels.
4. Sources of information concerning current issues, problems, and events.
5. Current issues, problems, and events that illustrate or point up the content of courses in history and the social sciences.
6. The skills necessary for studying and keeping informed about current issues, problems, and events. Among these skills are
   a. Ability to locate, gather, organize, and evaluate new material.
   b. Ability to judge factualness.
   c. Ability to read and interpret charts, graphs, diagrams, maps, tables, statistics, cartoons, illustrations.
   d. Ability to listen attentively and critically.
   e. Ability to read critically.
   f. Ability to think critically.
   g. Ability to discuss objectively.
   h. Ability to detect and evaluate propaganda, bias, and coloring of reports.

Criteria for Selecting Content for Current Events Teaching.   Perhaps the following criteria will help you select content for current events teaching. Essentially, they are the same as those for selecting any other course content.

1. Is it significant? What difference does it make?
2. How is it related to other subject matter? Is it pertinent to what is being studied? Is it pertinent to course objectives? Does it relate to other schoolwork?
3. Does it have motivational value? Could it be used as a springboard? Is it interesting?
4. Are sources of information readily available in sufficient quantity for pupils to study and understand the event, its background, and its implications?

ORGANIZING CURRENT EVENTS CONTENT

There are a number of ways to incorporate current events content into social studies courses:

1. Isolated topics. Sometime current events topics are studied separately as they come up. These topics can be studied as short units taking one or two periods. Although the topic can be studied in some depth, there is no attempt to tie it directly to other course work.
2. Correlated. Sometimes teachers attempt to correlate current events teaching with other social studies content by picking current events topics that are illustrative of what is being studied in the course and by pointing out the relationships between the current events happenings and the social studies course content.
3. Integrated. Sometimes teachers weld current events and social studies content into integrated lessons and units. In some cases, the social studies content is the basis of the course and the current events point it up. In other cases, current affairs may be the basis of the course, and history and the social science content

are used to explain the current issues, problems, or events being studied. Full integration of current events with the other subject matter to be taught in social studies courses is difficult to do well. It requires the teacher to be (1) well versed in his subject matter content, (2) awake to what is going on in the news, and (3) alert to see and help pupils find the relationships between today's news and academe. However, it seems to be a goal worth seeking.

4. Survey (shotgun). Perhaps the most common approach consists of discussing selected items in the news as they occur. This type of organization gives good coverage, but otherwise is not recommended as it tends to be superficial, inaccurate, tangential, and artificial.

5. Continuing issue. Sometime the class picks current topics, issues, or problems and follows them week after week as long as they remain important and pertinent. The topics can be followed by the whole class, or by committees, or by individuals who report to the class from time to time.

6. Combinations. The organizational categories listed are not mutually exclusive. You probably will find that you need to use a mixture of the various approaches.

Scheduling Current Events Weekly or Daily.   Current Events usually occupies about 20 per cent of the time allocated to social studies. In a large number of courses, current events is taught once a week, usually either Friday or Monday. In other courses, teachers give over the first few minutes of each class to current events. Neither of these approaches is very satisfactory, because the current events tend to become divorced from the rest of the social studies being taught.

Scheduling Current Events As the Occasion Warrants.   Still another way to teach is to discuss current events as opportunities present themselves. This approach is often associated with the integration of current events with other social studies. Teachers who are awake to the potential value of current events for illustrating, amplifying, and clarifying history and the social sciences, use this approach in their classes. However, to get reasonable continuity and organization is extremely difficult. If this approach seems to you to be too haphazard, as it does to many teachers, there is no reason why you cannot combine it with one or both of the organized schedules described in the preceding paragraphs.

A variation on this approach is the committee report type, one example of which was described earlier as the continuing issue approach. Here the teacher assigns specific topics to committees to study or follow in the news and to report at certain times or on call. This type of current events organization can be combined with any of the other types of organization for current events teaching. In conjunction with other types of current events teaching it can be quite effective.

METHODS OF TEACHING CURRENT EVENTS

Contrary to what many beginning teachers seem to think, current events, or contemporary affairs, is difficult to teach effectively. The fact that in current events teaching there is usually relatively little time to prepare, and that no teacher can possibly be an expert in all areas that might come up, makes current events classes especially trying. In addition, many schools have limited sources of information suitable for use in current events classes, and sometimes much of that information is biased, inaccurate, or too difficult for the pupils to read with understanding. Also, by their very nature, current events and contemporary affairs tend to be controversial. Although this factor tends to make current events and contemporary affairs exciting, it creates methodological problems for the teacher.[7]

To be effective, you must plan and teach current events at least as carefully as the other social studies content. However, if you and your pupils really try to answer carefully each of the following questions about every current event you study, you should do well.

1. What exactly happened?
2. Why did it happen?
3. What difference does it make?
4. If it makes a difference, what can be done about it?[8]

SPECIFIC TECHNIQUES AND TACTICS IN TEACHING CURRENT EVENTS AND CONTEMPORARY AFFAIRS

1. Use bulletin boards, flannel boards, or hook and loop boards to display materials to attract attention, to create interest, and to form a basis for current events lessons.
    a. Bulletin boards can be divided into sections; for example:

Current Events			
International	National	State	Local

   Other headings might be music, sciences, theater, and so on. Give the responsibility for certain sections of the bulletin board, or for the entire bulletin board, to committees or to individual pupils.
    b. Provide bulletin board space for a glossary of new words.
    c. Coordinate the bulletin board display with current events reports and discussions.
    d. Have pupils raise questions about the material being displayed. These can be added to the bulletin board or put on the chalkboard as the basis for discussion.
    e. Use the bulletin board as a basis for class discussion.
    f. Make a picture gallery of personalities in the news.
2. Let pupils prepare current events notebooks and scrapbooks.
    a. Current events notebooks could include such things as summaries of the news, discussion notes, glossaries of new or difficult words, and commentary and conclusions written by the pupils. The notebook can be organized in either chronological or topical form. Perhaps the best way is

---

[7] See Chapter 2 for a discussion of controversial issues and suggestions for handling them.
[8] Edgar Dale, "Six Basic Jobs for the Press," in William D. Boutwell, ed., *Using Mass Media in Schools* (New York: Appleton-Century-Crofts, 1962), p. 196.

to divide the notebook into sections by topics and then enter the events chronologically. Let the pupils make up a list of topics in a pupil-teacher planning session. Change the list when events make it seem desirable. Among the topics that might be included in current events notebooks are

Space	Our Town
The World	People in the News
The United States	The Arts
Foreign Affairs	Business and Finance
Domestic Affairs	Science
Politics	Religion
The State	Communications.

  b. Have pupils keep current events scrapbooks. Include in them such things as feature stories, cartoons, editorials, writings of featured columnists with suitable commentary by the pupils. Usually scrapbooks are made individually, but group scrapbooks can be quite successful. To be useful, the clippings and so forth must be organized and evaluated by the pupils. Scrapbooks can be generalized or specialized just as notebooks can be.

  c. Usually a combination scrapbook and notebook that draws heavily on the pupils' reactions, evaluations, interpretations, and organizations of scrapbook material is more successful than either a notebook or a scrapbook. Scrapbooks that do not contain commentary by the pupils are likely only to be busywork.

3. Have pupils collect clippings following a single topic, issue, or current events in general. These can be used as the basis for displays and reports. Sometimes clippings should be mounted and filed for a permanent collection.

4. Accompany all current events teaching with map and globe work.
  a. Have pupils locate where important events have occurred.
  b. Utilize newsmaps to illustrate what is happening in the world.
  c. Use outline maps.
  d. Have pupils construct their own news maps.
  e. Use map transparencies. Pupils can make flip-ons to illustrate, locate, and point out geographical elements in the news of the world.

5. Encourage pupils to discuss current events.
  a. Conduct class discussions of current topics in the news.
  b. Have pupils discuss reports brought in by individual pupils and small groups or committees.
  c. Use such formal discussion techniques as debate, panels, round tables, town meetings, forums, English debates, juries, trials, and so on. These are described in detail in Chapter 4.
  d. Discuss values.
    (1) Give the pupils an article to read.
    (2) Give them questions about the article to guide their thinking.
    (3) Have pupils give their reactions to the questions.
    (4) In discussion, examine the different viewpoints without advocating any position as right or wrong. Pupils should be able to understand their own thinking and values better as a result of this type of teaching.[9]

[9] Phyllis Lieberman and Sidney B. Simon, "Current Events and Values," *Social Education,* **29**:532–533 (Dec. 1965).

6. Utilize reports by individuals or committees. Have individual pupils or committees
    a. Interview someone who has special knowledge of a certain affair or event, and report to the class (for example, a legislator, world traveler, Vista or Peace Corps veteran, military veteran, and so on).
    b. Make special biographical studies of figures in the news and report on them.
    c. Investigate the background of a current event and brief pupils on what has led up to the event, and if possible, point out the probable causes and effects.
    d. Follow a certain story or issue for a period and report on the developments from time to time.
    e. Follow certain sections of a newspaper or magazine and brief pupils on what has appeared in them occasionally.
    f. Have committees be responsible for reading and reporting on one article. Let them look up and present the background of the article, the facts presented in the article, and their interpretation of the article. Encourage the class to question them on details.
    g. During periods of important news, divide the class into committees and assign each committee to follow the coverage of the key stories on a particular medium. The committees then should report to the entire class how the stories were reported on "their" medium. Each committee could use the following outline for a guide:
       (1) Story.
       (2) Reporter.
       (3) Facts presented.
       (4) Points emphasized.
       (5) Conclusions made, if any.
       (6) Comment.
7. Use cartoons and pictures.
    a. Have pupils interpret political cartoons in the press.
    b. Make a collection of cartoons, illustrations, and pictures applicable to current events lessons.
    c. Have pupils draw cartoons, posters, illustrations, comic strips, and other art work representing and interpreting current affairs.
    d. Have pupils assemble a pictorial essay explaining and illustrating current community problems.
8. Use dramatics and role playing.
    a. Let the pupils dramatize or role play events in the news.
    b. Let the pupils plan and present mock television or radio newscasts.
    c. Let the pupils present a television or radio news special in which the pupils analyze some current situation, issue, or problem facing the nation, community, or region.
    d. Let pupils see a film that presents a current issue or problem.
    e. Let pupils work out and present a weekly newscast to present to the entire school over the public address system, the dial access network, or the closed-circuit television system.
    f. Simulate legislative debates on current problems; that is, at mock sessions of Congress, the UN Assembly, the city council, or the legislature.
    g. Plan and present assembly programs on current affairs, issues, and

problems, such as international foreign policy, the economic situation, urban affairs, or political campaigns.

9. Use community resources.
   a. Have pupils interview local officials or experts.
   b. Invite a local authority or expert to speak to the class or to join in a class discussion.
   c. Encourage pupils to attend local meetings: hearings, council meetings, forums, discussion groups, citizens' committee meetings, and political meetings of civic and patriotic groups.
   d. Take field trips to sites currently in the news.
   e. Arrange for telephone interviews with local authorities. (It may be possible to arrange facilities, through the telephone company or the audiovisual department, so that everyone can hear and speak to the person being interviewed.)
10. Have pupils evaluate the news presented in the mass media. (See Chapter 14.)
11. Correlate and integrate with other social studies.
    a. Have pupils or committees
       (1) Figure out and report the historical, geographical, economic, sociological and/or political reasons why certain current events happened as they did.
       (2) Take a problem from some period of history and try to find out if the problem is still significant; if so, how is it being handled today; if not, how was the problem solved, or why is it no longer important?
       (3) Make generalizations on the basis of similarities between past and present situations.
    b. In your teaching
       (1) Refer to specific current happenings to bring out points in history and the social sciences (for example, federalism versus states' rights, civil rights, conservation, or protection versus free trade).
       (2) Trace the origins of current affairs in the past.
       (3) Refer to similar situations in either the past or present to illustrate what you are studying.
12. Use in-depth study to avoid superficiality.
    a. Tie current events study to
       (1) Map work.
       (2) Research projects.
       (3) Committee work.
       (4) Critical thinking.
    b. Fill in information missing in press accounts about a current affair.
    c. Require study in depth. Have certain people specialize on a topic, issue, or problem.
    d. Use an entire period for one topic rather than survey many topics.
    e. Have pupils follow one topic for a month or more.
13. Publish a class newspaper.
14. Record radio news broadcasts. Play these newscasts or portions of them during the current events class as a basis for discussion.
15. Videotape news telecasts for presentation during classes on current affairs or to show contemporary examples of historical or social science issues and problems.

16. Tape record short-wave English language newscasts of foreign radio stations and the Voice of America as a basis for class discussion. Note the difference in viewpoint presented by the foreign newscasters, the Voice of America, and the local press radio and television.

17. Adopt a sister school. Exchange news and information about the school and community.

SOURCES OF INFORMATION ABOUT CURRENT EVENTS

1. Maps and globes (absolutely essential).
2. Newspapers: dailies, weeklies, Sunday.
3. Newspaper supplement.
4. Radio.
5. Television.
6. News magazines (for example, *Time, Newsweek, U.S. News and World Report, The National Observer*).
7. General magazines (for example, *The Atlantic, Harpers, The World, The Reader's Digest*).
8. Interpretive magazines (for example, *The Nation, The New Republic*, liberal; *The National Review*, conservative).
9. Student current history publications (for example, *Scholastic*).
10. Pamphlet materials.
11. School assemblies.
12. Local organizations (for example, *League of Women Voters, Daughters of the American Revolution, Americans for Democratic Action*, unions, political parties). Beware of slanted material.
13. Community resources such as knowledgeable adults to be speakers or to be interviewed, political meetings, and so on.
14. Weekly news maps.
15. Filmstrips.[10]

WORLD AFFAIRS AND INTERNATIONAL UNDERSTANDING

In most schools, whatever is taught about world affairs, world understanding, and international relations is taught in the various social studies courses and sometimes in foreign language and literature courses, not in separate courses. One school system, in Glens Falls, New York, has made an all out effort to incorporate world understanding throughout its curriculum.[11] This experiment has proved, without a doubt, that world understanding can be taught in all subjects and at all levels. Few school systems make any special effort in this direction, however.

---

[10] A basic reference for teaching current events is John C. Payne, ed., *The Teaching of Contemporary Affairs*, Twenty-first Yearbook (Washington, D. C.: National Council for the Social Studies, 1950).

[11] Harold M. Long and Robert N. King, "Improving the Teaching of World Affairs: The Glens Falls Story," *Bulletin No. 35* (Washington, D. C.: National Council for the Social Studies, 1964).

OBJECTIVES OF WORLD AFFAIRS EDUCATION

World Affairs is taught at two levels:

1. International relations are taught in ways that show the pulling and tugging of nations as they try to implement their foreign policies and solve the various problems on the international scene.

2. World understanding is taught so as to create attitudes and understandings in citizens that will, presumably, eventually reduce the tensions among nations and so smooth the way toward world peace. To implement this objective much has been made of the value of person-to-person contacts, the theory being that, if people of different countries get to know each other, they will respect each other. Thus, for instance, the goals of the Glens Falls project were

   a. Increasing understanding of world affairs.
   b. Developing an appreciation of other peoples and cultures.
   c. Inculcating an attitude of respect toward foreign people.
   d. Promoting a sense of responsibility for furthering better understanding of foreign peoples and countries.[12]

BASIC STRATEGY FOR TEACHING INTERNATIONAL AFFAIRS AND WORLD UNDERSTANDING[13]

1. Basically one can best teach an understanding of international and world affairs through the use of problem-solving methods. Because this type of teaching takes time, it is most important to limit the content to a depth study of a few topics rather than a great number of topics. It is also better to study a single area or nation in depth rather than attempt to cover the entire globe.

2. Examples of topics that might be included in teaching international relations and world affairs:
   a. Problems of underdevelopment.
   b. Rich and poor countries.
   c. Overpopulation.
   d. The UN and its agencies.
   e. The waste of natural resources.
   f. NATO and pollution.
   g. Why nations disagree.

---

[12] Ibid., p. 46.

[13] The following lists are largely based on suggestions contained in James M. Becker and Howard D. Mehlenger, eds., *International Dimensions in the Social Studies,* Thirty-eighth Yearbook (Washington, D. C.: National Council for the Social Studies, 1968); Long and King, op. cit.; *Education for International Understanding* (Paris: Unesco, 1959); Mary Renaud, "Bringing the World into Your Classroom," *Curriculum Series No. 13* (Washington, D. C.: National Council for the Social Studies, 1968); and Samuel Everett and Christian O. Arndt, eds., *Teaching World Affairs in American Schools* (New York: Harper and Row Publishers, 1956). Consult these for more suggestions on content and methodology in teaching world affairs.

EXAMPLES OF TACTICS AND TECHNIQUES SUITABLE FOR TEACHING INTERNATIONAL RELATIONS AND WORLD UNDERSTANDING

Foreign Policy and International Relations

1. Study the program of United States foreign aid to a particular country.

2. Debate the role of the United States in Southeast Asia, the Middle East, or similar troubled areas.

3. Conduct a High School Conference on International Affairs.

4. Utilize simulation games that show the difficulties of conducting foreign policy, of arriving at sound decisions in foreign affairs, and of reaching agreements with other nations (for example, Inter-Nation, Crisis, or Dangerous Parallel).

5. Study cases of tense international situations or problems in depth, utilizing the case method, Foreign Policy Association, *Great Decisions* kits, *Crisis Papers* of the Atlantic Information Center for Teachers, and the like.

6. Conduct a model UN Assembly.

7. Invite speakers from the World Affairs Council, United Nations Association, and similar organizations.

8. Invite speakers from foreign consulates and the like to present the positions of their countries.

9. Invite speakers from industry to discuss problems of world trade.

10. Form a high school speakers' corps or debating teams to present programs on topics having to do with international relations to outside groups such as service clubs, PTAs, and the like.

11. Set up committees to research and report on specific questions in international affairs.

12. Have foreign language class pupils report on comments in foreign newspapers.

13. Encourage pupils to attend community meetings on foreign affairs conducted by such organizations as the United Nations Association, The World Affairs Council, and the League of Women Voters.

14. Conduct public opinion polls on problems of international relations.

15. Utilize International Relations Clubs, World Affairs Junior Councils, Junior Statesmen of America, and the like.

16. Study the United Nations and its role in world affairs.

17. Have pupils do reports, dramatizations, and stories on such topics as A Day in the Life of a Boy (Girl or Family) in _____.

18. Have pupils build a class file of information about other nations. They can write to foreign embassies, UNESCO, travel agencies, and the like for information.

19. Encourage pupils to write to pen pals in other countries.

20. Ask persons who have lived abroad to visit the class; for example:
    Immigrants.
    Exchange teachers.
    Exchange students.
    Businessmen.
    Government employees.

Press representatives.

Military personnel.

Foreign natives.

21. Adopt a foreign school affiliate: exchange letters, exchange art, exchange information about community life, the country, government, customs, recreation, dating, work, and so on. Exchange gifts (arrangements sometimes can be made through a consulate) and exchange newspapers.

22. Utilize the speakers and services of international service clubs (for example, Rotary).

23. Have pupils check to see where the food in the supermarket comes from.

24. Use fiction and other literature to give a picture of life in other countries.

25. Study biographies of heroes, leaders, and other people in foreign lands.

26. Have pupils make various kinds of maps (for example, flour maps, animated maps, charts, graphs, and murals).

27. In cooperation with art and music teachers, bring in examples or art and music of other lands.

28. Have pupils research, write, and conduct a puppet show, or other dramatization, depicting some aspect of living in another land.

29. Have pupils conduct style shows illustrating the dress of other lands, in cooperation with home economics teachers and classes.

30. Have each pupil become an expert on a country in the United Nations. It would be his responsibility to find out all he can about it, to follow it in the news, and to report on it.

31. Have pupils develop displays of materials, and so on, from a specific country or a group of countries.

32. Have pupils develop charts comparing the governments of different countries.

33. Have pupils write thumbnail sketches of other lands. Gather them into a booklet and publish it.

Extracurricular Activities for World Understanding

1. In an International Relations or World Affairs club, study aspects of another nation all year and then end up with a party or banquet that features the food and entertainment of that nation.
2. Help pupils collect, sort, package, and send off materials for children in a country where people are in need.
3. Conduct an international day and include
   a. Foreign students.
   b. Seminars. (If enough foreign students are available, each can be assigned to a classroom. Then classes of pupils can circulate in order to hear and see them all.)
   c. Film programs.
   d. Lectures.
   e. Exhibitions.
   f. Pageants.
   g. Posters.
4. Adopt a child in another land.
5. Conduct assembly programs such as a UN day assembly, or a town meeting assembly on the Middle-Eastern situation.

PART IV

Tools and Materials
of Instruction

CHAPTER 14

Mass Media[1]

THE mass media can contribute to the success of social studies courses in at least three ways. First, they make up part of the content of the social studies curriculum. Second, they can be vehicles for teaching much of the content of history, political science, sociology, problems of democracy, and current events. Third, they can be used to help pupils learn the methodology of history and the social sciences, particularly those skills necessary for determining and interpreting facts.

NEWSPAPERS

USING NEWSPAPERS

Every social studies classroom should be well stocked with newspapers and magazines. The collection should include both local and metropolitan dailies, including a newspaper of record, copies of *The New York Times, The Christian Science Monitor,* or another newspaper of similar reputation, and the local and state newspapers. If possible, a copy or two of reputable foreign newspapers (*The London Times* or *The Manchester Guardian*) would be helpful. In addition, other newspapers should be available for classroom use in the social studies resource center or school library. These newspapers, plus news magazines such as *Newsweek, Time,* or *U.S. News and World Report,* should be the basis of lessons that discuss current happenings.

ANALYZING THE NEWSPAPER

Part of the study of mass media should include the analysis of at least one newspaper. Such analysis will give the pupils a better understanding of newspapers and of news and increase their ability to judge the worth of news.

[1] Portions of this chapter have been adapted from Leonard H. Clark, *Social Studies and Mass Media,* originally printed in *The Mass Media in Secondary Education,* 1965 Yearbook (Plainfield, N. J.: New Jersey Secondary School Teachers Association, 1965), pp. 46–54.

Some Exercises for Use in Newspaper Analysis

1. Have pupils develop criteria for an analysis of newspapers.
2. Have pupils use these criteria to rate international, national, local, financial, sports, society, theater, movie, television, radio news, and editorials and advertising. Use a rating scale or A B C D F ratings.
3. Have pupils check the national and international news that are printed in a local newspaper against that in a metropolitan newspaper such as *The New York Times*. Let them compare both the space and the stories used. Also have them compare what actually came over the teletype with what the paper used.
4. Study the pictures and cartoons.
5. Have pupils discuss the newspaper audience. To whom is the newspaper addressed? What different publics are involved?

Other Activities for Pupils

1. Ask the editor of a local paper to brief you on his purposes and policies.
2. Discuss the educational value of a newspaper.
3. Discuss the importance of reading the newspapers.
4. Discuss what lay people expect of newspapers or what newsmen think the criteria of newsworthiness should be.
5. Discuss the influence the newspaper has in the community.

Learning How to Read a Newspaper

If pupils are ever to learn to use newspapers effectively and efficiently, they must be taught how to read them. Most of this task should be the responsibility of teachers of English. However, we in the social studies are also responsible for seeing to it that our pupils learn to read critically.

To read a newspaper critically one should consider these questions:

1. What is the purpose and general policy of the newspaper?
2. What editorial positions, stated or tacit, does the newspaper take (is it conservative or liberal)?
3. Does the information contained in particular news stories seem dependable?
   a. Who wrote the story? Can he be depended on? If it is a wire service story, does the reputation of the wire service indicate that it can be trusted? Does the paper, or the wire service, or the reporter have certain biases we should take into account?
   b. What is the source of the story? Does it seem reliable? In this connection how do we interpret such phrases as: a government official, a usually reliable source, and so on?
   c. Was the reporter on the scene or was his information secondhand or thirdhand — or perhaps bazaar rumor?
   d. Does the story seem factual? (See for ways to check facts.)
   e. Are there signs of coloring or managing the news? (See Chapter 5 for ways to detect slanting, coloring, or managing the news.)
      (1) Does the coverage reflect the real, relative importance of the stories?
      (2) Are controversial issues treated impartially?
      (3) Are facts distinguished from opinions?
      (4) Are the editorials important and effective?
      (5) Check on the predictions of columnists and correspondents.

To Motivate Pupils to Read Newspapers

1. Read unusual stories aloud.
2. Read old newspapers.
3. Display unusual headlines.
4. Read foreign papers.
5. Hang sections of newspapers on the wall of the classroom.
6. Make up questions and problems based on the day's news.
7. Discuss teen columns, letters to the editor, and so on.
8. Read and discuss the entertainment section.
9. Give an introductory quiz on Names in the News. Take the names from the news, editorials, sports section, columnists, and special features of your local newspaper.[2]

CINEMA

In spite of the inroads from television, movies still remain an important educational and recreational medium. They have been, and continue to be, quite influential in forming the standards and tastes of our young people (and of adults too, for that matter). They are also the basis of many of the ideas people have concerning other lands, other times, and other people.

Suggestions for Using Commercial Movies

Commercial films, such as those appearing in local theaters and on television, provide more social studies content than most teachers realize. All dramas — cinema, theatrical, or real — must take place in time and space, even if it is only "once upon a time" and "the land of make believe." Furthermore, dramas also draw their substance from the behavior of people and their relations with one another. Even when one eliminates the perversions and misrepresentations of reality — of which there are too many — a goodly number of films suitable for augmenting the social studies curriculum remain. Sometimes films whose relationships to the social studies seem distant, turn out to have excellent, useful material — especially films set abroad, which may have scenes depicting foreign lands and customs. The old movies that reappear on television are often the best suited for your purposes.

Learning About Commercial Films. It would be quite impossible for you to be knowledgeable about all the useful films that may come to local theaters and television stations. Fortunately, you do not have to be. Pupils can absorb some of the burden of bringing films to the attention of the class.

---

[2] For more complete information on the study of newspapers consult Edgar Dale, *How to Read a Newspaper* (Glenview, Ill.: Scott, Foresman and Company, 1941) and William A. Nesbit, *Interpreting the Newspaper in the Classroom,* 2nd ed. (New York: Thomas Y. Crowell Company, 1971). For more ideas on how to use the newspaper as a teaching tool consult Harry Bard, Claire Eckels, Sidney Blum, and Edyth Myers, *Learning from the Sun Papers,* 2nd ed. (Baltimore, Md.: The Sun, A. S. Abell Co., n.d.) and Howard H. Cummings and Harry Bard, "How to Use Daily Newspapers," *How to Do It Series No. 5* (Washington, D. C.: National Council for the Social Studies, 1964).

1. Let the pupils do the scouting necessary by reporting on the movie reviews and on movies they have seen that may be useful. Brief oral reports and bulletins or chalkboard notices will serve to alert other pupils when a likely movie with social studies impact is in town.

2. Scan the notices of coming attractions to find films that may be exploited.

3. Read the reviews in the local newspapers and newsmagazines.

4. Write or call on the local theater and television station managers; ask them to notify you of any film that may be appropriate for classroom use.

5. Sometimes, if asked, the theater manager or local television station can arrange for showings of classic films.

6. Many of the more famous movies have been made into 16 mm versions. These can be shown in the school on school equipment and so be made part of class assignments.[3]

7. Many films are available on television. One can find out about these as one would any other television program.

8. Many films are available from government agencies — national, state, and local. Films provided by chambers of commerce, industry, travel services, and the like are frequently useful and free from advertising.

Suggestions for Using Commercial Films

1. List the titles of useful films on the bulletin board, or chalkboard, as optional activities.

2. Announce the coming of films that seem worthwhile, and discuss how they might fit into the program.

3. Arrange theater parties for exceptional productions.

4. Use films as the basis for oral and written reports.

5. Use films that all can see as a basis for discussion.

6. Have a film section on the bulletin board giving information on appropriate films to be shown in local theaters and on television.

7. Assign exercises or reports similar to those to be suggested subsequently for *The Bridge Over the River Kwai.*

Using a Movie to Enrich Social Studies Teaching. The following activities are illustrative of the kinds of activities one might use in teaching via a feature film — in this case *The Bridge Over the River Kwai.*[4]

1. International affairs.
    a. Look up the Geneva Convention. What exactly is the law? Was Colonel Nickerson or Colonel Saito right? What countries had agreed to the Convention prior to World War II? When was it adopted? What is its present status? Do the countries of the Soviet Block subscribe to it? How about Red China? To what extent was it honored during World War II?
    b. Prepare a report on commando operations. Compare the operations of the Task Force with guerilla operations in South Vietnam. Why is it so difficult

---

[3] See David Mallory, *The School and the Art of Motion Pictures* (Boston: National Association of Independent Schools, 1964). This is probably the best reference on the use of films in teaching.

[4] Adapted from Leonard H. Clark, "Social Studies and The Bridge Over the River Kwai," *School Paperback Journal*, **2**:18–20 (Oct. 1965).

for any army to successfully combat troop operations like the one sent to
blow up the bridge?

2. Sociology. Note the difficulty the Japanese had in controlling the British captives. Why does it seem to be so difficult for conquerors to bend captives to
their will? Read Steinbeck's *The Moon Is Down* or see the movie and compare
it to *The Bridge Over the River Kwai.* How do the commanders try to control
their captives? Compare these efforts with those of the police in the United
States in their attempts to put down riots and stop demonstrations.

3. Geography. Where is the River Kwai (Khwae Noi)? Can you find it on a map?
Is there a railroad or highway there now? What type of terrain would you expect to find there? Is the scenery in the picture along the route accurate? Does
the picture portray the climate well? Look up the rainfall and temperature statistics for that part of the world and chart them.

4. Anthropology. Find out as much as you can about the people of the area.
What is their level of civilization? What is their religion? What are their
customs?

5. History. What was the military situation in the early part of World War II in
Southeast Asia? Why would the Japanese need a railroad from Rangoon to
Bangkok? What military value would it have? Did they really build one? Why
would the British want to destroy it? Report on the principal campaigns and
commanders in Southeast Asia. What was the strategic value of holding this
area?

6. Map work. Map out a route for the railroad from Bangkok to Rangoon using a
large-scale map. Draw a series of map overlays showing the position of the
various armies in Southeast Asia during the period from the fall of Burma on.
Make a terrain map showing the terrain, vegetation, and principal obstacles.

TELEVISION AND RADIO

There are at least four types of television programs suitable for use in social
studies courses.

1. Standard commercial programs.

2. Special events, such as the Republican and Democratic party conventions,
the Presidential inauguration, and so on.

3. General cultural, educational, informational, and enrichment programs.

4. Instructional programs designed for classroom use. Any of them can be
used to enrich the curriculum and help cut a window into the world outside the
school's academic ivory tower. They can be extremely useful for creating interest
in topics being studied, and as springboards for class discussion and inquiry
teaching.

SOURCES OF INFORMATION ABOUT TV PROGRAMS

Although it is true that much TV programming is fatuous, social studies teachers should try to become familiar with the programs that their pupils watch, especially those programs whose content may pertain to history or to one of the
social sciences — if for no other reason than to understand where the pupils may

be getting some of their misinformation. Therefore, keep track of what is slated for future productions on the local television channels. Such information may be found:

1. In the professional journals for example, *Today's Education, NEA Reporter, Social Education.*
2. In the local press.
3. In television guides.
4. In magazines.
5. By writing to the television stations and networks.

TAPING PROGRAMS

Television and radio programs that one wants to use in the classroom are seldom on the air when the class is in session. To overcome this difficulty one can rely, in part, on the use of pupil reports and summaries. Another solution is to tape the programs. Although video taping is necessary to make most television programs interesting and meaningful, audio tapes of such programs as the *President's News Conference* and *Meet the Press* are usually sufficient for classroom use.

USEFUL PROGRAMING

Educational and Informational Programs. Educational or informational programs can be a very good source of enrichment activity. Among the best are television travelogs, news specials, news commentaries, news programs, interview programs such as *Meet the Press, Face the Nation,* and portions of the *Today* show. Frequently, television stations while away the dull hours by running the publicity or training films of state, regional, or governmental agencies and commercial and industrial enterprises. Many of these films are surprisingly interesting and especially useful for social studies classes in geography, civics, and Problems of Democracy.

You can find out what will be shown locally by inquiring at your local stations. On occasion, a station might arrange to match its programing to the curriculum. Similar programs are frequently available over educational television stations in better hours. They can be used to advantage.

Newscasts and Public Affairs Programing. Perhaps the newscasts and public affairs specials are the most useful of the television programs being offered.

The study of news and current affairs should be much the same with radio and television as it is with newspapers and periodicals.

Instructional Programs. In many communities served by educational television stations, prime time is given to instructional programs designed for adults either for self-improvement or college credit. Often these programs can be used for high school classes. They can be assigned as the subjects of reports, or as supplementary assignments for certain individuals. At times these programs require a high level of viewing or listening skill, but often they do not.

Recreational Programs. Educational or cultural programs are natural material for classroom use. Such programs can be supplemented by many other programs that are basically recreational. For instance, any period drama, in addition to being theater, is also a representation of life taking place in historical time and may be useful for history classes.

PREPARING FOR THE PROGRAMS

To prepare specific activities for specific television programs requires that one know something of the content of the programs. Sharp eyes and attention to the TV news can ameliorate this problem. Often the announcement of planned programs in such periodicals as *TV Guide* give enough information to build activities. Sometimes it is possible to secure study guides through professional journals or through the telecasting station or network. Much can be gleaned also from the advertisements of the programs carried in newspaper Sunday supplements and entertainment sections. A good practice is to have a committee of pupils scout for useful programs.

For the most part, educational and cultural programs on both commercial and educational stations are far from popular with pupils. If you want the pupils to watch a specific program you must make viewing the program a definite assignment. Many teachers have success with bulletin board and chalkboard advertising and class discussion of selected programs.[5]

USE OF RADIO

The advent of television has sharply curtailed radio programing in some areas. However, many stations continue to feature excellent public interest programs in which matters of current importance in the community and in the nation are discussed. In some of the smaller communities, radio programing about the affairs and problems of the local community is much better than that of television. Programs sponsored by the state extension service, local institutions of higher learning, and civic organizations are frequently very useful. Because the cost of radio time is not so high as that of television time, some radio stations cover speeches, conventions, meetings, and other matters of local interest much more fully than television channels.

Shortwave Radio. Shortwave radio can be especially useful. Via shortwave it is possible to get the point of view of news reporting and commentary in other countries. The English language news commentaries from the BBC, CBC, Radio Havana, Radio Prague, and Radio Moscow are extremely interesting.

MAGAZINES

Magazines are similar to newspapers, but their authors and editors have the advantages of having time to prepare their stories carefully and of being free to concern themselves less with the news of the moment and more with matters of

---

[5] Gerald Leinwand and Daniel M. Feins, *Teaching History and the Social Studies in Secondary Schools* (New York: Pitman Publishing Corp., 1960), Chap. 15, contains an overview of the use of television in social studies teaching by a former television teacher.

wider import. The social studies class should have copies of news weeklies and other magazines readily available. These periodicals should furnish pupils with examples of both liberal and conservative viewpoints as well as those in the middle of the road.

Among the most useful periodicals are special purpose magazines such as *The National Geographic Magazine.* Less well known, but very useful and often beautifully illustrated, are the many magazines such as *Ford Times, Arizona Highways, Vermont Life, Coming Events in Britain, Steelways,* and other magazines published by bureaus of tourism, state development agencies, and the publicity departments of large industrial and commercial enterprises. These magazines often feature articles useful in classes in history, goegraphy, sociology, and economics.

Use news magazines to check the accuracy of news stories and to follow significant stories in depth. Their semipermanent format also makes back issues available for ready use. Thus, if a committee of pupils wanted to trace the progress of school integration since the famous 1954 Supreme Court decision, it would be much easier for them to do so in the back issue files of *Time* or *Newsweek* (although still a real job), than in the newspaper files.

WEEKLY NEWS MAGAZINES

Advantages. Several publishing houses specialize in providing weekly news magazines for pupils in junior and senior high schools. There are several advantages to them:

1. The reading level is controlled.
2. They supply background material to help pupils understand the stories.
3. They present both information and interpretation.
4. Being weeklies they are able to tie together, select, and evaluate the news so that events can be seen in perspective.
5. They are usually as objective, authoritative, and reliable as their editors can make them.
6. They are supported by teacher's editions and study helps that can be very useful to teachers. They attempt to appeal to young people and write stories in a way that will interest them.

Disadvantages. They also have disadvantages:

1. Because they are weeklies, the news may often be stale.
2. They tend to write down to the pupils.
3. They tend to take the life out of the stories by oversimplifying, glossing over, and predigesting.
4. Consciously or unconsciously, the papers tend to present a point of view — the result being a cumulative influence on the readers toward certain biases.

School Editions. A number of adult magazines publish pupil or school editions. Ordinarily, such editions are the regular adult editions with study guides bound into them. Such magazines have the same advantages and disadvantages of the periodicals written for the classroom, except that no attempt has been made to control the reading level or to simplify or tie together the stories for classroom use.

CHAPTER 15

Maps and Globes

Aʟʟ the studies of the social studies are dependent, at least in part, on maps and map reading, because maps are essential

1. To show locations.
2. To show size, shape, distances, and area.
3. To show slope and elevation.
4. To show distribution of phenomena.
5. To give a picture of places.
6. To motivate and create interest.
7. To show the arrangement of natural and other features.
8. To show relationships.
9. To illustrate the effects of events.
10. To orient the pupils.

Systematic training in the use of maps should probably be concentrated in the early secondary school years in order to ensure its use as a tool for the later years. The senior high school years should be devoted to maintaining and using the basic skills and gaining more proficiency and sophistication with maps and globes.

Nevertheless, few curricula include courses in map reading. In almost every instance, map reading is taught as part of other social studies courses. This practice may have merit. Even though special units and lessons should be turned over to the teaching of map skills, from time to time, it seems that skills taught in context stick better. Unfortunately, when map work is not a primary objective, there is always a tendency to skip over it. Consequently, you must guard against slighting map work and against the common fault of expecting pupils to use map skills no one has ever taught them. The ideal procedure seems to be for pupils to first learn map skills by direct instruction and then maintain these skills by frequent map work in succeeding social studies classes and courses.

OBJECTIVES OF MAP INSTRUCTION

Despite differences of opinion, authorities generally agree that map and globe work should achieve the following objectives:

1. Pupils will be able to picture mentally whatever it is the map portrays.
2. Pupils will be able to see relationships and draw inferences and conclusions from studying maps.
3. Pupils will know what is best expressed by maps.
4. Pupils will be able to translate information gained from actual firsthand study on the ground or from references or other written materials to suitable maps using appropriate symbols.
5. Pupils will habitually turn to maps as a source of information.

PLACEMENT OF CONTENT

Recent proposals for the placement of content in map and globe work assume a graded sequence beginning with the early elementary school years and carrying through to college. *The Rand McNally Handbook of Map and Globe Usage* recommends the following sequence for the secondary school:

Map Concepts and Skills   Grades 7–8

1. Shape and size of the earth.
   Converting degrees of latitude and longitude into miles.
   Proof of the earth's sphericity.
   Land survey as related to shape.
   Map projections.
2. Direction.
   Reading directions on maps of any projection.
   Change in direction along great circle routes.
   Plotting great circle routes on cylindrical projections.
3. Scale.
   How scales are expressed.
   Use of graduated scales (polar maps especially).
   Relation of scale to selection of data to be mapped.
4. Location.
   Continued use of latitude and longitude.
   Description and significance of relative position.
5. Earth and sun relationships.
   Use of International Date Line, eclipses, and analemma.
   Time around the world.
   Length of days.
   Time and place of sunrise and sunset.
   Apparent paths of sun at different latitudes.
6. Symbols.
   Relief shown by contours on topographic maps.

Layer tints to show elevation and slope.
International color scheme.
Importance of the legend in color interpretation.
7. Learning how to interpret information.
8. Using an atlas for research.[1]

Map Concepts and Skills
To Be Reviewed or Developed
Grades 9–12

1. Shape and size of the earth.
   Global studies for correct ideas of areas. (Incorrect ideas of the world may
      have been derived from study of the Mercator map.)
   Map projections (various devices for representing the curved surface or a
      place).
   Measurement of great circles.
2. Direction.
   True direction from study of the globe.
   Reading direction by use of parallels and meridians on any projection.
   Direction in space and direction on earth.
3. Scale.
   Correlation of maps of different scales.
   Drawing to scale.
4. Location.
   World patterns of land forms, climate, natural vegetation, transportation,
      and so on.
   Location of political divisions.
   Strategic location in the past and at present.
5. Earth, sun, and space relations.
   Review of rotation, revolution, and parallelism and their effects.
   Definition and illustration of orbits.
   Effects of rotation of earth or apparent change in orbits of satellites.
6. Symbols.
   Importance of key or legend in map reading.
   Analysis of historical maps.
   Conventional symbols on government maps.
   Use of color on physical maps.
7. Expression of ideas by making maps.[2]

The most practical suggestions for teaching maps and globes can be found in
The Rand McNally Handbook of Map and Globe Usage. Although this book is built
around Rand McNally products, the exercises and activities can be used with
any maps and globes.[3]

---

[1] Ruby M. Harris, *The Rand McNally Handbook of Map and Globe Usage,* 4th ed. (Chicago: Rand
McNally & Co., 1967), pp. 101–102.

[2] Ibid., pp. 143–144.

[3] If your map reading is unsure, see Department of the Army Field Manual FM 21–26, *Map
Reading* (Washington, D. C.: Government Printing Office, 1965); it will show you how to do it quickly
and easily.

TEACHING THE GLOBE

The globe is a spherical map of the world. It is the only map free of bothersome distortions. Give your pupils the opportunity to work with globes individually, in pairs, or in small groups. Globes are particularly useful in teaching

1. The real geographical relationships among nations and other areas or points in particular with respect to distance and direction.
2. The great circle routes.
3. The real shapes of continents, islands, oceans, and political units.
4. The rotation of the earth and its effects.
5. The revolution of the earth and its effects.
6. World patterns of various types.
7. International affairs.

EXAMPLES OF TACTICS AND TECHNIQUES TO USE WITH GLOBES

1. Use the globe as a world map.
   a. Center the place to be studied.
   b. Note the visible hemisphere.
   c. Note the position of the place to be studied relative to other places and physical features such as continents, rivers, mountains, and so on.
   d. Measure the direct distances to other places.
   e. Locate the great circle routes from the place to be studied to other places.
2. Use exercises in which pupils build world patterns on a slated globe.
3. Use exercises showing distance, direction, and relative position, for example:

> Find the azimuth in degrees from New York to Mecca.
> Which is farther from New York, London or Rio de Janeiro?
> What direction is it in degrees from New York to San Francisco?

4. Use exercises having to do with great circles, for example:

> An airline advertises that its route from New York to Tokyo via Anchorage is much shorter than other airline routes to Tokyo. Assuming that the plane must make at least one other stop en route, is there a possible shorter route?

5. Use exercises concerning the earth's rotation, for example:

> Darken the room. Shine a flashlight on the globe. Rotate the globe from east to west. This procedure will demonstrate many features having to do with night and day, time, and the like.

6. Use exercises concerning the earth's revolutions, for example:

> In a darkened room, place a lighted candle on a table where all can see it. Take a globe, tip it so that the axis is 22½° out of vertical. Keeping the axis at

the same angle, carry the globe full circle around the candle. This procedure demonstrates how the sunlight strikes the earth at different angles at different times of the year. Thus, it can be used to explain the seasons, the midnight sun, and other related phenomena.

MAP READING

The skills used in map reading are quite different from those used in ordinary reading. Instead of being linear, maps are patterns from which the reader selects information and draws relationships. If pupils are not proficient in the skills of map reading, you must begin with the fundamentals of mapping. To do this, start off with the construction of simple maps of the classroom, the school grounds, or the immediate environment. As the pupils become more competent, add instruction in details and in the use of map symbols until the pupils can describe the terrain reasonably accurately from the perusal of a topographic sheet.

Use large-scale (topographic) map sheets to make the learning of map reading realistic and interesting. If it is feasible, use local quadrangles because of their motivating aspects. Oblique aerial photographs and other pictures of the area being studied on the map can add reality and zest to the teaching. Stereo-pairs can be particularly exciting. Actually seeing the land or pictures of it will serve as a check of the pupils' interpretation of the map's representation.

In teaching maps to pupils, keep these principles in mind:

1. The title of the map limits and defines its purpose.
2. The key clues us to the meaning of the symbols and is essential for our interpretation.
3. The scale tells us distances and areas.
4. Height must be indicated in some way, either by color, shading, or contours.
5. Directions must be indicated to show the relationships of portions of the maps.
6. The projection allows for the representing of a curved surface on a flat sheet.[4]

In addition, pupils should learn something about the different kinds of maps and their functions.

General Suggestions for Teaching Map Reading

1. Use maps in as many ways as you can in all your classes.
2. Have pupils find on the map the places that are discussed in all classes. Don't do it yourself. Let the pupils do it.
3. Always use map coordinates to locate or to describe map locations.

[4] G. H. Gopsill, *The Teaching of Geography in School,* 2nd ed. (London: Macmillan & Company, Ltd., 1961), p. 47.

4. Always stress relative locations—location with reference to mountains, sea, trade routes, rivers, foreign countries, and so on.

5. Use many different map projections.

6. Use maps of imaginary places. Use appropriate symbols for manmade objects and natural features of the landscape. Have pupils describe the landscape pictured by the map.

7. Individualize map work. Start where the pupils are. Diagnose before you begin their map skills.

8. Use slated maps for tests, drills, and reviews.

9. Include some map work in every lesson.

10. Insist that pupils interpret what they read on maps.

11. Have pupils compare data and make inferences on the basis of these compared data.

12. Use noncaptioned maps to teach symbols.

13. Use different kinds of maps: road maps, topographic maps, city guide maps, and so on.

14. Introduce a map symbol only when needed.

15. Relate map work to pupils' lives.

16. Use maps of imaginary places for map-reading exercises so that the map reading will be all new material.

17. Select a point on a map. Have pupils describe the surrounding terrain, including waterways, boundaries, distances, and the like, and the presumable effect of these terrain features on whatever is located at the point selected.

18. Use photo maps.

To identify features on a photomap use (1) shape, (2) size, (3) tone, (4) patterns, (5) shadows, and (6) texture as clues.

SUGGESTIONS FOR TEACHING ELEVATIONS, CONTOURS, AND RELIEF

Because of its importance and difficulty, teaching pupils to read elevations and slopes from a map should be done very thoroughly. Early in their careers as map readers, pupils should learn the meanings of topographical terms such as ridge, escarpment, spur, and the like. Because this knowledge is of no value unless pupils can recognize the features when they see them, wherever possible, utilize field work and pictures. Once pupils can identify features on the ground and in pictures, they can proceed to identify them on maps.

Reading Relief Maps That Use Layer Tinting or Color. In teaching pupils to read elevations designated by color coding,

1. Emphasize that the color indicates a range of elevations. The land is not flat, but the elevations of all the hills and valleys are within the range indicated by the color. Note that high land is not necessarily mountainous.

2. Point out that the borders of the color bands do not indicate abrupt changes in elevation: the slope may be very gradual at this point.

3. Encourage pupils to check the legend to find the elevation range represented by each color.

Reading Relief Maps That Use Contour Lines. Each contour line represents an imaginary line on the ground along which all points are at the same elevation. This idea can be presented to the pupils in several ways:

1. It is the path one would make if he walked along a hill or valley always at the same elevation. (If you always walked 100 feet above sea level you would be walking on the 100-foot contour line.)

2. Teach by means of a straight-sided model. Cut the shapes out of heavy cardboard or plywood and glue them together. The edge of each layer is in effect a contour line because it is at the same height from the datum plane (in this case the bottom of the model) at every point.

3. Read such contour representations of single features as those represented in Figure 15-2.

4. Make relief models of single features from contour maps.

5. Read relief on simplified contour maps. (Make up maps of imaginary places yourself. Let pupils draw or describe what they see.)

6. Let pupils make up contour maps of an imaginary area. See if other pupils can describe the area from the map.

7. Read relief from topographic maps. Let pupils draw or describe what they see. (In this type of exercise it is better if pupils learn to work well with one scale before they change to a different one.)

8. Make profiles—that is, a side view of the terrain along a line between the points.

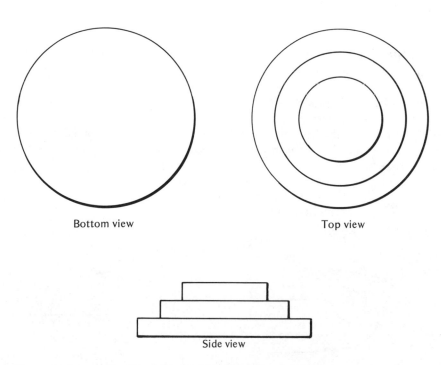

Bottom view   Top view

Side view

FIGURE 15-1. *Use Straight-sided Model to Teach Contours.*

Contours

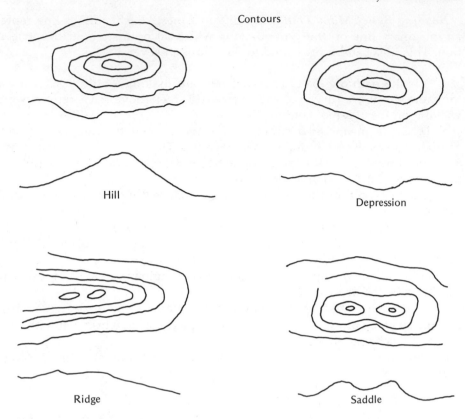

FIGURE 15-2. *Relief Features Shown by Contours. After U.S. Army.*

To Picture Slope. Pupils need to learn to picture slope from contour maps. For this purpose such tactics as the following are recommended:

1. Have pupils draw or describe the slopes represented on the map.
2. Have pupils make profiles.
3. Have pupils determine what can be seen or what is masked from a certain point. For example, what route could you take to get from *A* to *B* without being seen from *C*?
4. Utilize exercises such as these:

    a. In the following, which slope is steeper, *AB* or *CD*?

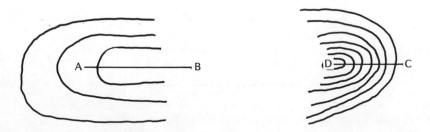

b. Which of the following profiles most closely represents the slope *AB?*
Which *CD?*

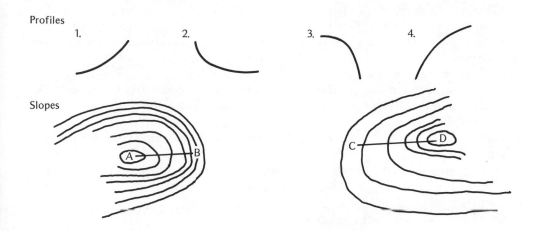

SUGGESTIONS FOR TEACHING PUPILS TO READ MAP DIRECTIONS

1. Pupils should be able to orient both large- and small-scale maps. To orient a map, put it flat on the floor or desk with the north index pointing north. Use the compass or noon shadows to find north. Correct the map's orientation for the magnetic inclination. Also, orient large-scale maps by matching terrain and pattern features on the map with those on the ground.

2. Never use the words *up, down, left,* or *right* when you mean *north, south, east,* or *west.* To cure pupils of the habit of confusing down, right, and left with compass directions, place the maps flat and read them from the north, east, or west sides. Using polar and other projections, in which north is at a point other than the top of the page, is also useful.

3. Be sure pupils know compass directions and how to read them off a map. Use such exercises as:

> Assuming you could travel in a straight line, which compass direction would you have to take to reach Buenos Aires from here? To reach Buenos Aires from Caracas, Venezuela?

4. Pupils should practice such exercises as the preceding ones on globes and maps that have various kinds of projections. (Note that in some map projections, directions are distorted. Remember, grid lines always follow cardinal directions!)

5. Have pupils learn to do exercises involving azimuths and bearings. For instance:

> If a ship were at Nantucket Island what bearing would it plot to reach Lands' End by the shortest route?

6. When teaching locations, have pupils learn directions, distances, and other relationships having to do with the locations being learned.

SUGGESTIONS FOR TEACHING SCALE

Sample Exercises in Using Scale

1. Make a scale map of the classroom.
   a. Measure the room.
   b. Select a scale. Let the pupils use one that is reasonable and will fit their paper.
   c. Put the scale on the map.
   d. Lay out the map and position objects in the room according to the scale. To do this one must measure the distances within the room and convert them to scale.
2. Have pupils compare maps of different scale but of the same size, as in a road atlas.
3. Have pupils measure the distances from place to place (for example, New York to Chicago) on maps of different scale.
4. Compare maps of different size but of the same scale.
5. Use such exercises as the following:

   If the range of the Minuteman is 8,000 kilometers (a kilometer is ⅝-miles), and Minutemen are stationed at Great Falls, Montana; Rapid City, South Dakota; Minot, North Dakota; Knob Noster, Missouri; Cheyenne, Wyoming; and Grand Forks, North Dakota, what parts of Europe and Asia can the United States bring under Minuteman fire from these missile sites?

GRID SYSTEMS

In order to make it easy to indicate the locations of places on maps and globes, cartographers have created grid systems. Plane grid systems are used for maps; spherical ones for globes. All of them are easy to use and understand. The grid most commonly recognized by adults consists of longitudes and latitudes.

Simple Grid Systems. Grid systems are easy to learn. The simplest type is used in the ordinary road map. In such a grid system the map is divided into squares. These squares are identified vertically by letters and horizontally by numbers (or vice versa). Points are identified by the intersections of the numbers and letters. (See Figure 15-3.)

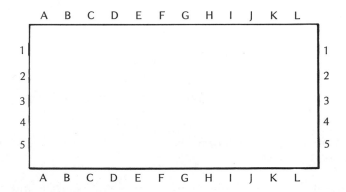

FIGURE 15-3. *A Simple Grid System.*

Complex Square Grid Systems. More complex grid systems are built on the same premises as the simple square grids. Examples of these systems are Universal Mercator Grid System and the Universal Polar Stereographic System. All of these systems are read in much the same manner.[5]

Latitude and Longitude. Latitude and longitude, really a spherical grid system, together form the grid system most commonly used in secondary school social studies classes. Latitude represents the arc on the earth's surface from the equator north or south to the point designated. Longitude represents the arc from the prime meridian east or west to the point designated. In most of the maps you will use the prime meridian is Greenwich, England.

The arcs of latitude and longitude are measured by degrees. In effect, they denote the size of the angle at the center of the earth from the point being located to the equator, if latitude, or to the prime meridian, if longitude. When considering latitude and longitude remember that

1. Each represents an angle or an arc cut by an angle.
2. The parallels are parallel.
3. The meridians converge at the poles.
4. The representation of parallels and longitudes on a flat surface is usually distorted in some respect.

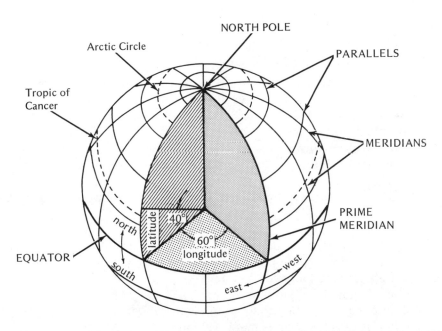

FIGURE 15-4. *The Earth's Grid.* [*Reprinted with the Permission of the National Council for the Social Studies and Lorrin Kennamer, from Helen McCracken Carpenter, ed.,* Skill Development in the Social Studies (*Washington, D.C.: National Council for the Social Studies,*) p. 154.]

[5] Techniques for using such grid systems can be found in such works as Department of the Army Field Manual, loc. cit.

Polar Coordinates. Polar coordinates consist of rays that emanate from a point of origin. Places are located by giving the distance and direction of the point being located from the point of origin. For example, X is 7,500 meters NNW of point Y. Polar coordinates are especially useful for field work.

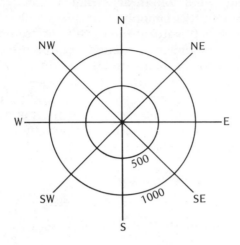

FIGURE 15-5. *Polar Coordinates.*

Techniques and Tactics for Teaching Grid Systems (Including Latitude and Longitude)

1. If pupils are not familiar with grid coordinates, first teach vertical grid lines, then in order teach horizontal grid lines, teach where the grid lines cross, drill them on these fundamentals, and finally reenforce by constantly using the grid coordinates in all map work.
2. Let pupils create their own grid systems. Grid systems can be laid out on the classroom floor. Figure 15-6 is a map and grid system of a classroom prepared by a pupil.
3. Use road maps, county maps, and city maps, until pupils learn the grid system well.
4. Use topographic maps.
5. Teach latitude and longitude in the same way as other grid systems. (Be careful that pupils include the directions in latitude and longitude.)
6. To illustrate the need for a grid system,
   a. Put an X on a slated globe.
   b. Ask pupils to describe the location of the globe.
   c. Let pupils develop a coordinate system.
7. Use such practice exercises as the following:
        a. What do you find located at: 135°W 20°S?
        b. Give the latitude and longitude of Rio de Janeiro.
        c. What are the coordinates of the westernmost point in the continental United States?

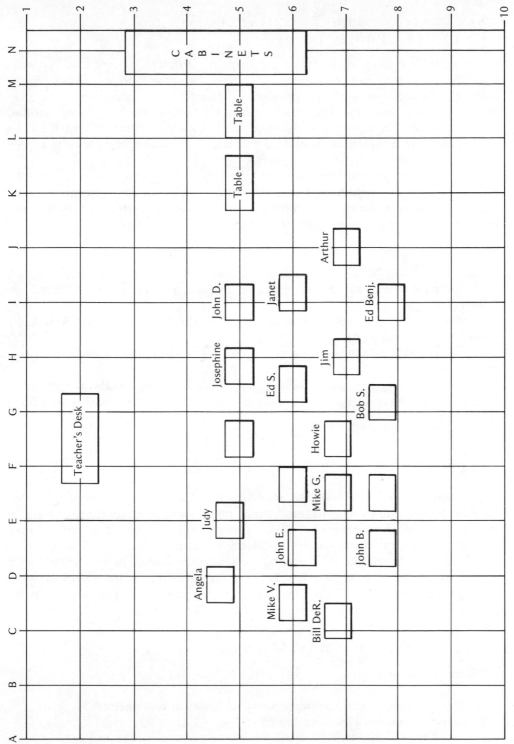

FIGURE 15-6. *The Concept of Longitude and Latitude.*

Suggestions for Teaching Pupils to Read Map Projections

The earth is a globe or a sphere. *All maps are distorted in some way,* because they are attempts to portray a spherical surface two dimensionally. Map projections are attempts to solve the problem of distortion. Usually, when the map maker succeeds in eliminating one kind of distortion, he introduces another kind. Therefore, there are many different map projections, each of which has its advantages and disadvantages, and each of which is more useful for certain purposes than others.

Pupils should become familiar with a variety of map projections. As a rule, pupils need not be held to learning the names and features of the projections, but they do need to know the different ways maps are distorted and understand what the map has to say in spite of its distortion.

Some Tactics and Techniques for Showing Distortion

1. Compare Greenland and Australia on the globe. Compare them on a Mercator projection.
2. Measure the distance from Cape Horn to the Cape of Good Hope on a globe. On a Mercator map.
3. Compare various projections to see the size, shapes, and directions of certain areas.
4. Cut a ball or an orange in half, try to flatten it out without cutting it.
5. Compare the converging meridians on the globe with the parallel meridians of the Mercator projection.

MAP MAKING

All pupils should have enough experience in drawing maps from observed statistical or reference data to understand how a map is made and to have at least some skill in making one. Making maps will also improve skill in map reading and the basic knowledges necessary for map study.

On no account should map making become busywork. For this reason it is foolish to ask pupils to copy maps. For the same reason, the free-hand drawing of maps has doubtful validity. *Therefore, the use of outline maps as a basis for making finished maps is strongly recommended.*

Guidelines for Map Making

When making a map:

1. Have a single specific purpose for what the map will portray.
2. State the purpose clearly in the title.
3. Avoid too much detail. (Too much detail results in clutter and confusion. It is better to make several maps than to overload one.)
4. Provide a clear key. Be sure the key is complete.
5. Make the map as accurate as you can.

Types of Maps Pupils Can Make

1. Sketch maps.
2. Original maps of local areas.
3. Distribution maps
   a. Surface conditions.
   b. Rainfall.
   c. Growing seasons.
   d. Population.
   e. Crops.
   f. Minerals.
   g. Animal products.
   h. Land use.
   i. Route maps.
   j. Transportation.
   k. Physical geography maps.
   l. Political boundary maps.
   m. Maps showing directions of movements.
   n. Outline maps.
   o. Puzzle maps (that is, jigsaw-puzzle made by cutting up a map securely, glued to a piece of thin plywood or heavy cardboard).
   p. Transparencies (for overhead projection).
   q. Glass slides (for slide projection).
   r. Relief maps.
   s. Azimuthal maps centering on local area (for advanced pupils only).
   t. Window shade maps.
   u. Map stencils.
   v. Map murals.
   w. Reproductions of an assigned map.

---

6. Indicate the scale and directions.
7. Make the map neat so that it will be legible.

TO MAKE SPECIFIC KINDS OF MAPS

1. Flat maps.
   a. Window shade map. Simply draw a map on a window shade. It then can be used as an ordinary roll-up map.
   b. Sketch maps. A sketch map is a map drawn quickly to give an impression or to aid memory of the landscape in an area. It should include
      (1) The limits of the area.
      (2) One or more meridians and parallels (to identify location).
      (3) North line.
      (4) Key.
      (5) Clear title.
      (6) Prominent physical features.
      (7) Names of features.
      (8) Water courses, road nets, and so on as necessary and desirable for one's purpose.

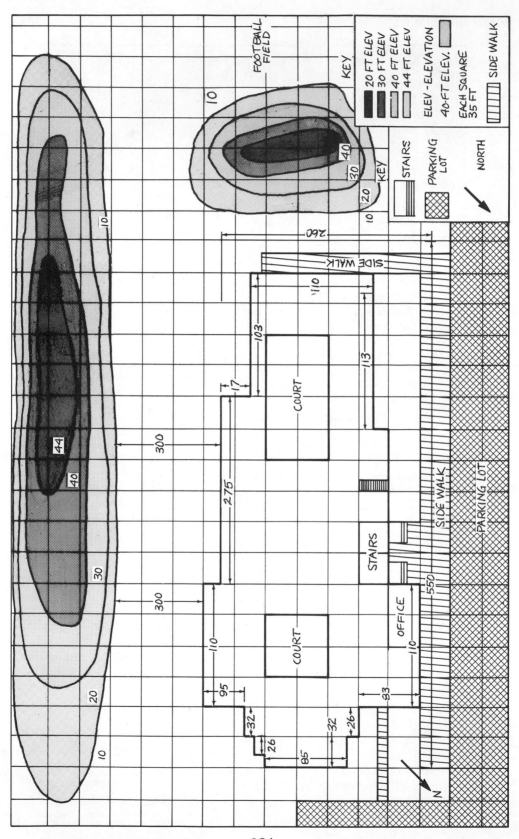

(9) Shadings, hachures, and other symbols to represent necessary and desirable information.

Sketch maps are made by laying out a sheet of paper in squares, locating the principal features within the squares, and then sketching in the detail as accurately as possible. Teachers should also make quick sketches on the blackboard to illustrate points in history, geography, and other social studies subjects.

c. Strip map — triptic. A strip map is a schematic road map depicting a route taken or to be taken. It contains only the detail necessary to identify the route. Perhaps the best known examples are the triptics used by the automobile clubs. Pupils can make strip maps by identifying the route from ordinary maps and then mapping the information on a strip of paper. In order to fit the strip, the directions in strip maps are often distorted, but the distances should be kept to scale as nearly as possible. The making of strip maps with annotations describing the areas the route passes through has interesting possibilities for both geography and history classes. It is especially useful in teaching history courses; for example, a strip map could describe the route from Mt. Vernon to New York taken by Washington on his way to his inauguration.

d. Distribution maps. Distribution maps are easy to make. Pupils should make them often as part of their work in geography, economics, problems of democracy, and other courses. In making distribution maps the following suggestions may prove helpful.

(1) It is best to use dot maps. (Maps based on shaded colors or color are not satisfactory because they are unnecessarily difficult to make and encourage copying.)

(2) Place only one variable on each map.

(3) Make dots of only one size and color. (One way to make dots of the same size is to make a template by punching a hole through a piece of cardboard. Place the template on the map with the hole at the spot desired. Fill in the exposed area of the map with a colored pencil.)

(4) Scatter the dots evenly, or — if you want to show concentration — according to the concentration you want to portray. Usually the latter method is too difficult for pupils to use accurately in the time available.

(5) Include at least one meridian and one parallel.

(6) Show only what is described in the title.

(7) Be sure the title adequately identifies what is being shown.

(8) Be sure there is an adequate key.

(9) Add any explanation and interpretation necessary to point up and explain what is being shown.

(10) Indicate the source of information.

e. Outline maps. Outline maps provide the structure for maps of various kinds. They are available for purchase from several sources, or they can be made locally on a duplicating machine. Stencils and masters for several types of duplicating machines are available commercially.

FIGURE 15–7. *One of the Maps of the School Grounds Prepared by Pupils in the Class of Edmund Vail, Avenel (N. J.) Junior High School, John La Polla, Student Teacher.*

Pupils should post data on the outline map from data they have gathered from their reading, studying, observation, and research. Posting data should not be an exercise in copying or coloring.

  f. Map stencils for chalkboard use. To make a map stencil:

    (1) Tape a large sheet of paper to the chalkboard.

    (2) Project a map image on to the paper using an overhead, opaque, or slide projector.

    (3) With a pin make holes in the paper along the outlines of the map. This completes your stencil.

    (4) Use this stencil to make chalkboard maps. To do this, stick the stencil up on the board with scotch tape or masking tape. Pat the holes with a chalky chalkboard eraser. Remove the stencil and connect the dots with a chalk line to make the outlines of the map..

  g. Maps of increased or diminished scale.

    (1) Maps can be enlarged by using the opaque projector or the overhead projector.

      (a) Project the image of the map on a chalkboard or on a large sheet of wrapping paper, on sheets of construction paper pasted together, on an old window shade, a large sheet of acetate, or what you will.

      (b) Trace the projected image. Include as much detail as you wish.

      (c) Fill in with color, symbols, and so on, as desired.

    (2) Maps can be enlarged or diminished by the method of proportional squares.

      (a) Set up a grid system on the map, if there is not one.

      (b) On a blank sheet make a similar grid system in which the size of the grid squares is larger or smaller.

      (c) Using the grids as guides, draw in the map outline and features on the grid as they were on the original map.

      (d) Add details, color, symbols, and the like as desired.

  h. Overlays. Overlays are excellent means of depicting information directly on a map without injuring the map.

    (1) Cover the map with transparent acetate. (Plastic drop cloths, old table covers, or garment bags will do for large maps; plastic wrapping is good for smaller ones).

    (2) With a grease pencil (china marking pencil) mark the intersection of grid lines at opposite corners of the map; that is, the top right-hand corner and bottom left-hand corner. Label them. These can be used as reference points when one wants to use the overlay again.

    (3) With a grease pencil put whatever information you want to record on the overlay.

Overlays prepared in this fashion can be saved for future use. The marks at the intersections of the grid lines will serve as guidelines for repositioning the overlay on the map.

2. Three-dimensional maps.

  a. Peg method.

    (1) Lay out contour lines on a base.

    (2) Drive brads, pegs, or stout pins into the base at points along the contour lines. The tops of the brads (pegs or pins) are to represent the

elevation at the contour line and so should be adjusted to scale (say ⅛ of an inch = 2,000 feet). If it seems too difficult to drive the nails to the proper height, you can cut them at the height required with a wire cutter.

   (3) Fill in the body of the map to the tops of the brads (pegs or pins) and shape.

  b. Materials suitable for making relief maps and models.

   (1) Nonoil-based clay (use heavy cardboard, hardboard, glass, or metal for a base).

   (2) Papier-mâché.

    (a) Tear newspaper into fine strips.

    (b) Soak for 24 hours.

    (c) Squeeze out water.

    (d) Mix with salt and flour (1 part salt, 3 parts flour, 9 parts paper).

   (3) Salt and flour. Mix 2 parts salt, one part flour, and enough water to make it doughy.

   (4) Liquid starch and detergent. Mix 4 tablespoons liquid starch with 1 cup of detergent.

CRITERIA FOR SELECTING MAPS

1. Is the content suitable for the use intended?
2. Is the map accurate?
3. Is the projection suitable?
4. Is the map information up-to-date?
5. Is the scale suitable? Is it large enough to give the necessary detail?
6. Can the map be used for several purposes?
7. Are the map symbols standard?
8. Is the legend correct, useful, and informative enough?
9. Is the map easy to read? Can the detail be seen? Is it free from clutter?
10. Is the map strongly made? Will it stand up under hard usage?
11. Is the price reasonable?
12. Is the map attractive? Is it colorful and interesting?

CHAPTER 16

Production and Use of Teaching Tools and Instructional Materials

In this part of the handbook some of the teaching tools and instructional materials and how to produce and use them will be discussed. Sources from which teaching tools and materials may be procured are listed in the appendixes.

PRINTED AND DUPLICATED MATERIALS

PAMPHLETS, BROCHURES, AND OTHER READING MATTER

Such an abundance of free and inexpensive reading matter is available that there is no reason why any social studies class should be short of things to read. *Every social studies teacher should start collecting for a classroom library before he begins to teach.*

A Few Tips on Collecting and Using Printed Matter

1. Write for material on school stationery. Explain why you need it. Let pupils write some of the letters.

2. Cut out and save magazine articles, newspaper articles, and excerpts from old books, as well as pamphlets and brochures.

3. Buy paperbacks, source materials, and so on in fives and sixes instead of entire sets.

4. Bind magazine articles and the like into homemade brochures by stapling them inside file folders or term-paper binders.

5. Evaluate materials. If they are not good, throw them away.

6. Let pupils evaluate materials. Have them put their comments on index cards for the guidance of future pupils.

7. Set up some sort of filing system. Used cardboard cartons from the supermarket make good filing and storage cabinets if other storage is not available.

8. Encourage pupils to search for and bring in suitable materials.

9. Duplicate and copy materials not available in print.

10. Write your own pamphlets and brochures.

DUPLICATED MATERIALS

The best social studies teachers use many duplicated materials. When making these materials try to make them clear, simple, neat, forceful, and attractive.

Types of Duplicated Materials. Several types of homemade duplicated materials are most useful to social studies teachers. Among them are

1. Study guides and learning packets.
2. Outline maps and other maps.
3. Copies of documents, quotations, speeches, anecdotes, and other supplementary reading matter.
4. Springboard materials: problems, situations, case studies, and the like.
5. Tests and quizzes.

Preparing Duplicated Materials. In most schools secretarial services are in short supply. Learn to use the spirit duplicator, the mimeograph machine, and copying machines as soon as you can.

If you want material to be run off by the secretarial staff, see to it that you get the copy to them early enough for them to do it without rushing.

Remember that most printed materials are copyrighted. You have no right to duplicate copyrighted material without permission, although you may be allowed to copy a reasonable amount under the free-use clause. Government publications, however, are in the public domain and may be copied freely, except for art work and quoted material that belongs to the artist or the original publisher.

Lighten up the duplicated material by using color, drawings, and plenty of white space. Spirit duplicators are very flexible and lend themselves to the use of color and drawings.

Preserving Duplicated Materials. Usually, duplicated material is given to the pupils to keep. In most cases this is wise. However, often it would be wiser to save duplicated exercises, problems, supplementary reading materials, and springboard materials for later use. To make this sort of material durable,

1. Bind the duplicated material in a stiff cover. Stapling it to a manila file folder or pieces of construction paper will do very well.
2. Caution pupils not to write on the duplicated sheets. Provide answer sheets. Let them provide notebooks or extra sheets for note taking, question answering, and the like.
3. Collect and store the materials when they are not being used by the pupils.

Special Study Guide. The purpose of a special study guide is to provide a means by which pupils can assume some of the responsibility for directing their own learning without floundering. It might consist of directions for the students to follow on a field trip, reaction questions for use in viewing a television program, or directions for carrying out an individual assignment. They are particularly useful for providing directions and guidance for pupils doing special assignments, supplementary reading, research, and any of the other individualized and independent study activities that are essential when one attempts to provide for individual differences via independent study and supplementary or optional assignments.

Special study guides do not fit into set forms. Design the form to do what you want it to do. You might want to include some or all of the following:

1. The purpose of the activity.
2. Directions for carrying out the activity.
3. Background information.
4. Problems to solve.
5. Exercises and drill material.
6. Fact questions and/or thought questions.
7. Suggested readings.
8. Follow-up activities.
9. Self-correcting material.

Instructional (Learning) Packets. Instructional packets are the heart of instruction in courses divided into modules or units as a part of continuous progress plans. Instructional packets consist of the materials necessary for the study of an individualized unit and a study guide.

To build an instructional packet,

1. Divide the course content or subject content into topics, if this has not already been done. Select the topic to be packeted.
2. Describe the learning objectives of the topic.
   a. General overview.
   b. Specific outcomes.
3. Select the activities and content by which pupils should be able to achieve these objectives.
4. Decide how to evaluate pupil achievement. Prepare the necessary instruments.
5. Gather and prepare the necessary instructional materials.
6. Set time limits and agendas.
7. Write the study guide. Include
   a. Topic.
   b. Rationale: what the teacher hopes the pupils will get out of studying the topic.
   c. Directions.
      (1) General directions: agenda, time limits (if any), requirements, and options.
      (2) Specific directions; that is, the direction and explanations for specific activities. For example,
         (a) Problem to be solved: What the problem is, what the background of the problem is, what requirements must be met to solve the problem successfully.
         (b) Reading: Purpose of the reading, what information is to be learned; what is to be done with the information; questions on the reading, exact citations.
         (c) Information to be learned: Possible sources of the information.
      (3) Where to go for materials and information.

    d. Bibliography.

    e. Instructional materials you have prepared for the module. (Include these with the study guide or distribute them separately.)

    f. Self-correcting, testing, and evaluating material. (Usually it is better to issue these separately as pupils become ready for them.)

DUPLICATED SPRINGBOARD MATERIALS

Springboards are materials, usually duplicated or printed, that can be used to start pupils thinking, discussing, and investigating. Usually they present a situation that has happened, or might have happened, and bring up a number of open-ended questions. They may consist of excerpts from historical accounts, news stories, bits from novels, documents, and so on, or they may be original matter prepared by the teacher. Many examples of this type of material are available commercially.

Not all springboard materials are duplicated. The material might also be presented by film or film clip, video tape, dramatization, role playing, or oral report.

THE CLASSROOM LIBRARY

Reading material, whether printed or duplicated, should be readily available to pupils. For this reason, it is recommended that the classroom be a classroom library. Collect all sorts of pertinent reading material: books, periodicals, pamphlets, brochures, duplicated materials, bound articles, and clippings. Let the pupils act as librarians.

For record keeping use a self-charging system. Prepare a card for each item. Place the card in a pocket at the back of the book or attach it to the material with a paper clip. Have the borrowers sign the cards and place them in a box prepared for that purpose. On returning the book, the borrower should cross his name off the card and place it back in the pocket or reattach it to the material. You or the pupil can easily manufacture cards and pockets out of stiff paper or cardboard such as used manila folders.

Book Title	
Borrower	Date

FIGURE 16-1. *A Library Card.*

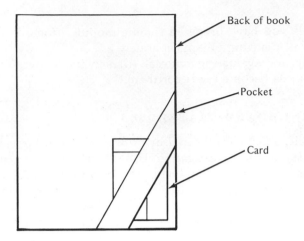

FIGURE 16-2. *A Library Card Pocket.*

PICTURES AND ILLUSTRATIONS

USING PICTURES AND ILLUSTRATIONS

Use pictures to clarify and add interest to your classes. Pictures are easy to obtain and handy to use. You really should assemble a sizable collection of suitable pictures as part of your personal stock of teaching materials. These should be stored in the classroom library where they will be used.

Suggestions for Using Pictures

1. Use the pictures and illustrations in books.
2. Use collections of pictures to tell a story or make a presentation (as in a film strip or slide program).
3. Use pictures with study guides as a basis for individual, independent study.
4. Use pictures as a basis for discussions and as springboards for further study and research.
5. Do not hesitate to build an entire class around the study of a single picture. Single pictures may have much information and many implications.
6. Do not pass pictures around the classroom during a class. Pupils cannot pay attention to the class discussion and study pictures at the same time. If you want the pupils to study a picture and learn from it, provide for study under guidance. One way is to project it via the opaque projector while you discuss it. Another is to provide study guides or exercises for individual study. Pictures for study can be placed on the chalk tray, displayed on a bulletin board, or attached to the chalkboard where pupils can go up to look at them.
7. Preserve pictures by mounting them. Covering the pictures with clear acetate or laminating them will give them additional protection.
8. Clip pictures and paste them on sheets. Have pupils write captions, commentary, and interpretations of the pictures. Having them write or discuss "how the picture affected you" can also be effective.

STUDYING CARTOONS

Cartoons make excellent teaching aids because sometimes they clinch an understanding when all else fails. Pupils need practice in using and interpreting them, however.

Make it a policy to collect and save good cartoons pertinent to the subjects you teach. If you make transparencies of them for the overhead projector, you will find the transparencies even more useful. File them away in the vertical file for use whenever necessary.

Some Activities Useful in Studying with Cartoons

1. Analyze cartoons—particularly political ones.
   a. What is the point?
   b. What mood does the cartoon try to create?
   c. Is the cartoon for or against?
   d. What use was made of propaganda or polemic strategies or devices?
   e. Was there an appeal to the emotions?
   f. Did the cartoon oversimplify?
   g. Did it reveal stereotype or bias? If so, what?
   h. What use was made of symbolism?
2. Evaluate cartoons. Check them against other information.
3. Find the news story or other factual account that fits the cartoon. Compare them. Analyze the cartoonist's position.
4. Have pupils volunteer to make their own cartoons of contemporary events at a school, community, state, national, or an international level.
5. Use cartoons to illustrate historical events. Let pupils make their own cartoons of historical happenings.

MOUNTING PICTURES AND CARTOONS

Pictures or cartoons worth saving should be mounted. To mount your pictures and cartoons,

1. Select a mat that is made of good material, allows for wide margins, and is of a color that will not overpower the picture.
2. Mount the picture by using a rubber cement or a dry mount process.

DISPLAY AND DISPLAY-TYPE DEVICES AND MATERIALS

GENERAL COMMENT

A few comments are applicable to all displays and display-type materials.

1. They should be clearly visible.
2. They should be attractive.
3. They should catch the eye.

4. They should be simple.
5. They should be clear.
6. They should make a point.
7. They should have a center of interest.
8. They should avoid clutter and confusion.

BULLETIN BOARDS

Good bulletin board displays can greatly enhance social studies classrooms. Use them to motivate, interpret, supplement, and reenforce your teaching as well as to dress up the classroom. Treat them as instructional tools. Aim them directly at your teaching objectives.

Suggestions for Using Bulletin Boards

1. Plan the bulletin board. Begin with an idea, gather materials, sketch out the plan. Try out the plan on the board before fastening anything.

2. Make the arrangement tell the story.

3. Have a center of interest. Limit the board to one central idea or theme. If several things must be presented, divide the board into sections. Use lines or arrows to draw the viewer's eye to the center of interest, if necessary.

4. Design the bulletin board to support the classwork. Use it as another audiovisual aid. Combine it with other activities such as oral reports, demonstrations, and discussions.

5. Have pupils or pupil committees plan and post the bulletin boards. Some teachers have competitions to see who does the best bulletin board.

6. Be sure it is visible. Make captions and use pictures large enough to be seen.

7. To attract attention use questions, action, and drama.

8. Utilize ideas from advertisements in magazines, newspapers, and television.

9. Use eye catchers. Have a line of movement to carry viewers through the details.

10. Use unusual material, three-dimensional objects, color, variety, and humor for spice. Match colors to the ideas being presented.

11. Give the bulletin board depth by combining it with a table display. Set the table directly in front of the board and coordinate the displays. Use colored strings from the board to the table to show relationships.

12. Leave plenty of white space. Do not crowd things. Avoid solid blocks of material. Avoid clutter. A few well-selected pictures usually are more forceful than many pictures.

13. Keep the captions brief and clear. Short captions may be all capitals, but usually one should use both upper and lower case letters for the sake of clarity.

14. Be careful of lettering. It should be attractive and eye catching.

15. Fasten materials securely and neatly. If possible, keep the fasteners out of sight, or use pins with colored heads to heighten interest.

16. Be sure all pictures are mounted securely.

17. Keep the board up-to-date. Do not let it get stale. Change it frequently. Have a calendar or schedule for changing it.

18. Build up a file of materials for bulletin board use. Encourage pupils to bring in interesting materials.

Where There Are No Bulletin Boards. Where bulletin boards are not available you can easily improvise them.

1. Use an extra chalkboard if there is one. Fasten material to the chalkboard with double-faced scotch tape or bulletin board wax. Or cover the chalkboard with construction paper, wrapping paper, or burlap to which material can be taped or pinned. Note that material attached by cementing one surface only can be removed easily.

2. Make a bulletin board of wallboard: cover the wallboard with burlap to give it a textured surface that is easy to paint.

3. If permitted, use a free wall as a bulletin board. Bulletin-board wax will not hurt the paint.

THE CHALKBOARD

Chalkboards are so ubiquitous that teachers tend to forget that they are teaching tools. Use them

To present new facts.

To clarify old ones.

To provide illustrations.

To reenforce ideas.

For practice exercise.

Using the Chalkboard

1. Be sure pupils can see it. Write and print legibly. Write large. Use the pointer.

2. Keep the board clean, neat, and orderly. Do not let the board become cluttered.

3. Avoid crowding. See that there is plenty of white space.

4. Keep the board work simple and tasteful.

5. Use underlining, color, and boxes to emphasize.

6. Plan and prepare your board work ahead of time, if at all possible.

7. Do not leave distracting work on the board while the class is doing something else. Cover the board work that is yet to come. Pull a map down over it or cover with wrapping paper taped to the board with masking tape. In lectures and discussions, dramatically uncovering material on the board as one tries to make a point reenforces learning. (However, the flannelboard works better for this type of thing.)

8. Use stencils, patterns, or projected images as guides when drawing on the board.

9. Project outline maps, pictures, and exercises on the chalkboard. The pupils can write directly on the chalkboard to fill in blanks, write comments, add detail to the map, and so on.

10. Use stickmen, diagrams, diagrammatic maps, and rough drawings to illustrate and clarify.

FLANNEL BOARDS, FELT BOARDS, HOOK AND LOOP BOARDS, AND MAGNETIC BOARDS

Using Flannel Boards and Similar Devices. Flannel boards, felt boards, hook and loop boards, and magnetic boards all serve the same purpose. They are really audiovisual aids rather than display devices. They are excellent for making or reenforcing points during a lesson or for showing change. Use them like chalkboards to make immediate presentations during a lesson: to tie them up with displays for a whole period or longer is to waste them.

They have several advantages over chalkboards:

1. Material can be prepared in advance.
2. Material can be saved; one does not have to redo his work after every class.
3. They have immediacy and drama. When you need to make a point, just stick it up on the flannel board.

Chalkboards are effective teaching tools

Flannelboards are 50% more effective

Some Techniques for Using Flannel and Felt Boards

1. Project a map onto the flannel board. Use wool yarn to outline the map. Or if you want a permanent map, outline the map with a felt-tipped pen. Fill in the outlines with colored material, if you wish.
2. Similarly, outline other figures, charts, graphs, and grids.
3. Use a flannel board to show change and development (for instance by adding and subtracting sections one can show the boundary changes in Europe resulting from the world wars).
4. Use it to reenforce points. As each point is made, put the appropriate word, caption, picture, or what have you, on the flannel board to drive the point home.

To Make a Flannel or Felt Board

1. Cut a piece of plywood or beaverboard to the size desired.
2. Cover the plywood or beaverboard with felt, suede, or long-napped flannel, nap side out. Tack or staple the cloth to the back of the top of the board, stretch it tight, and tack or staple it to the back of the bottom of the board. Use the same procedure on both sides.

To Make Display Materials for the Flannel Boards

1. Cut out pictures, figures, or what you will from magazines, books, paper, lightweight cardboard, flannel cloth, or similar materials.
2. Then use one of the following procedures.
   a. Glue, not paste, pieces of sandpaper, sand side out, to the back of the picture or figure. It is not necessary to cover the entire back. Sandpaper at the corners or strips crossed on the center of the back will usually do, but don't be too stingy.
   b. Cover the back of the material with rubber cement. Sprinkle sand on the rubber cement while it is still wet. Let it dry.
   c. If the letters, figures, and so on are made of felt, flannel, roughened construction paper, oil cloth, blotting paper, or light sponge, they do not need a sandpaper backing. Just press them on the flannel board as is.
3. Use strips of yarn for decoration and to show relationships or to make letters. The yarn will stick to the flannel board without backing.

Ready Made Boards

1. Stiff, felt-backed dining room table pads make excellent felt boards. Soft pads will serve if hung up tautly.

2. Hook and loop boards can be purchased. They are made from the same type of material as Velcro fasteners. Professional speakers and television studios use hook and loop boards.

To Make a Magnetic Board

1. Procure a thin sheet of iron or steel-based sheet metal (for example, galvanized iron or tin plate) and cut it to size.

2. Paint the metal with automobile enamel or blackboard paint.

3. If the sheet metal edges are sharp, tape them or nail them to a wooden frame made to size.

To Make Materials for Magnetic Boards

1. Glue materials to small magnets. Use heavy duty glue or mending cement. The size of the magnet depends on the weight of the material. Provide a stiff backing for thin materials such as paper or cloth.

2. If the metal board is enameled, you can write on it with a china marking pencil (grease pencil). If the board has been painted with chalkboard paint or other gritty paint, one can write on it with chalk.

CHARTS, POSTERS, AND GRAPHS

Charts, posters, and graphs are all illustrative and reenforcing teaching tools. They can be used as displays, such as bulletin boards are, but probably they are best suited for getting across points in specific lessons.

Material. Charts and posters can be made on newsprint, wrapping paper, chart or poster paper, and the like. One can also make charts on transparencies and project them or make them on flannel boards.

Some Types of Useful Charts

1. Lists.
2. Flow charts.
3. Organizational charts.
4. Graphs.
5. Multicolumned charts showing contrast or comparison.
6. Trees or branching streams, as in genealogical charts.
7. Illustrated or pictorial charts.
8. Time charts and time lines.

Suggestions for Making Charts, Graphs, and Posters

1. Most of the charts used in classrooms should be the work of pupils who have found the information, chosen the way to represent it, and executed the plan themselves.

2. Charts should be planned ahead. Sketch out the chart on a piece of paper before beginning the chart itself. Pencil in the details of the chart lightly before inking them in.

3. Make the chart simple. One major point is quite enough for a chart.

4. Make the chart clear. Avoid confusing detail. Do not crowd it. Use symbols one can understand.

5. Make charts eye catching. Use colors, pictures, and the like.

6. Make charts forceful. Emphasize the central idea in a center of interest.

7. Be sure charts are visible. Make letters and symbols large enough. Leave plenty of white space so the message stands out.

8. Keep everything in proportion. Be careful of the spacing.

9. Avoid too much printing and writing. Let the chart tell its own story. To avoid too much printing on the chart, use a legend and keyed symbols.

Tips on Graph Construction. In making graphs, follow the suggestions for chart construction. It is particularly important to keep the graph in proportion.

1. Don't try to show too much on the same graph. If you want to show several phenomena, use several graphs.

2. Be sure to select units that fit your idea and your paper. In making pie graphs (circle graphs) note that 1 per cent $= 3.6°$ (100 per cent $= 360°$).

3. Be sure that there is a common base line for all the phenomena represented. Have the base line start at zero.

4. Be sure the total to which individual items are compared is shown.

5. Use color coding to show contrast, comparisons, growth, and so on. Be sure the key tells exactly what each symbol represents.

6. Be sure to credit your sources.

7. Be sure the title is brief, but clear.

Flip Charts. Flip charts can be used to illustrate and explain points as a lesson progresses. Separate charts mounted one on top of the other, on an easel, or even in the chalk tray, will suffice. Proper flip charts are made on large pads, such as artists use, set on a tripod. When one has finished using a chart, he simply flips it over the top of the easel and proceeds to the next chart. These are very handy. High school teachers do not use them enough, although they are often found in the elementary schools and in television studios.

Poster Making. Poster making can be an interesting and worthwhile activity.

1. Discuss the possibilities with pupils.
2. Discuss the criteria of good poster making.
   a. Aim at getting one idea across.
   b. Use as few words as possible.
   c. Make key words stand out. Use contrast, size, or color for this purpose.
   d. Keep the design simple.
   e. Leave plenty of white space.
3. Have pupils block out their designs on paper, and get teacher approval of the design.
4. Let the pupils execute their designs.

FIGURE 16-3. *Pupil-made Posters Can Add Life to Your Classes.*

DESK MURALS, SHADOW BOXES, AND LAYOUTS

The making of desk murals, shadow boxes, and layouts can also be worthwhile activities, particularly in the junior high school grades. For information on making such displays, see such works as Jerold E. Kemp, *Planning and Producing Audiovisual Materials,* 2nd ed. (San Francisco: Chandler Publishing Company, 1968), and Leslie W. Nelson, *Instructional Aids . . .* (Dubuque, Iowa: William C. Brown Company, Publishers, 1958).

STILL PROJECTION

OVERHEAD PROJECTION

The overhead projector is extremely versatile. The list that follows is a very incomplete and sketchy compilation of ways in which you might use it.

1. Write on it as on a chalkboard as the class proceeds. When the time comes to move on, just roll up the acetate or take a new blank sheet. In this way you do not have to erase and so can come back to reconsider, if necessary.
2. Use it to emphasize points by projecting them as they come up in class.
   a. Write points on the transparency as you go along.
   b. Flip on preprinted materials at propitious moments.
   c. Uncover blocked out preprinted material as the points come up. (To keep preprinted material out of sight, simply cover it with opaque material until the proper moment.)
3. Present pictures, drawings, diagrams, outlines, printed matter, and maps.
4. Project an outline form. (Fill it in as you go along.)
5. Project an outline. Cover it. (As you proceed, uncover the points as they are made.)
6. Reproduce or enlarge maps.
7. Project grids for graphing, outline maps on the chalkboard.
8. Project silhouettes.
9. Project tests and quizzes.
10. Correct tests, quizzes, papers, and so on. Project the correct answers by writing on the transparency. Transparencies made on spirit duplicators are excellent for this purpose because one can also make duplicate copies. Thus, it is possible for the teacher to go over something projected on the screen or board while the pupils follow along on their own copies.

Preparation of Overhead Transparencies

1. Procedures for handmade transparencies.
   a. Ditto transparencies.
      (1) Make a spirit master just as you would for normal duplicating. Transparencies made by this method will project in color, so use color for the master, if you wish.
      (2) Place the master on the duplicator.
      (3) Run a few sheets of paper through to be sure it is feeding properly.
      (4) Handfeed a sheet of frosted acetate, frosted side up, through the duplicator.
      (5) Spray with clear plastic.
      (6) Mount it if desired, adding a sheet of clear plastic over the face of the transparency for protection.
   b. Transparencies made directly on acetate.
      (1) You can write, print, or draw on acetate directly with felt-tipped pens, drawing ink, India ink, or transparent color pencils.
         (a) Draw the sketch on a sheet of paper.
         (b) Place the acetate sheet on the drawing. (Frosted acetate seems to

work better than clear acetate. If it is used, it should be frosted side up.)

(c) Trace the drawing using drawing ink, either black or colored.

(d) Let it dry.

(e) Add color as you wish. Use colored inks, felt-tipped pens, or transparent color pencils.

(f) Spray with clear plastic.

(g) Mount it, if desired.

(2) You can also use dry-transfer letters to make captions and titles. Graphs, charts, and diagrams can be made with black or colored tapes. These seem to go best on clear plastic.

2. Machine made transparencies.

Several types of copying machines can be used to make transparencies. Basically the procedure is to

a. Print, draw, or type the material to be projected.

b. Run the material through the machine according to the instructions for that machine. These machines will also copy printed material: some from books; others from single sheets only.

3. To lift pictures for transparencies.

One can make transparencies for the overhead projector by lifting pictures from magazines, provided that the picture is printed on clay-coated paper. To test for clay-coated paper, wet the end of your finger and rub the border of the picture to be lifted. If the paper is clay coated, it will leave a grayish-white residue on your fingertip. There are a number of methods for lifting pictures, some of which need special equipment. A simple method uses clear Contact, purchasable in any store.

a. Cut the Contact to size.

b. Place the picture on a flat surface, face up.

c. Remove the covering from a sheet of Contact and place it on the picture, sticky side down.

d. Rub out and smooth down any creases with a straight edge or a rolling pin. Rub from top to bottom and left to right. Be sure to get a good bond all over.

e. Place it in a pan of water.

f. Add a teaspoonful of detergent.

g. Let it soak for half an hour.

h. Remove it from the pan. Pull the paper slowly and easily from the Contact.

i. Wipe off any clay or paper residue with a soft wet rag or piece of cotton.

j. Blot off any excess moisture with a paper towel and let it dry.

k. Spray it with clear plastic.

l. Mount it, if desired.

4. Transparency making with a Polaroid camera.

Polaroid sells a special film that allows one to make transparencies with a Polaroid camera.

Mounting Transparencies. Several types of commercial mounts for overhead transparencies are available. Except for transparencies made by certain copying machines, which are very thin, mounts are really unnecessary. In some cases, because of the added length and width, they make the transparency awkward to transport and file. They are necessary if one wants to hinge on a series of masks or overlays (flip-ons), however.

To Make Overlays or Flip-ons. Overlays (flip-ons) are made exactly the same way one makes a base transparency. They can be laid on top of the base transparency without being attached, if one wishes, but usually it is preferable to hinge the overlay to the mount of the base transparency. (Use a piece of tape or commercially prepared hinges.)[1] Put reference marks (+) at the top left and bottom right corners of the basic transparency and overlays in order to match them up quickly and easily.

Masks are pieces of opaque material that block out portions of the transparency so that they will not be projected. Make masks by simply laying pieces of paper over the areas to be blocked out, or by covering them with opaque, pressure-sensitive adhesive tape that you can rip off at the proper time. Sometimes it is more efficient to hinge masks to the basic transparency than to use separate masks. To give hinged masks some permanence, use light cardboard or opaque plastic.

USE OF MICROFILM

Use microfilm to bring documents, reports, and newspaper stories not ordinarily available into the school and classroom. Ordinarily, microfilm is best suited for individual and library work. It provides pupils with opportunities for depth studies of celebrated cases, congressional debates, development of policy, the course of events during critical periods, and so on. Microfilm can also be adapted for large-group use by means of a large-group microfilm reader, by clipping and mounting portions of microfilm for viewing via slide projection, or by copying and duplicating excerpts from the microfilm.

35 MM (2 × 2) SLIDES AND FILMSTRIPS

Thousands of 35 mm slides suitable for social studies classes are available commercially through school supply houses and photography and other stores. Thousands more are available from associates, friends, neighbors, and relatives. Almost everyone who goes on a vacation trip comes back with slides that contain geographical and historical content. Many teachers make their own slides. With only a little skill you can copy pictures, book pages, documents, maps, and the like, in addition to taking pictures of scenes and events. Photographic manuals and works on the use of audiovisual aids will give you all the information you need for copying documents as well as for taking ordinary pictures.[2]

Some Suggestions For Using Slides

1. Have pupils make slide programs and illustrated reports.
2. Cut up microfilm; mount and project it. This technique is useful for projecting documents, and so on.

[1] Technifax Corporation, 195 Appleton St., Holyoke, Mass.
[2] *Copying,* Eastman Kodak Publication M1 (Rochester, N. Y.: Eastman Kodak Co., 1969); *How to Make Good Pictures,* Eastman Kodak Publication AW1 (Rochester, N. Y.: Eastman Kodak Co. n.d.); Jerold E. Kemp, *Planning and Producing Audiovisual Materials,* 2nd ed. (San Francisco: Chandler Publishing Company, 1968); Nelson, loc. cit.; and *Slides with a Purpose,* Eastman Kodak Publication V1-15 (Rochester, N. Y.: Eastman Kodak Co. n.d.).

3. Use as springboards—as a basis for study, discussion, or research.
4. Use for motivation and summation.
5. Use as any other picture for illustrating and clarifying.

Using Filmstrips and Slide Programs

1. Project two or more filmstrips or slide pictures simultaneously to show comparisons.
2. Use filmstrips or slide programs for motivation.
3. Use filmstrips as reference works for individual study.
4. Use filmstrips for small group work.
5. Study individual frames separately. One frame or slide may be quite enough for the entire class period.

To Make a Slide Program. The basic procedure for preparing a slide program is to

1. Set up the objective.
2. Decide on the main points you want to make.
3. Block these points into an outline or scenario.
4. Select slides that will best make your points. Try to use only photographically good slides, but do not hesitate to use a slide that really helps make the point even if it is not quite up to par technically.
5. Arrange the slides in sequence in accordance with the scenario.
6. Make title and explanatory slides as needed and place them in the sequence.
7. Prepare an oral commentary, if desired.
8. Arrange the slides into the projector tray in the proper sequence. If you will be using a single-shot projector, place the slides in a file box in the proper order and number them so that they will be in sequence when you show them.

To Make a Filmstrip. One can make filmstrips from slides. To do this well requires considerable skill and patience. If one has good slide projection equipment, making filmstrips seems hardly worth the effort. Instructions for making them can be found in audiovisual texts and technical manuals.[3]

THE OPAQUE PROJECTOR

The opaque projector is unique in that it will project the image of opaque materials on to a screen or onto a wall or chalkboard. Unfortunately, most opaque projectors require almost complete darkness to be effective and even then are difficult to focus and are somewhat awkward to use. Use the opaque projector

1. To project pictures, maps, pages from books, pamphlets, and magazines, and other opaque material too small for pupils to see or read from their seats. Opaque projection is much preferred to passing such material around the class. You can point out what you want the pupils to see and be sure every one has a chance to see it.

[3] See Kemp, op. cit., Chap. 20, and *Producing Slides and Film Strips*, Publication S-8 (Rochester, N.Y.: Eastman Kodak Co., 1969).

2. To project realia, such as coins, and other three-dimensional objects.

3. To enlarge maps and the like by projecting them onto a suitable surface and copying them. (See Chapter 15.)

4. To project pupils' work for all to see.

5. As a basis for pupils' reports. Shy pupils are likely to do very well when they use the opaque projector in their reports because they will feel less embarrassed in the darkened classroom.

6. To project work on the chalkboard for evaluation and correction. Corrections and comments can be made directly on the board.

INSTRUCTIONAL FILMS AND INSTRUCTIONAL TELEVISION[4]

Next to the chalkboard, the classroom instructional moving picture is probably the most ubiquitous and misused of all teaching tools. For such a potentially useful tool to be used so poorly is wasteful.

Uses of Instructional Film.   Use instructional films

1. To motivate.
2. To clarify.
3. To change attitudes.
4. To stimulate thought and discussion.
5. To sum up.
6. To clinch ideas.
7. To dramatize and enforce.
8. To show how.

Procedures for Using Instructional Films

1. Select only films that are pertinent to your teaching objectives *at the time the film is to be shown.*

2. Preview the film. Note the important points and relationships. Note how it relates to your objectives.

3. Introduce the film. Tell the pupils what they should look for, what questions to think about, and so on. You may even want to give them a study guide. (Sometimes you may just want the pupils to react. In that case tell them that that is what you are after. Don't point them toward one reaction or another.) Be sure that they understand that this is not an entertainment period.

4. Follow it up. Discuss what the movie had to say. You may want to follow it up with written work, problems, reading on the topic, and so on. Make it evident to the pupils that films are not just recreation.

5. When it seems propitious, stop the film and discuss what has happened or what has been brought out so far.

6. If pupils do not get a point, show the film again. When teaching skills—for example, map reading—stop the film, let the pupils practice, and then go back over the film, if it is necessary.

[4] Comments in this section have to do only with classroom instructional films and instructional television. Other types of films and television are discussed in Chapter 14, Mass Media.

7. If only some parts are pertinent or good, show only those parts.

8. When a film is suitable for a small-group activity, plug earphones into a junction box connected to the speaker output and project the picture onto a small screen or a sheet of white paper or cardboard in a corner of the room for the small group alone.

9. Create a film evaluation form. Keep a record of the films you have used, what they were about, and how they rated on the evaluation form.

10. Be sure to order your rental films early.

11. Allow a little spare time in your film class. Give yourself time to introduce, set up film, follow up, and allow for emergencies. A 40-minute film is too long for a 45-minute period.

12. If a film breaks, wind the film up on the take-up reel a few times, mark the break by slipping a small sheet of paper in at the break, and then go on with the film. Notify your audiovisual people or the film library. Do not try to splice it. Do not try to pin it together with paper clips, pins, scotch tape, or the like. Doing so only spoils someone else's showing.

13. Run a little of the film before the showing to be sure everything is in order.

14. Stop the film when you want to make comments. Don't try to talk over the film. You disrupt the continuity and, besides, no one can hear you.

15. Don't forget the value of silent films. Many times the visual impact of a film is all that is needed. Sometimes your own commentary, or that of a pupil, is better than any that the film company is likely to provide. In fact, sometimes, turning off the sound and adding your own commentary, or having pupils add their commentary, is the best way to show a sound film.

16. Investigate the use of rear-view projection. It makes it possible to use films in lighted classrooms, thereby making it easier for note taking and similar activities.

Moving Picture Production. Making moving pictures can be an interesting, worthwhile activity in a history or social science class. With guidance, pupils can carry out all of the writing, production, directing, and acting assignments quite satisfactorily. Teachers who want to attempt such a program should consult their audiovisual directors and such books as Kemp's *Planning and Producing Audiovisual Materials*.[5]

Using a Film for Independent Study. To prepare a 16 mm projector for independent study:

1. Load the film and thread the projector.
2. Plug earphones into the speaker outlet.
3. Arrange a sheet of paper, or use a box, for a screen.
4. Give pupils directions in a written guide. Instruct them about how to turn on the machine, run it through, and stop it at the end of the film. A good technique is to have the pupils stop the film before it is completely run out and then back it up to the starting point so that the projector will be ready for the next user before they turn the machine off. This procedure is not necessary if the machine is

---

[5] Kemp., loc. cit.

FILM EVALUATION FORM

Title:

Showing Time

Content:

Producer:

Evaluation

   Good Points:

   Poor Points:

self-threading, although it may be helpful to use it so that no one will try to thread the machine with a film that has not been rewound.

To Make a Box Screen for Individual Instruction and Independent Study. Make screens for individualized instruction or independent study by placing white paper in the bottom of a cardboard box and project into the box. The sides of the box provide shade and so permit clearer pictures on the screen than ordinarily would be the case in a brightly lighted classroom.

INSTRUCTIONAL TELEVISION

The procedures for using instructional television are basically the same as those for use of instructional movies. Even though the television presentations are lessons being taught by a television teacher, the classroom teacher has to assume the bulk of the responsibility for the pupils' learning. He must plan, select, introduce, guide, follow up, fill in the gaps, correct misunderstandings, and, in general, guide the pupils.

Procedure for Using Instructional Television

1. Prepare yourself for the telecast. Preview it if possible. Study the guides and any other advance material available.
2. Prepare the setting.
   a. Arrange the classroom.
   b. Prepare and distribute any materials and supplies needed.
   c. Discuss the lesson to be viewed with the pupils. Teach any background vocabulary necessary for understanding the instruction telecast.
   d. Guide the pupils' learning.
      (1) In work-type lessons, circulate to help your pupils.
      (2) Take notes of pupil reactions and evidences of lack of understanding or misunderstanding.
   e. Follow up.
      (1) Question and discuss.
      (2) Reteach and clarify as necessary.
      (3) Provide additional experiences—particularly ones that will allow pupil participation, creativity, problem solving, and critical and creative thinking.

Video Taping. In most schools that use video taping, the care and maintenance of the tape deck is entrusted to the audiovisual director. Usually, he is more than willing to help teachers make tape programs or to televise special events and classes.

Single-Concept Films. The single-concept film and the 8 mm projector are superior tools for individualizing instruction. They are extremely easy to operate and require no additional equipment. The short single-concept film is effective because, when well done, it concentrates on a single point and drives it home. Use it for both individual and large-group instruction.

Dial Access. Dial access systems provide television, film, slides, and tape recordings on call to either individual receivers or large-group receivers. To use these devices with large groups, make arrangements ahead of time to be sure that the program desired will be available. For individual work, provide study guides that tell the pupil (1) how to prepare for the program, (2) how to dial for the program, (3) what to do while listening or watching the program, and (4) how to follow up the program.

TEACHING WITH TAPES AND RECORDS

Undoubtedly, the record player has a place among the social studies teacher's most valued tools. The tape recorder, with its ability to record both pupil activities and outside sources, makes the scope of listening activities in the social studies even wider.

SOME LISTENING AND RECORDING ACTIVITIES

1. Correlate music with the history of a period.
2. Play excerpts of speeches, newscasts, debates, and the like concerning historical events.
3. Play dramatizations or dramatic representations of historical or legislative events.
4. Tape record interviews.
5. Tape record class sessions, committee meetings, and the like as (a) a record of what happens, and/or, (b) a basis for evaluating procedures, techniques, and substance.
6. Use tape-recorded narrations instead of the sound on sound films and filmstrips so that the commentary will be more appropriate for the class or teaching objectives.
7. Use tape recorders to individualize instruction or for small-group work. Set up a listening corner. So that other people will not be disturbed, plug in a set of earphones, or a junction box and several sets of earphones.
8. Tape record radio presentations and audio portions of telecasts for use in class later.
9. Stimulate current events by taping news roundups, the Voice of America, foreign broadcasts, and so on.
10. Use tape recording to record programs in which pupils simulate the production of radio programs, television programs, debates, and so on.

TO MAKE TAPE RECORDINGS FOR INDIVIDUALIZED INSTRUCTION

1. Plan the strategy and tactics to be used.
2. Prepare a script. Include:
   a. Instructions for students.
   b. Presentation by teacher.
   c. Exercises, questions, and instructions. Be sure to allow pupils enough time

to participate. Either provide for a pause in the tape, or instruct the individual to turn the player off until he is ready for the next step.
  d. Answers to exercises for feedback.
  e. Summary and conclusion.
  f. Instructions for the next activity, if desired.
3. Tape record according to the script.
4. Make up a written study guide for the pupils to follow.

TEACHING MACHINES, TEACHING PROGRAMS, AND COMPUTER-ASSISTED INSTRUCTION

Teaching machines are devices for presenting teaching programs. There is no doubt that teaching programs can and do teach. Just how well they teach is still problematical. Computer-assisted instruction (CAI) is really highly sophisticated, intrinsic programing.

USES OF PROGRAMED INSTRUCTION

1. To individualize classwork.
2. To teach basic skills and information.
3. As a basis for discussion, inquiry, and problem-solving activities.
4. To free time so that you can give individual attention and can concentrate on developing higher learnings.

SOME SUGGESTIONS FOR USING PROGRAMED INSTRUCTION

1. Pupils need guidance and supervision. Don't expect to be able to turn the pupils over to the machine and have it solve all your problems.
2. Check the pupils' progress continually.
3. Select programs for individuals and see to it that each is in the right place in the program.
4. Provide for follow-up activities. Use programed activities for background and jump-off activities.
5. Do not overuse the machine. Too much of even a good thing quickly becomes boring.

SELECTING TEACHING PROGRAMS

We have had so little experience in this area that to select teaching programs intelligently is difficult. Under the circumstances, you would do well to

1. Survey the literature: find out what is available.
2. Select programs that seem compatible with your teaching objectives.
3. Try them out on a sampling of pupils.
4. Adopt programs that seem to be productive in test runs.
5. Use a variety of programs. Not every program is suited for every youth, evidently.

BUILDING TEACHING PROGRAMS

The construction of teaching programs is very difficult and time-consuming. Usually, the collaboration of several experts is needed to build a single teaching program. Very rarely do teachers have the time and expertise necessary to do the job well. One of the problems with the programs on the market is that they have been made hastily and amateurishly. Most teachers, teaching teams, and faculties would do better to spend their energy on more productive activities and leave the building of teaching programs to others.

THE COMMUNITY AS A RESOURCE

Every community is filled with teaching resources. The use of the community not only brings excitement, interest, and action into classes, but also brings classes down to earth. Every school should have a central file listing the resources available to social studies teachers. Such a file should be a cooperative effort. In it every teacher should be able to find information concerning resource persons, instructional material that can be obtained locally, possible field trips, and community projects that might be worthwhile.[6]

USING RESOURCE PERSONS

Use resource persons to help pupils with projects, as sources of information, as guest speakers, and as consultants for discussion groups.

Preparing for Guest Speakers

1. Check to find out what you can about the speaker and his potential.
2. Brief the speaker on the topic, the purpose of the talk, the type of class, the time, and the place.
3. Agree with him about (a) the length of talk, (b) a question and answer period, (c) the use of audiovisual aids, and the like.
4. Confirm these agreements in a letter.
5. Make provisions for welcoming the speaker at the school.
6. Prepare the pupils for the speech. Have pupils make up questions they would like to have answered. Send copies of these to the speaker in advance.
7. Introduce the speaker. Briefly note the plan for the class in your introduction. Tell the class something about the speaker. Often this introduction is best done by a pupil, but the teacher should check it so that it comes out right—allowing for pupil inexperience and nervousness.
8. Thank the speaker at the end of the period.
9. Thank him again by letter.
10. If possible, do something special for him. Be sure that he is introduced to the principal and others and is made to feel at home. Invite him to lunch in the cafeteria with some of the pupils or in the teachers' cafeteria with staff members.

---

[6] Collecting the information for such a file should be the job of every teacher. Maintaining the file should be the job of a teacher-aide or clerk.

To Conduct Field Trips

Of all the possible instructional activities, field trips must be the most carefully planned. In the course of the planning you will have to

1. Talk over the trip with your principal and department head.
2. Take the trip yourself, if feasible, to see how to make it most productive and to see what arrangements should be made.
3. Arrange for details at the place to be visited. These arrangements include a schedule; the briefing of the host, or tour personnel, on what you want and what type of group you are; provisions for eating and rest rooms; and so on. Get clear information about fees.
4. Arrange for permissions from the school authorities and parents.
5. Arrange for schedule changes, excuses from other classes, and so on.
6. Arrange for transportation.
7. Arrange for the collection of funds, payments, and so on.
8. Arrange for the safety of pupils.
9. Arrange the itinerary, including all stops—rest stops, meals, and so on. Do not plan to rush. Allow plenty of time. Figure that someone will get lost, or be late, or something!
10. Establish rules of conduct.
11. Brief the pupils. Give them directions: what to do if lost or left behind, what to take along, what they are going to do, what they should look for, what notes they should take, what materials they should bring back. Give them a duplicated study guide.
12. Provide for follow-up activities. Taking along tape recorders and cameras will allow you to bring back a record of what you did and saw. Tape record interviews, talks, questions and answers, and take pictures of the people, places, and things seen as the basis of a class follow-up.
13. Take steps to see that no one is left out because of lack of money, race, religion, or ethnic background.
14. Arrange for other teachers and parents to help you.

To Build a File of Community Resources

A file of community resources can be most helpful. In it include

1. Information on possible field trips.
   a. What is there.
   b. Where it is and how to get there.
   c. Whom to see about arrangements.
   d. Expense involved.
   e. Time required.
   f. Other comments.
2. Information concerning resource people.
   a. Who they are.
   b. How they can help.
   c. Addresses.
3. Information concerning resource material.

a. What it is.
b. How to procure it.
c. Expense involved.
4. Information concerning community groups.
   a. Names and addresses.
   b. Function and purpose.
   c. Type of project with which they can help.
5. Information concerning local offices and industries.
   a. Name.
   b. Address.
   c. Key personnel.

TO DEVELOP A SIMULATION MODEL[7]

1. Select the process to be simulated.
   a. Determine the specific objectives.
   b. Decide what type of simulation would bring out these objectives.
2. Select a situation.
   a. Historical or current event.
      (1) May give a better understanding of the situation and the problems.
      (2) May be difficult to present because of biases, emotions, or lack of information.
   b. Hypothetical situation.
      (1) Good for demonstrating specific processes, skills, and pressures.
      (2) Likely to involve emotion and bias.
      (3) Teacher can control the variables easier—thus making the simulation simpler and clearer.
3. Research the situation in depth.
4. Develop the essential elements to be replicated.
   a. Try to keep all unessential elements out of the simulation model, for they tend to confuse and obscure the essential elements and complicate the simulation.
   b. Establish the relationships between the various roles (for example, power relationships).
5. Prepare the draft scenario.
   a. Read several other simulations to see how they have been developed. This may give you ideas.
   b. Set up some criteria or media for showing relationships.
   c. Try to keep the simulation from being too simple or too complicated.
   d. Write the draft scenario.
   e. Try out the draft scenario.
   f. Rewrite the draft scenario.
   g. Repeat (e) and (f) until you get a satisfactory draft.
   h. Present it to the class.
   i. Rewrite it (or junk it).

[7] Based on Dale M. Garvey and Sancha K. Garvey, *Simulation, Role Playing, and Sociodrama in the Social Studies,* The Emporia State Research Studies (Emporia: Kansas State Teachers College, 1957), Vol. 16, No. 2.

APPENDIXES

Sources of Information and Teaching Materials

T ODAY there are so many materials available for the teaching of social studies classes that no social studies class need be narrow, dry, or textbook-ridden. In the appendixes that follow you will find a sampling of the various materials and sources of materials available to you.

SOURCES OF INFORMATION ABOUT MATERIALS AND METHODS

Probably the most useful sources of information for teaching materials and methods of teaching are the curriculum guides and bulletins, syllabuses, and resource units that have been published by school districts, state departments of education, and sometimes by professional associations, and the professional journals such as *Social Education* and *The Social Studies*.

CURRICULUM GUIDES

Courses of studies, curriculum guides, or syllabuses usually outline what it is hoped the pupils will learn from the course and also give some indication of the content, material, and methods that should bring about the desired objectives.

In some cases, the guides set down the objectives, the scope, and the sequence of the course very explicitly, and teachers are expected to follow the line set forth very closely. Sometimes the guides even go so far as to indicate when and how long each topic should be taught. Other guides are very loose. Some schools have no guides or courses of study at all. Where curriculum guides are available, use them.

APPENDIX A

Resource Units

R ESOURCE units are just what the name implies. They are resources that you can mine for use in your teaching units and lessons. Go to them for suggestions concerning teaching objectives, content, teaching-learning activities, and materials of instruction on a topic.

To prepare a resource unit

1. Prepare an overview in which you point out the rationale for studying the topic, how it could fit into the curriculum, its importance, and so on.

2. Prepare suggested major objectives (for example, the principal generalizations to be learned; terminal behavior expected; attitudes, appreciations, or ideals to be encouraged, developed, and cultivated; and skills to be developed).

3. Prepare a list of specific objectives (concepts, terminal behavior, attitudes, appreciations, ideals, and skills) that might be suitable for teaching units or lessons on the topic.

4. Prepare an outline of content appropriate for the objectives.

5. Prepare a list of activities that might be used to achieve the suggested objectives.

6. Prepare a list of materials, films, film strips, records and games that might be useful for teaching the concepts, skills, attitudes, and behaviors that are listed as suggested objectives.

7. Prepare bibliographies for use by pupils and teachers.

Remember that in the resource unit the objectives, content, activities, and materials are not part of a plan, but are merely a collection from which teachers can select goals, content, activities, and materials when they are planning units or lessons. What format one uses does not really matter, as long as it is easy for teachers to find the help they seek.

APPENDIX B

Professional Societies

American Geographical Society, 156th St. and Broadway, New York, NY 10032.

American Historical Association, 400 A St., S.E., Washington, DC 20003.

American Sociological Association, 503 First National Building, Ann Arbor, MI 48108.

Association for Supervision and Curriculum Development, 1201 16th St., N.W., Washington, DC 20036.

The Association of American Geographers, 1710 16th St., N.W., Washington, DC 20009. (High School Geography Project publications, lists.)

National Association for Core Curriculum, 40 F Education Building, Kent State University, Kent, OH 44240.

National Association of Secondary School Principals, 1201 16th St., N.W., Washington, DC 20036. (Publications, films, filmstrips, catalog.)

National Catholic Educational Association, Suite 350, 1 Dupont Circle, Washington, DC 20036. (Publications, lists.)

National Council for Geographic Education, Room 1532, 111 West Washington St., Chicago, IL 60602.

National Council for the Social Studies, 1201 16th St., N.W., Washington, DC 20036. (*The* association for social studies teachers. Makes available many materials useful for teachers of social studies.)

National Education Association, 1201 16th St., N.W., Washington, DC 20036.

APPENDIX C

Social Studies Education Projects

American Liberties Project: c/o Harry C. Luccock, Asst. Director of Education for Curriculum Development, Hartford Board of Education, 249 High St., Hartford, CT 06103. (Booklets and visuals on constitutional cases for twelfth-grade nonacademic classes.)

Anthropology Curriculum Study Project: School of Education, University of California, Berkeley, CA 94720.

Asian Studies Project: Ohio State University, 1945 North High St., Columbus, OH 43210. (Newsletter giving information on developments and resources on Asian studies.)

Basic Concepts in History and Social Studies: Edwin C. Rozwenc, Director, Amherst College, Amherst, MA 01002. (Supplementary paperbacks on American history and culture available from Heath.)

Black History Project: Pacific Educational Projects, 3516 Sacramento St., San Francisco, CA 94118. (Slide presentations.)

Boston University School of Law, Law and Poverty Project: William M. Gibson, Director, 765 Commonwealth Ave., Boston, MA 02215. (Course materials and curriculum guide for use in teaching legal issues.)

Brevard County Schools Project: Marion Brady, Director, North Area Superintendent's Office, Brevard County Schools, 700 Sycamore St., Titusville, FL 32780. (Materials for sociology, K–12.)

Center for Research and Education in American Liberties: Alan F. Westin, Director, Teachers College, Columbia University, 501 W. 121st St., New York, NY 10027.

Center for Teaching International Relations: Maurice A. East, Director, Graduate School of International Studies, University of Denver, Denver, CO 80210. (Various materials, bibliographies and source lists.)

Chicago Social Studies Project: Edgar Bernstein, Director, University Laboratory School, University of Chicago, 1362 East 59th St., Chicago, IL 60637. (Ninth- and tenth-grade world history materials.)

Committee on Civic Education: Richard P. Longaker and Charles Quigley,

Directors, Committee on Civic Education, School of Law, University of California, Los Angeles, CA 90024. (Casebook and guide available from Ginn.)

Committee on the Study of History: Richard H. Brown, Director, Box 93, Amherst, MA 01002. ("Units" available from Heath and Addison-Wesley.)

Constitutional Rights Foundation: Vivian Monroe and Todd Clark, Directors, Suite 1012, 609 South Grand Ave., Los Angeles, CA 90017. (Casebooks.)

Council on Civic Education: Henry Toy, Jr., Director, 1735 De Sales St., N.W., Washington, DC 20036.

A Cultural Approach to the Study of History in Grades Seven and Eight: Winthrop S. Alden, Mt. Greylock Regional School District, Green River Rd., Williamstown, MA 01267. (Course of study.)

Dayton Negro History Program: June Marabb, Director, Dayton Board of Education, 348 West First St., Dayton, OH 45402. (Bibliography of materials and paperbacks.)

Development of Guidelines and Resource Materials on Latin America for Use in Grades 1–12: Clark C. Gill and William B. Conroy, Directors, University of Texas, 403 Sulton Hall, Austin, TX 78712. (Materials available from ERIC.)

Developmental Economic Education Program: John E. Mahler, Director, c/o Joint Council on Economic Education, 1212 Avenue of the Americas, New York, NY 10036. (Many materials.)

Econ–12, San Jose State College: John E. Sperling and Suzanne Wiggins Hilburn, Directors, Economic Education Center, San Jose State College, San Jose, CA 95114. (Several units available from Addison-Wesley.)

Educational Programming of Cultural Heritage (EPOCH): Jay Montfort, Berkeley Unified School District, 1033 Heinz Ave., Berkeley, CA 94710. (Multimedia clearing house on new resources.)

An Experimental Course in History-Oriented Humanities: Morris Buske, Director, Oak Park and River Forest High School, 201 North Scoville Ave., Oak Park, IL 60302. (Outlines and other material available.)

Harvard Social Studies Project: Donald Oliver and Fred Newmann, Graduate School of Education, 210 Longfellow Hall, Harvard University, Cambridge, MA 02138. (Public issues materials available from American educational publications.)

A High School Curriculum Center in Government: Shirley Engle and Howard Mehlinger, Directors, 1129 Atwater, Bloomington, IN 47401. (Ninth-grade course available from ERIC.)

High School Geography Project: Dana Kurfman, Director, P.O. Box 1095, Boulder, CO 80302. (Units available from Macmillan.)

A High School Social Studies Curriculum for Able Students: Edwin Fenton, Director, Carnegie Education Center, Carnegie-Mellon University, Schenley Park, Pittsburgh, PA 15213. (Material available from Holt.)

Human Dignity Through American History: Arthur L. Satterlee, Director, Vallejo Unified School District, 211 Valle Vista Ave., Vallejo, CA 94590. (Includes material on black Americans.)

Inquiry into Social Issues in Secondary Schools: Byron G. Massialas, Director, Department of Social Studies Education, 302 Education Bldg., Florida State University, Tallahassee, FL 32306. (Materials and units available.)

Intercultural Studies Program: Wallace L. Anderson, Director, University of Northern Iowa, Cedar Falls, IA 50613. (Intercultural studies materials.)

Intercultural Understanding Project: Melvin H. Samuels, Director, Allegheny County Schools, 100 Ross St., Fourth Floor, Pittsburgh, PA 15219. (Units and bibliographies.)

Janesville Social Studies Project: Kugh Hubel, Director, Janesville Social Studies Project, 3125 Mineral Pt. Ave., Janesville, WI 53545. (Three-year course sequence. Man Thru Time Publishing Co.)

Law in American Society Project: Robert H. Ratcliffe, Director, Law in American Society, Room 850, 29 South LaSalle St., Chicago, IL 60603. (Casebooks and handbooks available from Houghton.)

Lincoln Filene Center Program for Research and Development in the Social Studies: John S. Gibson, Lincoln Filene Center, Tufts University, Medford, MA 02155. (Many materials, catalog.)

Minnesota Social Studies Curriculum Project: Edith West, Director, College of Education, 350 A Peck Hall, University of Minnesota, Minneapolis, MN 55455. (K–12 curriculum materials available from Green Printing Co.)

Minority History and Culture Project: Norma Jean Anderson, Consultant, Intercultural Education, St. Paul Public Schools, 615 City Hall, St. Paul, MN 55102. (Guides on Afro-American and Mexican-American history.)

NCA Foreign Relations Project: Jerry R. Moore, Director, Room 740, 53 West Jackson Blvd., Chicago, IL 60603. (Eleven units available from Laidlaw.)

New Social Studies for the Slow Learner: A Junior High School American History Course: Edwin Fenton, Director, Social Studies Curriculum Center, Carnegie-Mellon University, Pittsburgh, PA 15213. (Available from Holt.)

New York University Center for Economic Education: George Dawson, Director, New York University, School of Education, Washington Square, New York, NY 10003. (Studies and materials.)

A Program for Learning in Accordance with Needs: John C. Flanagan, Director, American Institute for Research, P.O. Box 1113, Palo Alto, CA 94302. (Distributed by Westinghouse Learning Corp.)

Project Africa: Barry K. Beyer, Carnegie-Mellon University, Schenley Park, Pittsburgh, PA 15213. (Course of study and curriculum guide, grades 7–10.)

Providence Social Studies Curriculum Project: Ridgway F. Shinn, Jr., Rhode Island College, Providence, RI 02908. (Curriculum guides and resource units, Rhode Island College Bookstore.)

Religion–Social Studies Curriculum Project: Robert A. Spivey, Director, Florida State University, Tallahassee, FL 32301. (*Religious Issues in the Social Studies,* and manuals.)

Research Program in the Effects of Games with Simulated Environment in Secondary Education: Michael Inbar and James S. Coleman, Center for Study of Social Organization of Schools, The Johns Hopkins University, Baltimore, MD 21218. (Simulations available from Western Publishing Co. and Social Studies School Service.)

A Secondary School Social Studies Curriculum Focused on Thinking Reflectively About Public Issues: James P. Shaver, Director, Bureau of Educational Research, Utah State University, Logan, UT 84321. (Material for Analyses of Public Issues, Houghton.)

Social Sciences: Concepts and Values: Paul Brandwein, Director, Center for the Study of Instruction, Harcourt Brace Jovanovich Bldg., Polk and Geary Sts., San Francisco, CA 94109.

Social Studies Curriculum Center: Roy A. Price, 409 Maxwell Hall, Syracuse University, Syracuse, NY 13210. (Classroom materials and position papers.)

Social Science Curriculum Study Center: Ella C. Leppert, Director, University of Illinois, Curriculum Laboratory, 1212 West Springfield Ave., Urbana, IL 61803. (A sequential social studies course for the secondary school.)

Social Science Education Consortium: Irving Morrisett, Director, 970 Aurora, Boulder, CO 80302. (Monographs, newsletter, list of materials.)

Social Studies Curriculum Center: John R. Lee, Director, Northwestern University, Evanston, IL 60201. (Sequential curriculum on American history.)

Social Studies Curriculum Program: Peter B. Dow, Director, EDC Social Studies Curriculum Program, 15 Mifflin Place, Cambridge, MA 02138. (Units and courses.)

Social Studies Project of the APSA: American Political Science Association, 1527 New Hampshire Ave., N.W., Washington, DC 20036. (Assistance.)

Sociological Resources for Secondary Schools: Robert C. Angell, Director, 503 First National Bldg., Ann Arbor, MI 48108. (Episodes, readings, and sociology course.)

Task Force on Minority Cultures: Christian K. Skjernold, Work Opportunity Center, 107 S.E. 4th St., Minneapolis, MN 55414. (Micro units.)

World History Project: L. S. Stravianos, Department of History, Northwestern University, Evanston, IL 60201. (Interdisciplinary courses and world history.)

World Law Fund: Betty Reardon, Director, 11 West 42nd St., New York, NY 10036. (Syllabus, readings, case studies, films, simulations.)

World Studies Inquiry Program: Robin J. McKeown and John Michaelis, School of Education, Tolman Hall, University of California, Berkeley, CA 94720. (Materials for poor readers, available from Field Educational Publishers.)

APPENDIX D
Reference Works

THE social studies deal with such a mass of information that social studies teachers and pupils in live classes must look up a tremendous amount of information. You will find the standard encyclopedias extremely helpful. In addition, fact books such as *The World Almanac* and *Information Please Almanac* are absolutely essential and should be readily available in every social studies classroom.

The following is a sampling of useful reference works.

The Book of the State. Chicago: Council of State Governments, biennial.

The Education Index.

Educational Media Index: Geography and History. New York: McGraw-Hill, 1964.

Information Please Almanac Atlas and Yearbook. New York: Simon & Schuster, annual.

The Municipal Yearbook. Chicago: International City Managers Association, annual.

National Geographic Index. Washington, D. C.: National Geographic Society.

The New York Times Index.

Official Congressional Directory. Washington, D. C.: Government Printing Office, biennial.

Production Yearbook. New York: United Nations Publishing Service, annual.

The Readers Guide to Periodical Literature. State and local government annual or biennial reports.

The Statesman's Yearbook. Ed. by J. H. Paxton. New York: St. Martin's, annual.

Statistical Abstract of the United States. Washington, D. C.: Government Printing Office, annual.

Statistical Yearbook. New York: United Nations Publishing Service, annual.

Textbooks in Print. New York: R. R. Bowker Co., annual.

United States Government Organization Manual. Washington, D. C.: Government Printing Office, annual.

The World Almanac and Book of Facts. Garden City, N. Y.: Doubleday, School and Library Division.

Yearbook of the United Nations. New York: Columbia University Press, annual.

APPENDIX E

Periodicals Useful for Teachers

PERIODICALS are the most promising source of up-to-date information on social studies topics. The two most important periodicals in social studies education are *Social Education* and *The Social Studies*. Every social studies teacher owes it to himself to subscribe to both of them. *Social Education* is the journal of the National Council for the Social Studies. Membership in the Council includes a subscription to *Social Education*. *The Social Studies* is published by the McKinley Publishing Company.

The American Behavioral Scientist
The American Economics Review (Research reports.)
The American Historical Review
The American Political Science Review
American Sociological Review
Annals of the Association of American Geographers
The Annals of the American Academy of Political and Social Science
Audio-Visual Instruction
AV Communications Review
Bulletin of the National Association of Secondary School Principals (General professional.)
The Clearing House (General professional.)
Congressional Quarterly
The Core Teacher (Information on teaching social studies and general education courses.)
Economic Topics
Educational Leadership (General professional.)
Educational Theory
Focus (Geography, background information, and maps.)
Focus on Asian Studies, Service Center for Asian Studies Newsletter (Information on curriculum material, etc.)
Foreign Affairs

Geographic Bulletin. The Geographer, U.S. Department of State.

Geographical Review

Harvard Educational Review (General professional.)

The High School Journal (General secondary education.)

Information Notes. Office of Media Services, U.S. Department of State (Notes on countries and territories.)

Intercom (Useful in teaching world geography, cultures, and world affairs.)

The Journal of Economic Education

The Journal of Geography (Articles on geography and teaching of geography.)

Newsletter. Joint Council on Economic Education (Information on materials and methods of teaching economics.)

Progress in Economic Education (Information *re* economics education, teaching, and activities of the JCEE.)

Review of Educational Research (Research reports.)

Scholastic Teacher (Ideas for teaching.)

School and Society

Simulation and Games. Palo Alto, CA: Sage Publications.

Social Education (Social studies curriculum and methods.)

Social Studies. Brooklawn, N.J.: McKinley Publishing Co. (Social studies curriculum and methods.)

Teachers College Record (General professional. High quality.)

Today's Education (General articles on education.)

Urban Education

The World and the School (Current international affairs.)

APPENDIX F

Bibliographies and Lists of Resources[1]

An Annotated Bibliography of Audiovisual Materials Related to Understanding and Teaching the Culturally Disadvantaged. Washington, D. C.: National Education Association, Division of Educational Technology, 1969.

Annual Paperbound Book Guide for High Schools. New York: R. R. Bowker Co.

Asian Studies. Cambridge, Mass.: Harvard University Press, 1971.

Bibliography of Free and Inexpensive Materials for Economic Education. New York: Joint Council for Economic Education.

BROWN, RALPH A., AND MARIAN R. BROWN (eds.). "American History Booklist for High Schools." *Bulletin 42.* Washington, D. C.: National Council for the Social Studies, 1969.

CONNERY, ROBERT H., RICHARD H. LEACH, AND JOSEPH H. ZIKMUND. "Reading Guide in Politics and Government." *Bulletin 38.* Washington, D. C.: National Council for the Social Studies, 1966.

Educators' Guide to Free Films. Randolph, Wis.: Educators' Progress Service.

Educators' Guide to Free Film-strips. Randolph, Wis.: Educators' Progress Service.

Educators' Guide to Free and Inexpensive Teaching Materials. Randolph, Wis.: Educators' Progress Service.

Educators' Guide to Free Social Studies Materials. Randolph, Wis.: Educators' Progress Service.

Educators' Guide to Free Tapes. Randolph, Wis.: Educators' Progress Service.

EMBREE, AINSLIE (ed.). *A Guide to Paperbacks on Asia Selected and Annotated.* New York: The Asia Society, 1964.

FAISSLER, MARGARETA. *Key to the Past: History Books for Pre-College Readers.* Washington, D. C.: Service Center for Teachers of History, 1963.

Free and Inexpensive Learning Materials. Nashville, Tenn.: George Peabody College.

---

[1] Dates of publications have been omitted from bibliographies and lists that are subject to periodic up-dating, and to series that consist of a number of books or booklets published at different times.

Free and Inexpensive Materials on World Affairs. New York: Teachers College Press, 1968.

GALL, MORRIS, AND ARTHUR F. SODERLIND (co-chairmen). "World Civilization Booklist: Supplementary Reading for Secondary Schools." *Bulletin 41.* Washington, D. C.: National Council for the Social Studies, 1968.

HERSKOWITZ, HERBERT, AND BERNARD MARLIN. *A Guide to Reading in American History: The Unit Approach.* New York: The New American Library, 1966.

Index to Multi-Ethnic Teaching Materials and Teaching Resources. Washington, D. C.: National Education Association, 1967.

IRWIN, LEONARD B. *Guide to Historical Fiction.* Brooklawn, N. J.: McKinley Publishing Co., 1971. (This is the tenth edition of this guide, which was formerly prepared by the late Hannah Logasa.)

_____. *Guide to Historical Reading: Non-Fiction,* 9th ed. Brooklawn, N. J.: McKinley Publishing Co., 1970.

KENWORTHY, LEONARD S. *Studying Africa in Elementary and Secondary Schools,* 3rd ed. New York: Teachers College Press, 1970.

_____. *Studying South America in Elementary and Secondary Schools.* New York: Teachers College Press, 1970. (Guide to pamphlets, aids, etc.)

Latin America Curriculum Project. "Teaching About Latin America in the Secondary School: An Annotated Guide to Instructional Resources." *Bulletin 2.* (ED-012-832), ERIC, 1967.

LIMBACHER, JAMES L. *Feature Films on 8mm and 16mm,* 3rd ed. New York: R. R. Bowker Co., 1971.

List of Free Materials Available to Secondary School Instructors. New York: The Educational Service of Dow Jones and Company, Inc., 1968–1969.

The Mexican American: A Selected and Annotated Bibliography. Palo Alto, Calif.: Center for Latin American Studies, Stanford University, 1969.

MILLER, BRUCE. *Sources of Free and Inexpensive Pictures for the Classroom.* Riverside, Calif.: The Bruce Miller Publications, n.d.

_____. *Sources of Free Travel Posters.* Riverside, Calif.: The Bruce Miller Publications, n.d.

_____. *So You Want to Start a Picture File?* Riverside, Calif.: The Bruce Miller Publications, n.d.

New Educational Materials, 1970. Englewood Cliffs, N. J.: Citation Press, 1970. (Annual compilation.)

The Negro American in Paperback, rev. ed. Washington, D. C.: National Education Association, 1968.

Paperback Books in Economics. Syracuse, N. Y.: New York State Council on Economic Education, 1967.

ROGERS, VINCENT R. *A Sourcebook for Social Studies.* New York: Macmillan, 1970.

Some Sources of 2 × 2 Inch Color Slides. Rochester, N. Y.: Eastman Kodak Co., 1969. (S–2.)

Sources of Free and Inexpensive Pictures for the Classroom. Randolph, Wis.: Educators' Progress Service.

Sources of Slides and Filmstrips. Rochester, N. Y.: Eastman Kodak Co., 1969. (S–9.)

SPIESEKE, ALICE W. "World History Book List for High Schools: A Selection for Supplementary Reading." *Bulletin 31,* rev. ed. Washington, D. C.: National Council for the Social Studies, 1962.

Studying Africa in Elementary and Secondary Schools. New York: Teachers College Press, 1970.

Studying the Middle East in Elementary and Secondary Schools. New York: Teachers College Press, 1970.

Studying South America in Elementary and Secondary Schools. New York: Teachers College Press, 1970.

Studying the USSR in Elementary and Secondary Schools. New York: Teachers College Press, 1969.

Studying the World: Selected Resources. New York: Teachers College Press, 1970.

Supplement to A Guide to Paperbacks on Asia, Selected and Annotated. New York: The Asia Society, 1966.

Textbooks in Print. New York: R. R. Bowker Company, annual.

TURNER, MARY JANE. *Materials for Civics, Government, and Problems of Democracy.* Boulder, Colo.: Social Science Education Consortium, 1971.

TWELKER, PAUL A. *Instructional Simulation Systems: An Annotated Bibliography.* Corvallis, Ore.: Oregon State System of Higher Education, 1969.

U.S. Government Films for Public Education Use. Superintendent of Documents. Washington, D. C.: Government Printing Office.

APPENDIX G

International Agencies

Food and Agricultural Organization, Press and Publications Unit, United Nations, New York, NY 10017.

Food and Agriculture Organization of the United Nations, Liaison Office for North America, 1325 C St., S.W., Washington, DC 20437. (Leaflets and visual aids about food and population.)

General Agreement on Tariffs and Trade, GATT Secretariat, Villa le Bocage, Palais des Nations 1211, Geneva 10, Switzerland.

Inter-American Development Bank, 808 7th St., N.W., Washington, DC 20577.

International Atomic Energy Agency, Kaerntnerring 11, Vienna, Austria.

International Bank for Reconstruction and Development, 1818 H St., N.W., Washington, DC 20433.

International Bank for Reconstruction and Development, 20 Exchange Place, New York, NY 10015. (World Bank.)

International Civil Aviation Organization, International Aviation Bldg., 1080 University St., Montreal, P.Q., Canada. For information write to Aviation Programs and Policy Division, Department of State, Washington, DC 20520.

International Development Association, 1818 H St., N.W., Washington, DC 20025. (World Bank group.)

International Finance Corporation, 1818 H St., N.W., Washington, DC 20025. (World Bank group.)

International Labor Office, Washington Branch, 666 11th St., N.W., Washington, DC 20001. (Publications and posters.)

International Labor Organization, Washington Branch, 917 15th St., N.W., Washington, DC 20005.

International Monetary Fund, 19th and H St., N.W., Washington, DC 20431.

International Telecommunication Union, Place des Nations, Geneva, Switzerland. Information also available from Office of Telecommunication, Department of State, Washington, DC 20520.

The North Atlantic Treaty Organization, Brussells 39, Belgium. (Publications.)

Organization of American States, Pan American Union, 17th St., between Constitution Ave. and C St., N.W., Washington, DC 20006. (Many publications, catalog, list.)

Organization for Economic Cooperation and Development, Publications Center for USA, 1750 Pennsylvania Ave., N. W. Washington, DC 20006.

Pan American Health Organization, Pan American Sanitary Bureau, Regional Office of the World Health Organization, 525 23rd St., N.W., Washington, DC 20037.

United Nations, Office of Public Information, New York, NY 10017, or UN Information Center, Suite 714, 1028 Connecticut Ave., N.W., Washington, DC 20006.

UNESCO Publications Center, P.O. Box 433, New York, NY 10016. (Numerous publications, catalog.)

UNESCO, Branch Office, 2201 UN Building, 42nd St. and East River, New York, NY 10017.

United Nations Publications, Room LX, 2300 UN Building, New York, NY 10017. (Many publications and aids, catalog and brochures.)

United States Committee for UNICEF, 331 East 38th St., New York, NY 10016.

United States National Commission for UNESCO, Department of State, Washington, D. C. 20025.

Universal Postal Union, International Bureau, Schosshaldenstrasse 46, Bern 15, Switzerland.

Write for information to Office of International Economic and Social Affairs, Department of State, Washington, DC 20520.

World Bank Group, 1818 H St., N.W., Washington, DC 20433. (Booklets about World Bank, International Finance Corporation, and International Development Association.)

World Health Organization, Regional Office, Pan American Sanitary Bureau, 23rd St. and Virginia Ave., N.W., Washington, DC 20036.

World Meteorological Organization, United Nations, New York, NY 10017.

World Meteorological Organization, 41 Avenue Giusseppe Motta, Geneva, Switzerland.

Write for information to Office of International Economic and Social Affairs, Department of State, Washington, DC 20520.

APPENDIX H

Agencies of Foreign Governments[1]

Afghanistan: Royal Afghan Embassy, 2341 Wyoming Ave., N.W., Washington, DC 20008. (Pamphlet, limited supply.)

Arab Information Center, 757 Third Avenue, New York, NY 10017.

Australia: Australian News and Information Bureau, 636 Fifth Ave., New York, NY 10020. (Australian Handbook, films, bibliography, fact sheets, and brochures.)

Austria: Austrian Information Service, 31 E. 69th St., New York, NY 10021. (Maps, fact sheet, and brochures.)

Burundi: Burundi Embassy, 2717 Connecticut Ave., N.W., Washington, DC 20009. (Fact sheets.)

Canada: Canadian Consulate General, 500 Boylston St., Boston, MA 02116. (Many and various materials.)

Canadian Government Travel Bureau, Ottawa, Canada; also 680 Fifth Ave., New York, NY 10019.

Newfoundland & Labrador Tourist Development Office (TB), Confederation Bldg., St. John's, Newfoundland, Canada.

Department of Tourist Development, Prince Edward Travel Bureau (TB), Charlottetown, Prince Edward Island, Canada.

Nova Scotia Travel Bureau (TB), 5670 Spring Garden Road, Halifax, Nova Scotia, Canada.

Department of Natural Resources, Travel and Tourist Development Branch (TB), 796 Queen Street (P.O. Box 1030), Fredericton, New Brunswick, Canada.

Department of Tourism, Fish and Game; Tourism Branch (TB), 930 St. Foy Road, Quebec, Quebec, Canada.

Department of Tourism & Information (TB), 185 Bloor St. East, Toronto 5, Ontario, Canada.

Department of Tourism and Recreation (TB), 408 Norquay Bldg., 401 York Ave., Winnipeg 1, Manitoba, Canada.

---

[1] The word "list" or "catalog" following an entry indicates that a list or catalog of materials for distribution is available.

Tourist Development Branch (TB), Saskatchewan Industry Department, Power Building, Regina, Saskatchewan, Canada.

Alberta Government Travel Bureau (TB), 1629 Centennial Bldg., Edmonton 15, Alberta, Canada.

Department of Travel Industry (TB), Victoria, British Columbia, Canada.

Travelarctic, Tourist Development Section (TB), Yellowknife, Northwest Territories, Canada.

Department of Travel and Information (TB), P.O. Box 2703, Whitehorse, Yukon Territory, Canada.

Chad: Embassy of the Republic of Chad, Washington, DC. (Map, fact sheets, brochures.)

Chile: Consulado General de Chile, 809 UN Plaza, New York, NY 10017. (Fact sheets.)

Colombia: Colombia Information Service, 140 East 57th St., New York, NY 10022. (Many free booklets, maps, general information, *Colombia Today*.)

Congo: Embassy of the Democratic Republic of the Congo, Cultural Center, 4800 16th St., N.W., Washington, DC 20011. (Booklets, guide.)

Costa Rica: Instituto Costarricense de Turismo, San José, Costa Rica.

Cyprus: Embassy of Cyprus, 2211 R St., N.W., Washington, DC 20008. (Political booklets.)

Czechoslovakia: Embassy of Czechoslovak Republic, 3900 Lennean Ave., N.W., Washington, DC 20008. (Maps, tourist information.)

Denmark: Danish Information Office, 280 Park Ave., New York, NY 10017. (Map, fact sheet, time chart.)

Ecuador: Embassy of Ecuador, 2535 15th St., N.W., Washington, DC 20009. (Pamphlets.)

Estonia: The Consulate General of Estonia, 9 Rockefeller Plaza, New York, NY 10020. (Pamphlets about Estonian freedom.)

Ethiopia: Ethiopian Tourist Organization, P.O. Box 2183, Addis Ababa, Ethiopia.

Finland: Embassy of Finland, 1900 24th St., N.W., Washington, DC 20008. (Booklet, special information.)

France: Ambassade de France, Service de Presse et d'Information, 972 Fifth Ave., New York, NY 10021. (Various publications, lists.)

Germany (West): German Information Center, 410 Park Ave., New York, NY 10022. (Pamphlets, audiovisual materials, catalog. Free "sets of information.")

Ghana: Embassy of Ghana, 2460 16th St., N.W., Washington, DC 20009. (Fact sheet.)

Guinea: Embassy of the Republic of Guinea, 2112 LeRoy Place, N.W., Washington, DC 20008.

Guyana: Embassy of Guyana, 1701 Pennsylvania Ave., N.W., Room 404, Washington, DC 20006. (Single copies of materials on Guyana.)

Haiti: Ambassade de Haiti, Washington, DC. (Booklet.)

Iceland: Embassy of Iceland, 2022 Connecticut Ave., N.W., Washington, DC 20008. (General information.)

India: The Information Service of India, 2107 Massachusetts Ave., N.W., Washington, DC 20008. (Booklets, Reference Annual.)

Indonesia: Embassy of Indonesia, Information Section, 2020 Massachusetts Ave., N.W., Washington, DC 20036. (Map, periodical.)

Iran: Imperial Embassy of Iran, Washington, DC 20008. (Booklet.)

Ireland: Irish Tourist Board, 590 Fifth Ave., New York, NY 10036. (Pamphlets, map.)

Israel: Consulate General of Israel, Information Office, 11 E. 70th St., New York, NY 10021. (Various.)

Italy: Istituto Italiano Di Cultura, 685 Park Ave., New York, NY 10021. (Fact book.)

Jamaica: Embassy of Jamaica, 166 Connecticut Ave., N.W., Washington, DC 20009. (Fact sheets.)

Japan: Japan Information Service, Consulate General of Japan, 235 E. 42nd St., New York, NY 10017. (Pamphlet, fact sheets.)

Jordan: Jordan Tourist Information Center, 866 UN Plaza, Room 552, New York, NY 10017.

Korea: The American-Korean Foundation, Inc., 345 E. 46th St., New York, NY 10017. (Fact book, bibliography, pamphlets.) Korean Information Office, Embassy of Korea, 1145 19th St., N.W., Suite 312, Washington, DC 20036. (Pamphlets and booklets.)

Latvia: Legation of Latvia, 4325 17th St., N.W., Washington, DC 20011. (Booklet.)

Lithuania: Lithuanian Legation, 2622 16th St., N.W., Washington, DC 20009. (*The Story of Captive Lithuania* and *Lithuania, How Much Do We Know About Her?*)

Luxembourg: Luxembourg Consulate General, Economic and Tourist Dept., 200 E. 42nd. St., New York, NY 10017. (Brochure, map, films.)

Malaysia: Embassy of the Federation of Malaysia, Information Attaché, 2401 Massachusetts Ave., N.W., Washington, DC 20008. (Geographical, historical, political information.)

Mali: Embassy of Republic of Mali, 2130 R St., N.W., Washington, DC 20008. (Fact sheet.)

Nepal: Royal Nepalese Embassy, 2131 Leroy Place, N.W., Washington, DC 20008. (Brochures.)

Netherlands: Netherlands Information Service, 711 Third Ave., New York, NY 10017. (Booklets, posters, photoprints.)

New Zealand: New Zealand Embassy, 19 Observatory Circle, N.W., Washington, DC 20008. (Fact books and sheets, maps, films, filmstrips, records, lists.)

Nicaragua: Embassy of Nicaragua, 1627 New Hampshire Ave., N.W., Washington, DC 20009. (Pamphlets, brochures.)

Niger: Embassy of the Republic of Niger, 2204 R St., N.W., Washington, DC 20008. (Pamphlets.)

Norway: Norwegian Embassy Information Service, 825 Third Ave., New York, NY 10022. (Brochures, fact books.)

Pakistan: Embassy of Pakistan, 2315 Massachusetts Ave., N.W., Washington, DC 20008. (Pamphlets, fact sheets.)

Peru: Embassy of Peru, 1320 16th St., N.W., Washington, DC 20036. (Various pamphlets.)

Philipines: Embassy of the Philipines, 1617 Massachusetts Ave., N.W., Washington, DC 20038. (Map, brochures, fact sheet.)

Poland: Embassy of the Polish People's Republic, Press Office, 2640 16th St., N.W., Washington, DC 20009. (Booklets.)

Portugal: Casa De Portugal, 570 Fifth Ave., New York, NY 10036. (Map and fact sheet.)

Romania: Embassy of the Socialist Republic of Romania, Washington, DC 20008. (Booklets, statistics, archeological information.)

Saudi Arabia: Embassy of Saudi Arabia, Saudi Information Section, 1520 18th St., N.W., Washington, DC 20036. (Single copies, lists.)

Singapore: Embassy of the Republic of Singapore, 1824 R St., N.W., Washington, DC 20009. (Facts, maps, brochures.)

South Africa: Information Service of South Africa, 655 Madison Ave., New York, NY 10021. (Publication, films, filmstrips, magazines, lists, film catalog.) South African Tourist Corporation, 610 Fifth Ave., New York, NY 10020. (Posters, maps, tourist brochures.)

Spain: Spanish Embassy, Cultural Relations, Washington, DC 2009. (Booklets, information sheets.)

Sweden: Swedish Information Service, 825 Third Ave., New York, NY 10022. (Fact sheets, list; other materials on request.)

Syria: Embassy of Pakistan, Syrian Interest Section, 2315 Massachusetts Ave., N.W., Washington, DC 20008.

Thailand: Office of Public Relations Attaché, The Royal Thai Embassy, Washington, DC 20008. (Booklets, pamphlet, map, poster. Send self-addressed, 7½ × 10½ inch clasp envelope with twenty-four cents in postage stamps.)

Togo: Embassy of Togo, 2208 Massachusetts Ave., N.W., Washington, DC 20008. (Brochures.)

Trinidad and Tobago: Embassy of Trinidad and Tobago, 2209 Massachusetts Ave., N.W., Washington, DC 20008. (Brochures, pamphlets.)

USSR: Embassy of the USSR Information Department, 1706 18th St., N.W., Washington, DC 20009. (Many publications.)

Venezuela: Embassy of Venezuela, Institute of Information and Culture, 2437 California St., N.W., Washington, DC 20008. (Pamphlets, fact sheets.)

Yugoslavia: Yugoslav Information Center, 488 Madison Ave., New York, NY 10022. (Factual material and general information.)

APPENDIX I

Agencies of the
Federal Government[1]

THE United States Government publishes thousands of books, pamphlets, and papers on a range of topics covering every aspect of the social studies. Most of these publications are on sale by Superintendent of Documents, Government Printing Office, Washington, DC 20402. (Free publications may be obtained from the various governmental offices and from Congressmen. Addresses of the various federal agencies are contained in the *United States Government Organization Manual.*)

Administrative Office of the United States Courts, United States Supreme Court Building, 1 First St., N.E., Washington, DC 20544.

Appalachian Regional Commission Technical Information Director, 1666 Connecticut Ave., N.W., Washington, DC 20235.

Bureau of the Census, Office of Assistant Director for Statistical Information, Washington, DC 20233.

Bureau of Customs, Washington, DC 20226.

Bureau of Indian Affairs, Office of Public Information, 1951 Constitution Ave., Washington, DC 20242.

Delaware River Basin Commission, Department of the Interior Bldg., Washington, DC 20240.

Department of Agriculture, Information Office, 14th and Independence Ave., S.W., Washington, DC 20250.

Department of Defense, Directorate of Defense Information, Office of The Assistant Secretary of Defense (Public Affairs), The Pentagon, Washington, DC 20301.

Department of Health, Education, and Welfare, Information Center, 330 Independence Ave., S.W., Washington, DC 20201.

Department of Housing and Urban Development, Office of Information, 451 7th St., S.W., Washington, DC 20410.

[1] The word "list" or "catalog" following an entry indicates that a list or catalog of materials for distribution is available.

Department of the Interior, Washington, DC 20230.

Department of Labor, Office of Information, 14th St. and Constitution Ave., N.W., Washington, DC 20210.

Department of State, Office of Media Services, Bureau of Public Affairs, Washington, DC 20520. (*Background Notes, Current Foreign Policy,* Department of State *Bulletin,* audio visuals. Department of State materials are available through the Superintendent of Documents. However, it is possible to get on mailing lists that provide for free distribution.)

Environmental Science Services Administration, Office of Public Information, Rockville, MD 20852.

Federal Aviation Administration, 800 Independence Ave., S.W., Washington, DC 20590.

Federal Highways Administration, Management Systems Branch, 6th and D Sts., S.W., Washington, DC 20591.

Federal Railroad Administration, 400 6th St., S.W., Washington, DC 20591.

Federal Reserve Bank, Public Information Department, Federal Reserve Post Office Station, New York, NY 10045.

Federal Reserve Bank of Atlanta, 104 Marietta St., Atlanta, GA 30303.

Federal Reserve Bank of Chicago, 230 South LaSalle St., Chicago, IL 60690.

Federal Reserve Bank of Cleveland, East 6th St. and Superior Avenue, Cleveland, OH 44101.

Federal Reserve Bank of Minneapolis, 73 South 5th St., Minneapolis, MN 55440.

Federal Reserve Bank of New York, 33 Liberty St., New York, NY 10045.

Federal Reserve Bank of Richmond, 9th and Franklin Streets, Richmond, VA 23213.

Federal Reserve Bank of San Francisco, 400 Sansome St., San Francisco, CA 94120.

Federal Reserve Bank of St. Louis, P.O. Box 442, St. Louis, MO 63166.

Federal Trade Commission, Office of Administration, Pennsylvania Ave. at 6th St., N.W., Washington, DC 20580.

Federal Water Quality Administration, U.S. Dept. of the Interior, Washington, DC 20242.

Food and Drug Administration, Bureau of Education and Voluntary Compliance, Division of Consumer Education, U.S. Dept. of Health, Education, and Welfare, Washington, DC 20204.

Geological Survey, Information Office, GSA Building, Washington, DC 20242.

Interstate Commerce Commission, Public Information Office, 12th St. and Constitution Ave., N.W., Washington, DC 20423.

Maritime Administration, Office of Public Information, GAO Building, 5th and G Sts., N.W., Washington, DC 20235.

National Aeronautics and Space Administration, Washington, DC 20546. (Educational Publications, Code FAD-1.) (Many booklets and folders. Write for *NASA Educational Publications,* their catalog.)

National Air Pollution Control Administration, Publications Unit, Rm. 17-0-31, Public Health Service, U.S. Department of Health, Education, and Welfare, 5600 Fisher's Lane, Rockville, MD 20852.

National Endowment for the Humanities, Washington, DC 20506.

National Park Service, Division of Information, Interior Building, Washington, DC 20240.

Office of Conservation Education, Interior Building, Washington, DC 20240.

Office of Territories, Administrative Offices, Interior Building, Washington, DC 20240.

Organization for Economic Cooperation and Development, OECD Publications Center, Suite 1305, 1705 Pennsylvania Ave., N.W., Washington, DC 20006. (Makes available a large number of publications on international economic problems.)

Small Business Administration, 1441 L St., N.W., Washington, DC 20416.

Tennessee Valley Authority, Public Information Office, Knoxville, TN 37902.

United Savings Bond Division, 1111 20th St., N.W., Washington, DC 20226. (Write to state directors for free films and materials.)

United States Arms Control and Disarmament Agency, Office of the Public Affairs Advisor, Washington, DC 20451. (Publications and lists.)

U.S. Coast Guard, Management and Organization Branch, 1300 E St., N.W., Washington, DC 20591.

United States National Commission for UNESCO, Department of State, USA, Washington, DC 20520. (Publications and list; free mailing list for *Memo, UNESCOPE,* and *UNESCO Features.*)

U.S. Postal Service, Office of Public Information, 12th St. and Pennsylvania Ave., N.W., Washington, DC 20260.

United States Tariff Commission, E St., between 7th and 8th Sts., N.W., Washington, DC 20436.

U.S. Treasury Department, Public Affairs Office, Washington, DC 20220.

Urban Mass Transportation Administration Director, Government Relations, 800 Independence Ave., S.W., Washington, DC 20590.

APPENDIX J

Agencies of State Governments[1]

Alabama: Bureau of Publicity and Information, Montgomery, AL 36104. (*The Alabama Story,* vacation guides.)

Alaska: Alaska State Travel Division, Pouch E, Juneau, AK 99801.

Arkansas: Department of Parks and Tourism, 149 State Capitol, Little Rock, AR 72201. (Brochures, map.)

California: California Chamber of Commerce, 455 Capitol Mall, Sacramento, CA 95814. (Brochures of California statistics, film sources, and tourism.)

Hawaii: Hawaii Visitors Bureau, 2270 Kalakaua Ave., Honolulu, HI 96815. (Brochure, *Hawaii The Aloha State.*)

Idaho: Department of Highways, P.O. Box 7129, Boise, ID 83707. (Maps, brochures.)

Indiana: State Highway Commission, 100 North Senate Ave., Indianapolis, IN 46204. (Maps, personnel charts, etc.)

Maine: Maine Vacation Service, Galiway Circle, Portland, ME 04102. (Map, brochure.)

Maryland: Division of Tourism, State Office Building, Annapolis, MD 21401. (Map, brochure.)

Massachusetts: Massachusetts, Box 1775, Boston, MA 02105. (Map, brochures.)

Minnesota: Department of Economic Development, 51 East 8th St., St. Paul, MN 55101. (Brochures.)

Missouri: Division of Commerce and Industrial Development, P.O. Box 118, Jefferson Bldg., Jefferson City, MO 65101. (Pamphlet.)

Montana: Montana Highway Commission, Advertising Dept., Helena, MT 59601. (Teachers' kit, maps, brochures.)

Nebraska: Nebraskaland, Nebraska Game and Parks Commission, Information and Tourism Division, State Capitol, Lincoln, NB 68509. (Pamphlets, brochures, maps, fact sheets.)

[1] The word "list" or "catalog" following an entry indicates that a list or catalog of materials for distribution is available.

Nevada: Department of Economic Development, Carson City, NV 89701. (Map, brochures, fact sheets.)

New Mexico: Department of Development, 113 Washington Ave., Santa Fe, NM 87501. (Map, brochures, fact sheets.)

New York: State Department of Commerce, 112 State St., Albany, NY 12207. (Information about N. Y. government and history.)

North Carolina: North Carolina State Library, Raleigh, NC 27601. (Brochures, publications, lists.)

Ohio: Development Department, 65 South Front St., Box 1001, Columbus, OH 43216. (Pamphlets.)

Oklahoma: Tourism and Information Division, 500 Will Rogers Bldg., Oklahoma City, OK 73105. (Pamphlet, *A Brief History.*)

Oregon: State Highway Division, Travel Information, Salem, OR 97310. (Pamphlet, map.)

Pennsylvania: Department of Commerce, Harrisburg, PA 17120. (Pamphlets.)

Rhode Island: Rhode Island Development Council, Roger Williams Bldg., Providence, RI 02908. (Vacation, historical and geographic information, map, films.)

South Dakota: Department of Highway, Travel Div., Pierre, SD 57501.

Tennessee: Department of Conservation, 2611 West End Ave., Nashville, TN 37203. (Fact sheets.)

Utah: Utah Travel Council, Council Hall, Salt Lake City, UT 84114. (Map, fact sheets, brochure.)

Vermont: Agency of Development and Community Affairs, Montpelier, VT 05602. (School Kit.)

Virginia: State Travel Service, 911 East Broad St., Richmond, VA 23219. (Pamphlets, map.)

Washington: Department of Commerce and Economic Development, General Administration Bldg., Olympia, WA 98501. (Pamphlets, map.)

APPENDIX K

Organizations and Associations[1]

Ad Hoc Committee for Peace Studies, Horace Mann School, 231 W. 246 St., Bronx, NY 10471. (Bibliographies, film listings, newsletter.)

The African-American Institute, School Services Division, 866 UN Plaza, New York, NY 10017. (Information about teaching materials.)

Africa Research Group, P.O. Box 213, Cambridge, MA 02101.

African Studies Center, University of California, Los Angeles, CA 90024. (Occasional papers.)

AFS International Scholarships, 313 East 43rd St., New York, NY 10017. (Will arrange for high school age people from other countries to visit classes.)

American Assembly, Columbia University, New York, NY 10027. (Various books and pamphlets, list.)

American Association of University Women, Sales Office, 2401 Virginia Ave., N.W., Washington, DC 20037. (Various publications, catalog.)

American Civil Liberties Union, 156 Fifth Ave., New York, NY 10010.

American Committee on Africa, 164 Madison Ave., New York, NY 10016. (Various publications about Southern Africa and U.S. relations.)

American Federation of Labor and Congress of Industrial Organizations, 815 16th St., N.W., Washington, DC 20006. (Numerous publications, fact sheets, films, lists.)

American Freedom from Hunger Foundation, 1717 H St., N.W., Washington, DC 20006. (Unit, guide to films, monthly newsletter, films, packets on issues.)

American Friends of the Middle East, 1717 Massachusetts Ave., N.W., Washington, DC 20036. (Publications, maps, list.)

American Friends Service Committee, Inc., 160 N. 15th St., Philadelphia, PA 19102. (Numerous publications about peace, list.)

American Friends of Vietnam, 342 Madison Ave., New York, NY 10001. (Printed articles.)

[1] The word "list" or "catalog" following an entry indicates that a list or catalog of materials for distribution is available.

American Geographical Society, Broadway at 156th St., New York, NY 10032. (Issues of *Focus,* background information on many countries, list.)

American Institute of Cooperation, Board of Trade Building, 1129 20th St., N.W., Washington, DC 20036. (Materials about cooperatives, catalog.)

American Insurance Association, 86 John St., New York, NY 10038. (Publications, list.)

The American Jewish Committee, Institute of Human Relations, 165 E. 56 St., New York, NY 10022. (Many publications about Jews, Judaism, and human relations; catalog.)

American Jewish Congress, 15 East 84th St., New York, NY 10028. (Free or inexpensive books, pamphlets, and brochures, on Israel, Soviet Jewry, the Jewish community in the U.S., civil rights and civil liberties, church-state constitutional law, the improvement of race and intergroup relations, and so on. Specify particular area and whether you require materials in bulk.)

The American Legion, National Headquarters, 700 N. Pennsylvania St., Indianapolis, IN 46206. (Fact sheets, brochures, scholarship information.)

American Library Association, American Assoc. of School Librarians, 50 E. Huron St., Chicago, IL 60611. (Various publications, list.)

American Medical Association, 535 North Dearborn St., Chicago, IL 60610. (Numerous publications, list.)

American Newspaper Publishers Association Foundation, 750 Third Ave., New York, NY 10017.

American Society for Eastern Arts, 405 Sansome St., San Francisco, CA 94111. (Resource guide.)

American Trucking Associations, Inc., Educational Services, Public Relations Department, 1616 P St., N.W., Washington, DC 20036. (Classroom publications.)

Anti-Defamation League of B'nai B'rith, 315 Lexington Ave., New York, NY 10016. (Many publications, materials, catalog.)

Asian Studies Project, 1945 North High St., Columbus, OH 43210. (Newsletter about teaching materials and the like.)

Association for Asian Studies, 48 Lane Mall, University of Michigan, Ann Arbor, MI 48104. (Research materials; bibliographies; a periodical: *Journal of Asian Studies,* newsletter.)

Atlantic Council of the United States, 1616 M St., N.W., Washington, DC 20006. (*Atlantic Community Newsletter* and *NATO Letter,* subscription free.)

Atlantic Information Center for Teachers, 23–25 Abbey House, 8 Victoria St., London SW1, England. (Information service, periodicals: *World Survey, Crisis Papers, Correspondents World Wide.*)

Board of Missions of the United Methodist Church, Service Center, 7820 Reading Road, Cincinnati, OH 45237. (Publications, audiovisual materials concerning social problems and foreign lands, catalog.)

California Redwood Association, 617 Montgomery St., San Francisco, CA 94111. (Pamphlets, films, list, posters.)

Canadian Peace Research Institute, Oakville, Ontario, Canada. (Booklets.)

CARE/MEDICO World Headquarters, 660 1st Ave., New York, NY 10016. (Free films, filmstrips available from nearest field office.)

Carnegie Endowment for International Peace, UN Plaza at 46th St., New York, NY 10017. (Many publications, catalog.)

Center for Information on America, Washington, CT 06793. (*Vital Issues, Grass Root Guides,* list.)

Center for Inter-American Relations, 680 Park Ave., New York, NY 10021. (Many publications.)

Center for Strategic and International Studies, Georgetown University, 1800 K St., N.W., Washington, DC 20006. (Reports and monographs.)

Center for the Study of Democratic Institutions, P.O. Box 4546, Santa Barbara, CA 93103. (Various publications, list.)

The Center for Teaching About Peace and War, 754 University Center Bldg., Wayne State University, Detroit, MI 48202. (Educational materials.)

Center for Teaching International Relations, The Graduate School of International Studies, University Park, Denver, CO 80210. (Various materials, units.)

Center for War/Peace Studies, 218 E. 18th St., New York, NY 10003. (*Intercom,* Curriculum Materials Collection Project.)

Church Center for the United Nations, 777 UN Plaza, Room 10-E, New York, NY 10017. (Simulations for rent.)

CIRUNA, 833 UN Plaza, New York, NY 10017. (Publications about international affairs, list.)

Commission to Study the Organization of Peace, 866 UN Plaza, Room 405, New York, NY 10017. (Reports on international affairs.)

Committee for Economic Development, 477 Madison Ave., New York, NY 10022. (Publications, catalog.)

Committee for a National Trade Policy, Inc., 1028 Connecticut Ave., N.W., Washington, DC 20036. (Numerous publications on foreign trade.)

Conference on Peace Research in History, c/o Blanche W. Cook, John Jay College of Criminal Justice, CUNY, 315 Park Avenue South, New York, NY 10010. (Bulletins.)

The Conservation Foundation, 1250 Connecticut Ave., N.W., Washington, DC 20036. (Publications and a listing.)

Council for Family Financial Education, Twin Towers, Silver Spring, MD 20910. (Resource manual and bibliography.)

The Economic Club of Detroit, 920 Free Press Bldg., Detroit, MI 48226. (Reprints of speeches.)

European Community Information Service, Suite 707, 2100 N St., N.W., Washington, DC 20037. (General materials, maps, etc.)

Ford Foundation, Office of Reports, 320 East 43rd St., New York, NY 10017. (Many publications, lists.)

Foreign Policy Association, School Services Division, 345 East 46th St., New York, NY 10017. (Publications, bibliographies, simulations, etc.; probably the best source on foreign affairs.)

The Foundation for Economic Education, Inc., Irvington-on-Hudson, NY 10533. (Various publications, lists, catalog.)

Freedom House, Willkie Memorial Bldg., 20 West 40th St., New York, NY 10018. (Various publications.)

Friends Committee on National Legislation, 245 2nd St., N.W., Washington, DC 20002. (*Washington Newsletter,* various publications, price list.)

The Garden Club of America, 598 Madison Ave., New York, NY 10022. (Conservation packet.)

Hadassah Order Department, 65 East 52nd St., New York, NY 10022. (Publications, film strips, films, list.)

Institute of International Education, 809 UN Plaza, New York, NY 10017. (Various publications, price list.)

Inter-American Association for Democracy and Freedom, 20 West 40th St., New York, NY 10018. (*Hemispherica,* a monthly.)

International Chamber of Commerce, 1212 Avenue of the Americas, New York, NY 10036. (Various publications.)

International Council for Educational Development, 522 Fifth Ave., New York, NY 10036. (Studies, reports, speeches.)

International Friendship League, 40 Mount Vernon St., Boston, MA 02108. (Pen pals.)

International Student Service, 291 Broadway, New York, NY 10007. (Student exchange.)

International Studies Association, 2000 5th St. South, Minneapolis, MN 55904. (Teaching Kits for members.)

Japan Society, Inc., 833 East 47th St., New York, NY 10017. (*What Shall I Read on Japan?* Bibliography.)

Joint Council on Economic Education, 1212 Avenue of the Americas, New York, NY 10036. (Many various materials, *Checklist.*)

Keep America Beautiful, Inc., 99 Park Ave., New York, NY 10016. (Brochure and newsletter.)

League for Industrial Democracy, Inc., 112 East 19th St., New York, NY 10003. (Books, pamphlets, a news bulletin about government and economics, catalog.)

League of Women Voters of the United States, 1730 M St., N.W., Washington, DC 20036. (Various publications, films, tapes about governmental problems, catalog.)

Lincoln Filene Center for Citizenship and Public Affairs, c/o Tufts University, Medford, MA 02155. (Many various materials, catalog.)

The Middle East Institute, 1761 N St., N.W., Washington, DC 20036. (Free films, also various publications for sale.)

Minnesota World Affairs Center, c/o Mrs. Ruth Shipley, Public Service Director, Minneapolis Tribune, 425 Portland Ave., Minneapolis, MN 55415.
    Center Address: 3300 University Ave. S.E., Minneapolis, MN 55414. (Materials on public affairs for junior and senior high school social studies.)

Money Management Institute, Prudential Plaza, Chicago, IL 60601. (Booklets and filmstrips about money management.)

National Association of Counties, Suite 522, 1001 Connecticut Ave., N.W., Washington, DC 20036. (Variety of materials.)

The National Association for Mental Health, Inc., 1800 North Kent St., Rosslyn, VA 22209. (Publications, films, lists.)

National Audubon Society, 1130 Fifth Ave., New York, NY 10028.

National Committee on U.S.–China Relations, Inc., 777 UN Plaza, 9B, New York, NY 10017. (Resource guides, annotated bibliographies, list of units and tapes.)

National Conference of Christians and Jews, 43 West 57th St., New York, NY 10019. (Reprints, articles, books, and pamphlets about intergroup relations; catalog.)

National Congress of Parents and Teachers, 700 North Rush St., Chicago, IL 60611. (Various publications, catalog.)

National Council of Catholic Laity, 1312 Massachusetts Ave., N.W., Washington, DC 20005.

National Federation of Temple Sisterhoods, 838 Fifth Ave., New York, NY 10021. (Study guides on Jewish history and customs.)

National Geographic Society, Washington, DC 20036. (*School Bulletin*, various publications, globes, maps, list.)

National Parks Association, 1701 18th St., N.W., Washington, DC 20009. (Pamphlets, and the like.)

National Planning Association, 1606 New Hampshire Ave. N.W., Washington, DC 20009. (Many publications, list.)

National Recreation and Park Association, 1700 Pennsylvania Ave., N.W., Washington, DC 20006. (Publications.)

National Wildlife Federation, 1412 16th St., N.W., Washington, DC 20036. (Free newsletter, list.)

The Nature Conservancy, 1522 K St., N.W., Washington, DC 20005. (Publication.)

Open Space Institute, 145 East 52nd St., New York, NY 10022. (Publications.)

Overseas Development Council, 1717 Massachusetts Ave., N.W., Washington, DC 20036. Attention: Deborah H. Proctor. (Various free and inexpensive publications.)

Planned Parenthood–World Population, 810 Seventh Ave., New York, NY 10019. (Films, booklets, catalog.)

The Population Council, 245 Park Ave., New York, NY 10017. (Studies, reports, bibliographies.)

Population Crisis Committee, 1730 K St., N.W., Washington, DC 20006. (Newsletter, reports, list.)

Population Reference Bureau, Inc., 1755 Massachusetts Ave., N.W., Washington, DC 20036. (Many publications.)

Public Affairs Committee, Inc., 381 Park Avenue South, New York, NY 10016. (*Public Affairs Pamphlets*, catalog.)

Resources for the Future, Inc., 1755 Massachusetts Ave., N.W., Washington, DC 20036. (Publications.)

SANE, 378 Massachusetts Ave., N.E., Washington, DC 20002. (Publications, films, list.)

Service Center for Teachers of Asian Studies, Association for Asian Studies, 29 West Woodruff Ave., Columbus, OH 43210. (Newsletter including information on teaching materials.)

Service Center for Teachers of History, 400 A St., S.E., Washington, DC 20003. (Pamphlets about historical topics, list.)

Sierra Club, 1050 Mills Tower, San Francisco, CA 94104. (Publications and audiovisuals.)

Social Science Education Consortium, Inc., 970 Aurora, Social Science Bldg., Boulder, CO 80302. (Various materials, newsletter.)

Southern Africa Committee, 637 W. 125th St., New York, NY 10027.

Student Forum, 410 Dean St., Brooklyn, NY 11217. (Film and publications about peace; list.)

Tax Foundation, Inc., 50 Rockefeller Plaza, New York, NY 10020. (Research studies, briefs, bibliographies, list.)

The Twentieth Century Fund, 41 East 70th St., New York, NY 10021. (Research studies about economics, political and social issues, and institutions; newsletter, lists.)

United Nations Association of the United States of America, 833 UN Plaza, New York, NY 10017. (Publication, film strips, etc. on the UN.)

U.S. Committee for UNICEF, 331 East 38th St., New York, NY 10016. (Publications, films, materials, lists.)

"Voices from Developing Nations," Leyden High Schools, 3400 Rose St., Franklin Park, IL 60131. (Tapes by Peace Corps returnees.)

World Affairs Council, 70 Hereford St., Boston, MA 02115. (Bibliographies, film guides.)

World Federalist Youth, USA, 72-A Mariposa Ave., San Anselmo, CA 94960. (Various publications, list.)

World Law Fund, 11 West 42nd St., New York, NY 10036. (Many and various materials; information re teaching materials.)

World Neighbors, 5116 North Portland Ave., Oklahoma City, OK 73112. (Pamphlets.)

World Tapes for Education, P.O. Box 15703, Dallas, TX 75215. (Class-to-class correspondence by tape recordings, tape programs.)

World Without War Council, 1730 Grove St., Berkeley, CA 94709. (Publications.)

Young Women's Christian Association, National Board, 600 Lexington Ave., New York, NY 10022. (Publications.)

Young World Development, Freedom from Hunger Federation, 1717 H St., N.W., Washington, DC 20006. (Annotated bibliographies.)

APPENDIX L
Business and Industry[1]

Air World Education, TWA, 605 Third Ave., New York, NY 10016. (Pamphlets on aviation.)

American Advertising Federation, 1225 Connecticut Ave., N.W., Washington, DC 20036. (Booklets, list.)

The American Bankers Association, 1120 Connecticut Ave., N.W., Washington, DC 20036. (Booklets.)

American Bar Association, Public Relations Department, 1155 East 60th St., Chicago, IL 60637. (Film list; *Law and the Courts.*)

American Iron and Steel Institute, Teaching Aids Distribution Center, Bedford Hills, NY 10507. (Booklets, films, film strips.)

American Newspaper Publishers Association Foundation, 750 Third Ave., New York, NY 10017. (*Your Future in Daily Newspapers.*)

American Stock Exchange, 86 Trinity Place, New York, NY 10006. (Publications and films.)

American Trucking Association, Inc., 1616 P St., N.W., Washington, DC 20036. (Various free publications.)

The Anaconda Company, Advertising Department, Room 2145, 25 Broadway, New York, NY 10004. (Information about the copper industry.)

Armour and Company, Public Relations Department, P.O. Box 9222, Chicago, IL 60690. (Articles about meat packing and the meat packing industry; food source map.)

Association of American Railroads, Public Relations Department, American Railroads Bldg., Washington, DC 20036. (Various publications, list.)

Automobile Manufacturers Association, Inc., 320 New Center Bldg., Detroit, MI 48202. (Maps, bulletin board kits, booklets.)

Chamber of Commerce of the United States, 1615 H St., N.W., Washington, DC 20006. (*Understanding Economics,* publications, films, slides, catalog.)

[1] The word "list" or "catalog" following an entry indicates that a list or catalog of materials for distribution is available.

Chicago Board of Trade, Library and Literature Services, LaSalle at Jackson, Chicago, IL 60604. (Free publications.)

Cooperative Recreation Service, Inc., Radnor Rd., Delaware, OH 43015. (Folk lore, songs, games.)

Corn Refiners Association, Inc., 1001 Connecticut Ave., N.W., Washington, DC 20036. (Brochures, statistics.)

CUNA International, Inc., Public Relations Department, P.O. Box 431, Madison, WI 53701. (Publications, teachers' guide about credit unions.)

Delta Steamship Lines, Inc., 1700 International Trade Mart, P.O. Box 5250, New Orleans, LA 70150. (Photographic material, magazines, brochures about shipping and Latin America.)

E. I. du Pont de Nemours and Co., Public Relations Department, Wilmington, DE 19898. (Various publications.)

The Firestone Tire and Rubber Co., Akron, OH 44317. (*Rubber,* teachers' manual.)

First National City Bank, Public Relations, 399 Park Ave., New York, NY 10022. (*Economic Letter,* free; economic studies; urban studies; studies of countries; etc.)

Ford Motor Co., Educational Affairs Department, The American Rd., Dearborn, MI 48121. (Pamphlets, charts.)

General Motors Corporation, Public Relations Staff, Room 1–101, General Motors Bldg., Detroit, MI 48202. (Films, booklets, catalog.)

The Goodyear Tire and Rubber Co., Akron, OH 44316. (Leaflets.)

Hammermill Paper Co., Educational Service, East Lake Rd., Erie, PA 16512. (Film, exhibits, and brochure on making paper.)

Hershey Foods Corp., Hershey Chocolate and Confectionery Division, Education Department, Hershey, PA 17033. (Publications and film on chocolate, cocoa, and the industry.)

Industrial Forestry Association, 1410 S.W. Morrison St., Portland, OR 97205. (Publications, film about forestry, forest industries, and ecology.)

Inland Steel Co., 30 W. Monroe St., Chicago, IL 60603. (Booklets, pamphlets, annual report.)

Institute of Scrap Iron and Steel, Inc., 1729 H St., N.W., Washington, DC 20006. (Publications.)

International Commercial Exchange, Inc., 2 Broadway, New York, NY 10004. (Information on currency exchange.)

The International Paper Co., Public Relations Department, 220 East 42nd St., Room 1805, New York, NY 10017. (Various pamphlets.)

John Hancock Mutual Life Insurance Co., Department MA, Boston, MA 02117. (Booklets on history and government.)

Kaiser Aluminum and Chemical Corp., 300 Lakeside Dr., Oakland, CA 94604. (*Kaiser News;* list.)

Libbey-Owens-Ford Co., Department GMW, Public Relations Department, 811 Madison Ave., Toledo, OH 43624. (*Glass, The Miracle Worker.*)

Merrill Lynch, Pierce, Fenner, and Smith, Inc., 70 Pine St., New York, NY 10005. (Pamphlets and booklets on investing.)

Mirro Aluminum Co., Manitowoc, WI 54220. (*The Story of Aluminum.*)

National Association of Broadcasters, 1771 N St., N.W., Washington, DC 20036. (Bibliography.)

National Association of Securities Dealers, Inc., 1735 K St., N.W., Washington, DC 20006. (Books and pamphlets.)

National Coal Association, Coal Bldg., 1130 17th St., N.W., Washington, DC 20036. (Pamphlets about mining, coal, environment, etc.)

National Consumer Finance Association, 7th Floor, Solar Bldg., 1000 16th St., N.W., Washington, DC 20036. (Teachers' kit.)

National Cotton Council of America, P.O. Box 12285, Memphis, TN 38112. (Pamphlets.)

Pacific Coast Stock Exchange, 301 Pine St., San Francisco, CA 94104. (Various publications.)

Pan American Airways, Educational Services, Pan Am Bldg., New York, NY 10017. (Publications and films.)

State Mutual of America, Public Relations Branch, Worcester, MA 01605. ("Fifty State Flags," brochure.)

Sugar Information, Inc., 52 Wall St., New York, NY 10015. (Fact sheet.)

Union Pacific Railroad, 1416 Dodge St., Omaha, NB 68102. (Map, pictures, brochures.)

United States Beet Sugar Association, Educational Materials, P.O. Box 500, Dansville, NY 14437. (Teaching kits.)

United States Steel Corp., 71 Broadway, New York, NY 10006. (Publications, films, catalogs.)

Western Wood Products Association, Yeon Bldg., Portland, OR 97204. (Fact sheets and pamphlets on forestry.)

Weyerhauser Company, P.O. Box A, Tacoma, WA 98401. (Booklets, etc.)

APPENDIX M

Pen-Friend Services

	Ages Served	Charges
Letters Abroad 209 E. 56th Street New York, NY 10022	15–60 years or more	Self-addressed, stamped envelope.
World Pen Pals World Affairs Center University of Minnesota Minneapolis, MN 55455	12–20	35¢ service charge.
International Friendship League 40 Mount Vernon Street Boston, MA 02108	7–75	Self-addressed, stamped envelope; $1.00 membership fee.
The League of Friendship P.O. Box 509 Mount Vernon, OH 43050	12–20	35¢ charge; self-addressed, stamped envelope.
Student Letter Exchange R.R. No. 4 Waseca, MN 56093	10–19	30¢ each for *foreign* names; 10¢ each and self-addressed envelope for *U.S.* names.

For the best possible match, an application should include age, sex, hobbies, and other pertinent information. Also, except as noted, these agencies supply *only foreign correspondents*, not correspondents from other areas in the United States.

Addresses of
Publishers and Distributors

Abelard-Schuman Ltd., An Intext Publisher, 257 Park Avenue South, New York, NY 10010.

Abingdon Press, 201 Eighth Avenue South, Nashville, TN 37202.

Harry N. Abrams, Inc., 110 East 59th St., New York, NY 10022.

Aero Service Corp., P.O. Box 7600, Chicago, IL 60680.

Aldine Publishing Company, 529 South Wabash Ave., Chicago, IL 60605. (Distributors of Teachers Practical Press.)

Allyn & Bacon, Inc., 470 Altantic Ave., Boston, MA 02210.

American Book Company, 450 West 33rd St., New York, NY 10001.

American Education Publications, Inc., Education Center, Columbus, OH 43216.

American Heritage Publishing Co., 551 Fifth Ave., New York, NY 10017.

Appleton-Century-Crofts, Division of Meredith Corporation, 440 Park Avenue South, New York, NY 10016.

The Asia Society, 112 East 64th St., New York, NY 10021.

Association Press, 291 Broadway, New York, NY 10007.

Atherton Press, Inc., 70 Fifth Ave., New York, NY 10011.

Avon Book Division, The Hearst Corporation, 959 Eighth Ave., New York, NY 10019.

Bantam Books, Inc., 666 Fifth Ave., New York, NY 10016.

Barnes & Noble, Inc., 10 East 53rd St., New York, NY 10003.

Barron's Educational Series, Inc., 113 Crossways Park Drive, Woodbury, NY 11797.

Basic Books, Inc., Publishers, 404 Park Avenue South, New York, NY 10016.

Beacon Press, 25 Beacon St., Boston, MA 02108.

Behavioral Research Laboratories, P.O. Box 577, Palo Alto, CA 94302.

Blaisdell Ginn, 275 Wyman St., Waltham, MA 02154.

The Bobbs-Merrill Co., Inc., 4300 West 62nd St., Indianapolis, IN 46268.

R. R. Bowker Co., 1180 Avenue of the Americas, New York, NY 10036.

The Brookings Institution, 1775 Massachusetts Ave., N.W., Washington, DC 20036.

Bruce Books, 866 Third Ave., New York, NY 10022.

Cambridge Book Co., 488 Madison Ave., New York, NY 10022.

Cambridge University Press, 32 East 57th St., New York, NY 10022.

Carmen Educational Associates, Inc., P.O. Box 205, Youngstown, NY 14174.

Center for Inter-American Relations, 680 Park Ave., New York, NY 10021.

Chandler Publishing Co., Oak St. and Pawnee Ave., Scranton, PA 18515.

Chilton Book Co., 401 Walnut St., Philadelphia, PA 19106.

Citation Press, 50 West 44th St., New York, NY 10036.

Civic Education Service, 1733 K St., N.W., Washington, DC 20006.

College Entrance Book Co., Inc., 104 Fifth Ave., New York, NY 10011.

College Entrance Examinations Board, 888 Seventh Ave., New York, NY 10019.

Columbia University Press, 562 West 113rd St., New York, NY 10025.

Committee for Economic Development, 711 Fifth Ave., New York, NY 10022.

Congressional Quarterly, Inc., 1735 K St., N.W., Washington, DC 20006.

The Continental Press, Inc., Elizabethtown, PA 17022.

David C. Cook Publishing Co., School Products Division, 850 North Grove Ave., Elgin, IL 60120.

Council for Advancement of Secondary Education, 1201 Sixteenth St., N.W., Washington, DC 20036.

Coward-McCann and Geoghegan, Inc., 200 Madison Ave., New York, NY 10016.

Cowles Educational Corp., 480 Madison Ave., New York, NY 10022.

George F. Cram Co., 730 East Washington St., Indianapolis, IN 46202.

Criterion Books, Inc., 257 Park Ave. South, New York, NY 10010.

Thomas Y. Crowell Company, 666 Fifth Ave., New York, NY 10019.

The John Day Company, Inc., An Intext Publisher, 257 Park Avenue South, New York, NY 10010.

Dell Publishing Co., Inc., 245 E. 47th St., New York, NY 10017.

Denoyer-Geppert, 5235 Ravenswood Ave., Chicago, IL 60640.

The Dial Press, 750 Third Ave., New York, NY 10017.

Dodd, Mead & Co., 79 Madison Ave., New York, NY 10016.

The Dorsey Press, 1818 Ridge Rd., Homewood, IL 60430.

Doubleday & Company, Inc., School and Library Division, Garden City, L.I., NY 11530.

Doubleday Anchor Books, Garden City, L.I., NY 11530.

Dow Jones and Company, Inc., Educational Service Bureau, 200 Burnett Rd., Chicopee, MA 01021.

E. P. Dutton & Co., Inc., 201 Park Avenue South, New York, NY 10003.

Education Development Center, Social Studies Curriculum Program, 15 Mifflin Place, Cambridge, MA 02138.

Educational Testing Service, Princeton, NJ 08540.

Educators Publishing Service, Inc., 75 Moulton St., Cambridge, MA 02138.

Enrichment Testing Materials, 246 Fifth Ave., New York, NY 10001.

ERIC/ChESS, 970 Aurora, Boulder, CO 80302.

ERIC Document Reproduction Service, NCR Company, P.O. Box 2206, Rockville, MD 20832.

Farrar, Straus & Giroux, Noonday Paperbacks Book Publishers, 19 Union Square West, New York, NY 10003.

Fawcett Publications, Inc., Fawcett Place, Greenwich, CT 06830.

Fearon Publishers, Inc., 6 Davis Drive, Belmont, CA 94002.

Fearon Publishers, Inc., 2165 Park Blvd., Palo Alto, CA 94306.

The Fideler Co., Grand Rapids, MI 49502.

Field Educational Publications, Inc., 2400 Hanover St., Palo Alto, CA 94304.

Field Enterprises Educational Corp., Merchandise Mart Plaza, Chicago, IL 60654.

Follett Educational Corp., 1010 W. Washington Blvd., Chicago, IL 60607.

The Free Press, 866 Third Ave., New York, NY 10022.

Funk & Wagnalls Distributed by Thomas Y. Crowell Co., 201 Park Ave. South, New York, NY 10003.

Ginn and Company, 125 Spring St., Lexington, MA 02173.

Globe Book Co., 175 Fifth Ave., New York, NY 10010.

Government Printing Office, Washington, DC 20401.

Grolier Education Corp., 575 Lexington Ave., New York, NY 10022.

Grosset & Dunlap, Inc., 51 Madison Ave., New York, NY 10010.

Grove Press, Inc., Education Department, 53 East 11th St., New York, NY 10003.

E. M. Hale and Co. Publishers, 1201 South Hastings Way, Eau Claire, WI 54701.

Hammond Incorporated, Education Division, Dept. ED-4, Maplewood, NJ 07040.

Harcourt Brace Jovanovich, Inc., 757 Third Ave., New York, NY 10017.

Harper and Row, Publishers, 49 East 33rd St., New York, NY 10016.

Harvey House, Inc., Irvington-on-Hudson, NY 10533.

Hastings House, Publishers, Inc., 10 East 40th St., New York, NY 10016.

D. C. Heath & Company, 285 Columbus Ave., Boston, MA 02116.

Holt, Rinehart & Winston, Inc., 383 Madison Ave., New York, NY 10017.

Houghton Mifflin Company, 110 Tremont St., Boston, MA 02107.

International Textbook Co., Publishing Division of Intext, Scranton, PA 18515.

The Interstate Printers and Publishers, Inc., Jackson at Van Buren, Danville, IL 61832.

The Johns Hopkins University Press, Baltimore, MD 21218.

Joint Council on Economic Education, 2 West 46th St., New York, NY 10036.

The Junior Literary Guild, Doubleday & Company, Inc., School and Library Division, 501 Franklin Ave., Garden City, L.I. NY 11530.

The KAGG Press, P.O. Box 264, Wilmette, IL 60091.

Alfred A. Knopf, Inc., 201 East 50th St., New York, NY 10022.

Laidlaw Brothers, A Division of Doubleday & Company, Thatcher and Madison Sts., River Forest, IL 60305.

Life, Time and Life Bldg., Rockefeller Center, New York, NY 10020.

Life Educational Reprint Program, P.O. Box 834, Radio City Post Office, New York, NY 10019.

Lincoln Filene Center for Citizenship and Public Affairs, Tufts University, Medford, MA 02156.

J. B. Lippincott Co., Educational Publishing Division, East Washington Square, Philadelphia, PA 19105.

Little, Brown and Company, 34 Beacon St., Boston, MA 02106.

Lothrop, Lee & Shepard Company, Inc., 381 Park Avenue South, New York, NY 10016.

Lyons and Carnahan, Educational Division, Meredith Corp., 407 East 25th St., Chicago, IL 60610.

Macmillan Publishing Co., Inc., 866 Third Ave., New York, NY 10022.

Macrae Smith Co., 225 South 15th St., Philadelphia, PA 19102.

Massachusetts Institute of Technology Press, 50 Ames St., Cambridge, MA 02412.

McCormick-Mathers Publishing Co., 450 West 33rd St., New York, NY 10001.

McGraw-Hill Book Company, 330 West 42nd St., New York, NY 10036.

David McKay Co., Inc., 750 Third Ave., New York, NY 10017.

McKinley Publishing Co., 112 South New Broadway, Brooklawn, NJ 08030.

Memphis State University Press, Memphis State University, Memphis, TN 38111.

Charles E. Merrill Publishers, 1300 Alum Creek Dr., Columbus, OH 43216.

Julian Messner, Division of Simon & Schuster, Inc., 1 West 39th St., New York, NY 10018.

William Morrow & Co., Inc., 105 Madison Ave., New York, NY 10016.

National Academy of Sciences, Printing and Publishing Office, 2101 Constitution Ave., N.W., Washington, DC 20418.

National Council for Geographic Education, Publications Center, Illinois State University, Normal, IL 61761.

National Press, Books, 850 Hansen Way, Palo Alto, CA 94304.

NCR–ERIC Document Reproduction Service, 4936 Fairmount Ave., Bethesda, MD 20014.

Thomas Nelson Inc., Copewood and Davis Sts., Camden, NJ 08103.

The New American Library, Inc., The Education Division, 1301 Avenue of the Americas, New York, NY 10019.

New York Graphic Society Ltd., Education Department, 140 Greenwich Ave., Greenwich, CT 06830.

The New York Times, Book and Education Division, 330 Madison Ave., New York, NY 10017.

New York Times Library and Information Services Division, 330 Madison Ave., New York, NY 10017.

New York University Press, Washington Square, New York, NY 10003.

Northwestern University Press, 1735 Benson Ave., Evanston, IL 60201.

W. W. Norton & Co., Inc., 55 Fifth Ave., New York, NY 10003.

A. J. Nystrom and Co., 3333 Elston Ave., Chicago, IL 60618.

Oceana Publications, Inc., 40 Cedar St., Dobbs Ferry, NY 10522.

Ohio State University Press, 2070 Neil Ave., Columbus, OH 43210.

Oxford Book Co., 387 Park Ave. South, New York, NY 10016.

Oxford University Press, Inc., 1600 Pollitt Drive, Fairlawn, NJ 07410.

Pacific Coast Publishers, Campbell at Scott Dr., Menlo Park, CA 94025.

Paperback Library, Inc., 315 Park Avenue South, New York, NY 10010.

Parents' Magazine Press, A Division of Parents' Magazine Enterprises, Inc., 52 Vanderbilt Ave., New York, NY 10017.

Penguin Books, Inc., 39 West 55th St., New York, NY 10019.

Pitman Publishing Corp., 6 East 43rd St., New York, NY 10017.

Pocket Books, Inc., 1 West 39th St., New York, NY 10018.

Portal Press, Inc., Publishers, A Subsidiary of John Wiley & Sons, Inc., 605 Third Ave., New York, NY 10016.

Praeger Publishers, Inc., 111 Fourth Ave., New York, NY 10003.

Prentice-Hall, Inc., Educational Books Division, Englewood Cliffs, NJ 07632.

Public Affairs Press, 419 New Jersey Ave., S.E., Washington, DC 20003.

G. P. Putnam's Sons, 200 Madison Ave., New York, NY 10016.

Ramapo House, 235 East 45th St., New York, NY 10017.
Rand McNally & Co., P.O. Box 7600, Chicago, IL 60680.
Random House, Inc., 501 Madison Ave., New York, NY 10022.
Random House, School and Library Service, Inc., 457 Madison Ave., New York, NY 10022.
Random House, Inc., Alfred A. Knopf, Inc., The College Department, 201 East 50th St., New York, NY 10022.
Henry Regnery Co., 114 West Illinois St., Chicago, IL 60610.
Republic Book Co., 104–16 Roosevelt Ave., Flushing, NY 11368.
The Ronald Press Company, 79 Madison Ave., New York, NY 10016.
Sage Publications, Inc., 275 South Beverly Dr., Beverly Hills, CA 90212.
W. B. Saunders Company, West Washington Square, Philadelphia, PA 19105.
Schenkman Publishing Co., Inc., 3 Revere St., Cambridge, MA 02318.
Warren Schloat Productions, Inc., Pleasantville, NY 10570.
Scholastic Book Services, 904 Sylvan Ave., Englewood Cliffs, NJ 07632.
Science Research Associates, 259 East Erie St., Chicago, IL 60611.
Scott, Foresman and Company, 1900 East Lake Ave., Glenview, IL 60025.
Charles Scribner's Sons, 597 Fifth Ave., New York, NY 10017.
Service Center for Teachers of History, 400 A St., S.E., Washington, DC 20003.
Silver Burdett Co., Morristown, NJ 07960.
Simon & Schuster, Inc., 630 Fifth Ave., New York, NY 10020.
Simon & Schuster, Inc., Education and Library Department, 1 West 39th St., New York, NY 10018.
Social Studies School Service, 10000 Culver Blvd., Culver City, CA 90230.
Steck-Vaughn Co., Publishers, Vaughn Bldg., P.O. Box 2028, Austin, TX 78767.
Stryker-Post Publications, 6330 Utah Ave., N.W., Washington, DC 20015.
Superintendent of Documents, Washington, DC 20402.
Syracuse University Press, Syracuse, NY 13210.
Taplinger Publishing Co., 200 Park Ave. South, New York, NY 10003.
Teachers College Press, Teachers College, Columbia University, 1234 Amsterdam Ave., New York, NY 10027.
Teacher's Practical Press, 47 Frank St., Valley Stream, NY 11580. Distributed by Aldine Publishing Company.
Charles E. Tuttle Co., Inc., Rutland, VT 05701.
UNESCO Publications Center, 317 East 34th St., New York, NY 10016.
UNIPUB, 650 First Ave., New York, NY 10016.
United Nations Publications, United Nations Sales Section, New York, NY 10017.
University of Chicago Press, 5801 Ellis Ave., Chicago, IL 60637.
University of Minnesota Press, 2037 University Ave., S.E., Minneapolis, MN 55455.
The University of North Carolina Press, Chapel Hill, NC 27514.
University of Notre Dame Press, Notre Dame, IN 46556.
University of Toronto Press, 33 East Tupper St., Buffalo, NY 14203.
The University of Wisconsin Press, P.O. Box 1379, Madison, WI 53701.
Van Nostrand Reinhold Company, 450 West 33rd St., New York, NY 10001.
The Viking Press, Inc., School and Library Department, 625 Madison Ave., New York, NY 10022.

Henry Z. Walck, Inc., 19 Union Square West, New York, NY 10003.

Frederick Warne and Co., Inc., 101 Fifth Ave., New York, NY 10003.

Franklin Watts, Inc., 845 Third Ave., New York, NY 10022.

Webster Division, McGraw-Hill Book Company, Manchester Rd., Manchester, MO 63011.

Webster Publishing Co., 1154 Reco Ave., St. Louis, MO 63126.

The Westminster Press, Witherspoon Bldg., Philadelphia, PA 19107.

John Wiley & Sons, Inc., 605 Third Ave., New York, NY 10016.

The H. W. Wilson Co., 950 University Ave., Bronx, NY 10452.

World Affairs Book Center, 345 East 46th St., New York, NY 10017. (A service of the Foreign Policy Association.)

World Book Encyclopedia, Field Enterprises Corp., Merchandise Mart, Chicago, IL 60654.

World Publishing Company, 110 East 59th St., New York, NY 10022.

The Zaner-Bloser Co., Dept. EL, 612 North Park St., Columbus, OH 43215.

APPENDIX O

Audiovisual Producers and Suppliers

A C I Films, Inc., 35 West 45th St., New York, NY 10036. (Films.)

AEVAC Inc., 500 Fifth Ave., New York, NY 10036. (Overhead transparencies.)

Allyn & Bacon, Inc., Rockleigh, NJ 07647. (Transparencies.)

Alpha Corp. of America, Educational Division, 520 North Michigan Ave., Chicago, IL 60611. (35mm filmstrips with sound and study guide; Alpha cone concept motion pictures; and super 8 movie loops.)

American Documentary Films, Inc., 336 West 84th St., New York, NY 10024. (Films on social and political issues.)

Associated Sterling Films, Inc., 600 Grand Ave., Ridgefield, NJ 07657; 561 Hillgrove Ave., La Grange, IL 60525; 2221 South Olive St., Los Angeles, CA 90007. (Free films.)

Audio Book Co., 4430 West Jefferson Blvd., Los Angeles, CA 90016. (Tapes and records.)

Audio-Visual Div., Popular Science Publishing Co., Inc., 353 Lexington Ave., New York, NY 10017. (Transparencies.)

Audio-Visual Enterprises, 911 Laguna Rd., Pasadena, CA 91105. (Films, study prints, multimedia kits, models.)

The Avalon Hill Co., 4517 Harford Rd., Baltimore, MD 21214. (Games.)

Bear Films, Inc., 805 Smith St., Baldwin, NY 11510.

Beckley-Cardy, 1900 N. Narragansett, Chicago, IL 60639. (Transparencies, charts, and other materials.)

Behavioral Research Laboratories, P. O. Box 577, Palo Alto, CA 94302. (Programed texts.)

Herbert Budek, P.O. Box 307, Santa Barbara, CA 93102. (American Geographical Society filmstrips.)

Caedmon Records, Inc., 505 Eighth Avenue, New York, NY 10018. (Records and tapes.)

Charles Cahill and Associates, Inc., P.O. Box 3220, Hollywood, CA 90028. (Films, filmstrips.)

Canadian Travel Film Library, 680 Fifth Ave., New York, NY 10019. (Films of Canada, some free.)

Capital Film Laboratories, 470 E St., S.W., Washington, DC 20024.

Carousel Films, Inc., 1501 Broadway, Suite 1503, New York, NY 10036. (Educational and documentary 16mm sound films.)

Castle Films, 1445 Park Ave., New York, NY 10029. (Government films.)

CCM Films Inc., Dept. S.E., 866 Third Ave., New York, NY 10022.

CEBCO, Division of Standard Publishing, P.O. Box 31138, Cincinnati, OH 45231. (Overhead projection transparencies, master sheets for spirit duplicators, and prerecorded audio tapes.)

Charad Motion Pictures, 2110 East 24 St., Brooklyn, NY 11229. (Free pictures.)

Churchill Films, 662 North Robertson Blvd., Los Angeles, CA 90069. (Films.)

Civic Education Service, 1733 K St., N.W., Washington, DC 20006. (Transparencies.)

John Colburn Associates, Inc., 1215 Washington Ave., Wilmette, IL 60091. (16mm and 8mm films, filmstrips, transparencies, multimedia kits, etc.)

College Entrance Book Co., 104 Fifth Ave., New York, NY 10011. (Tapes, booklets, and spirit duplicator master books.)

Columbia Records, Special Products, 8th Floor, 51 West 52nd St., New York, NY 10019. (Tapes and records.)

Contemporary Films, Inc., 267 West 25th St., New York, NY 10001. (United Nations 16mm film catalog.)

Coronet Learning Programs, Coronet Bldg., 65 E. So. Water St., Chicago, IL 60601. (Programed learning units, films, filmstrips, etc.)

Current Affairs Films, 527 Madison Ave., New York, NY 10022. (Current affairs filmstrips.)

Decca Records, 445 Park Ave., New York, NY 10022.

Denoyer-Geppert, 5235 Ravenswood Ave., Chicago, IL 60640. (Transparencies, filmstrips, maps.)

Walt Disney 16mm Films, 477 Madison Ave., New York, NY 10022. (Films, loops, etc.)

Display Corporation of America, 4865 Stinton Ave., Philadelphia, PA 19144. (Transparencies.)

DuKane Corp., AV Division, St. Charles, IL 60174. (Audiovisual source directory of educational sound films.)

Ealing Film Loops, 2225 Massachusetts Ave., Cambridge, MA 02140. (Film loops.)

EDCOM Systems, Inc., Princeton, NJ 08540. (Globes, slides, and supplementary material.)

Educational Division, Imperial Productions, Inc., Dept. K, Kankakee, IL 60901. Filmstrips and tape sets.)

Educational Film Library Association, Inc., 250 West 67th St., New York, NY 10019. (Catalog of feature-length 16mm films.)

Educational Record Sales, 157 Chambers St., New York, NY 10007. (Records, projectuals, tapes, and filmstrips.)

Educators Progress Service, Box 497, Randolph, WI 53956. (Catalogs of free films, etc.)

Encyclopaedia Britannica Educational Corp., 425 North Michigan Ave., Chicago, IL 60611. (Filmstrips, teaching transparencies, records, study prints, books, multimedia materials.)

Encyclopaedia Britannica Films, 1150 Wilmette Ave., Wilmette, IL 60091.

Enrichment Materials, Inc., A Division of Scholastic, 50 W. 44th St., New York, NY 10036. (Enrichment records and filmstrips with study guides.)

Film Associates, 11559 Santa Monica Blvd., Los Angeles, CA 90025. (Films, filmstrips, etc.)

Filmstrip House, Inc., 432 Park Avenue South, New York, NY 10016. (Filmstrips.)

Folkways/Scholastic Records, 906 Sylvan Ave., Englewood Cliffs, NJ 17632. (Recordings.)

Gateway Educational Films, Ltd., 470–472 Green Lanes, Palmers Green, London N13, England. (Filmstrips, 8mm film loops, and 16mm films.)

General Aniline and Film Corp., 140 West 51st St., New York, NY 10020. (Transparencies.)

Guidance Associates, Pleasantville, NY 10570. (Sound filmstrips, slide libraries, etc., some coordinated with social studies textbooks.)

Hammond, Inc., 515 Valley St., Maplewood, NJ 17040. (Transparencies and maps.)

Hi Worth Pictures, P.O. Box 6, Altadena, CA 91001.

Holt, Rinehart & Winston, Inc., 383 Madison Ave., New York, NY 10017. (Programed units, academic games, films, filmstrips, and film loops.)

T. N. Hubbard Scientific Co., 2855 Shermer Rd., Northbrook, IL 60062. (Multimedia "Urban Studies System.")

Instructional Materials and Equipment Distributors, 1415 Westwood Blvd., Los Angeles, CA 90024. (Study prints.)

International Communication Films, Division of Doubleday & Company, Inc., Garden City, L.I., NY 11530. (8mm films, sound-color filmstrips, multimedia kits.)

International Film Bureau, Inc., 332 South Michigan Ave., Chicago, IL 60604. (Films and filmstrips.)

International Film Foundation, Inc., 475 Fifth Ave., Suite 916, New York, NY 10017. (Films.)

Jossey-Bass, Inc., 615 Montgomery St., San Francisco, CA 94111.

Keuffel and Esser Co., Educational Audiovisual Division, Hoboken, NJ 07030. (Materials for making transparencies in black and white and in color, transparencies, lettering sets, French curves, etc.)

Key Productions, Inc., 527 Madison Ave., New York, NY 10022. (Filmstrips.)

Keystone View Co., Division of Mast Development Co., P.O. Drawer 466, Meadville, PA 16335.

The Lansford Publishing Co., 2516 Lansford Ave., San Jose, CA 95125. (Charts, transparencies, and special aids.)

Learning Through Seeing, Inc., 8138 Foothill Blvd., Sunland, CA 91040. (Transparencies, duplicating books.)

Library Filmstrips Center, 140 North Old Manor, Wichita, KS 67208. (Color sound filmstrips.)

Life, Time and Life Bldg., Rockefeller Center, New York, NY 10020. (Filmstrips, reprints, tearsheets.)

Listening Library, Inc., 1 Park Ave., Old Greenwich, CT 06870. (Recordings, tapes, filmstrips.)

Mailbox Buyers' Service, A Division of Scholastic, 904 Sylvan Ave., Englewood Cliffs, NJ 07632. (Mail order service of Scholastic. Maps, etc.)

McGraw-Hill Films, 330 West 42nd St., New York, NY 10036. (Films, filmstrips, etc.)

Milton Bradley Co., Springfield, MA 01101. (Flannelboards.)

Modern Learning Aids, 1212 Avenue of the Americas, New York, NY 10036. (Films, filmstrips.)

Modern Talking Picture Service, 1212 Avenue of the Americas, New York, NY 10036. (Films.)

National Film Board of Canada, P.O. Box 6100, Montreal 3, Quebec. Also, 680 Fifth Ave., New York, NY 10019. (Geography, history, and social science films for rent or purchase.)

National Tape Repository, Bureau of Audio-Visual Instruction, Stadium Bldg., Rm. 348, University of Colorado, Boulder, CO 80301.

New York Times, Library Services and Information Division, Dept. SE, 229 West 43rd St., New York, NY 10036. (Microfilm.)

A. J. Nystrom and Co., 3333 Elston Ave., Chicago, IL 60618.

Pathescope Educational Films, Inc., 71 Weyman Ave., New Rochelle, NY 10802. (Filmstrips.)

Popular Science Publishing Co., Inc., Audio-Visual Division, 355 Lexington Ave., New York, NY 10017. (Filmstrips with teaching guides.)

Portal Study Graphics, 777 Bridgeway, Sausalito, CA 94965. (Pictures.)

Rand McNally & Co., P.O. Box 7600, Chicago, IL 60680. (Maps, globes, and books.)

Raytheon Learning Systems Co., 475 South Dean St., Englewood, NJ 07631.

RCA Record Division, Attention: Educational Department, 1133 Avenue of the Americas, New York, NY 10036.

Revell Educational Systems, 1216 Fifth St., Santa Monica, CA 90401. (Recordings, tapes, filmstrips, model kits, and simulation games; multimedia.)

SANDAK, 4 East 48th St., New York, NY 10017. (Slides of art works.)

Scholastic Audio-Visual Materials, 906 Sylvan Ave., Englewood Cliffs, NJ 07632.

Scholastic Book Services, 904 Sylvan Ave., Englewood Cliffs, NJ 07632. (Multimedia.)

School Marketing, Inc., 1414 Sixth Ave., New York, NY 10019.

School Service Co., 4233 Crenshaw Blvd., Los Angeles, CA 90008. (Flannelboards.)

Science Research Associates, Inc., 259 East Erie St., Chicago, IL 60611. (Map and globe skills, simulations.)

Scott Educational Division, Scott Graphics, Inc., Holyoke, MA 01040. (Jam Handy, Tecnifax, EML, filmstrips, overhead transparencies, multimedia, etc.)

Scott, Foresman and Company, 1900 East Lake Ave., Glenview, IL 60025. (Transparencies, supplementary readings.)

Screenscope, Inc., 3518 P St., N.W., Washington, DC 20007. (Films.)

Silver Burdett Co., Morristown, NJ 07960. (Various.)

Society for Visual Education, Inc., 1345 Diversey Parkway, Chicago, IL 60614. (Filmstrips, multimedia kits, pictures, slide sets, 8mm loops, records.)

Spoken Arts, Inc., 59 Locust Ave., New Rochelle, NY 10801. (Recordings, tapes, filmstrips.)

Stanton Films, 7934 Santa Monica Blvd., Los Angeles, CA 90046. (Films.)

Sterling Educational Films, 241 East 34th St., New York, NY 10016. (Films.)

Superintendent of Documents, U.S. Government Printing Office, Washington, DC 20402. (U.S. Office of Education Radio Scripts.)

Supply Room, Garden Grove Blvd., Garden Grove, CA 92641. (Flannelboards.)

Thorne Films, 1229 University Ave., Boulder, CO 80302. (Film loops, etc.)

Universal Color Slide Co., 136 West 32nd St., New York, NY 10001.

Universal Education and Visual Arts, 221 Park Avenue South, New York, NY 10003. (Films, filmstrips, recordings, and film loops.)

U.S. Department of State, Films Librarian, Distribution Control Division, Rm. 5819 (A), Office of Media Services, Washington, DC 20520. (Films and filmstrips.)

Visual Products Division, 3M Company, 3M Center, St. Paul, MI 55101. (Transparencies, transparency-making materials, etc.)

Visual Sciences, P.O. Box 599 A, Suffern, N.Y. 10901. (Filmstrips.)

Warren Schloat Productions, Inc., Pleasantville, NY 10570. (Filmstrips.)

Western Publishing Co., School and Library Department, 850 Third Ave., New York, NY 10022. (Materials, including visual aids, having to do with prejudice, civil rights, civil liberties, and race and intergroup relations.)

World Tapes for Education, P.O. Box 15703, Dallas, TX 75214.

Young America Films, 330 West 42nd St., New York, NY 10036.

APPENDIX P

Some Producers and Distributors of Simulation Games

Abt Associates, Inc., 55 Wheeler St., Cambridge, MA 02138.

Academic Games Associates, 430 East 33rd St., Baltimore, MD 21218.

American Educational Publications (AEP), Education Center, Columbus, OH 43126.

Paul S. Amidon and Associates, Inc., 5408 Chicago Ave. South, Minneapolis, MN 54417.

Avalon Hill Co., 4517 Harford Rd., Baltimore, MD 21214.

Baldicer Games, P.O. Box 1176, Richmond, VA 23209.

Benefic Press, 10300 West Roosevelt Rd., Westchester, IL 60153.

BOCES, 845 Fox Meadow Rd., Yorktown Heights, NY 10598.

Changing Times Education Service, 1729 H St., N.W., Washington, DC 20006.

Didactic Systems, Inc., P.O. Box 500, Westbury, NY 11590.

Division of Educational Services, University of Alberta, Edmonton, Alberta, Canada.

Dynasty International, Inc., 815 Park Ave., New York, NY 10021.

Educational Development Center, 15 Mifflin Place, Cambridge, MA 02138.

Educational Games Co., P.O. Box 363, Peekskill, NY 10566.

Educational Methods, Inc., 20 East Huron, Chicago, IL 60611.

Elementary Games Project, Industrial Relations Center, University of Chicago, 1225 East 60th St., Chicago, IL 60637.

Entelek, Inc., 42 Pleasant St., Newburyport, MA 01950.

Environmetrics, Inc., Suite 900, 1100 17th St., N.W., Washington, DC 20036.

Federal Reserve Bank of Minneapolis, Director of Public Information, Minneapolis, MN 55440.

The Free Press, 866 Third Ave., New York, NY 10022.

Good Time Educators, 5530 Zealand Ave. N., New Hope, MN 55428.

Instructional Simulations, Inc., 2147 University Ave., St. Paul, MN 55104.

Instructor Publications, Inc., Dansville, NY 14437.

Interact, P.O. Box 262, Lakeside, CA 92040.

Richard W. Irwin, Inc., 1818 Ridge Rd., Homewood, IL 60430.

Joint Council on Economic Education, 1212 Avenue of the Americas, New York, NY 10036.

The Macmillan Company, 866 Third Ave., New York, NY 10022.

Mental Health Research Institute, University of Michigan, Ann Arbor, MI 48104.

Portola Institute, 1115 Merrill St., Menlo Park, CA 94025.

Prentice-Hall, Inc., Englewood Cliffs, NJ 07631.

Proctor and Gamble Co., P.O. Box 599, Cincinnati, OH 45201.

Random House, Inc., 201 East 50th St., New York, NY 10022.

Science Research Associates, 165 University Ave., Palo Alto, CA 94031.

Simile II, 1150 Silverado Rd., P.O. Box 1023, La Jolla, CA 92037.

Systems Gaming Associates, A 1-2 Lansing Apartments, 20N Triphammer Rd., Ithaca, NY 14850.

Urban Systems, Inc., 1033 Massachusetts Ave., Cambridge, MA 02138.

Western Publishing Co., Inc., School and Library Department, 850 Third Ave., New York, NY 10022.

Xerox Education Sciences, Xerox Education Group, 600 Madison Ave., New York, NY 10022.

APPENDIX Q

Suppliers of Maps, Globes, and Allied Materials

TECHNOLOGICAL advances in learning materials and equipment have caused an explosion in the amount and kinds of materials for map study on the market. Almost all school publishing and supply houses now sell map transparencies, spirit masters, and the like. Look through their catalogs for aids of this sort — particularly for aids tied into textbooks and readings to form the beginning of instructional systems. However, for really good maps and globes, one still must depend largely on the established map makers, such as Cram, Hammond, Denoyer-Geppert, Rand McNally, and the government map services. Government topographical maps can be obtained from map stores as well as from federal centers, such as U.S. Geological Survey, Washington, DC 20242; and Federal Center, Denver, CO 80225. The U.S. Geological Survey provides indexes of available topographical maps for all the states, Puerto Rico, The Virgin Islands, Guam, and American Samoa, free of charge. These indexes also contain lists of special maps, addresses of local map dealers, and federal map distribution centers. Free and inexpensive maps are available from many sources.

1. Foreign embassies, information bureaus, and Bureaus of Tourism.
2. Newspapers and magazines.
3. State Highway agencies.
4. State Tourist and Development Agencies.
5. Airlines, and other transportation companies.
6. Oil company highway maps.
7. Automobile Association Highway Maps.

Aeronautical Chart and Information Center, U.S. Air Force, St. Louis, MO 63118.
American Map Co., 347 Madison Ave., New York, NY 10017. (Maps, globes, etc.)
Carman Educational Associates, Inc., P.O. Box 205, Youngstown, NY 14174. (Filmstrips, transparencies, maps, and photographs, etc.)
Coast and Geodetic Survey, U.S. Department of Commerce, Washington, DC 20230. (Maps.)

George F. Cram Co., Inc., 730 E. Washington St., Indianapolis, IN 46206. (Maps, globes, spirit masters, map-reading material, outline maps, etc.)

Denoyer-Geppert Co., 5235 Ravenswood Ave., Chicago, IL 60640. (Maps, globes, map-reading material, transparencies, etc.)

EdCom Systems, Inc., Princeton, NJ 08450. (Globes, maps, and slides, etc.)

Farquhar Transparent Globes, 3727 Spruce St., Philadelphia, PA 19104. (Maps, globes, and map-reading material.)

Hagstrom Map Co., Inc., 450 West 33rd St., New York, NY 10001. (Maps, globes, and map-reading material.)

Hammond Inc., Educational Division, 515 Valley St., Maplewood, NJ 07040. (Transparencies, maps, globes, atlases, etc.)

McKinley Publishing Co., 112 S. New Broadway, Brooklawn, NJ 08030. (Maps, outline maps, books, bibliographies, games.)

Map Distribution Office, Surveys and Mapping Branch, Department of Mines and Technical Surveys, Geographical Branch, 601 Booth St., Ottawa 4, Ontario, Canada.

National Geographic Society, 17th and N St., N.W., Washington, DC 20036. (Maps, globes and map-reading material.)

A. J. Nystrom and Co., 3333 Elston Ave., Chicago, IL 60618. (Maps, globes, map-reading material, transparencies, outline maps, etc.)

W. H. Olsen and Co., Inc., Providence, RI 02900. (Maps, globes, and map-reading material.)

Rand McNally & Co., P.O. Box 7600, Chicago, IL 60680. (Maps, globes, map-reading material, transparencies, etc.)

U.S. Department of the Army, Army Map Service, Corps of Engineers, Washington, DC 20315.

U.S. Department of Commerce, Geography Division of the Census Bureau, Washington, DC 20230. (Maps.)

United States Travel Service, Commerce Department, Washington, DC 20230.

U.S. Geological Survey, Department of the Interior, Washington, DC 20242.

Weber Costello and Co., Chicago Heights, IL 60411. (Maps, globes, and map-reading materials.)

APPENDIX R
Bibliography for Teachers

THIS bibliography contains works on general methods of teaching, the social studies disciplines, and how to teach the social studies. Reference works, bibliographies, and secondary school textbooks will be found in separate appendixes.

FOUNDATIONS OF METHODS

ASCHNER, MARY JANE, AND CHARLES E. BISH (eds.) *Productive Thinking in Education*, rev. ed. Washington, D. C.: NEA, 1968.

BERMAN, LOUISE M. (ed.) *The Humanities and the Curriculum*. Washington, D. C.: Association for Supervision and Curriculum Development, 1967.

BIDDLE, BRUCE J., AND WILLIAM J. ELLENA (eds.) *Contemporary Research in Teacher Effectiveness*. New York: Holt, 1964.

BIGGE, MORRIS L. *Learning Theories for Teachers*. New York: Harper, 1964.

BLOOM, BENJAMIN S., et al. *Taxonomy of Educational Objectives, The Classifications of Educational Goals, Handbook I: Cognitive Domain*. New York: McKay, 1956.

BRUNER, JEROME S. *The Process of Education*. Cambridge, Mass.: Harvard U. P. 1960. (Also a Vintage paperback.)

_____. *The Relevance of Education*. New York: Norton, 1971.

_____. *Toward a Theory of Instruction*. Cambridge, Mass.: Harvard U. P., 1966.

DUNFEE, MAXINE (ed.) *Ethnic Modification of the Curriculum*. Washington, D. C.: Association for Supervision and Curriculum Development, 1970.

EURICH, ALVIN C. *High School 1980*. New York: Pitman, 1970.

GAGNE, ROBERT M. *The Conditions of Learning*. New York: Holt, 1965.

GETZELS, JACOB W., AND PHILIP W. JACKSON. *Creativity and Intelligence: Explorations with Gifted Students*. New York: Wiley, 1962.

HOLT, JOHN. *How Children Fail*. New York: Pitman, 1964.

JOHNSON, P. E. *Psychology of School Learning*. New York: Wiley, 1971.

KRATWOHL, DAVID R., BENJAMIN S. BLOOM, AND BERTRAM B. MASIA. *Taxonomy of Educational Objectives, Handbook II: Affective Domain*. New York: McKay, 1964.

MARX, MELVIN H., AND TOM N. TOMBAUGH. *Motivation: Psychological Principles and Educational Implications*. San Francisco, Calif.: Chandler, 1967.

RUBIN, LOUIS J. *Life Skills in School and Society.* Washington, D. C.: Association for Supervision and Curriculum Development, 1969.

RUSSELL, IVAN L. *Motivation.* Dubuque, Iowa: Wm. C. Brown, 1971.

SMITH, B. OTHANEL, AND ROBERT H. ENNIS. *Language and Concepts in Education.* Chicago: Rand McNally, 1969.

THOMAS, R. M., AND S. M. THOMAS. *Individual Differences in the Classroom.* New York: McKay, 1965.

VARS, GORDON F. (ed.) *Common Learning: Core and Interdisciplinary Team Approaches.* Scranton, Pa.: International Textbook, 1969.

GENERAL METHODS

ALCORN, MARVIN D., JAMES S. KINDER, AND JIM R. SCHUNERT. *Better Teaching in Secondary Schools,* 3rd ed. New York: Holt, 1970.

BISHOP, LLOYD K. *Individualizing Educational Systems.* New York: Harper, 1970.

BLAIR, GLENN MYERS, AND WILLIAM POWELL. *Diagnostic and Remedial Teaching,* 2nd ed. New York: Macmillan, 1967.

BLOUNT, NATHAN S., AND HERBERT J. KLAUSMEIER. *Teaching in the Secondary Schools,* 3rd ed. New York: Harper, 1968.

BURTON, WILLIAM. *The Guidance of Learning Activities.* New York: Appleton, 1962.

CALLAHAN, STERLING G. *Successful Teaching in Secondary Schools,* 2nd ed. Chicago: Scott, Foresman, 1971.

CHESLER, MARK, AND ROBERT FOX. *Role-Playing Methods in the Classroom.* Chicago: Science Research Associates, 1966.

CLARK, LEONARD H. (ed.) *Strategies and Tactics in Secondary School Teaching.* New York: Macmillan, 1968.

CLARK, LEONARD H., AND IRVING S. STARR. *Secondary School Teaching Methods,* 2nd ed. New York: Macmillan, 1967.

Controversial Issues in the Classroom. Washington, D. C.: NEA, 1961.

EBOCH, SIDNEY C., AND GEORGE W. COCHERN. *Operating Audio-Visual Equipment.* 2nd ed. San Francisco: Chandler, 1968.

FARR, ROGER, AND JAMES LAFFEY. "Reading in the High School." *What Research Says to the Teacher, No. 11,* rev. ed. Washington, D. C.: Association of Classroom Teachers, 1970.

FOX, ROBERT, MARGARET B. LUSZKI, AND RICHARD SCHMUCK. *Diagnosing Classroom Learning.* Chicago: Science Research Associates, 1966.

GRAMBS, JEAN D., JOHN C. CARR, AND ROBERT M. FITCH. *Modern Methods in Secondary Education,* 3rd ed. New York: Holt, 1970.

GROISSER, PHILIP. *How to Use the Fine Art of Questioning.* Englewood Cliffs, N. J.: Prentice-Hall, 1964.

GRONLUND, NORMAN E. *Stating Behavioral Objectives for Classroom Instruction.* New York: Macmillan, 1970.

HAAS, GLEN, KIMBALL WILES, AND ARTHUR ROBERTS. *Readings in Secondary Teaching.* Boston: Allyn, 1970.

HAMACHEK, DON E. "Motivation in Teaching and Learning." *What Research Says to the Teacher, No. 34.* Washington, D. C.: Association of Classroom Teachers, 1968.

HANEY, JOHN B., AND ELDON J. ULLMER. *Educational Media and The Teacher.* Dubuque, Iowa: Wm. C. Brown, 1970.

HILL, WILLIAM FAWCETT. *Learning Through Discussion: Guide for Leaders and Members of Discussion Groups.* Beverly Hills, Calif.: Sage, 1969.

HIPPLE, THEODORE W. *Secondary School Teaching: Problems and Methods.* Pacific Palisades, Calif.: Goodyear, 1970.

HOCK, LOUISE. *Using Committees in the Classroom.* New York: Holt, 1961.

HOOVER, KENNETH H. *A Handbook for High School Teachers.* Boston: Allyn, 1970.

———. *Readings on Learning and Teaching in the Secondary School,* 2nd ed. Boston: Allyn, 1971.

HOWES, VIRGIL M. *Individualization of Instruction: A Teaching Strategy.* New York: Macmillan, 1970.

INLOW, GAIL M. *Maturity in High School Teaching,* 2nd ed. Englewood Cliffs, N. J.: Prentice-Hall, 1970.

KIBLER, ROBERT J., LARRY L. BARKES, AND DAVID T. MILES. *Behavioral Objectives and Instruction.* Boston: Allyn, 1970.

MAGER, ROBERT F. *Preparing Instructional Objectives.* San Francisco: Fearon, 1962.

McASHAN, H. H. *Writing Behavioral Objectives.* New York: Harper, 1970.

NOAR, GERTRUDE. *Teaching and Learning the Democratic Way.* Englewood Cliffs, N. J.: Prentice-Hall, 1963.

———. "Teaching the Disadvantaged." *What Research Says to the Teacher, No. 33.* Washington, D. C.: Association of Classroom Teachers, 1967.

PARRISH, LOUISE, AND YVONNE WASKIN. *Teacher-Pupil Planning.* New York: Harper, 1958.

POPHAM, W. JAMES, AND EVA L. BAKER. *Planning an Instructional Sequence.* Englewood Cliffs, N. J.: Prentice-Hall, 1970. (Programed text.)

———. *Systematic Instruction.* Englewood Cliffs, N. J.: Prentice-Hall, 1970. (Companion to *Planning an Instructional Sequence.*)

RATHS, LOUIS E. *et al. Teaching for Thinking.* Columbus, Ohio: Merrill, 1967.

RATHS, LOUIS E., MERRILL HARMIN, AND SIDNEY B. SIMON. *Values and Teaching.* Columbus, Ohio: Merrill, 1966.

ROOT, J. H., *et al. Diagnostic Teaching, Methods and Materials.* Syracuse, N. Y.: Syracuse U. P., 1965.

ROSSI, PETER (ed.) *New Media and Education.* Chicago: Aldine, 1966.

SANDERS, NORRIS M. *Classroom Questions: What Kinds?* New York: Harper, 1966.

SCHMUCK, RICHARD, MARK CHESSLER, AND RONALD LIPPITT. *Problem Solving to Improve Classroom Learning.* Chicago: Science Research Associates, 1966.

SCHMUCK, RICHARD, AND PATRICIA SCHMUCK. *Group Processes in the Classroom.* Dubuque, Iowa: Wm. C. Brown, 1971.

SHAFTEL, FANNIE R., AND GEORGE D. SHAFTEL. *Role-Playing for Social Values: Decision-Making in the Social Studies.* Englewood Cliffs, N. J.: Prentice-Hall, 1967.

STRANG, RUTH. "Guided Study and Homework." *What Research Says to the Teacher, No. 8,* rev. ed. Washington, D. C.: Association of Classroom Teachers, 1968.

TORRANCE, E. PAUL. *Encouraging Creativity in the Classroom.* Dubuque, Iowa: Wm. C. Brown, 1971.

DISCIPLINE

BROWN, DUANE. *Changing Student Behavior: A New Approach to Discipline.* Dubuque, Iowa: Wm. C. Brown, 1971.

CLARIZIO, H. F. *Toward Positive Classroom Discipline.* New York: Wiley, 1971.

GNAGEY, WILLIAM J. "Controlling Classroom Misbehavior." *What Research Says to the Teacher, No. 32.* Washington, D. C.: Association of Classroom Teachers, 1965.

JESSUP, M., AND M. KELLEY. *Discipline: Positive Attitudes for Learning.* Englewood Cliffs, N. J.: Prentice-Hall, 1971.

MADSEN, CHARLES H., JR., AND CLIFFORD K. MADSEN. *Teaching Discipline.* Boston: Allyn, 1969.

EVALUATION AND STATISTICS

BERG, HARRY D. (ed.) *Evaluation in Social Studies.* Thirty-fifth Yearbook. Washington, D. C.: NCSS, 1965.

BUROS, OSCAR. *Mental Measurements Yearbook.* Highland Park, N. J.: Gryphon (Various noncumulative editions.)

CRONBACH, L. J. *Essentials of Psychological Testing,* 3rd ed. New York: Harper, 1970.

DIZNEY, HENRY. *Classroom Evaluation for Teachers.* Dubuque, Iowa: Wm. C. Brown, 1971.

_____. *Evaluation in the Classroom.* Dubuque, Iowa: Wm. C. Brown, 1971.

GOROW, FRANK F. *Better Classroom Testing.* San Francisco: Chandler, 1966.

GRONLUND, NORMAN E. *Measurement and Evaluation in Teaching,* 2nd ed. New York: Macmillan, 1971.

KURFMAN, DANA (ed.) "Teacher Made Test Items in American History: Emphasis Junior High School." *Bulletin No. 40.* Washington, D. C.: NCSS, 1968.

MORSE, HORACE T., AND GEORGE H. McCUNE. "Selected Items for the Testing of Study Skills and Critical Thinking." *Bulletin No. 15.* Washington, D. C.: NCSS, 1964.

Multiple Test Items, A Close Look. Princeton, N. J.: Educational Testing Service, 1963.

PAYNE, D. A., AND R. F. McMORRIS (eds.) *Educational and Psychological Measurement.* Waltham, Mass.: Ginn/Blaisdell, 1967.

SCHOER, LOWELL A. *Test Construction: A Programed Guide.* Boston: Allyn, 1970.

SCRIVEN, MICHAEL. *The Methodology of Evaluation.* Lafayette, Ind.: Social Science Education Consortium, 1966. (Mimeo.)

STODOLA, Q. *Making the Classroom Test.* Princeton, N. J.: Educational Testing Service, 1961.

TATE, MERLE W., AND RICHARD C. CLELLAND. *Nonparametric and Shortcut Statistics.* Danville, Ill.: Interstate Printers and Publishers, 1957.

THORNDIKE, ROBERT L. (ed.) *Educational Measurement.* Washington, D. C.: American Council on Education, 1971.

THORNDIKE, ROBERT L., AND ELIZABETH HAGER. *Measurement and Evaluation in Psychology and Education,* 3rd ed. New York: Wiley, 1969.

TYLER, RALPH W. *Educational Evaluation: New Roles, New Means,* Part II, 68th Yearbook. National Society for the Study of Education. Chicago: U. of Chicago, 1969.

TEACHING THE GIFTED

Almost all the methodology described in methods books was originally conceived with gifted or better-than-average pupils in mind. Consequently, one hardly needs a special book on teaching the gifted, except to read about what others have done or are doing.

COPLEY, FRANK O. *The American High School and the Talented Student.* Ann Arbor, Mich.: U. of Michigan, 1961.

GALLAGHER, JAMES J. *Teaching Gifted Students: A Book of Readings.* Boston: Allyn, 1965.

KLEIN, MILTON M. *Social Studies for the Academically Talented in the Secondary School.* Washington, D. C.: NEA, 1960.

KOUGH, JACK. *Practical Programs for the Gifted.* Chicago: Science Research Associates, 1960.

SLOW LEARNERS

ABRAHAM, WILLARD. *The Slow Learner.* New York: Center for Applied Research in Education, 1964.

ABRAMOWITZ, JACK. *Diary of a Slow Learning Class.* Chicago: Follett, 1963.

BIENVENU, MILLARD, SR. *Helping the Slow Learner.* New York: Public Affairs Committee, 1967. (Pamphlet.)

HOWITT, LILLIAN C. *Creative Techniques for Teaching the Slow Learner.* Chicago: Teachers Practical Press, 1964.

JOHNSON, G. ORVILLE. *Education for the Slow Learners.* Englewood Cliffs, N. J.: Prentice-Hall, 1963.

KARLIN, MURIEL, AND REGINA BERGER. *Successful Methods for Teaching the Slow Learner.* Englewood Cliffs, N. J.: Prentice-Hall, 1969.

SHELTON, B. *Teaching and Guiding the Slow Learner.* Englewood Cliffs, N. J.: Prentice-Hall, 1971.

YOUNIE, WILLIAM J. *Instructional Approaches to Slow Learning.* New York: Teachers College Press, 1967.

TEACHING THE CHILDREN OF THE POOR

BOTTOM, R. *The Education of Disadvantaged Children.* Englewood Cliffs, N. J.: Prentice-Hall, 1970.

LORETAN, JOSEPH O., AND SHELLEY UMANS. *Teaching the Disadvantaged.* New York: Teachers College Press, 1966.

MOSTELLER, FREDERICK, AND DANIEL P. MOYNIHAN. *On Equality of Educational Opportunities.* New York: Random, 1971.

NOAR, GERTRUDE. *Teaching the Disadvantaged.* Washington, D. C.: NEA, 1967.

ORNSTEIN, ALAN C., AND PHILIP D. VAIRO (eds.) *How to Teach Disadvantaged Youth.* New York: McKay, 1969.

PASSOW, A. HARRY (ed.) *Education in Depressed Areas.* New York: Teachers College Press, 1963.

STROM, ROBERT D. *Teaching in the Slum School.* Columbus, Ohio: Merrill, 1965.

TABA, HILDA, AND DEBORAH ELKINS. *Teaching Strategies for the Culturally Disadvantaged.* Chicago: Rand McNally, 1966.

PROGRAMED INSTRUCTION

DETERLINE, WILLIAM A. *An Introduction to Programed Instruction.* Englewood Cliffs, N. J.: Prentice-Hall, 1962.

LYSAUGHT, JEROME P., AND CLARENCE M. WILLIAMS. *A Guide to Programed Instruction.* New York: Wiley, 1963.

SIMULATION

BOOCOCK, SARANE S., AND E. O. SCHILD (eds.) *Simulation Games in Learning.* Beverly Hills, Calif.: Sage, 1968.

CARLSON, ELLIOT. *Learning Through Games.* Washington, D. C.: Public Affairs Press, 1968.

GUETZKOW, HAROLD S. (ed.) *Simulation in Social Science: Readings.* Englewood Cliffs, N. J.: Prentice-Hall, 1962.

NESBIT, WILLIAM A. *Simulation Games for the Social Studies Classroom.* New York: Crowell, 1970.

AUDIOVISUAL MATERIALS

In this bibliography you will find books on the use of audiovisual or media devices and materials. Works listing sources of materials will be found in the lists and bibliography section.

Adapting Your Tape-Recorder to the Kodak Carousel Programer, SC-1. Rochester, N. Y.: Eastman Kodak, 1969.

Applied Color Photography Indoors, E-76. Rochester, N. Y.: Eastman Kodak, 1968.

Audiovisual Projection, S-3. Rochester, N. Y.: Eastman Kodak, 1969.

Basic Copying, AM-2. Rochester, N. Y.: Eastman Kodak, 1966.

Basic Developing, Printing and Enlarging, AJ-2. Rochester, N. Y.: Eastman Kodak, 1969.

Better Bulletin Boards. Austin, Tex.: Instructional Media Center (VIB), U. of Texas at Austin.

Better Movies in Minutes, AD-4. Rochester, N. Y.: Eastman Kodak, 1970.

BROWN, JAMES W., RICHARD B. LEWIS, AND FRED F. HARCLEROAD. *A-V Instruction: Materials and Methods,* 3rd ed. New York: McGraw-Hill, 1969.

Color Photography Outdoors, E-75. Rochester, N. Y.: Eastman Kodak, 1968.

Composition, AC-11. Rochester, N. Y.: Eastman Kodak, 1968.

COPLAN, KATE. *Poster Ideas and Bulletin Board Techniques: For Libraries and Schools.* Dobbs Ferry, N. Y.: Oceana, 1962.

Copying, M-1. Rochester, N. Y.: Eastman Kodak, 1969.

DAVIDSON, RAYMOND L. *Audiovisual Machines.* Scranton, Pa.: International Textbook, 1969.

Designing Instructional Visuals. Austin, Tex.: Instructional Media Center (VIB), U. of Texas at Austin, 1968.

Educational Displays and Exhibits. Austin, Tex.: Instructional Media Center (VIB), U. of Texas at Austin, 1966.

Effective Lecture Slides, S-22. Rochester, N.Y.: Eastman Kodak, 1970.

ELY, DONALD, AND VERNON S. GERLACH, *Teaching and Media.* Englewood Cliffs, N.J.: Prentice-Hall, 1971.

ERICKSON, CARLTON W. H., AND DAVID H. CURL. *Fundamentals of Teaching with Audiovisual Technology,* 2nd ed. New York: Macmillan 1972.

FREEDOM, FLORENCE B., AND ESTHER L. BERG. *Classroom Teachers' Guide to Audio-Visual Material.* Philadelphia: Chilton, 1971.

GASKILL, ARTHUR, AND DAVID ENGLANDER, *How to Shoot a Movie Story.* New York: Duell Sloane and Pearce, 1960.

Good Color Pictures—Quick and Easy, AE-10. Rochester, N.Y.: Eastman Kodak, 1969.

HAEMER, K. W. *Making the Most of Charts.* Holyoke, Mass.: Tecnifax, 1960.

Instructional Display Boards. Austin, Tex.: Instructional Media Center (VIB), U. of Texas at Austin, 1968.

KELLEY, GAYLIN B., AND PHILIP J. SLEEMAN. *A Guide to Overhead Projection and Practical Preparation of Transparencies.* Leeds, Mass.: Chart Pak, 1967.

KEMP, JERROLD E. *Planning and Producing Audiovisual Materials,* rev. ed. Scranton, Pa.: International Textbook, 1968.

KOSKEY, THOMAS ARTHUR. *Bulletin Boards for Subject Areas: A Handbook for Teachers.* Palo Alto, Calif.: Fearon, 1962.

LACEY, RICHARD A. *Films in the Classroom: Seeing with Feeling.* Philadelphia: Saunders, 1971.

LOUGHARY, JOHN (ed.) *Man-Machine Systems in Education.* New York: Harper, 1966.

Making Black and White Transparencies for Overhead Projection, S-7. Rochester, N. Y.: Eastman Kodak, 1970.

MINOR, ED. *Simplified Techniques for Preparing Visual Instructional Materials.* New York: McGraw-Hill, 1962.

Models for Teaching. Austin, Tex.: Instructional Media Center (VIB), U. of Texas at Austin, 1956.

MORLAND, JOHN E. *Preparation of Inexpensive Teaching Materials.* San Francisco: Chandler, 1966.

The Overhead System. Austin, Tex.: Instructional Media Center (VIB), U. of Texas at Austin, n.d.

Planning and Producing Visual Aids, S-13. Rochester, N. Y.: Eastman Kodak, 1969.

Producing Slides and Filmstrips, S-8, 4th ed. Rochester, N. Y.: Eastman Kodak, 1969.

Production of 2 × 2 Inch Slides. Austin, Tex.: Instructional Media Center (VIB), U. of Texas at Austin, 1970.

RING, ARTHUR E., AND WILLIAM J. SKELLEY. *Creative Teaching with the Overhead Projector.* Scranton, Pa.: International Textbook, 1969.

SCHILLACI, ANTHONY, AND JOHN M. CULKEN. *Films Deliver.* Englewood Cliffs, N. J.: Citation, 1970.

SCHULTZ, MORTON J. *The Teacher and Overhead Projection: A Treasury of Ideas, Uses, and Techniques.* Englewood Cliffs, N. J.: Prentice-Hall, 1965.

SCUORZO, HERBERT E. *The Practical Audio-Visual Handbook for Teachers.* Englewood Cliffs, N. J.: Prentice-Hall, 1967.

The Tape Recorder. Austin, Tex.: Instructional Media Center (VIB), U. of Texas at Austin, n.d.

TAYLOR, C. W., AND FRANK E. WILLIAMS (eds.) *Instructional Media and Creativity.* New York: Wiley, 1966.

Using Tear Sheets. Austin, Tex.: Instructional Media Center (VIB), U. of Texas at Austin, n.d.

WITTICH, WALTER ARNO, AND CHARLES FRANCIS SCHULLER. *Audiovisual Materials: Their Nature and Use,* 4th ed. New York: Harper, 1967.

SOCIAL STUDIES: GENERAL

ALDRICH, JULIAN C., AND EUGENE COTTLE (eds.) *Social Studies for Young Adolescents: Programs for Grades 7, 8, and 9,* Series No. 6, 3rd ed. Washington, D. C.: NCSS, 1967.

ALLEN, RODNEY F., JOHN V. FLECKENSTEIN, AND PETER M. LYONS (eds.) "Inquiry in the Social Studies: Theory and Examples for Classroom Social Studies." *Social Studies Readings No. 2.* Washington, D. C.: NCSS, 1968.

American Council of Learned Societies and the National Council for the Social Studies. *The Social Studies and the Social Sciences.* New York: Harcourt, 1962.

Association of Teachers of Social Studies of the City of New York. *Handbook for Social Studies Teaching.* New York: Holt, 1967.

BERG, HARRY D. (ed.) *Evaluation in Social Studies.* Thirty-fifth Yearbook. Washington, D. C.: NCSS, 1965.

BEYER, BARRY K., AND ANTHONY N. PENNA. "Concepts in the Social Studies." *Bulletin No. 45.* Washington, D. C.: NCSS, 1971.

BROWN, CHARLES, W. ROYCE ADAMS, AND ROLLAND C. ROGERS. *How to Read the Social Sciences.* Glenview, Ill.: Scott, Foresman, 1968.

BRUBAKER, DALE L. *Alternate Directions for the Social Studies.* Scranton, Pa.: International Textbook, 1967.

BRUBAKER, DALE L. (ed.) *Innovations in the Social Studies.* New York: Crowell, 1968.

――――. *Social Studies in a Mass Society.* Scranton, Pa.: International Textbook, 1969.

CARR, EDWIN R. *The Social Studies.* New York: Library of Education, Center for Applied Research in Education, 1966.

COX, C. BENJAMIN, AND BYRON G. MASSIALAS. *Social Studies in the United States: A Critical Appraisal.* New York: Harcourt, 1967.

ESTVAN, FRANK J. *Social Studies in a Changing World.* New York: Harcourt, 1968.

FAIR, JEAN, AND FANNIE R. SHAFTEL (eds.) *Effective Thinking in the Social Studies.* Thirty-fifth Yearbook. Washington, D. C.: NCSS, 1967.

FANCET, VERNA, *et al. Social Science Concepts in the Classroom.* Syracuse, N. Y.: Syracuse U. P., 1968.

FELDMAN, MARTIN, AND ELI SEIFMAN. *The Social Studies: Structure, Models, and Strategies.* Englewood Cliffs, N. J.: Prentice-Hall, 1969.

FENTON, EDWIN. *Teaching the New Social Studies—An Inductive Approach.* New York: Holt, 1966.

――――. *The New Social Studies.* New York: Holt, 1967.

FRASER, DOROTHY McCLURE (ed.) *Social Studies Curriculum Development: Prospects and Problems.* Thirty-ninth Yearbook. Washington, D. C.: NCSS, 1969.

FRASER, DOROTHY McCLURE, AND SAMUEL P. McCUTCHEON. "Social Studies in Transition: Guidelines for Change." *Curriculum Series No. 12.* Washington, D. C.: NCSS, 1965.

FRASER, DOROTHY McCLURE, AND EDITH WEST. *Social Studies in Secondary Schools: Curriculum and Methods.* New York: Ronald, 1961.

GARDNER, WILLIAM E., AND FRED A. JOHNSON (eds.) *Social Studies in the Secondary Schools: A Book of Readings.* Boston: Allyn, 1970.

GIBSON, JOHN. *New Frontiers in the Social Studies.* New York: Citation, 1967 (2 Vols.).

GROSS, RICHARD E., WALTER E. McPHIE, AND JACK R. FRAENKEL. *Teaching the Social Studies: What, Why, and How.* Scranton, Pa.: International Textbook, 1969.

GROSS, RICHARD E., RAYMOND H. MUESSIG, AND GEORGE L. FERSH (eds.) "The Problems Approach and the Social Studies." *Curriculum Series No. 9,* rev. ed. Washington, D. C.: NCSS, 1960.

HERBERT, LOUIS J., AND WILLIAM MURPHY (eds.) "Structure in Social Studies," *Social Studies Readings No. 3.* Washington, D. C.: NCSS, 1968.

HOWES, VIRGIL M. *Individualizing Instruction in Reading and Social Studies.* New York: Macmillan, 1970.

HUNT, ERLING M., *et al. High School Social Studies Perspectives.* Boston: Houghton, 1962.

HUNT, MAURICE P., AND LAWRENCE METCALF. *Teaching High School Social Studies,* 2nd ed. New York: Harper, 1968.

JOHNSON, HENRY. *Teaching of History,* rev. ed. New York: Macmillan, 1940.

KELLUM, DAVID F. *The Social Studies: Myths and Realities.* New York: Sheed and Ward, 1969.

KENWORTHY, LEONARD S. *Background Papers for Social Studies Teachers.* Belmont, Calif.: Wadsworth, 1966.

_____. *Guide to Social Studies Teaching in Secondary Schools,* 3rd ed. Belmont, Calif.: Wadsworth, 1970.

KRUG, MARK M. *History and the Social Sciences.* Waltham, Mass.: Ginn/Blaisdell, 1967.

KRUG, MARK M., JOHN B. POSTER, AND WILLIAM B. GILLIES III. *The New Social Studies.* New York: F. E. Peacock, 1970.

LEINWAND, GERALD, AND DANIEL M. FEINS. *Teaching History and the Social Studies in Secondary Schools.* New York: Pitman, 1968.

LEWENSTEIN, MORRIS R. *Teaching Social Studies in Junior and Senior High School.* Chicago: Rand McNally, 1963.

LOWE, WILLIAM T. *Structure and the Social Studies.* Ithaca, N. Y.: Cornell U. Press, 1969.

MADGE, JOHN. *The Tools of the Social Sciences.* Garden City, N. Y.: Anchor Doubleday Books, 1965.

MASSIALAS, BYRON G., AND C. BENJAMIN COX. *Inquiry in Social Studies.* New York: McGraw-Hill, 1966.

MASSIALAS, BYRON C., AND ANDREAS M. KAZAMIAS. *Crucial Issues in the Teaching of the Social Studies: A Book of Readings.* Englewood Cliffs, N. J.: Prentice-Hall, 1964.

MASSIALAS, BYRON C., AND F. R. SMITH (eds.) *New Challenges in the Social Studies: Implication of Research for Teaching.* Belmont, Calif.: Wadsworth, 1965.

McCRACKEN, HELEN (ed.) *Skill Development in Social Studies.* Thirty-fifth Yearbook. Washington, D. C.: NCSS, 1963.

McLENDON, JONATHON C. *Readings on Social Studies in Secondary Education.* New York: Macmillan, 1966.

_____. *Social Studies in Secondary Education.* New York: Macmillan, 1965.

_____. "Teaching the Social Studies." *What Research Says to the Teacher,* No. 20. Washington, D. C.: Association for Classroom Teaching, 1968.

MICHAELIS, JOHN U. *Social Studies for Children in a Democracy: Recent Trends and Developments,* 3rd ed. Englewood Cliffs, N. J.: Prentice-Hall, 1963.

MICHAELIS, JOHN U., AND A. MONTGOMERY JOHNSTON. *The Social Sciences—Foundations of the Social Studies.* Boston: Allyn, 1965.

MOFFAT, MAURICE P. *Social Studies Instruction,* 3rd ed. Englewood Cliffs, N. J.: Prentice-Hall, 1963.

MORELAND, WILLIS D. (ed.) "Social Studies in the Senior High School: Programs for Grades Ten, Eleven and Twelve." *Curriculum Series No. 7,* rev. ed. Washington, D. C.: NCSS, 1965.

MORRISSETT, IRVING (ed.) *Concepts and Structure in the New Social Science.* New York: Holt, 1967.

MORRISSETT, IRVING, AND W. WILLIAM STEVENS. *Social Science in the Schools: A Search for a Rationale.* New York: Holt, 1971.

MUESSIG, RAYMOND H. "Social Studies Curriculum Improvement: A Guide for Local Committees." *Bulletin No. 36.* Washington, D. C.: NCSS, 1965.

NEWMAN, FRED M., AND DONALD W. OLIVER. *Clarifying Public Controversy.* Boston: Little, Brown, 1970.

OLIVER, DONALD W., AND JAMES P. SHAVER. *Teaching Public Issues in the High School.* Boston: Houghton, 1966.

PATRICK, JOHN J. "Political Socialization of American Youth: Implications for Secondary School Social Studies." *Research Bulletin No. 3.* Washington, D. C.: NCSS, 1967.

POWELL, THOMAS F. (ed.) "Humanities and the Social Studies." *Bulletin No. 44.* Washington, D. C.: NCSS, 1969.

PRESTON, RALPH C., J. WESLEY SCHNEYER, AND FRANC J. THYNG. "Guiding the Social Studies Reading of High School Students." *Bulletin No. 34.* Washington, D. C.: NCSS, 1963.

PRICE, ROY A., GERALD R. SMITH, AND WARREN L. HICKMAN. *Major Concepts for the Social Studies.* Syracuse, N. Y.: Social Studies Curriculum Center, Syracuse University, 1965.

ROGERS, VINCENT R. *A Sourcebook for Social Studies.* New York: Macmillan, 1969.

SELAKOVICH, DANIEL. *Problems in Secondary Social Studies.* Englewood Cliffs, N. J.: Prentice-Hall, 1965.

SMITH, FREDERICK R., AND C. BENJAMIN COX. *New Strategies and Curriculum in Social Studies.* Chicago: Rand McNally, 1969.

TOOZE, RUTH, AND BEATRICE PERKUM KRONE. *Literature and Music As Resources for Social Studies.* Englewood Cliffs, N. J.: Prentice-Hall, 1955.

WESLEY, EDGAR B., AND STANLEY P. WRONSKI. *Teaching Social Studies in High Schools,* 5th ed. Lexington, Mass.: Heath, 1964.

WOMACK, JAMES G. *Discovering the Structure of the Social Studies.* New York: Benziger, 1966.

BLACK STUDIES

BINKLEY, JOANNE. *Off the African Shelf.* Boulder, Colo.: ERIC/ChESS, 1971.

CLARK, KENNETH. *Dark Ghetto.* New York: Harper, 1965.

CRUDEN, ROBERT. *The Negro in Reconstruction.* Englewood Cliffs, N. J.: Prentice-Hall, 1969.

CURTIN, PHILIP D. (ed.) *Africa Remembered: Narratives by West Africans from the Era of the Slave Trade.* Madison, Wis.: U. of Wisconsin Press, 1970.

DOUGLASS, FREDERICK. *Narrative of the Life of Frederick Douglass, An American Slave.* New York: New American Library, 1968. (Originally published in 1845.)

DUCAS, GEORGE (ed.) *Black Dialogues: Topics in Afro-American History.* Chicago: Encyclopaedia Britannica Educational Corporation, 1970.

FANON, FRANTZ. *Black Skin, White Masks.* New York: Grove, 1967.

HATCH, JOHN. *Africa: The Rebirth of Self-Rule.* New York: Oxford U. P., 1968.

KATZ, WILLIAM LOREN. *Teachers' Guide to American Negro History.* Chicago: Quadrangle, 1968.

MIERS, E. S. *Story of the American Negro.* New York: Grosset, 1965.

MILLER, J. D. B. *The Politics of the Third World.* New York: Oxford U. P., 1967.

Multi-Ethnic Teaching Materials and Teacher Resources. Washington, D. C.: NEA, n.d.

MYRDAL, GUNNAR. *An American Dilemma.* New York: Harper, 1944.

OLIVER, ROLAND. *The Dawn of African History,* 2nd ed. New York: Oxford U. P., 1968.

———. *The Middle Age of African History.* New York: Oxford U. P., 1967.

OTTLEY, ROI, AND WILLIAM J. WEATHERBY. *The Negro in New York.* Dobbs Ferry, N. Y.: Oceana, 1967.

PINKNEY, ALPHONSO. *Black Americans.* Englewood Cliffs, N. J.: Prentice-Hall, 1969.

ROSENTHAL, RICKY. *The Splendor That Was Africa.* Dobbs Ferry, N. Y.: Oceana, 1967.

ROUX, EDWARD. *Time Longer than Rope: A History of the Black Man's Struggle for Freedom in South Africa,* 2nd ed. Madison, Wis.: U. of Wisconsin Press, 1970.

SALK, E. A. (ed.) *A Layman's Guide to Negro History.* Chicago: Quadrangle, 1966.

SLOAN, IRVING J. *The American Negro: A Chronological Factbook,* 2nd ed. Dobbs Ferry, N. Y.: Oceana, 1968.

WASHINGTON, BOOKER T. *Up From Slavery.* New York: Doubleday, 1901, also a Bantam paperback.

WOODWARD, C. VANN. *The Strange Career of Jim Crow.* New York: Oxford U. P., 1966.

CITIZENSHIP AND POLITICAL SCIENCE

BOTTER, DAVID. *Politicians and What They Do.* New York: Franklin Watts, 1960.

CAMPBELL, ANGUS, *et al. The American Voter.* New York: Wiley, 1960.

CARPENTER, HELEN M. "Skills for Democratic Citizenship in the 1960s." in Helen M. Carpenter (ed.) *Skill Development in Social Studies.* Thirty-eighth Yearbook. Washington, D. C.: NCSS, 1963.

CLAPP, CHARLES. *The Congressman—His Work As He Sees It.* Washington, D. C.: Brookings, 1963.

COHEN, WILLIAM, MURRAY SCHWARTZ, AND DE ANNE SOBUL. *The Bill of Rights: A Source Book.* New York: Benziger, 1968.

CONNERY, ROBERT H., RICHARD H. LEACH, AND JOSEPH ZIKMUND II. "Reading Guide in Politics and Government." *Bulletin No. 38.* Washington, D. C.: NCSS, 1966.

DAHL, ROBERT. *Who Governs?* New Haven, Conn.: Yale, 1961.

DAVIS, ELMER. *But We Were Born Free.* Indianapolis: Bobbs, 1954.

DIMOND, STANLEY E. *Schools and the Development of Good Citizenship.* Detroit, Mich.: Wayne State University, Citizenship Education Project, 1953.

Guide to Current American Government. Washington, D. C.: Congressional Quarterly, 1971.

HINES, PAUL D., AND LESLIE WOOD. "A Guide to Human Rights Education." *Bulletin No. 43.* Washington, D. C.: NCSS, 1969.

HYNEMAN, CHARLES S. *The Study of Politics.* Urbana, Ill.: U. of Illinois Press, 1959.

JAMES, LEONARD F. *The Supreme Court in American Life.* Chicago: Scott, Foresman, 1964.

Joint Committee of the National Education Association and the American Legion. *Teaching About Communism: Guidelines for Junior and Senior High School Teachers.* Indianapolis: The American Legion, 1962.

KEY, V. O. *Public Opinion and American Democracy.* New York: Knopf, 1961.

Laboratory Practices in Citizenship Education. New York: Institute for Administrative Research, Teachers College, Columbia University, 1958. (Hundreds of suggestions for teaching citizenship.)

LIPSET, SEYMOUR MARTIN. *Political Man: The Social Bases of Politics.* Garden City, N. Y.: Doubleday, 1959.

MACNEIL, NEIL. *Forge of Democracy.* New York: McKay, 1963.

McCLOSKEY, ROBERT G. *The American Supreme Court.* Chicago: U. of Chicago, 1960.

MEHLINGER, HOWARD D. "The Study of Totalitarianism: A Guide for Teachers." *Bulletin No. 37.* Washington, D. C.: NCSS, 1965.

MILLS, C. WRIGHT. *The Power Elite.* New York: Oxford U. P., 1956.

MORGAN, JOY ELMER (ed.) *The American Citizens Handbook,* 6th ed. Washington, D. C.: NCSS, 1968.

NEUSTADT, RICHARD E. *Presidential Power.* New York: Wiley, 1964.

NEWMAN, EDWIN S. *The Freedom Reader,* 2nd ed. Dobbs Ferry, N. Y.: Ocear. 1963.

NEWMAN, EDWIN S. *Civil Liberty and Civil Rights,* 4th ed. Rev. by Norman C. Amaker. Dobbs Ferry, N. Y.: Oceana, 1967.

OLIVER, DONALD W., FRED W. NEWMANN, AND MARY JO BANE. *Cases and Controversy: Guide to Teaching the Public Issues Series/Harvard Social Studies Project.* Middletown, Conn.: American Educational Publications, 1967.

OLIVER, DONALD W., AND JAMES P. SHAVER. *Teaching Public Issues in High School.* Boston: Houghton, 1966.

PATTERSON, FRANKLIN. *High Schools for a Free Society.* New York: Free Press, 1960.

RIDDLE, DONALD H., AND ROBERT E. CLEARY (eds.) *Political Science in the Social Studies.* Thirty-sixth Yearbook. Washington, D. C.: NCSS, 1960.

ROBINSON, DONALD W., *et al. Promising Practices in Civic Education.* Washington, D. C.: NCSS, 1967.

SCHATTSCHNEIDER, E. E. *Party Government.* New York: Holt, 1942.

SHAVER, JAMES R., AND HAROLD BERLAK. *Democracy, Pluralism and the Social Studies, Readings and Commentary, An Approach to Curriculum Decisions in the Social Studies.* Boston: Houghton, 1968.

SORAUF, FRANCIS J. *Political Science: An Informal Overview.* Columbus, Ohio: Merrill, 1965.

Student Activities for Civic Education. Washington, D. C.: National Council for Social Education, 1967.

TURNER, MARY JANE. *Materials for Civics, Government, and Problems of Democracy: Political Science for New Social Studies.* Boulder, Colo.: Social Science Education Consortium, 1971.

United States Government Organization Manual. Washington, D. C.: Government Printing Office, annual. (Official information.)

WHITE, WILLIAM S. *Home Place: The Story of the U.S. House of Representatives.* Boston: Houghton, 1965.

CURRENT EVENTS
(SEE ALSO MASS MEDIA)

BARD, HARRY, AND CLAIRE ECKELS. *Learning Through the Sun Papers,* 2nd ed. Baltimore: The Baltimore Sun, n.d.

Editors of Civic Education Service. *Teaching Current Affairs.* Washington, D. C.: Civic Education Service, 1963.

HOWITT, LILLIAN C. *Enriching the Curriculum with Current Events.* New York: Atherton, 1964.

The Lincoln Filene Center for Citizenship and Public Affairs and Newsweek Magazine Educational Program. *Current Affairs and the Social Sciences: A Program for Social Studies Educators.* Medford, Mass.: Lincoln Filene Center, Tufts University, 1968.

PAYNE, JOHN C. (ed.) *The Teaching of Contemporary Affairs.* Twenty-first Yearbook. Washington, D. C.: NCSS, 1950.

ROEHM, A. WESLEY. "The Teaching of Contemporary Affairs: A Teacher's Point of View." *Social Education,* **30:**513–520 (Nov. 1966).

WASS, PHILMORE B. "Improving Current Events Instruction." *Social Education,* **36:**79–81 (Feb. 1961).

ECONOMICS

The following recommendations include works both on economics and the teaching of economics. The best source for information and materials on the teaching of economics is the Joint Council on Economic Education. Among the materials they publish are

Progress in Economic Education (Newsletter.)
Checklist (A list of materials and sources.)
Personal Economics (Series of booklets for consumer education classes.)
Economic Topics (Collected articles on contemporary economic issues.)
Economic Education Experiences of Enterprising Teachers (Books on how to do it.)
The Journal of Economic Education (Semiannual.)
Filmstrips
Games—simulations

Other works are

ALEXANDER, ALBERT. *Economics.* New York: Franklin Watts, 1963.

AMMER, DEAN S. *Readings and Cases in Economics.* Boston: Ginn, 1966.

BACH, GEORGE L. *Economics: An Introduction to Analyses and Policy*, 6th ed. Englewood Cliffs, N. J.: Prentice-Hall, 1968.

BUEHR, WALTER. *Treasure: The Story of Money and Its Safe-keeping.* New York: Putnam, 1955.

BYE, RICHARD T., AND WILLIAM W. HEWETT. *The Economic Process: Its Principles and Problems.* New York: Appleton, 1963.

CALDERWOOD, JAMES D., *et al. Economic Ideas and Concepts: Teachers Guide to Developmental Economic Education Program, Part I.* New York: Joint Council on Economic Education, 1964.

DAWSON, GEORGE G. *Research in Economic Education.* New York: New York University Center for Economic Education, 1969.

DE RYCKE, LAURENCE (ed.) *Beginning Readings in Economics.* New York: McGraw-Hill, 1962.

"Economic Education Experiences of Enterprising Teachers." New York: Joint Council on Economic Education and the Calvin K. Kazanjian Economic Foundation, annual since 1963.

Economic Literary for Americans, A Program for Schools and for Citizens. A Statement on National Policy by the Research and Policy Committee of the Committee for Economic Development, February, 1962. New York: Committee on Economic Development, 1962.

Educating for Economic Competence, A Report Prepared by the ASCD Commission on Education for Economic Competence. Washington, D. C.: Association for Supervision and Curriculum Development, 1960.

The Federal Reserve System Purposes and Functions. Washington, D. C.: Board of Governors of the Federal Reserve System, 1963.

GALBRAITH, JOHN K. *American Capitalism: The Concept of Countervailing Power.* Boston: Houghton, 1956.

————. *The New Industrial State.* New York: Houghton, 1967.

————. *The Affluent Society.* New York: Houghton, 1958.

HANSEN, ALVIN H. *The American Economy.* New York: McGraw-Hill, 1957. (Also in paperback.)

HARRIS, SEYMOUR E. "Economics" in *High School Social Studies Perspectives.* Ed. by Erling Hunt. Boston: Houghton, 1962.

HARRIS, C. LOWELL. *The American Economy: Principles, Practices, and Poucies.* Homewood, Ill.: Richard D. Irwin, 1962.

HEILBRONNER, ROBERT L. *The Making of Economic Society.* Englewood Cliffs, N. J.: Prentice-Hall, 1962.

————. *The World of Economics.* New York: Public Affairs Committee, 1963.

————. *The Worldly Philosophers: The Lives, Times, and Ideas of the Great Economic Thinkers.* New York: Simon & Schuster, 1953.

HELBURN, SUZANNE WIGGINS. *Preparing to Teach Economics: Sources of Approaches.* Boulder, Colo.: Social Science Education Consortium, 1971.

HOMAN, PAUL T., ALBERT G. HART, AND WILLIAM W. SAMETZ. *The Economic Order: An Introduction to Theory and Policy.* New York: Harcourt, 1958.

Joint Council on Economic Education. *Suggestions for a Basic Economics Library, A Guide to the Building of an Economics Library for School, Classroom, or Individual.* New York: The Council, 1965.

————. *Study Materials for Economic Education in the School.* New York: The Council, 1970.

KLEIN, LAWRENCE R. *The Keynesian Revolution.* New York: Macmillan, 1964.

LEWIS, DARRELL R., AND DONALD WENTWORTH. *Games and Simulation for Teaching Economics.* New York: Joint Council on Economic Education, 1971.

LEWIS, BEN W. "Economics." *The Social Studies and the Social Sciences.* Washington, D. C.: American Council of Learned Societies and the National Council for the Social Studies, 1962.

LINDHOLM, RICHARD W., AND PAUL DRISCOLL. *Our American Economy.* New York: Harcourt, 1962.

MAHER, JOHN E. *What is Economics?* New York: Wiley, 1969.

National Task Force on Economic Education. *Economic Education in the Schools.* New York: Committee for Economic Development, 1961.

Office of Public Affairs, U.S. Department of Commerce. *Do You Know Your Economic ABC's?* Washington, D. C.: Superintendent of Documents, Government Printing Office. (Series of pamphlets.)

PHELPS, EDMUND S. *The Goal of Economic Growth: An Introduction to a Current Issue of Public Policy.* New York: Norton, 1962.

PREHN, EDWARD C. *Teaching High School Economics: The Analytical Approach.* New York: Pitman, 1968.

ROBINSON, M. A., H. C. MORTON, AND J. V. CALDERWOOD. *An Introduction to Economic Reasoning.* Washington, D. C.: Brookings, 1956. (Also a Doubleday Anchor paperback.)

ROSTOW, W. W. *The Stages of Economic Growth.* New York: Cambridge U. P., 1960. (Also in paperback.)

SAMUELSON, PAUL A. *Economics: An Introductory Analysis.* 5th ed. New York: McGraw-Hill, 1970.

SAYRE, J. WOODROW. *Paperbound Books In Economics.* An Annotated Bibliography. Albany, N. Y.: Center for Economic Education, State University of New York at Albany, 1965.

SCHOENFELD, DAVID, AND ARTHUR A. NATELLA. *The Consumer and His Dollar.* Dobbs Ferry, N. Y.: Oceana, 1966.

SCHUMPETER, JOSEPH A. *Business Cycles.* New York: McGraw-Hill, 1937. (Also in paperback.)

SELIGMAN, EDWIN R. A. *The Economic Interpretation of History.* New York: Columbia U. P., 1961.

SOULE, GEORGE. *Ideas of the Great Economists.* New York: Mentor, 1963.

"Teachers Guide to Developmental Economic Education Program." New York: Joint Council for Economic Education, 1964.

VILLARD, HENRY H. *Economic Performance: An Introduction to Economics.* New York: Holt, 1961.

WARD, BARBARA. *The Rich Nations and Poor Nations.* New York: Norton, 1962.

ENVIRONMENT

CALDWELL, LYNTON KEITH. *Environment: A Challenge to Modern Society.* New York: Natural History Press, 1970.

DISCH, ROBERT (ed.) *The Ecological Conscience: Values for Survival.* Englewood Cliffs, N. J.: Prentice-Hall, 1970.

FABUN, DON. *The Dynamics of Change.* Englewood Cliffs, N. J.: Prentice-Hall, 1970.

JOHNSON, HUEY D. (ed.) *No Deposit–No Return, Man and His Environment.* New York: U.S. National Commission for UNESCO, 1970.

MUMFORD, LEWIS. *The Myth of the Machine.* New York: Harcourt, 1970.

NASH, RODERICK. *The American Environment: Readings in the History of Conservation.* Reading, Mass.: Addison-Wesley, 1968. (Also in paperback.)

OPPENHEIMER, VALERIE K. "Population." *Headline Series, No. 206.* New York: Foreign Policy Association, 1971.

PLATT, JOHN R. *Perception and Change: Projections for Survival.* Ann Arbor, Mich.: U. of Michigan Press, 1970.

REVELLE, ROGER, AND HANS H. LANDSBERG (eds.) *America's Changing Environment.* Boston: Houghton, 1970.

GEOGRAPHY

BACON, PHILIP (ed.) *Focus on Geography: Key Concepts and Teaching Strategies.* Fortieth Yearbook. Washington, D. C.: NCSS, 1970.

BROEK, JAN M. *Geography.* Columbus, Ohio: Merrill, 1965.

CAREY, GEORGE W., AND JULIE SCHWARTZBERG. *Teaching Population Geography.* New York: Teachers College Press, 1969.

Geographic Reports. Bureau of Census Reports of Department of State, Interior, and Agriculture. Washington, D. C.: Government Printing Office.

"Geography in the High School." *The Bulletin of the National Association of Secondary-School Principals*, **51**:1–70 (Feb. 1967).

GRECO, PETER. *Geography.* Lafayette, Ind.: Social Science Education Consortium, 1966.

GRIFFIN, PAUL F. *Geography of Population—A Teachers Guide.* 1970 Yearbook of the National Council for Geographic Education. Palo Alto, Calif.: Fearon, 1969.

HANNA, PAUL R., *et al. Geography in the Teaching of Social Studies.* Boston: Houghton, 1966.

HIGHSMITH, RICHARD M., JR. *Case Studies in World Geography.* Englewood Cliffs, N. J.: Prentice-Hall, 1961.

HILL, WILHELMINA (ed.) *Curriculum Guide for Geographic Education.* Normal, Ill.: Council for Geographic Education, 1964.

JAMES, PRESTON E. *A Geography of Man,* 3rd ed. Boston: Ginn, 1966.

———. *New Viewpoints in Geography.* Washington, D. C.: NCSS, 1959.

KENDALL, HENRY MADISON, ROBERT M. GLENDINNING, AND CLIFFORD H. MAC-FADDEN. *Introduction to Geography,* 4th ed. New York: Harcourt, 1967.

KOHN, CLYDE F. (ed.) "Selected Classroom Experiences: High School Geography Project." *Geographic Education Series No. 4.* Normal, Ill.: Publications Center, National Council for Geographic Education, 1964.

LOGAN, MARGUERITE. *Geographic Techniques.* Ann Arbor, Mich.: Edwards Brothers, 1958.

MAYER, H. M., AND C. F. KOHN (eds.) *Readings in Urban Geography.* Chicago: U. of Chicago, 1959.

MURPHY, RHOADS. *An Introduction to Geography.* Chicago: Rand McNally, 1961.

National Council for Geographic Education. *Do It This Way Series.* Normal, Ill.: The Council, various.

———. *Inventories of Source Materials.* Normal, Ill.: The Council, various.

———. *Professional Papers.* Normal, Ill.: The Council, various.

PRICE, ROY A. (ed.) *New Viewpoints in the Social Studies.* Washington, D. C.: NCSS, 1958.

RAY, JOHN B. *Materials of Geography for Educational Use.* Minneapolis: Burgess, 1963.

SCARFE, NEVILLE V. *Geography in School.* Normal, Ill.: National Council for Geographic Education, 1965.

————. *A Handbook of Suggestions on the Teaching of Geography.* Paris: UNESCO, 1951.

SCARFE, NEVILLE V. (ed.) *Report of the Commission on the Teaching of Geography in Schools.* Chicago: Denoyer-Geppert, 1956.

Sydney Teachers College, Faculty of Geography. *Local Geography in the Secondary School.* Sydney, NSW, Australia: Sydney Teachers College, 1962.

THRALLS, ZOE A. *The Teaching of Geography.* New York: Appleton, 1958.

WAGNER, P. L., AND M. W. MIKESELL (eds.) *Reading in Cultural Geography.* Chicago: U. of Chicago, 1962.

WARNTZ, WILLIAM. *Geographers and What They Do.* New York: Franklin Watts, 1964.

WHEELER, JESSE H., JR., J. TRENTON KOSTBADE, AND RICHARD S. THOMAS. *Regional Geography of the World.* rev. ed. New York: Holt, 1961.

Periodicals:
The Professional Geographer
Annals of the Association of American Geographers
Geographical Review
Focus
Journal of Geography
Social Education

HISTORY AND HISTORIOGRAPHY (GENERAL)

ARON, RAYMOND. *Introduction to the Philosophy of History.* Boston: Beacon Press, 1961.

BARNES, HARRY ELMER. *An Intellectual and Cultural History of the Western World,* 3rd ed. New York: Dover, 1965.

BARRACLOUGH, GEOFFREY. *Introduction to Contemporary History.* Baltimore: Penguin, 1967.

BENNS, F. LEE. *European History Since 1870.* New York: Appleton, 1955.

BUTTERFIELD, HUBERT. *Man on His Past.* Boston: Beacon Press, 1960.

CARR, E. HALLETT. *What Is History?* New York: Knopf, 1964.

COLLINGWOOD, R. G. *The Idea of History.* New York: Oxford U. P., 1946.

DANIELS, ROBERT V. *Studying History: How and Why.* Englewood Cliffs, N. J.: Prentice-Hall, 1966.

DEAN, VERA. *The Nature of the Non-Western World.* New York: New American Library, 1957.

DOUCH, ROBERT. *Local History and the Teacher.* New York: Humanities Press, 1967; also London: Routledge and Kegan Paul, 1967.

EISEN, SYDNEY, AND MAURICE FILLER. *The Human Adventure: Readings in World History.* New York: Harcourt, 1965. (Source materials in 2 Vols.)

ENGLE, SHIRLEY (ed.) *New Perspectives in World History.* Thirty-fourth Yearbook. Washington, D. C.: NCSS, 1964.

GIBBON, EDWARD. *The Decline and Fall of the Roman Empire.* London, 1776, 1781, 1788. (6 vols.) (Various editions.)

GOTTSCHALK, LOUIS (ed.) *Generalizations in the Writing of History.* Chicago: U. of Chicago, 1963.

GRAY, WOOD, *et al. Historians Handbook,* 2nd ed. Boston: Houghton, 1964.

GRIFFIN, BULKLEY S. *Offbeat History.* New York: World, 1967.

GUSTAVSON, CARL G. *A Preface to History.* New York: McGraw-Hill, 1955.

HANSCOM, JAMES, *et al.* (eds.) *Voices of the Past.* New York: Macmillan, 1955, (Paperback, in 3 Vols.)

HAWKES, JACQUETTA, AND LEONARD WOOLLEY. *History of Mankind: Pre-History and the Beginnings of Civilization.* New York: Harper, 1963.

HEPWORTH, PHILIP. *How to Find Out in History.* Elmsford, N. Y.: Pergamon, 1966.

KENT, SHERMAN. *Writing History,* 2nd ed. New York: Appleton, 1967.

KROEBER, A. L. *An Anthropologist Looks at History.* Berkeley, Calif.: U. of California Press, 1963.

LANGER, WILLIAM L. *An Encyclopedia of World History: Ancient, Medieval, and Modern,* 5th ed. Boston: Houghton, 1972.

LIPSET, SEYMOUR MARTIN. *The First New Nation.* Garden City, N. Y.: Doubleday Anchor Books, 1963.

MCNEIL, WILLIAM H. *The Rise of the West: A History of the Human Community.* Chicago: U. of Chicago, 1963.

MULLER, HERBERT J. *The Uses of the Past.* New York: Oxford U. P., 1952. (Also a Mentor paperback.)

NEVINS, ALLAN. *The Gateways of History.* Lexington, Mass.: Heath, 1962.

SHOTWELL, JAMES T. *The Long Road to Freedom.* Indianapolis: Bobbs, 1960.

SMITH, PAGE. *The Historians and History.* New York: Random, 1960.

SNYDER, LOUIS L., MARVIN PERRY, AND BENJAMIN MAZEN. *Panorama of the Past.* Boston: Houghton, 1966. (Readings in 2 Vols.)

STERN, FRITZ R. *The Varieties of History.* New York: Meridian Books, 1956.

TOYNBEE, ARNOLD J. *A Study of History.* London: Oxford U. P., 1947. (A single-volume abridgment.)

WELLS, H. G. *Outline of History.* (Numerous editions.)

WEST, RALPH O. (ed.) *The Human Side of World History.* Boston: Ginn, 1963.

AMERICAN HISTORY AND HISTORIOGRAPHY

ADAMS, JAMES TRUSLOW. *The Epic of America.* Boston: Little, Brown, 1932.

American Service Center for History Pamphlets. New York: Macmillan, Various. (Authoritative pamphlets on many subjects.)

ANDERSON, FRANK S. *The Macmillan Syllabus in American History,* 3rd ed. New York: Macmillan, 1967.

BENNETT, LERONE, JR. *Before the Mayflower: A History of the Negro in America.* Baltimore: Penguin, 1962.

BOORSTIN, DANIEL. *The Colonial Experience.* New York: Random, 1965.

BREMNER, ROBERT. *From the Depths.* New York: New York U. P., 1956.

BURNS, JAMES M. *Roosevelt: The Lion and the Fox.* New York: Harcourt, 1956.

CARTWRIGHT, WILLIAM H., AND RICHARD L. WATSON (eds.) *Interpreting and Teaching American History.* Thirty-first Yearbook. Washington, D. C.: NCSS, 1961.

CHAMBERLAIN, JOHN. *The Enterprising Americans: A Business History of the United States.* New York: Harper, 1963.

COMMAGER, HENRY S. *The American Mind.* New Haven: Yale, 1950.

————. *Living Ideas in America.* New York: Harper, 1951.

CUNLIFFE, MARCUS. *The Nation Takes Shape.* Chicago: U. of Chicago, 1959.

DEGLER, CARL N. *Out of Our Past: The Forces that Shaped Modern America.* New York: Harper, 1959.

FORBES, JACK. *The Indian in America's Past.* Englewood Cliffs, N. J.: Prentice-Hall, 1964.

GOLDMAN, ERIC. *The Crucial Decade and After.* New York: Knopf, 1956.

————. *Rendezvous with Destiny.* New York: Knopf, 1952.

HERSKOWITZ, HERBERT, AND BERNARD MARLIN. *A Guide to Reading in American History: The Unit Approach.* New York: New American Library, 1966.

HIGHAM, JOHN. *The Reconstruction of American History.* New York: Harper, 1962.

————. *Strangers in the Land.* New Brunswick, N. J.: Rutgers U. P., 1955.

HOFSTADTER, RICHARD. *Age of Reform.* New York: Knopf, 1955.

————. *The American Political Tradition.* New York: Knopf, 1968.

————. *Great Issues in American History.* New York: Vintage Books, 1958. (Documents in 2 Vols.)

HOFSTADTER, RICHARD, WILLIAM MILLER, AND AARON DANIEL. *The Structure of American History.* Englewood Cliffs, N. J.: Prentice-Hall, 1964.

KELLUM, DAVID F. *American History Through Conflicting Interpretations.* New York: Teachers College Press, 1969.

LEUCHTENBERT, WILLIAM EDWARD. *The Perils of Prosperity.* Chicago: U. of Chicago, 1958.

LORD, CLIFFORD (ed.) *Localized History Series.* New York: Teachers College Press, various.

MEYERS, MARVIN. *The Jacksonian Persuasion.* Stanford, Calif.: The Stanford U. P., 1957.

MORRIS, RICHARD B., AND HENRY STEELE COMMAGER. *Encyclopedia of American History.* New York: Harper, 1953.

MORISON, SAMUEL ELIOT. *The Oxford History of the American People.* New York: Oxford U. P., 1965.

MORGAN, EDMUND S. *The Birth of the Republic.* Chicago: U. of Chicago, 1958.

NEVINS, ALLAN, AND HENRY S. COMMAGER. *The Pocket History of the United States.* New York: Pocket Books, 1943.

POTTER, DAVID M. *People of Plenty.* Chicago: U. of Chicago, 1954.

QUARLES, BENJAMIN. *The Negro in the Making of America.* New York: Collier Books, 1964.

RANDALL, JAMES, AND DAVID DONALD. *Civil War and Reconstruction.* Lexington, Mass.: Heath, 1961.

SCHLESINGER, ARTHUR M., JR. *Age of Roosevelt.* Boston: Houghton, 1957.

SMITH, HENRY NASH. *Virgin Land.* Cambridge, Mass.: Harvard U. P., 1950.

WILLIAMS, WILLIAM A. *The Tragedy of American Diplomacy.* New York: World, 1959.

WOODWARD, C. VANN (ed.) *The Comparative Approach to American History.* New York: Basic Books, 1968.

INTERNATIONAL RELATIONS AND WORLD AFFAIRS

Tremendous amounts of material on international relations and the teaching of international relations are available from such organizations as the United Nations; UNESCO; Department of State, Office of Media Services; The World Law Fund; and Center for War/Peace Studies. Probably the best source is the Foreign Policy Association.

BASIUK, VICTOR. *Technology and World Power*. New York: Foreign Policy Association, 1970.

BECKER, JAMES M., AND HOWARD P. MEHLINGER (eds.) *International Dimensions in the Social Studies*. Thirty-eighth Yearbook. Washington, D. C.: NCSS, 1968.

BLOOMFIELD, LINCOLN P. "The UN and World Order." *Headline Series No. 197.* New York: Foreign Policy Association, October 1969.

COEDÈS, GEORGES. *The Making of South East Asia*. Trans. by H. M. Wright. Berkeley and Los Angeles: U. of California Press, 1966.

Crisis Papers. London: Atlantic Information Center for Teachers. (Periodical.)

Education for International Understanding: Examples and Suggestions for Classroom Use. Paris: UNESCO, 1959.

ELLIS, JOSEPH A. *Latin America*. New York: Macmillan, 1971.

EVERETT, SAMUEL, AND CHRISTIAN O. ARNDT. *Teaching World Affairs in American Schools: A Case Book*. New York: Harper, 1956.

FISHER, ROGER (ed.) *International Conflict for Beginners*. New York: Harper, 1969.

Foreign Policy Association. *Great Decisions*. (Annual.)

FULLER, R. BUCKMINSTER. *Operating Manual for Spaceship Earth*. Carbondale, Ill.: Southern Illinois University Press, 1969.

The Geographer, U.S. Department of State. "Profiles of Newly Independent States." *Geographic Bulletin No. 1*. Washington, D. C.: Government Printing Office, 1965.

HERMANN, CHARLES F. *Crises in Foreign Policy*. Indianapolis: Bobbs, 1969.

The International Dimension in Education. Washington, D. C.: The Association for Supervision and Curriculum Development, 1970.

Issues in United States Foreign Policy, U.S. Department of State. Washington, D. C.: Government Printing Office. (Periodical.)

JACOBS, NORMAN, *et al.* "Making Foreign Policy in a Nuclear Age: 1. Government and Public Opinion." *Headline Series, No. 171*. New York: Foreign Policy Association, 1965.

KENWORTHY, LEONARD S. *World Affairs Guides*. New York: Teachers College Press, various dates.

KING, DAVID C. *International Education for Spaceship Earth*. New York: Crowell, 1970.

KUBLIN, HYMAN. *What Shall I Read on Japan?* 10th ed. New York: Japan Society, 1971. (Revised frequently.)

Latin America Curriculum Project. "Key Ideas About Latin America." *Bulletin No. 4*, 1967 (ED-013-342). Rockville, Md.: ERIC.

Life series on individual countries. Morristown, N. J.: Silver Burdett Co., various.

LONG, HAROLD M., AND ROBERT N. KING. "Improving the Teaching of World Affairs: The Glens Falls Story." *Bulletin No. 35*. Washington, D. C.: NCSS, 1964.

LOVELL, JOHN P. *Foreign Policy in Perspective*. New York: Holt, 1970.

MALLERY, DAVID. *Africa and Asia in the Study of History: Examples of School Programs Seeking to Teach Students to Think Historically About Non-Western Civilizations*. Boston: National Association of Independent Schools, 1964.

Materials on Japan. New York: Japan Society, 1964.

NESBITT, WILLIAM A. *Teaching About War and War Prevention.* New York: Crowell, 1971.

Other Lands, Other Peoples, 5th ed. Washington, D. C.: NEA, 1969. (Factbook.)

RENAUD, MARY (ed.) "Bringing the World Into Your Classroom: Gleanings from GLENS FALLS." *Curriculum Series No. 13.* Washington, D. C.: NCSS, 1968.

ROGERS, WILLIAM C. *A Guide to Understanding World Affairs.* Dobbs Ferry, N. Y.: Oceana, 1966.

ROLFE, SIDNEY I. "The Multinational Corporation." *Headline Series No. 199.* New York: Foreign Policy Association, February 1970.

SEABERG, STANLEY. *Teaching the Comparative Approach to American Studies.* New York: Crowell, 1969.

STEPHEN, ROBERT H. *Case Studies in International Law.* Dobbs Ferry, N. Y.: Oceana, 1968.

The Study of World Cultures in Secondary Schools. Report of a Conference Conducted by South Penn School Study Council and the Philadelphia Suburban School Study Council, Group B. Danville, Ill.: Interstate Printers and Publishers, 1962.

Teachers Packet on Southeast Asia. New York: The Asia Society, 1966. (Other kits are also available.)

WOODWARD, C. VANN (ed.) *The Comparative Approach to American History.* New York: Basic Books, 1968.

The World and the School. London: Atlantic Information Center for Teachers. (Periodical.)

MAP STUDY

Cartocraft Teachers Manuals. Geographical Research Institute. Chicago: Denoyer-Geppert, various.

FORSYTHE, ELAINE. "Map Reading: A Series of Lessons for Use in the Junior High School." *Geographic Education Series No. 1.* Normal, Ill.: National Council for Geographic Education, 1964.

GREENHOOD, DAVID. *Mapping.* Chicago: U. of Chicago, 1964.

HARRIS, RUBY M. *The Rand McNally Handbook of Map and Globe Usage,* 4th ed. Chicago: Rand McNally, 1967.

JAMES, PRESTON E., AND SHIRLEY HESS. *Better Teaching with Relief Maps.* Philadelphia: Aero Service Corp., 1962.

Map Reading, Department of the Army Field Manual FM21-26. Washington, D. C.: Government Printing Office, 1965.

RAISZ, ERWIN. *Principles of Cartography.* New York: McGraw-Hill, 1962.

MASS MEDIA

American Newspaper Publishers Association Foundation Booklets:

The Daily Newspaper in the School Curriculum: A Manual for Teachers and Newspapermen on the Use of Newspapers in the Classroom.

The Teacher and the Newspaper: A Guide to its Use.

How to Get More out of Your Newspapers.

Units on the Study of the Newspaper for English Classes, Grades 7–12.

The Faculty Speaks.

Suggested Plans for the Study of the Newspaper in the Classroom.

Race Against Time.

BARD, HARRY, CLAIRE ECKELS, *et al. Learning Through the Sunpapers,* 2nd ed. Baltimore: The Baltimore Sun, nd.

BROWN, DONALD E. *How America Gets Its News.* Chicago: Rand McNally, 1967.

CATER, DOUGLASS. *The Fourth Branch of Government,* rev. ed. New York: Vintage Books, 1965.

COHEN, BERNARD C. *The Press and Foreign Policy.* Princeton, N. J.: Princeton University Press, 1963.

Commission on Freedom of the Press. *A Free and Responsible Press.* Chicago: U. of Chicago, 1947.

Communications in the Space Age. Paris: UNESCO, 1968.

CUMMINGS, HOWARD H., AND HARRY BARD. "How to Use Daily Newspapers." *How To Do It Series, No. 5.* Washington, D. C.: NCSS, 1964.

DALE, EDGAR. *How to Read a Newspaper.* New York: Scott, Foresman, 1941.

DALE, EDGAR, *et al. Mass Media and Education.* Fifty-third Yearbook of the National Society for the Study of Education, Part II. Chicago: U. of Chicago, 1954.

DIZARD, WILSON P. *Television: A World View.* Syracuse, N. Y.: Syracuse University Press, 1966.

DOOB, LEONARD W. *Public Opinion and Propaganda,* rev. ed. Hamden, Conn.: Shoe String Press, 1966.

HOFFMAN, ARTHUR S. (ed.) *International Communication and the New Diplomacy.* Bloomington, Ind.: Indiana University Press, 1968.

HOHENBERG, JOHN. *The News Media: A Journalist Looks at His Profession.* New York: Holt, 1968.

KAYSER, JACQUES. *One Week's News: Comparative Study of Seventeen Major Dailies for a Seven Day Period.* Paris: UNESCO, 1953.

LIEBLING, A. J. *The Press,* rev. ed. New York: Ballantine Books, 1964.

LIPPMANN, WALTER. *Public Opinion.* New York: Free Press, 1965.

MINOW, NEWTON N. *Equal Time: The Private Broadcaster and the Public Interest.* New York: Atheneum, 1964.

NESBITT, WILLIAM A. *Interpreting the Newspaper in the Classroom: Foreign News and World News.* New York: Crowell, 1971.

RESTON, JAMES. *The Artillery of the Press: Its Influence on American Foreign Policy.* New York: Harper Colophon Books, 1966.

ROWSE, ARTHUR (ed.) *One Day in the World's Press.* Stanford, Calif.: Stanford University Press, 1959.

SCHRAMM, WILBUR, *et al. The Science of Human Communication.* New York: Basic Books, 1963.

Teachers' Guide to Television, P.O. Box 5641, Lenox Hill Station, New York, N. Y. 10021. (Information and suggestions for teaching television programs to be shown on major networks.)

TORKELSON, GERALD M. "Educational Media." *What Research Says to the Teacher, No. 14.* Washington, D. C.: Association of Classroom Teachers, 1968.

SOCIOLOGY

BOHANNAN, PAUL. *Anthropology.* Lafayette, Ind.: Social Science Education Consortium, 1966.

DOBZHANSKY, THEODOSIUS. *Mankind Evolving.* New Haven, Conn.: Yale, 1962.

HIMES, JOSEPH S. *The Study of Sociology.* Chicago: Scott, Foresman, 1968. (A college text.)

HOEBEL, E. ADAMSON. *Man in the Primitive World,* 2nd ed. New York: McGraw-Hill, 1958.

HORTON, PAUL B., AND CHESTER L. HUNT. *Sociology,* 2nd ed. New York: McGraw-Hill, 1968. (A college text.)

INKELES, ALEX. *What Is Sociology?* Englewood Cliffs, N. J.: Prentice-Hall, 1964. (Paperback.)

KLUCKHOHN, CLYDE. *Mirror for Man: The Relation of Anthropology to Modern Life.* New York: McGraw-Hill, 1949. Also Fawcett Publications, 1960.

KROEBER, A. L. *Anthropology, Biology and Race,* Vol. I, *Anthropology, Culture Patterns and Processes,* Vol. II. New York: Harbinger Paperbacks, 1963.

LEAKEY, L. S. B. *Adam's Ancestors.* New York: Harper Torchbook, 1963.

LINTON, RALPH. *The Tree of Culture.* New York: Vintage Books, 1959. (Abridged.)

MALINOWSKI, BRONISLAW. *Argonauts of the Western Pacific.* New York: Dutton, 1961.

MANDELBAUM, DAVID G., GABRIEL W. LASKER, AND ETHEL M. ALBERT (eds.) *Resources for the Teaching of Anthropology.* Berkeley, Calif.: University of California Press, 1964.

MCKEE, JAMES B. *Introduction to Sociology.* New York: Holt, 1969. (A college text.)

MCNALL, S. G. *The Sociological Experience.* Boston: Little, Brown, 1969. (Paperback.)

OLIVER, DOUGLAS. *Invitation to Anthropology.* Garden City, N. Y.: Natural History Press, 1964.

PELTO, PERTTI J. *The Study of Anthropology.* Columbus, Ohio: Merrill, 1965.

PERRUCCI, ROBERT. *Sociology.* Lafayette, Ind.: Social Science Education Consortium, 1966.

ROSE, CAROLINE B. *The Study of Sociology.* Columbus, Ohio: Merrill, 1966.

SCHULER, EDGAR A., THOMAS F. HOULT, DUANE L. GIBSON, AND WILBUR B. BROOKOVER (eds.) *Readings in Sociology,* 4th ed. New York: Crowell, 1971.

SHOSTAK, ARTHUR B. (ed.) *Sociology in Action.* Homewood, Ill.: Dorsey Press, 1966.

SPINDLER, GEORGE, AND LOUISE SPINDLER. *Case Studies in Cultural Anthropology.* New York: Holt. (A series of short works on different cultures.)

TAX, SOL (ed.) *Anthropology Today—Selections.* Chicago: U. of Chicago, 1962.

_____. *Horizons of Anthropology.* Chicago: Aldine, 1964.

APPENDIX S

Textbooks and Other Teaching Materials

T H E following lists include some of the textbooks and supplementary materials available for use in secondary school social studies classes. These lists are not all-inclusive; in fact, they do not necessarily include all the best items available. They are just a sampling. The copyright dates of the works have not been included because of the policy of continuously revising texts, common to many publishers. Consult the publishers' catalogs to find the latest editions.

You should also consult catalogs to find out about what aids are available with the various textbooks. It has become quite common for publishers to furnish (for a price) all sorts of multimedia teaching aids with their textbooks. In some cases, the text and supporting materials have been designed as a sort of instructional system. Therefore, to purchase only one part of the system may be wasteful. Some instances, but not all instances, in which audiovisual or multimedia materials are available with the text have been noted. Others have been noted in the lists of supplementary materials.

To find out about new textbooks, consult (1) reviews and announcements in such professional journals as *Social Education, The Social Studies,* and *Journal of Geography;* (2) *Textbooks in Print;* (3) advertisements and catalogs of the publishers; (4) booths at educational conventions; and (5) curriculum libraries and resource centers of school systems, universities, and state departments of education.

The lists of supplementary materials are also only samplings. There are far too many films, film strips, paperback books, and other materials on the market to include them all in a handbook such as this. Consult the catalogs and listings, such as those of the Educators' Progress Service. Do not forget to check your local film library catalogs for films. Films are not included in these lists.

PERIODICALS

Periodicals are the most promising source of up-to-date information on social studies topics. The following list includes scholarly and popular periodicals. Use the more popular journals with all your pupils. Bright, advanced pupils will find the scholarly journals useful too, although oftentimes the articles tend to be esoteric. In the majority of cases, the title of the periodical gives a good indication of its content. In other cases, the type of content is indicated in parenthesis following the listing.

American Heritage. American Heritage Publishing Co., Inc. (Monthly articles on history.)

Atlantic Monthly. 8 Arlington St., Boston, Mass. 02116. (General.)

Atlas Magazine. Subscription Department, 368 West Center St., Manor, Ohio 43302. (Commentary from abroad.)

Current History. Current History, Inc. (World affairs, monthly.)

Ebony. 55 West 42nd St., New York, N. Y. 10036. (General.)

Focus. American Geographical Society, Broadway at 156th St., New York, N. Y. 10032. (Monthly issues devoted to single nations or regions.)

Foreign Affairs. 58 E. 68th St., New York, N. Y. 10021.

The Nation. 333 Avenue of the Americas, New York, N. Y. 10017.

National Geographic Magazine. National Geographic Society. (Useful in geography and world cultures, pictures and maps, monthly.)

NATO Letter. NATO, also Department of State. (Articles and documentation on NATO and NATO countries, monthly.)

New Republic. 1244 19th St. N.W., Washington, D. C. 20036.

Newsweek. 444 Madison Ave., New York, N.Y. 10022.

Time. Time and Life Building, Rockefeller Center, New York, N. Y. 10020.

Transaction. P.O. Box 43, Washington University, St. Louis, Mo. 63130.

U.S. News and World Report, 2300 N St., N.W., Washington, D. C. 20037.

Vista. UN Association. (World affairs and UN.)

UN Monthly Chronicle. United Nations Publications.

World Survey Monthly. The Atlantic Education Trust, 23/21 Abbey House, 8 Vitoria St., London SW1, England.

UNITED STATES HISTORY: TEXTS

ABRAMOWITZ. *American History.* Follett. (10–11. Slow.)

ALLEN AND BETTS. *History, USA.* American Book, 2 Vols. (SHS.)

BETTERSWORTH, PATRICK, AND STEEN. *New World Heritage.* Steck-Vaughn. (7–8.)

BRAGDON AND McCUTCHEON. *A History of a Free People,* Macmillan. (SHS.)

BRANSON. *American History for Today.* Ginn. (JHS; educationally disadvantaged; hard to motivate.)

BRANSON. *Inquiry Experiences in American History.* Ginn. (JHS; hard to motivate; paper.)

BIDNA, GREENBERG, AND SPITZ. *We, the People.* Heath. (JHS; slow.)

BRONZ, *et al. The Challenge of America.* Holt. (7–8.)

BROWN, LANG, AND WHEELER. *The American Achievement.* Silver Burdett.

CASNER, *et al. Story of the American Nation.* Harcourt.

CHAPLIN, McHUGH, AND GROSS. *Quest for Liberty.* Field Educational Publications. (8.)

CURRY, SPROAT, AND CRAMER. *The Shaping of America.* Holt. (7–12; readings and AV available.)

DAVIS, ARNOF, AND DAVIS. *Background for Tomorrow.* Macmillan. (JHS.)

EIBLING, KING, AND HARLOW. *History of Our United States.* Laidlaw. (7–8.)

EIBLING, KING, AND HARLOW. *The Story of America.* Laidlaw. (7–8; slow.)

FEDER. *Viewpoints, USA.* American Book. (HS; obtainable as separate units.)

FENTON, et al. *The Americans: A History of the United States.* Holt. (7–8; AV.)

FENTON, FOWLER, AND MANDELBAUM. *A New History of the United States.* Holt. (9–12; AV.)

FORCEY. *A Strong and Free Nation.* Macmillan. (8.)

FROST, BROWN, ELLIS, AND FINK. *A History of the United States.* Follett. (HS.)

GARDNER. *The Story of Our Country.* Allyn. (HS.)

GAVIAN, HAMM, AND FREIDEL. *United States History.* Heath. (HS.)

GAWRONSKI. *Out of the Past: A Topical History of the United States.* Macmillan. (HS.)

GLANZROCK AND GLANZROCK. *Adventures in American History.* Silver Burdett. (JHS.)

GRAFF. *The Free and the Brave.* Rand McNally. (JHS; Diamond edition for slow readers available.)

GROSS AND MADGIC. *Profile of America Series.* Field Educational Publications. (9–12, ten separate units.)

HELLER AND POTTER. *One Nation Indivisible.* Merrill. (SHS.)

HOVENIER, et al. *Perspectives in United States History.* Field Educational Publications. (SHS.)

KANE AND GLOVER. *Inquiry USA.* Globe. (J and SHS; slow.)

KOWNSLAR AND FRIZZLE. *Discovering American History.* Holt. (7–12; student activity kit and individual units available.)

MACKEY. *Your Country's History.* Ginn. (7–9.)

O'CONNOR, GALL, AND GOLDBERG. *Exploring the Urban World.* Globe. (J and SHS; slow.)

PLATT AND DRUMMOND. *Our Nation From Its Creation.* Prentice-Hall. (SHS.)

REICH AND BILLER. *Building the American Nation.* Harcourt.

SANDLER, ROZWENC, AND MARTIN. *The People Make a Nation.* Allyn. (HS.)

SCHWARTZ. *Exploring American History.* Globe. (JHS; slow.)

SCHWARTZ. *Exploring Our Nation's History.* Globe. (J and SHS; slow; both single- and two-volume editions.)

SHAFER, et al. *A High School History of Modern America.* Laidlaw. (HS.)

SHAFER, AUGSPURGER, AND McLEMORE. *1865 to Present.* Laidlaw. (HS.)

SILVER. *The United States Yesterday and Today.* Ginn. 2 Vols. (JHS; slow.)

TODD AND CURTI. *Rise of the American Nation.* Harcourt. (HS.)

WADE, WILDER, AND WADE. *A History of the United States with Selected Readings.* Houghton. 2 Vols. (Vol. 1 to 1877; Vol. 2 1865–1970.)

WILDER, LUDLUM, AND BROWN. *This Is America's Story.* Houghton. (Visuals and filmstrips available.)

WILLIAMS AND WOLF. *Our American Nation.* Merrill. (SHS.)

WINTHER AND CARTWRIGHT. *The Story of Our Heritage.* Ginn. (7–8; also available in 2 Vols.)

U.S. HISTORY: SUPPLEMENTARY MATERIALS

ALLEN. *Documents, USA.* American Book. (35 pamphlets.)

America in Crisis Series. Wiley. (Paperbacks dealing with the United States in conflict with other powers.)

American Adventure Series. Scholastic. (Program consisting of paperbacks, plus audiovisual materials for slow readers.)

American Heritage Pictorial Atlas of United States History. American Heritage Press/McGraw-Hill.

American History 400. Harcourt. (A slide system.)

American History Transparencies. A. J. Nystrom.

Amherst Problems in American Civilization Series. Heath. (Source materials.)

ARNOF. *A Sense of the Past: Readings in American History,* rev. ed. Macmillan.

Arts of the Home in Early America. Merrill. (Filmstrips, records, or cassettes; resource book.)

BROWN. *The Human Side of American History.* Ginn. (Excerpts of documents, newspapers, etc.)

Case Studies in American History. Educators Publishing Service. (Booklet of 14 case studies.)

Cartocraft History Map Studies. Denoyer-Geppert. (Desk-sized maps.)

Discovering American History Through Art. Rand McNally. (Multimedia program: filmstrips, record, printed reproductions, manual.)

Donald. *A Documentary History of American Life Series.* Webster/McGraw-Hill. (Selections of documents.)

The 8mm Document Project. Thorne Films. (8mm film loops.)

Growth of American History Transparencies. A. J. Nystrom.

History Transparencies. Civic Education Service.

In America Series. McCormack-Mathers. (J and SHS.)

Landmark Enrichment Films. Enrichment Materials.

Life History of the U.S. Series. Silver Burdett. (Books plus LP records; e.g., The Age of Steel and Steam.)

Milestones in History Series. Messner.

A Miscellany of History. Steck-Vaughn. (Pamphlet series.)

New Dimensions in American History. Heath. (Paperbacks in depth in primary sources; SHS.)

New Perspectives in American History. Macmillan. (Paperbacks.)

Our America. Denoyer-Geppert. (Maps, atlas, and transparencies.)

Overhead Visuals in American History. Houghton.

Promise of America Series. Scott, Foresman, Spectre. (For low-performing high school pupils.)

Rand McNally Classroom Library, Rand McNally. (Illustrated paperbacks.)

ROBINSON. *As Others See Us: International Views of American History.* Houghton.

Service Center for Teachers of History Pamphlets. American Historical Association.

Slavery, The Civil War, and Reconstruction. Crowell. (Multimedia.)

Squire. *British Views of the American Revolution.* Heath.

STARR, CURTI, AND TODD. *Living American Documents.* Harcourt.

Time-Life Library of America Series, Silver Burdett. (E.g., *Border States* and *District of Columbia*.)

Time Line and Date Charts: American History. Merrill.

U.S. History Transparencies. Universal Education and Visual Arts.

Viewpoints Kits. Random House/Singer. (Multimedia kits; e.g., *Viewpoints on American Abolition* and *Viewpoints on American Labor*.)

Yesterday Today. Merrill. (Facsimiles of newspaper accounts and overhead visuals.)

WORLD HISTORY, WORLD STUDIES, AND WORLD CULTURES: TEXTS

ABRAMOWITZ. *World History.* Follett. (9–10; slow.)
BECKER AND COOPER. *Modern History Since 1600.* Silver Burdett. (HS.)
BLACK. *Our World History.* Ginn. (9–12; for general students.)
CASSIDY AND SOUTHWORTH. *Long Ago in the Old World.* Merrill.
EWING. *Our Widening World.* Rand McNally. (HS.)
FORD. *Tradition and Change in Four Societies.* Holt. (9–12; AV kit.)
GOOD. *The Shaping of Western Society.* Holt. (9–12; AV kit.)
HABBERTON, ROTH, AND SPEARS. *World History and Cultures.* Laidlaw.
HOLT AND O'CONNOR. *Exploring World History.* Globe. (Slow.)
KOLEVZON. *The Afro-Asian World: A Cultural Understanding.* Allyn. (HS.)
LOGAN AND COHEN. *The Old World Background and New World Experience.* Houghton. (HS.)
MAGENIS AND APPEL. *A History of the World.* American Book. (Text plus coordinated filmstrips.)
MAGOFFIN AND DUNCALF. *Ancient and Medieval History.* Silver Burdett. (HS.)
MASSIALAS AND ZEVIN. *World History Through Inquiry.* Rand McNally. (Nine multimedia units.)
NEILL. *Story of Mankind.* Holt. (9–11.)
PETROVICH AND CURTIN. *The Human Achievement, Cultural Area Approach to World History.* Silver Burdett. (SHS.)
PLATT AND DRUMMOND. *Our World Through the Ages.* Prentice-Hall.
REICH, BILLER, AND KRUG. *Building the Modern World.* Harcourt. (SHS; slow.)
ROEHM, *et al. The Record of Mankind.* Heath.
ROGERS, ADAMS, AND BROWN. *Story of Nations.* Holt. (9–11.)
ROSELLE. *A World History — A Cultural Approach.* Ginn. (9–12.)
SCHWARTZ. *Exploring the Western World.* Globe. (JHS; slow.)
SNYDER, PERRY, AND MAZEN. *Panorama of the Past: Readings in World History.* Houghton. 2 Vols. (Vol. 1, Ancient Times to 1815; Vol. 2, 1815 to the present.)
STAVRIANOS, *et al. A Global History of Man.* Allyn. (HS.)
WARREN, LEINENWEBER, AND ANDERSON. *Our Democracy at Work.* Prentice-Hall.
WELTY. *Man's Cultural Heritage: A World History.* Lippincott. (HS.)

WORLD HISTORY AND CULTURES: SUPPLEMENTARY MATERIALS

Alva Museum Replicas. Silver Burdett. (Replicas of classic sculptures, etc.)
Area Studies Series. Franklin Watts.
Atlas of World History. Rand McNally.
Berkshire Studies in European History. Holt.
Breasted-Huth-Harding. *World History Maps.* Denoyer-Geppert.
Contemporary Civilization Series. Holt. (9–12; paperbacks.)
Culture Regions of the World. Interdisciplinary Paperback Series. Macmillan. (HS.)
Ginn Studies in Depth. Ginn. (7–8; studies of nations or areas; e.g., Israel.)
Global Culture Series. McCormack Mathers. (JHS.)
Global History Series. Prentice-Hall.
Great Ages of Man Series. Time-Life Books. Silver Burdett. (E.g., African Kingdoms, Age of Enlightenment.)

Hanscom, Hillerman, and Posner. *Voices of the Past.* Macmillan. 3 Vols.

Historical Atlas. Hammond.

Historical Atlas of the World. Rand McNally.

Kohn and Drummond. *World Patterns Transparency Program.* Webster/McGraw-Hill.

Life World Library. Time-Life Books. Silver Burdett. (E.g., The Andean Republics, The Arab World.)

Major Cultures of the World Series. World.

Merrill and Teall. *Atlas of World History.* Ginn.

Milestones in History Series. Messner.

National Geographic School Bulletin. National Geographic Society. (Pictures and articles, world geography.)

Our Widening World Paperbacks. Rand McNally.

The Oxfan Series: Case Studies of Developing Nations. Houghton. (HS.)

Problems in Asian Civilization Series. Heath. (SHS.)

Problems in European Civilization Series. Heath.

Regions of Our World Series. Oxford Book.

Source Problems in World Civilizations. Holt.

Stavrianos, *et al. Culture in Perspective Series.* Allyn. (Separate units from *A Global History of Man.*)

Stavrianos, *et al. Readings in World History.* Allyn. (Primary and secondary source material.)

This Fabulous Century Series. Time-Life Books. Silver Burdett. (E.g., Vol. 1, 1900–1910.)

Time Capsule Series. Silver Burdett. (Excerpts from *Time;* annual volumes since 1923.)

Time Line and Date Charts, World Civilization. Merrill.

World Affairs Materials. Brooklyn College.

World Affairs Multi-Texts. Scholastic. (7–10; paperback on regional approach to world history.)

Watts Focus Books. Franklin Watts. (Books that focus on historical events.)

World History Filmstrips. Follett.

World History Map Filmstrips. Silver Burdett.

World History 400. Harcourt. (Slide series.)

World History Map Transparencies. Rand McNally.

World Landmark Enrichment Records. Enrichment Materials.

World Study Inquiry Series. Field Educational Publishing. (7–12; slow.)

GEOGRAPHY TEXTS

Bradley. *World Geography.* Ginn.

Glendenning. *Your Country and the World.* Ginn.

Haft. *World Geography.* Simon & Schuster.

High School Geography Project. *Geography in an Urban Age.* Macmillan. (Multimedia course.)

Holt. *World Geography and You.* American Book.

Israel, Roemer, and Durand. *World Geography Today.* Holt. (7–12.)

James and Davis. *The Wide World: A Geography.* Macmillan.

Jones and Murphy. *Geography and World Affairs.* Rand McNally. (Units available in paperback.)

KOHN AND DRUMMOND. *The World Culture Today*. Webster/McGraw-Hill.
KOLEVZON AND HEINE. *Our World and Its Peoples*. Allyn.
MICHAELIS AND MCKEOWN. *20th Century Asia: An Anthropology*. Hammond.
PRESTON AND TOTTLE. *Geography—United States and Canada*. Heath.
SAVELAND. *World Resources*. Ginn. (7–9.)
SCHWARTZ. *Exploring a Changing World*. Globe. (Slow.)
SORENSON. *A World View*. Silver Burdett. (JHS.)
VAN CLEEF AND FINNEY. *Global Geography*. Allyn.

CIVICS, GOVERNMENT, PROBLEMS OF AMERICAN DEMOCRACY, AND CURRENT ISSUES: TEXTS

ALILUNAS AND SAYRE. *Youth Faces American Citizenship*. Lippincott.
BALL AND ROSCH. *Civics*. Follett.
BARD, MORELAND, AND CLINE. *Citizenship and Government in Modern America*. Holt. (7–12.)
BOHLMAN. *Democracy and Its Competitors*. Merrill.
BROWN, PELTIER, AND FARNER. *Government In Our Republic*. Macmillan.
BRUNTZ AND EDGERTON. *Understanding Our Government*. Ginn. (9–12; for general students.)
CLARK, *et al. Civics for Americans*. Macmillan. (JHS.)
DIMOND AND PFLEIGER. *Civics for Citizens*. Lippincott.
DUNWIDDIE. *Problems of Democracy*. Ginn.
Eagleton Institute of Politics. *American Society in Action*. Webster/McGraw-Hill. (Readings; 9–12.)
Eagleton Institute of Politics. *Contemporary Issues in American Democracy*. Webster/McGraw-Hill. (9–12.)
Eagleton Institute of Politics. *Man, Society, and Social Order*. Webster/McGraw-Hill. (9–12.)
Eagleton Institute of Politics. *The Problems and Promises of American Democracy*. Webster/McGraw-Hill.
EBENSTEIN AND MILL. *American Government in the Twentieth Century*. Silver Burdett.
FELDER AND DELL. *The Challenge of American Democracy*. Allyn.
Government for Americans. Harper. (11–12.)
GROSS AND DEVEREAUX. *Civics in Action*. Field Educational Publications. (JHS.)
HARTLEY AND VINCENT. *American Civics*. Harcourt.
HUGHES. *American Government*. Bruce.
KARLEN. *The Patterns of American Government*. Glencoe.
Lincoln Filene Center. *Practical Political Action*. Houghton.
MCCLENAGHAN. *Magruder's American Government*. Allyn. (Revised annually.)
MCCROCKLIN. *Building Citizenship*. Allyn.
MCCUTCHEN AND FERSH. *Goals of Democracy: A Problem Approach*. Macmillan.
PAINTER AND BEXLER. *Citizenship in Action*. Follett. (8–9.)
REED. *Today's Problems*. Allyn.
RESNICK AND NERENBERG. *American Government in Action*. Merrill. (SHS.)
RIENOW. *American Government in Today's World*. Heath.
SMITH. *Your Life As a Citizen*. Ginn. (9.)
STEEN AND FAULK. *Government by the People*. Steck-Vaughn. (7–9.)

CIVICS, GOVERNMENT,
PROBLEMS OF AMERICAN DEMOCRACY,
AND CURRENT ISSUES:
SUPPLEMENTARY MATERIALS

AEP Booklets. American Education Press.

American Government Series. Curriculum Resources.

American Problems Series. Holt. (Paperbacks.)

American Problems Studies. Holt.

BRAGDON, McCUTCHEN, AND BROWN. *Frame of Government: Documents on Constitutional Development.* Macmillan.

The Changing City. Ginn. (Programed text.)

The Constitution. Ginn. (Programed text.)

DORF, LEAVITT, AND PFAFF. *Visualized American Government.* Oxford Book.

Editorial Research Reports. Congressional Quarterly. (High-level pamphlets on current issues.)

Foreign Policy Headline Books. Foreign Policy Association.

Government in a Free Society. Rand McNally. (Charts and transparencies.)

Great Decisions. Foreign Policy Association. (Annual.)

Great Issues Series. Scholastic. (Inquiry-oriented paperbacks.)

The Great Law of Our Land. Merrill. (JHS; 48 pp., skill texts.)

HANNA. *Teenagers and the Law.* Ginn. (Supplementary reading.)

HART. *Visualized Problems of American Democracy.* Oxford Book.

HATCH. *Urban Action.* Ginn. (Multimedia course.)

Headline Series. Foreign Policy Association. (Booklet.)

How a Bill Becomes a Law. Ginn. (7–8; programed text.)

Inquiry Into Crucial American Problems Series. Prentice-Hall. (POD Teachers Manual.)

The Insight Series: Studies in Contemporary Issues. Macmillan. (Source books.)

Intercom. Center for War/Peace Studies. (Every other month. Relates classroom materials to topical concerns.)

Issues in United States Foreign Policy. U.S. Department of State. (With discussion guide.)

McCLOSKEY. *United States Constitution.* Behavioral Research Laboratories. (Programed text.)

Merrill Studies of American Documents. Merrill. (Series of booklets.)

MILL. *Liberty and Law.* Silver Burdett. (Readings.)

MILL. *Politics and Progress.* Silver Burdett. (Readings.)

NCA Foreign Relations Series. Laidlaw. (Paperback.)

New Dimensions Series. Foreign Policy Association.

Our Democracy Series. Denoyer-Geppert. (Charts and transparencies.)

Paperbacks on Communism and Democracy. Scholastic.

PENN. *Every Four Years: A Programed Text on the Presidential Electoral System.* Allyn. (Programed text.)

Propaganda Techniques. Coronet Films. (11 min.; black and white, or color.)

The Real World Books. McCormack Mather. (E.g., *The Stock Market, American Economics History*.)

Social Education Judgment Series. Scholastic. (Legal cases.)

Social Studies Supplement Kit. League of Women Voters. (Prepared for American Government and Citizenship courses.)

Studies in Political Science Series. Allyn. (Paper.)

Synopsis. Curriculum Innovations. (Magazine-style booklets that update contemporary problems, etc.)

Taped Lectures on World Order. World Law Fund.

UNESCOPE. United States National Commission for UNESCO. Washington, D. C. 20520.

The United States in World Affairs. Follett. (Visuals.)

ECONOMICS: TEXTS

ALEXANDER, PREHN, AND SAMETZ. _The Modern Economy in Action, An Analytical Approach._ Pitman.

CALDERWOOD AND FERSH. _Economics in Action._ Macmillan.

COLEMAN. _Comparative Economic Systems._ Holt. (9–12; AV kit, part of Fenton Program.)

DODD, KENNEDY, AND OLSON. _Economics._ Southwestern.

GORDON AND WITCHEL. _An Introduction to the American Economy: Analysis and Policy._ Heath.

HOLT. _Economics and You._ Follett. (11–12.)

HURWITZ AND SHAW. _Mastering Basic Economics._ Oxford Book.

LINDHOLM AND DRISCOLL. _Our American Economy._ Harcourt.

MCCONNELL. _Economics: Principles, Problems, and Policies._ Webster/McGraw-Hill. (9–10; supplementary materials and visuals available.)

OVARD AND DAVIES. _Economics and the American System._ Lippincott.

SAMUELSON. _Economics._ Webster/McGraw-Hill. (For advanced pupils only.)

SMITH. _Economics for Our Times._ Webster/McGraw-Hill. (Accompanying filmstrips.)

THAI. _Your Family and Its Money._ Houghton. (Consumer education.)

WRONSKI, DOODY, AND CLEMENCE. _Modern Economics._ Allyn.

ECONOMICS: SUPPLEMENTARY MATERIALS

Accent/Family Finances Series. Follett. (11–12; slow.)

American Economics Charts. Denoyer-Geppert.

Area Studies in Economic Progress. Scott, Foresman.

ATTIYEH, LUMSDEN, AND WERNER. _The American Economics Series._ Behavioral Research Laboratories. (Seven programed texts.)

CASE Economic Series. Webster/McGraw-Hill. (9–12.)

Economic Forces in U.S. History Series. Scott, Foresman.

Modern Economic Issues. Prentice-Hall.

SILK AND SAUNDERS. _The World of Economics Transparency Program._ Webster/McGraw-Hill.

SLOAN. _Viewpoints on American Labor._ Random House/Singer. (Multimedia.)

ANTHROPOLOGY AND SOCIOLOGY: TEXTS

Anthropology Curriculum Study Project. _Patterns in Human History._ Macmillan. (Multimedia course.)

BROOM AND SELZNICK. _Sociology._ Harper. (Text plus readings.)

COLE AND MONTGOMERY. _High School Sociology._ Allyn.

CURTIS, LANE, AND COLEMAN. _Sociology: An Introduction._ Bruce.

DOWNS AND BLEIBTREU. _Human Variation: An Introduction to Anthropology._ Macmillan.

GREEN. *Sociology: An Analysis of Life in Modern Society.* Webster/McGraw-Hill. (Advanced.)

HORTON AND HUNT. *Sociology.* Webster/McGraw-Hill.

KOLLER AND COUSE. *Modern Sociology.* Holt. (11–12.)

LANDIS. *Sociology.* Ginn.

QUINN. *Living in Social Groups.* Lippincott.

SANDBERG. *Introduction to the Behavioral Sciences.* Holt. (9–12; AV; part of Fenton program.)

SANKOWSKY. *Sociology for High School.* Oxford Book.

SCHULTZ. *Comparative Political Systems.* Holt. (9–12; AV kit; part of Fenton program.)

Sociological Resources for the Social Studies. *Inquiries in Sociology.* Allyn.

ANTHROPOLOGY AND SOCIOLOGY: SUPPLEMENTARY MATERIALS

The Anthropological Curriculum Study Project. Anthropology Paperbacks. Macmillan.

DOWNS. *Cultures in Crisis.* Macmillan. (Paperbacks.)

Man in His World Series. McGraw-Hill. (16 mm films on anthropology.)

Sociological Resources for the Social Studies. *Episodes in Inquiry Series.* Allyn. (Short paperbacks.)

Sociology Resources for the Social Sciences. *Readings in Sociology Series.* Allyn.

Urban Plight Series. McGraw-Hill. (Films.)

PSYCHOLOGY

BRANCA. *Psychology: The Science of Behavior.* Allyn.

BRENNECKE AND AMICK. *The Struggle for Significance.* Glencoe.

ENGLE AND SNELLGROVE. *Psychology: Its Principles and Applications.* Harcourt.

GORDON. *Psychology for You.* Oxford Book.

HERSHEY AND LUGO. *Living Psychology.* Macmillan.

AFRO, BLACK, AND ETHNIC SOURCES

Americans All Series. Webster/McGraw-Hill. (Paperbacks on minorities.)

BEYER AND HICKS. *Africa Inquiry Maps.* Crowell.

The Black American. Alpha Corp. of America. (Sound filmstrip series.)

Black Heritage Series. Warren Schloat. (Color sound filmstrips.)

Black Studies. NEA. (Multimedia kit.)

CLIFFORD AND ROSS. *Noble and Noble African Studies Program.* Noble. (64-page paperbacks and duplicating masters; e.g., The African Environment, The Voices of Africa.)

DASILVA, FINKELSTEIN, AND LOSHEN. *The African American in United States History.* Globe. (7–12; slow.)

DAVIDSON. *Discovering Our African Heritage.* Ginn. (HS; paperback.)

FINKELSTEIN, SANDIFER, AND WRIGHT. *Minorities USA.* Globe. (7–12; slow.)

FRAZIER. *Afro-American History: Primary Sources.* Harcourt. (SHS.)

GOLDSTON. *The Negro Revolution: From Its African Genesis to the Death of Martin Luther King.* Macmillan. (7–12.)

Historical Highlights in the Education of Black Americans. NEA. (Multimedia kit.)
Minorities in Contemporary American Society. Lincoln Filene Center. (Booklets.)
MORSBACH. *The Negro in American Life.* School Edition. Harcourt.
The Negro in American History Paperbacks. Scholastic.
The Negro in U.S. History Film Strips. Scholastic.
SCHWARTZ. *Exploring Africa South of the Sahara.* Globe.
Slavery, Civil War, and Reconstruction. Crowell. (7–12; multimedia kits.)
Starter Kit for Teaching About Africa. Social Studies School Services.
STEINFIELD. *Cracks in the Melting Pot: Readings in Racism and Discrimination in American History.* Glencoe.
Tapes About Developing Nations. Tapes from Developing Nations. 6245 South Brainard Ave., LaGrange, Ill. 60525.

CURRENT EVENTS

The primary sources of current events materials are, of course, the various news media. However, a number of firms provide specialized programs for school classes. Some of these specialized materials are included here.

American Observer. Scholastic. (9–12.)
Current Affairs Case Study Series. Newsweek Educational Division. (Free materials developed by Lincoln Filene Center, Tufts University.)
Current Affairs Filmstrips. Current Affairs Films.
Current Events. American Educational Publications. (7–8; weekly.)
Headline Focus Wall Maps. Scholastic. (Biweekly.)
Issues Today. American Educational Publications. (9–12; twice monthly.)
Junior Scholastic Magazine. Scholastic. (6–8.)
The Manchester Guardian. 20 East 53rd St., New York, N. Y. 10022 (Includes articles from *Le Monde.*)
Le Monde. Le Monde, 5, Rue des Italiens, Paris 9^e, France. (Weekly selections in English.)
The National Observer. Dow Jones and Co. (Weekly, reduced rates.)
Newsweek. Newsweek. (Also teaching aids, spirit masters, news quiz, Map of the Month.)
The New York Times. The New York Times. (School weekly, transparencies, filmstrips, etc. also available.)
Senior Scholastic Magazine. Scholastic. (10–12.)
Synopsis. Curriculum Innovations. (One current social issue every other week.)
Time Magazine. Time Inc. (*Time,* plus teaching aids.)
Urban World. American Educational Publications. (8–12; twice monthly.)
Vital Issues. (Readings for teachers and students, eight times a year, with teacher's guide.)
The Wall Street Journal. Dow Jones and Co. (Daily; reduced rates.)
World News of the Week. World News of the Week. (Map.)
World Week Magazine. Scholastic. (6–8.)
You and Your World. American Educational Publications. (Weekly; for poor readers.)

ATLASES

Academic World Atlas. Hammond.
Ambassador World Atlas. Hammond.

American Heritage Pictorial Atlas. American Heritage.
Atlas of the World. National Geographic Society.
Citation World Atlas. Hammond.
Classroom Atlas. Rand McNally. (Paperbound.)
Cosmopolitan World Atlas. Rand McNally.
Cram's Student Quick-Reference Atlas. Cram.
ESPENSHADE, EDWARD B. (ed.) *Goode's World Atlas.* Rand McNally.
Hammond's Comparative World Atlas. Hammond.
The International Atlas. Rand McNally.
International World Atlas. Denoyer-Geppert.
Locations and Boundaries. Rand McNally. (Paperbound atlas of political world.)
The Odyssey World Atlas. Denoyer-Geppert.
Philips' New School Atlas. Denoyer-Geppert.
Regional Atlas. Rand McNally. (Paperback abridgment of Goode's.)
World Atlas. Denoyer-Geppert.
World Atlas for Students. Hammond.
The World—Its Geography in Maps. Denoyer-Geppert. (Paper.)
A World of Maps. Rand McNally. (Paper.)

SOME SIMULATION GAMES
FOR SOCIAL STUDIES CLASSES

Adventuring. Abt Associates. (English Civil War, JHS.)
Atlantis. Portola Institute. (Archeologists at work, SHS.)
Balance. Interact. (Ecology, economic goals and decisions, SHS.)
Baldicer. Baldicer Games. (World economy, SHS.)
BMG. Western Behavioral Sciences Institute. (Simplified economic market, JHS, SHS.)
Budgeting Games. Changing Times Education Service. (Budgeting, JHS, SHS.)
Buy. Simile II. (Management team at work, SHS.)
The Cities Game. The Cities Game. (Groups attempt to solve urban problems, JHS, SHS.)
The City Model. Environmetrics. (Urban and suburban problems, SHS.)
CLUG. Systems Gaming Associates. (Private enterpreneurs, SHS.)
Collective Bargaining. Science Research Associates. (Economics, SHS.)
The Community. Science Research Associates. (Economics, SHS.)
Community Disaster. Western Publishing. (Problems resulting from a natural disaster, JHS, SHS.)
Compass—Community Priority Assessment Simulation, Instructional Simulation. (Urban groups interact, JHS, SHS.)
Conflict. World Law Fund. (Keeping the peace.)
Confrontation: The Cuban Missile Crisis. School Marketing. (A nuclear confrontation, mixed media, SHS.)
Consumer. Western Publishing. (Consumer buying, SHS.)
Crisis. Simile II. (International crisis, JHS, SHS.)
Crisis. Western Behavioral Sciences Institute. (International crisis, SHS.)
Dangerous Parallel. Scott, Foresman. (International crisis, SHS.)
Democracy. Western Publishing. (Legislative process, JHS, SHS.)
Destiny. Interact. (Cuban crisis, SHS.)
Development. Science Research Associates. (Major powers and developing nations, JHS, SHS.)

Dirty Water. Urban Systems. (Problems of water pollution, JHS, SHS.)

Disunia. Interact. (Problems of disunited country, JHS, SHS.)

Division. Interact. (Problems of a divided nation, SHS.)

Dynasty Game. Dynasty International. (Pushing and tugging for social position, JHS, SHS.)

Economic System. Western Publishing. (Interrelationships in the economic system, JHS, SHS.)

Empire. Educational Development Center. (Mercantilism, American Colonists and the British Empire, JHS.)

The English Civil War Unit. Abt Associates. (King Charles, traitor or martyr, JHS.)

Environmental Games. Simulation Systems Program. (Problems of pollution, JHS, SHS.)

Firm. Science Research Associates. (Running a business firm, SHS.)

FLIP. Instructional Simulations. (Coping with family financial problems, SHS.)

Free Enterprise. Instructional Innovations. (Corporations in action, JHS.)

Frontier. Science Research Associates. (Early American expansion, JHS, SHS.)

Ghetto. Western Publishing. (Pressures of the urban poor and how to improve their lot, JHS, SHS.)

Impact. Instructional Simulations. (Group relations in the community, SHS.)

Inner City Planning. Macmillan. (Problems of urban renewal, SHS.)

Inter-Nation Simulation. Science Research Associates. (Decision making in international affairs, SHS.)

Intervention. Science Research Associates. (Foreign affairs, JHS, SHS.)

Kolkhoz. Abt Associates. (Collective farm, JHS.)

Labor vs Management, Social Education. October, 1966. (Labor management relations, SHS.)

Low Bidder. Didactic Systems. (Company managers, self-business, SHS.)

Manchester. Abt Associates. (Industrial Revolution, SHS.)

Market. Science Research Associates. (Supply and demand, economics, SHS.)

Market Game. Joint Council on Economic Education. (Supply and demand, JHS, SHS.)

Marketplace. Joint Council on Economic Education. (Basic economic concepts, SHS.)

Mr. Banker. Federal Reserve Bank of Minneapolis. (Money and credit, JHS, SHS, loan.)

Mulberry. Paul S. Amidon. (Urban renewal, JHS, SHS.)

Napoli. Western Behavioral Sciences Institute. (Legislative process, JHS, SHS.)

National Economy. Science Research Associates. (Growth, inflation, income, unemployment, SHS.)

Panic. Interact. (Economic crisis 1920–1940; Depression; JHS, SHS.)

Plans. Simile II. (Pressure groups, JHS, SHS.)

Potlatch. Anthropology Curriculum Project. (Kwakiutl Indians, JHS.)

Production. Good Time Educators. (Participation in market economy, JHS, SHS.)

Railroad Game. American Educational Productions. (Railroads compete for business, JHS, SHS.)

Rand Political Games. Rand Corp. (Cold War, SHS.)

Reconstruction. Science Research Associates. (Post Civil War reform, JHS, SHS.)

Revolution. Abt Associates. (English Civil War, SHS.)

Scarcity and the Market. Good Time Educators. (Resources, their relative value and scarcity, JHS, SHS.)

Simulation: The Decision-Making Model. World Affairs Council of Philadelphia. (International decision making, SHS.)

Sitte. Didactic Games. (Activist interest groups, SHS.)

Star Power. Simile II. (Distribution of wealth, JHS, SHS.)

Stockmarket Game. Avalon Hill Co. (Security investing, JHS, SHS.)

Strike. Interact. (Labor management in nineteenth century, JHS, SHS.)

Strike. Macmillan. (Labor management, SHS.)

Sunshine. Interact. (Urban problems, JHS, SHS.)

Tracts. Instructional Simulations. (Urban land development, SHS.)

Trade and Develop. Academic Games Project. (International trade, JHS, SHS.)

Trade and Develop. Western Publishing. (Developing a national economy, JHS, SHS.)

Index